D0201281

HUMAN RIGHTS

and

RESPONSIBILITIES

in the world religions

"The Universal Declaration of Human Rights by the World's Religions has gone beyond the U.N. Universal Declaration of Human Rights by establishing an unambiguous link between religion and a just society. It has also explored how one balances rights with duties, one of the most complex challenges facing humankind."

Chandra Muzaffar,
President, International Movement for a Just World,
Kuala Lumpur

THE LIBRARY OF GLOBAL ETHICS AND RELIGION
General Editors: Joseph Runzo and Nancy M. Martin

Volume I, *The Meaning of Life in the World Religions*, ISBN 1–85168–200–7
Volume II, *Love, Sex and Gender in the World Religions*, ISBN 1–85168–223–6
Volume III, *Ethics in the World Religions*, ISBN 1–85168–247–3
Volume IV, *Human Rights and Responsibilities in the World Religions*,
   ISBN 1–85168–309–7

RELATED TITLES PUBLISHED BY ONEWORLD

Avatar and Incarnation, Geoffrey Parrinder, ISBN 1–85168–103–2
Believing: An Historical Perspective, Wilfred Cantwell Smith, ISBN 1–85168–166–3
The Call of the Minaret, Kenneth Cragg, ISBN 1–85168–210–4
Celebrate!, Margo Westrheim, ISBN 1–85168–199–X
Christianity and Other Religions, Edited by John Hick and Brian Hebblethwaite,
   ISBN 1–85168–279–1
Common Prayer, Kenneth Cragg, ISBN 1–85168–181–7
Concepts of God, Keith Ward, ISBN 1–85168–064–0
Faith and Belief: The Difference Between Them, Wilfred Cantwell Smith,
   ISBN 1–85168–165–5
The Fifth Dimension, John Hick, ISBN 1–85168–191–4
Global Philosophy of Religion: A Short Introduction, Joseph Runzo,
   ISBN 1–85168–235–X
God: A Guide for the Perplexed, Keith Ward, ISBN 1–85168–323–2
God and the Universe of Faiths, John Hick, ISBN 1–85168–071–3
God, Chance and Necessity, Keith Ward, ISBN 1–85168–116–7
God, Faith and the New Millennium, Keith Ward, ISBN 1–85168–155–8
In Defence of the Soul, Keith Ward, ISBN 1–85168–040–3
Interfaith Theology: A Reader, Edited by Dan Cohn-Sherbok,
   ISBN 1–85168–276–7
Inter-religious Dialogue: A Short Introduction, Martin Forward,
   ISBN 1–85168–275–9
Jesus and the Muslim, Kenneth Cragg, ISBN 1–85168–180–9
Muhammad and the Christian, Kenneth Cragg, ISBN 1–85168–179–5
Muslims and Christians Face to Face, Kate Zebiri, ISBN 1–85168–133–7
Paths from Science Towards God, Arthur Peacocke, ISBN 1–85168–245–7
Patterns of Faith Around the World, Wilfred Cantwell Smith, ISBN 1–85168–164–7
The Phenomenon of Religion, Moojan Momen, ISBN 1–85168–161–2
Pluralism in the World Religions: A Short Introduction, Harold Coward,
   ISBN 1–85168–243–0
Religious Truth for our Time, William Montgomery Watt, ISBN 1–85168–102–7
Scripture in the World Religions: A Short Introduction, Harold Coward,
   ISBN 1–85168–244–9
The Sense of God, John Bowker, ISBN 1–85168–093–4
September 11: Religious Perspectives on the Causes and Consequences, Edited by Ian
   Markham and Ibrahim M. Abu Rabi', ISBN 1–85168–308–9
Sexual Morality in the World Religions, Geoffrey Parrinder, ISBN 1–85168–108–6
Sin and Salvation in the World Religions: A Short Introduction, Harold Coward,
   ISBN 1–85168–319–4
Wilfred Cantwell Smith: A Reader, Edited by Kenneth Cracknell,
   ISBN 1–85168–249–X

HUMAN RIGHTS

and

RESPONSIBILITIES

in the world religions

EDITED BY

Joseph Runzo, Nancy M. Martin,

and Arvind Sharma

Volume IV
in
The Library of Global Ethics and Religion
General Editors: Joseph Runzo and Nancy M. Martin

ONEWORLD

OXFORD

HUMAN RIGHTS AND RESPONSIBILITIES IN THE WORLD RELIGIONS

Oneworld Publications
185 Banbury Road
Oxford OX2 7AR
England
www.oneworld-publications.com

ISBN 978–1–85168–309–3

Cover design by Design Deluxe
Typeset by Saxon Graphics Ltd, Derby, UK
Printed and bound in Great Britain by Biddles Ltd, Kings Lynn

This volume is dedicated to

NINIAN SMART AND VASUDHA NARAYANAN

*friends who share the vision of
interreligious understanding*

The path of Truth is as narrow as it is straight. Even so is that of ahimsa. It is like balancing oneself on the edge of a sword. By concentration an acrobat can walk on a rope. But the concentration required to tread the path of Truth and ahimsa is far greater. The slightest inattention brings one tumbling to the ground. One can realize truth and ahimsa only by ceaseless striving...

The principle of ahimsa is hurt by every evil thought, by undue haste, by lying, by hatred, by wishing ill of anybody. It is also violated by our holding on to what the world needs.

(Mahatma Gandhi
Excerpt from a Letter to Narandas Gandhi
[July 28–31, 1930])

"I was hungry and you gave me food, I was thirsty and you gave me drink, I was a stranger and you welcomed me, I was naked and you clothed me, I was sick and you visited me, I was in prison and you came to me." Then the righteous will answer him, "Lord, when did we see thee hungry and feed thee, or thirsty and give thee drink? And when did we see thee a stranger and welcome thee, or naked and clothe thee? And when did we see thee sick or in prison and visit thee?" And the King will answer them, "Truly, I say to you, as you did it to one of the least of these my brethren, you did it to me."

(Matthew 25:35–40 RSV)

CONTENTS

Part III A DECLARATION OF HUMAN RIGHTS

BY THE WORLD'S RELIGIONS

Part IV RIGHTS AND RELIGIOUS TRADITIONS

ILLUSTRATIONS

Photographs: Nancy M. Martin and Joseph Runzo

CONTRIBUTORS

KHALED ABOU EL FADL is Professor of Law at the University of California, Los Angeles, where he is the Omar and Azmeralda Alfi Distinguished Fellow in Islamic Law. A leading authority in Islamic law in the United States and Europe, he works with various human rights organizations, such as Human Rights Watch and the Lawyers' Committee for Human Rights and often serves as an expert witness in international litigation involving Middle Eastern law. His many publications include *Rebellion and Violence in Islamic Law*; *Speaking in God's Name: Islamic Law, Authority and Women*; and *And God Knows the Soldiers: The Authoritative and Authoritarian in Islamic Discourse*.

ABDULLAHI A. AN-NA'IM is Charles Howard Candler Professor of Law and Fellow of the Law and Religion Program of Emory University. An internationally recognized scholar of Islam and human rights and human rights in cross-cultural perspectives, he has held numerous fellowships and visiting professorships and served as the Executive Director of Human Rights/Africa. He is author or editor of nine books, including *Universal Rights, Local Remedies*; *The Cultural Dimensions of Human Rights in the Arab World*; *Human Rights in Cross-Cultural Perspectives*; *Human Rights and Religious Values*; and *The Politics of Memory: Truth, Healing and Social Justice*.

JOHN BERTHRONG is Associate Dean for Academic and Administrative Affairs, Assistant Professor of Comparative Religion, and Director of the Institute for Dialogue Among Religious Traditions in the School of Theology at Boston University. As a leading proponent of interreligious dialogue and a renowned scholar of Confucian studies, his most recent books include *All Under Heaven: Transforming Paradigms in Confucian–Christian Dialogue; Transformations of the Confucian Way; Confucianism: A Short Introduction;* and *Confucianism and Ecology: The Interrelation of Heaven, Earth, and Humans,* which he edited with Mary Evelyn Tucker.

ARINDAM CHAKRABARTI is Professor of Philosophy at the University of Hawaii. After being trained as an analytic philosopher of language at Oxford, he spent several years receiving traditional training in Indian logic (Navya Nyaya) and metaphysics. In addition to numerous articles and reviews, he has authored or edited four books including *Denying Existence: The Logic, Epistemology, and Pragmatics of Negative Existentials and Fictional Discourse,* and *Knowing from Words: Western and Indian Philosophical Analysis of Understanding and Testimony,* and he is currently working on a book on moral psychology.

DAVID CHAPPELL is Professor of Comparative Religion at Soka University of America and Professor Emeritus of the University of Hawaii. He was the founding editor of the journal *Buddhist–Christian Studies,* founding director of the Buddhist Studies Program at the University of Hawaii, and co-founder and former president of the Society of Buddhist–Christian Studies. His five books include *Buddhist Peacework: Creating Cultures of Peace,* and he is currently exploring the changing relationships between religion, business, and government in our global society.

CHRISTOPHER KEY CHAPPLE is Professor of Theological Studies and Director of Asian Pacific Studies at Loyola Marymount University in Los Angeles. He has published ten books, including *Karma and Creativity; Ecological Prospects: Scientific, Religious, and Aesthetic Perspectives;* and *Nonviolence to Animals, Earth, and Self in Asian Traditions.* He has just completed editing two volumes for Harvard University's Center for the Study of World Religions: *Hinduism and Ecology: The Intersection of Earth, Sky, and Water,* and *Jainism and Ecology: Nonviolence in the Web of Life,* and is engaged in a long-term study of Haribhadra's Jaina analysis of Yoga.

ELLIOT DORFF is Rector and Professor of Philosophy at the University of Judaism. The leading spokesperson for ethics in Conservative Judaism today, he is the author of over one hundred articles and eight books on Jewish theology, Jewish law, and Jewish ethics. His books include *Matters of Life and Death; Contemporary Jewish Theology: A Reader; To Do the Right and the Good: A Jewish Approach to Modern Social Ethics;* and *A Living Tree: The Roots and Growth of Jewish Law.* He has served

on the ethics committee of the national health care task force and testi-
fied before the President's National Bioethics Advisory Committee, in
addition to being a regular lecturer at UCLA's Law School.

CHARLOTTE FONROBERT is Assistant Professor of Religious Studies at
Stanford University. With expertise in Judaism, particularly talmudic
literature and the construction of gender in this literature, her current
work focuses on the cultural strategies the talmudic rabbis employ to
construct their identity as the only valid Jewish identity and on the
parallel rabbinic strategies of delegitimizing Jewish cultural alternatives.
She is the author of *Menstrual Purity: Rabbinic and Christian Recon-
structions of Biblical Gender*.

JAMES FREDERICKS is Associate Professor of Theological Studies at
Loyola Marymount University. A specialist in Japanese Buddhism and
comparative theology and an active participant in Buddhist–Christian
dialogue, he has worked closely with Masao Abe and translated his
writings. His publications include the book *Faith Among Faiths: Christian
Theology and the Non-Christian Religions*.

AMIR HUSSAIN is Assistant Professor of Islamic Studies at California
State University, Northridge. He received his Ph.D. at the University of
Toronto, studying Comparative Religion and Islam with Wilfred
Cantwell Smith. His research focuses on contemporary Muslim
societies in North America, and he is currently writing a book on Muslim
communities in Toronto and completing work on the *Encyclopedia of
Islam in the United States*.

JERRY IRISH is Professor of Religious Studies at Pomona College. He has
been Vice President and also acting President of Pomona College. His
fields are philosophy of religion, theology, and ethics, and he is particularly interested in the social and ethical issues facing our contemporary
pluralistic society. He has published two books and a number of articles
on historical and systematic theology and religious ethics.

JAMES KELLENBERGER is Professor of Philosophy at California State
University, Northridge. He has published eight books including *The
Cognitivity of Religion: Three Perspectives*; *God-Relationships With and
Without God*; *Inter-Religious Models and Criteria: Relationship Morality*;
Kierkegaard and Nietzsche: Faith and Eternal Acceptance; and most
recently *Moral Relativism, Moral Diversity, and Human Relationships*.

BRIAN LEPARD is Associate Professor of Law at the University of
Nebraska. An international human rights law specialist, he was the
editor of the *Yale Journal of International Law* and has served at the

United Nations office of the Bahá'í International Community. His most recent book, titled *Rethinking Humanitarian Intervention: A Fresh Legal Approach Based on Fundamental Ethical Principles in International Law and World Religions*, is available from Penn State University Press.

PHILIP QUINN is John A. O'Brien Professor of Philosophy at the University of Notre Dame. He taught at Brown University before assuming his current position. Having published over one hundred articles and reviews in various areas of philosophy, he is also the author of *Divine Commands and Moral Requirements*, and *The Philosophical Challenges of Religious Diversity* as well as the co-editor of *A Companion to Philosophy of Religion*.

GERRIE TER HAAR is Professor of Religion, Human Rights, and Social Change at the Institute of Social Studies in The Hague, the Netherlands. Her publications include *The Freedom to Do God's Will: Religious Fundamentalism and Social Change*; *World Religions and Community Religions: Where does Africa Fit in?*; *Halfway to Paradise: African Christians in Europe*; and *Strangers and Sojourners: Religious Communities in the Diaspora*. She is the secretary for the Dutch Association for the Study of Religion and the Deputy Secretary-General of the International Association for the History of Religions.

SUMNER B. TWISS is Distinguished Professor of Human Rights, Ethics, and Religion at Florida State University and Professor Emeritus of Religious Studies at Brown University. Co-editor of the *Journal of Religious Ethics* and the author of numerous articles on comparative ethics, philosophy of religion, biomedical ethics, and intercultural human rights, he is co-author or co-editor of six books including *Comparative Religious Ethics: A New Method*; *Religion and Human Rights*; and *Explorations in Global Ethics: Comparative Religious Ethics and Interreligious Dialogue*.

The Editors

NANCY M. MARTIN received her M.A. from the University of Chicago Divinity School and her Ph.D. from the Graduate Theological Union, Berkeley. An Associate Professor of Religious Studies at Chapman University, she is a historian of religion with expertise in Asian religions, gender issues, and comparative mysticism. Involved in extensive fieldwork in Rajasthan, her research focuses on devotional Hinduism, women's religious lives, and the religious traditions of low-caste groups in India. As the co-editor of the Library of Global Ethics and Religion, she has published *The Meaning of Life in the World Religions; Love, Sex, and Gender in the World Religions;* and *Ethics in the World Religions,* and she has just completed a book on the sixteenth-century saint Mirabai, forthcoming from Oxford University Press.

JOSEPH RUNZO received his Ph.D. in philosophy from the University of Michigan and his M.T.S. in theological studies from Harvard Divinity School. He is Professor of Philosophy and Religious Studies at Chapman University and Life Fellow at Clare Hall, Cambridge University. He is the recipient of six National Endowment for the Humanities fellowships and awards. Working in the fields of philosophy of religion, epistemology, and religious ethics, he has published nine books: *Reason, Relativism, and God; Religious Experience and Religious Belief; Is God Real?; Ethics, Religion and the Good Society; World Views and Perceiving God;* and (co-editor with Nancy M. Martin) *The Meaning of Life in the World Religions; Love, Sex and Gender in the World Religions;* and *Ethics in the World Religions.* He has recently published *Global Philosophy of Religion: A Short Introduction,* and is currently working on a book on the ethics of war, entitled *War and the Destruction of the Soul.*

ARVIND SHARMA received his M.T.S. from Harvard Divinity School and his Ph.D. in Sanskrit and Indian Studies from Harvard University. Having taught at the University of Queensland and the University of Sydney in Australia, he is now the Birks Professor of Comparative Religion at McGill University in Canada. A renowned scholar of comparative religion, Indian philosophy and ethics, Hinduism, and issues concerning women and religion, he has received numerous awards and fellowships including being named a Fellow of the Royal Asiatic Society. Among the more than thirty-five books he has published are *Our Religions; A Dome of Many Colors: Studies in Religious Pluralism, Identity and Unity; Feminism and World Religions; Fragments of Infinity: Essays in Religion and Philosophy*; and *Hinduism for Our Times.* He is currently engaged in promoting the working document, "A Universal Declaration of Human Rights by the World's Religions," published herein, for discussion and revision by scholars and religious leaders and within religious communities around the globe.

ACKNOWLEDGMENTS

This is the fourth volume in Oneworld's Library of Global Ethics and Religion, offering a pluralistic and global perspective on ethical issues through original essays by foremost scholars of the world religions. The editors wish to thank Novin Doostdar and Juliet Mabey of Oneworld Publications for their continued support for this project. We also would like to thank Helen Coward, Victoria Roddam, Rebecca Clare, Sarah McKeown, and Alex Ivey at Oneworld for their superb work on this volume. In preparing this volume, we owe a special debt of gratitude to Jessie Stevens and Vanessa Pfleger, and to Niki Heurlin, Geeti Rajadhyaksha, Linda Mandala, and Josh Farrar, whose hard work, dedication, and good humor made the completion of the manuscript possible.

This book benefited from the cooperative efforts of the Global Ethics and Religion Forum (www.GERForum.org), an international society of scholars which is committed to promoting a wider understanding both of religious pluralism and of global ethical issues. We wish to thank our friends in the Forum, many of whom have essays in the present volume, for their steadfast support.

The Universal Declaration of Human Rights by the World's Religions which is presented and assessed in this volume evolved from its original form, first drafted at McGill University, through a number of public discussions. These included three conference presentations by participants in the Global Ethics and Religion Forum at international conferences at Chapman and Loyola Marymount Universities, and at the meetings in 2000 of the International Association for the History of Religion in Durban, South Africa.

The present volume is dedicated to two scholars who served successively as Presidents of the American Academy of Religion. Ninian Smart was one of the founding members of the International Board of Consultants of the Forum, and his untimely death in 2001 was a great blow to all of us concerned about the importance of interreligious understanding for human rights. We trust that the essay which Ninian intended to contribute to this volume is here in spirit if not in fact. Vasudha Narayanan is not only an outstanding scholar of Hindu ethics, she exemplifies a new generation of leadership in interreligious understanding as a basis for global ethical responsibility. Vasudha now brings this expertise and leadership to the International Board of Consultants of the Global Ethics and Religion Forum.

INTRODUCTION

Religions have too often been used to justify the violation of human rights, in part through the hierarchical and selective use of role ethics and the postponement of temporal justice to divine judgment or future karmic consequences. Yet the world religions have also provided a constant voice of critique against the violation of human rights by calling for equality, and universal compassion and love, calls which reach far beyond the mere protection of human rights. The essays in this volume offer a diversity of perspectives from the world religions and multiple dimensions of the view that religion can – and indeed must – play an important role in promoting human rights on a global scale.

Yet what is that role, and what ought it to be? What can the world religions contribute positively to our understanding of human rights and human responsibilities and to our active fulfillment of both? Further, what can each world religion in itself and the religious perspective in general add to this? These are the questions taken up in this volume, and in addressing them, the authors must also address the relationship between the secular and the religious, the foundations for rights, the very real differences among different religious perspectives on rights and responsibilities, the problem of reaching consensus and what that consensus might look like, and finally the practical considerations of how to implement the protection of human rights and to respond to violations.

The initial essays in part I address the relationship between secular and religious ethics. In the first chapter, after giving a brief history of the development of the notion of human rights, Joseph Runzo argues that the common perception at the start of the twenty-first century that religion is an enemy of human rights is both mistaken and detrimental to the positive role religion can have. He identifies a "religious point of view" which is common to the world religions and which promotes relationality and moral responsibility. He further suggests that the interpersonal relatedness and responsibility that religion is meant to promote can provide another balance with regard to the egocentric tendencies of a purely secular emphasis on rights and the rule of law.

In the next chapter Abdullahi An-Na'im advocates a synergy or inter-dependence between human rights, religion, and secularism, such that religions can offer moral foundations for the protection of human rights and mobilize adherents, even as secularism mediates between various reli-gious and non-religious groups to allow for a united political community which can uphold human rights. It is, An-Na'im suggests, essential that each society and each group within a given society embrace the struggle for human rights as their *own* struggle, rather than as an importation from the so-called West or some other hegemonic power, and that freedom of expression and belief within religious traditions be permitted to allow for needed transformation from within.

Arindam Chakrabarti then takes up the issue of the relationship between adherents of different religious traditions, which is a precursor for global ethical cooperation and a universal affirmation of human rights. Unmasking the actual lack of faith exhibited when religion is used to advo-cate violence against members of its own or another religious community (with particular reference to the situation in his homeland of India), he takes a position of faith that our global community can reach an acceptance and celebration of divergent philosophical, religious, and cultural orienta-tions marked by "a moral overlap at the bottom and a supra-rational (mystical) experimental overlap at the top." Concluding this section, Arvind Sharma addresses the question of what religion in general can contribute to thinking about human rights and argues for human dignity as the foundation and source for human rights – a foundation which at once fills a void in a legalistic reading of rights and allows for the religious grounding of dignity in relationship to a transcendent dimension.

The three chapters in part II of the volume address the issue of being human and having rights. Gerrie ter Haar takes up cultural relativism and the challenge of arriving at a common moral language while at the same time honoring the right to cultural and religious difference in the complex context of multicultural societies and contemporary globalization.

Acknowledging the motivational power of religion and the ways in which religion has sometimes been used in an exclusionary way as part of a process of dehumanizing others and perpetrating violence and the violation of human rights, she recognizes that religion, like all human institutions, can be used for either destructive or constructive purposes and advocates that its positive resources be marshaled in support of human rights. Finally, she challenges us to delve more deeply into the question of how we understand what a human being is, given the claim that we have rights by virtue of being "human."

Brian Lepard, in the next chapter, addresses the thorny question of humanitarian intervention by the United Nations and what guidance the world religions might offer in this regard. When (if ever), how, and on what grounds should we intervene to stop human rights violations? Drawing on international law and the texts of the world religions, Lepard bases his argument for intervention on the affirmation of relationship, of the unity of the human family even in our diversity, and of our resulting ethical obligation to help those in need. Further, he seeks to demonstrate that the world religions can be seen to advocate open-minded consultation and the use of force only as a last resort in the carrying out of the obligation to help those in need and to offer guidance in, for example, balancing national sovereignty with the universal dignity of human beings.

In the final essay in this section James Kellenberger analyzes in greater depth the understanding of rights being used in the United Nations Universal Declaration of Human Rights, asserting that "rights" as they are used in this context are moral rather than merely legal; recognized, not invented; and real, not fictions. Further, he asserts that rights in this context do not necessitate an atomistic view of the self nor an assertion that rights are the basis of all morality. Instead, Kellenberger argues that relationships are the basis of all morality and therefore of human rights, relationships which he calls person–person relationships. He then raises the issue of whether there is also a similar fundamental person–environment relationship which would serve as the basis for environmental rights, concluding his discussion with an analysis of whether Christian and Jewish traditions allow for environmental rights.

Part III of the volume presents a Universal Declaration of Human Rights by the World's Religions. This creative and concrete attempt to address the contribution that religions can bring to the question of human rights is a working document, first drafted on the occasion of the fiftieth anniversary of the United Nations Declaration at McGill University in 1998 and initiating a global process of dialogue and consensus building. Initiated by scholars, the document is intended to be circulated among scholars, religious leaders, and religious communities, bringing people within religious traditions and across religious traditions together to address human rights and responsibilities.

The attempt to craft such a universal declaration immediately leads us into the challenging terrain of searching for a universality that also honors and celebrates particularity, and requires us to be cognizant of the ways that perceived rights violations (particularly those concerning gender and regarded as religiously based) were used to rationalize colonialization in the past as well as cultural, economic, and military domination in the present. The document as it stands in this volume is the latest draft of the Declaration and is followed by a series of responses to this current draft as well as the overall project, from the perspectives of Judaism, Christianity, Islam, Buddhism, Hinduism, and Confucianism.

The Declaration and responses are followed in part IV by a series of six essays, addressing human rights in specific religious traditions in greater depth. From a Jewish perspective, Elliot Dorff explains, human rights are grounded in understandings of human beings as created "in the image of God" and as unique individuals. Commandments within the Torah guarantee those rights and make cherishing them the responsibility of Jews and a form of worship of God. As an example of what Judaism might bring to the discussion of human rights, he then examines in detail Jewish teachings on the right to privacy. Philip Quinn analyzes Louis Henkin's negative assessment of the relations between religion and human rights and then demonstrates how human rights can be supported from a Christian ethical perspective.

The next chapter carries the question of Christian ethics forward in a comparison with Buddhist ethics. James Fredericks details the ongoing debate regarding whether or not human rights discourse is compatible with Buddhist teachings. From a Buddhist perspective rights discourse is often too individualistic and self-oriented in terms of rights, too adversarial and too strictly focused on human rights, and too concerned with symptoms rather than root problems. Fredericks presents an alternate Buddhist notion of rights and then applies the insights gleaned from the Buddhist debate about rights to the Christian context.

Nancy M. Martin then turns to rights and roles in the Hindu tradition. Elucidating Hindu understandings of dharma, she suggests that Hinduism challenges an individualistic notion of equality as a basis for human rights and offers an alternate vision of egalitarian complementarity which preserves and celebrates differences and distinctions while at the same time valuing and honoring the dignity and rights of all. Just as Martin confronts conceptions of Hinduism as irrevocably hierarchical, Sumner Twiss takes on the image of Confucianism as authoritarian, meritocratic, and antithetical to human rights. He presents an overview of the development of Confucian thought and then offers explicit examples of analogues to human rights within the Confucian tradition.

The final chapter in this volume, written by Khaled Abou El Fadl, is a tour de force analyzing human rights commitments and Islam. Within his extended analysis, Abou El Fadl clearly lays out the challenges to human rights discourse within contemporary Muslim society, particularly in the wake of colonialization and the perceived onslaught of cultural imperialism from the West. He then addresses in detail the nature of Islamic law or Shari'a and the history of its interpretation, and argues persuasively that support of human rights is not only consistent with Islam but a fulfillment of the teachings of Islam.

It is the hope of the editors and authors of this volume that these essays might open new dimensions in the contemporary dialogue on human rights and on human rights and religion and so bring us another step closer as a global community to establishing a world where we will all take responsibility to uphold the dignity, rights, and opportunity to flourish of every person equally.

Part I

SECULAR AND RELIGIOUS ETHICS

Plate 1 Statue of Mahatma Gandhi in Pietermaritzburg, South Africa, commemorating the beginning of his *satyagraha* or non-violence movement. Pietermaritzburg is the city where Gandhi, as a young lawyer, was thrown out of his train compartment because of his lower social standing as an Indian in the era of apartheid. Photo: *Joseph Runzo*

1

SECULAR RIGHTS *and* RELIGIOUS RESPONSIBILITIES

Joseph Runzo

No other issue in the twenty-first century may be more crucial than human rights, and no other aspect of more practical importance for this issue than the positive role that religion can play in human rights. While the stirrings of war and, even more, the nuclear posturing that have already marked the beginning of the century remind us of the one issue that might supersede human rights – that is, war – paramount issues of human rights and responsibilities are at the heart of any ethics of war. And just as the sincere religious perspective has done much to mitigate the call to war, sincere religious perspectives can greatly lessen the violation of human rights. The lives and work of Mohandas Gandhi and Martin Luther King, Jr. are paradigms of the powerful transformation toward a just world which secular law and religious sensitivity can achieve together as positive partners. The work of Gandhi and King (and others like them) should serve as examples of the means to an interrelational global community, a means which recognizes both human rights and human responsibility.

In the last century, the exemplary leadership of figures like Gandhi, King, Archbishop Tutu, Mother Teresa, and the Fourteenth Dalai Lama set a positive tone for the contribution that the spiritual and moral resources of the world religions could bring to human rights in the secular and political world. Yet, as we enter the twenty-first century, religion is now often seen as an enemy of human rights. "Religion is the cause of wars" has become an unfounded but frequent mantra of the anti-religious, and religion has moved from its characterization in the anti-religious imagination as "opiate of the people" to "cause of oppression." But this attitude not only belies the actual history of the religious life of humankind, it also stands as an impediment to accessing the rich positive resources for human rights and responsibilities that the world religions do have to offer. And while secularism is meant to provide the negative function of protecting everyone's individual rights in society, the world religions are meant at their core to provide a positive vision of human interdependence and a compelling motivation for moral responsibility. Both may fail at their respective core goals. But it is a tragedy of our contemporary world that the moral/legal structure of the secular and the moral/spiritual commitments of the religious might be seen as acting in opposition even as they need each other if we are to move toward a better world of global justice and care within the community of humankind.

Humankind forms a global community, a community of persons with inherently shared needs and interests, even if those shared needs are approached through often opposing and culturally diverse desires and attitudes. In order to achieve a stable society, any community must develop consensus on a unified vision both of the common good and of the good in common. If the global community of humankind is ever going to achieve a vision of the common good, if global humanity is ever going to see itself as a "community of ends," as Kant would say, we must not only (1) seek commonality on a global scale but (2) tolerate and even cherish human differences.

Genuine religion supports global community on both counts, and as such, genuine religion is not only a necessary part of, but will also make a significant contribution to, a just world incorporating both human rights and human responsibilities. For despite the bad press in the popular media about religion, despite violence and oppression and acts of hatred carried out in the name – but not the spirit – of religion, I will argue that what I shall call "the religious point of view" provides a foundational under-standing of the commonality and interdependence of humankind. In my own country, the United States, there is a particular phobia about allowing the "private" concerns of religion into the "public" spaces of law and social ordering. As the thoroughly secular U.N. Declaration on Human Rights of 1948 evidences, this pattern is paralleled in contemporary international law. So to convince the skeptical about the role of religion, the question is whether religion has anything important to add – and not just reinforce – about human rights and responsibilities.

THE IDEA OF RIGHTS

The first modern use of the term "rights" to designate a legal status – that is, to designate something enforceable under law – can be found in the English Bill of Rights of 1688. By 1779 Thomas Jefferson had turned this political/legal/philosophical notion into a cornerstone concept of the nascent American Republic: "We hold these truths to be self-evident, that all men are created equal; that they are endowed by their Creator with certain inalienable rights; that amongst these are life, liberty, and the pursuit of happiness."[1] To this theistic – or at least deistic – view of the origin of rights, Alexander Hamilton added in 1787: "The sacred rights of mankind are not to be rummaged for amongst old parchments or musty records. They are written, as with a sunbeam, in the whole volume of human nature by the hand of divinity itself, and can never be erased or obscured."[2]

However, these pious underpinnings to early American "rights" talk[3] carried the early seed of the danger of identifying state ends with God's ends, an identification which not only suffers from hubris and the epistemological problem of whether humans can ever actually know with certainty what God intends, but also has more recently run headlong into the claim that the contemporary United States is a pluralistic nation, a nation with sizable populations of both religious and non-religious citizens who do not believe in the God of the Judeo-Christian tradition. Moreover, as the British philosopher Jeremy Bentham said in the nineteenth century: "When I hear of natural rights, I always see in the background a cluster of daggers and pikes introduced into the National Assembly…for the avowed purpose of extermination of the King's friends."[4] It is all too easy to use talk of "rights" as a cudgel against others, either to upset or to sustain the status quo. And of course even in the early American Republic, the "inalienable" rights of all men as created equal did not apply to slaves in America or to American women.

As Geoffrey Robertson observes in *Crimes Against Humanity: The Struggle for Global Justice* regarding these earlier attempts to give a metaphysical grounding to the notion of rights:

> "Natural rights" were of uncertain provenance: if from God, their content (apart from biblical injunctions) was unknowable; if from "nature" they were unprovable and unpredictable. The force of Bentham's arguments was partly responsible for "natural rights" falling out of fashion in the nineteenth century and the first half of the twentieth century. When they returned, it would be as "*human* rights" rather than "natural rights", sourced in the nature of humans rather than in the laws of God or the seasons.[5]

Moreover, "The force of this early critique [also] led Marxist thinkers in the next century to characterize human rights as a device to universalize capitalist values, notably freedom of enterprise without social responsibility."[6]

However, war, as I observed, forces us – perhaps more than anything else – to think about rights. After the disheartening world disaster of the "war to end all wars" and the rise of the Axis powers only two decades later in the 1930s, Robertson suggests:

> The revival of the human rights idea in the twentieth century really began at the instigation and inspiration of the British author H.G. Wells, in the months immediately following the declaration of the Second World War. It can be traced to letters he wrote to *The Times* in October 1939, advocating the adoption by "parliamentary peoples" of a Declaration of Rights – a fundamental law defining their rights in a democracy and drafted to appeal "to every spirit under the yoke of the obscurantist and totalitarian tyrannies with which all are in conflict."[7]

This new talk of human rights spread, so that by the end of the Second World War, the victorious Allied Nations were to declare that "complete victory over their enemies is essential…to preserve human rights and justice in their own lands as well as in other lands."[8]

After the horrific slaughter and mass violation of rights during the Second World War, the U.S. was one of the leaders in placing the language of human rights in the U.N. charter. The preamble affirms "faith in fundamental human rights, in the dignity and worth of the human person, in the equal rights of men and women," and article I sets out this purpose of the U.N.: "To achieve international co-operation in solving international problems of an economic, social, cultural or humanitarian character, and in promoting and encouraging respect for human rights and for fundamental freedoms for all without distinction as to race, sex, language or religion."[9] In an important further development in this international support for human rights, the Universal Declaration of Human Rights was adopted by the General Assembly in 1948.[10] However, the continued large-scale violation of human rights forced a continual reassessment of these documents so that a number of specific types of rights needed to be more exactly delineated in a series of refinements rooted in the U.N. Charter and the 1948 Declaration. These conventions and declarations notably included:

- 1959 – Declaration of the Rights of the Child
- 1963 – Declaration on the Elimination of All Forms of Racial Discrimination

- 1967 – Declaration on the Elimination of Discrimination Against Women
- 1987 – Declaration on the Elimination of All Forms of Intolerance and of Discrimination Based on Religious Belief
- 1992 – Declaration on the Rights of Persons Belonging to National or Ethnic, Religious and Linguistic Minorities

However, even the 1987 and the 1992 Declarations, which deal specifically with religion, offer a secular or extra-religious prohibition against discrimination, not an appeal to religions as an ally of the legal and moral. As the 1987 Declaration states:

> For the purposes of the present Declaration, the expression "intolerance and discrimination based on religion or belief" means any distinction, exclusion, restriction or preference based on religion or belief and having as its purpose or as its effect nullification or impairment of the recognition, enjoyment or exercise of human rights and fundamental freedoms on an equal basis.

While many of the framers of these international rights documents were themselves either religious or influenced by the religious traditions of their cultures, these are purely secular documents. As Abdullahi A. An-Na'im suggests in his essay, "The Synergy and Interdependence of Human Rights, Religion, and Secularism" (chapter 2 in this volume), the notion of human rights articulated in the 1948 Declaration is that such rights

> are universal claims of rights that are due to all human beings by virtue of their humanity, without distinction on such grounds as race, sex (gender), religion, language, or national origin. The key feature of human rights in this specific sense is universality, in the sense that they are rights due all human beings, everywhere.[11]

This secular conception of rights which has been developed in the modern era offers the restrictive legal and moral parameter that there should be no discrimination on the basis of religion. It offers a protection for religion, but it does not envision a positive rights role for religion.

In view of this, a number of scholars around the world – including those in the Global Ethics and Religion Forum – have worked under the leadership of Arvind Sharma to produce a counterpart to the 1948 U.N. Declaration on Human Rights, namely A Universal Declaration of Human Rights by the World's Religions.[12] The purpose of the framers of the latter document is neither to circumvent nor to counter the 1948 U.N. Declaration (and the refinements in subsequent declarations), but to enhance the moral force and broaden both the appeal and the perview of the 1948 Declaration. This raises the question of the proper relationship between religion and morality regarding questions of rights, i.e. the proper relationship between the religious point of view and the moral point of view.

RIGHTS AND THE MORAL POINT OF VIEW

To answer this question, let us look first at morality itself. Individual moral decisions are often difficult, requiring a weighing of alternatives. When we think globally, the situation is made more complex by the fact that particular moral imperatives and values vary among individuals and cultures. As a result, considerations of global morality should not be conceived of in terms of a set of categorical imperatives. For example, the 1993 document "Towards a Global Ethic: An Initial Declaration," which came out of the Second Parliament of the World Religions, echoes Kant when it states that "No woman or man, no institution, no state or church or religious community has the right to speak lies to other humans." But surely such a categorical imperative is mistaken, as ethicists as diverse as Aristotle and W.D. Ross have pointed out. Normally humans should not lie, but if I am a woman of the underclass and mercenaries come to my door, demanding to know where my child is in order to kill him or her, I not only have a right but a moral duty to lie and misdirect the mercenaries away from my child. As this example demonstrates, categorical imperatives do not provide any means to resolve moral dilemmas in which two *prima facie* moral duties – such as not lying and protecting a life – come into conflict.

However, the very possibility that moral dilemmas could be adjudicated presupposes a foundational ethical commonality. Underlying the various moral systems – or else they would not be systems of the same type – is what we may call "the moral point of view." The most important feature of what it means to take the moral point of view is to take others into account in one's actions because one respects them as persons.[13] But what is the origin or source of this obligation to take others into account because one respects them as persons?

I do not think that respect for others as persons amounts to their possession of moral rights.[14] It seems to me that there are objections on both ethnocentric and egocentric grounds to treating rights as the most foundational element of morality. To take the ethnocentric objection, the notion of inalienable moral rights is, as we have seen, historically a fairly recent Western conception – highly motivated by politics and based on a notion of humans (at least some humans) as a community of rational, autonomous individuals with competing interests which need to be adjudicated. Moreover, this notion of rights is not even a Western concept, for it is decidedly European Christian. Even Islam, one of the great Western traditions and the second-largest religious tradition in the world with a billion adherents, did not figure importantly in the development of this notion. And as Khaled Abou El Fadl notes in "The Human Rights Commitment in Modern Islam" (chapter 21 in this volume):[15]

> Muslims did not first encounter Western conceptions of human rights in the form of the Universal Declaration of Human Rights of 1948, or in the form of negotiated international conventions. Rather, Muslims encountered such conceptions as part of the "White Man's Burden" or the "civilizing mission" of the colonial era, and as a part of the European natural law tradition, which was frequently exploited to justify imperialistic policies in the Muslim world.

In contrast to the European Christian language of "rights," in the South and East Asian societies of Hinduism, Buddhism, Jainism, Confucianism, and Taoism, the elemental moral notion traditionally is not one of rights but rather of one's role in society, a matter of obligations to the society and so to others. I am not suggesting that "rights" is an unimportant moral category – indeed, it might be among the best moral categories for articulating some salient features of morality. But, as close attention to the great Asian cultural traditions of humanity helps us see, I am suggesting that the notion of rights should not supersede other moral notions such as obligation or role or moral responsibility. Indeed, I would suggest not only that possessing rights implies having duties to others and having duties to others implies rights, but that the notion of responsibilities should be given precedence as the moral wellspring of rights, though I will not specifically argue for the last point here.

Another point is this. Rights talk is egocentric, and if it is taken as the primary moral category, then it is egoistic. For a salient emphasis on one's rights presents a self-interested and self-centered conception of the self and a conception of society as a group of individuals each protecting their own self-interest and each a victim of the greed of others. This is not to say that self-interest is immoral, just that it should not be taken as the essential and unregulated generative principle of morality. A good ethics slogan would be "no rights without responsibilities and no responsibilities without rights." Indeed, with respect to the project to develop a rights document which takes account of the religious perspective, my own view is that we should be more explicitly developing a "Universal Declaration of Rights *and Responsibilities* by the World's Religions." For the individual should not be subject to the tyranny of the "rights" of the majority (or the powerful minority masquerading as representing the universal), and the claim to universal rights should not be taken as a substitute for the call to universal responsibilities.

This still leaves us with the question of the source for the obligation to take the moral point of view. Now, one often-recognized characteristic of moral agency is autonomy. The ability to make rational and responsible decisions on one's own obviously does not in itself produce a moral point of view or a sense of obligation or sense of moral responsibility; an amoral, sociopathic person such as Stalin can be perfectly autonomous. However, as the Christian ethicist Margaret Farley argues, "the capacity for relationship is as significant a characteristic of human persons as the capacity for self-determination."[16] Relationality, which requires autonomy – or, perhaps better, is the morally and spiritually appropriate expression of autonomy – is a defining characteristic of persons as social beings. Relationality is a character trait, the willingness to be open and interact fully with others as persons. Relationality is the wellspring of the felt obligation to take others into account as persons in one's actions.

The character trait of relationality is encapsulated in the imperative to do unto others as you would have them do unto you, a universal moral principle found in variant forms in all the world's great religious traditions. In the *Analects*, Confucius says, "Do not impose on others what you yourself do not desire."[17] The monumental Hindu epic the *Mahabharata* expresses a similar idea: "One should never do that to another which one regards as injurious to one's own self. This, in brief, is the rule of the dharma."[18] In the West, Kant's ethical dictum to "always treat others as ends in themselves and not merely as means to an end" requires relationality, and an obligation to develop the character trait of relationality continually is reflected in the Jewish thinker Martin Buber's justly famous notion of the "I–thou" perspective: "When I confront a human being as my You and speak the basic word I–You to him, then he is no thing among things nor does he consist of things."[19] For to relate to persons as persons is different in kind from treating something as an "it," and Buber insists that anyone who treats everything as an "it" "is not human," though we should amend this to "is not a fully realized human." Nero, Stalin, Pol Pot, and Idi Amin were human, but not fully realized humans, lacking as they did a well-developed character trait of relationality.

Alan Donagan explicates Kant's ethics this way:

> No rational being may be simply a means to benefiting another, but every rational being is required, so far as it is in his or her power, to be a means for the good of others. Yet the benefits anyone confers on anyone else must be in a system of social relations in which those who confer them are ends equally with those on whom they are conferred.[20]

An obvious human rights example of this Kantian point about cases in which those who confer benefits are not equal with those upon whom they are conferred is slavery. Slavery precludes – in fact destroys – relationality and is not other regarding. This is why the early American Republic's avowal of a commitment to inalienable rights was contradicted by the possession of slaves, i.e. human beings who were not treated as persons, not treated as ends in themselves with rights equal to those of their "masters." To the extent that relationality is a defining characteristic of how a person exercises his or her autonomy, it is the wellspring of the person's felt obligation to take the moral point of view.

RIGHTS AND THE RELIGIOUS POINT OF VIEW

We are now ready to address the question of how religion relates to morality in general and to human rights in particular. While being moral is not sufficient for being religious, to be genuinely religious entails being moral, such that religion supervenes on morality. And just as there is a "moral point of view" which underlies the diversity of human moral outlooks, there is a "religious point of view" which underlies the diversity of religious worldviews among the world religions and which supervenes upon the moral point of view. I do not mean that there is only one correct or appropriate religious perspective, for religious values are, to some extent, irreducibly variant and relative to each particular religious worldview. But one does not have a specifically religious perspective unless one shares a fundamental "religious point of view" with others having quite different specific religious perspectives. The religious point of view is the point of commonality and the manifestation of universality in religion.

As James Kellenberger has argued, what is fundamental to the moral point of view is the realization of a "person–person relationship" which creates "a sense of duty grounded in a recognition of the intrinsic worth of persons."[21] So to be genuinely religious requires both a realization of this person–person relationship, which underlies the moral point of view, and also a supervening sense of a relationship of humankind to the Transcendent.

Consequently, the ultimate grounding of spirituality is the felt realization of a single universal relationship among all persons as spirits – what we might call a spirit–spirit relationship – and the Transcendent.

Taking the religious point of view in one's thought and actions means treating others as having the same spiritual value as oneself, as being on the same spiritual quest as oneself, and with the same potential for salvation or liberation.[22] This underlying religious point of view among the world religions entails both religious tolerance and an acceptance of diversity within the spiritual community of humankind; as such it can provide one of the underpinnings for a universal or global ethics of human rights and responsibilities.

RELIGIOUS EXCLUSIVISM AND RELIGIOUS EGOISM

However, as we noted, religion is now often seen not as a force for understanding and global justice – the model presented by Gandhi and King – but as a divisive force. The potential for divisiveness can be seen even in the characterization of religion offered by a sympathetic voice like that of Abdullahi A. An-Na'im:

> Religion can be defined as a system of belief, practices, institutions and relationships that is used by a community of believers to identify and distinguish itself from other communities. The key feature of religion in this specific sense is the exclusivity of the community of believers, as defined by its own religious faith and practice.[23]

So if the religious ethics of the world religions is to be taken seriously and have any chance of being ultimately efficacious in the global arena of secular ethics, religious ethics needs to have a global outlook and be universally applicable. And no religious ethics could be universal unless in some sense religion can be universal.

The adherents of each of the great religious traditions naturally believe that their own religious worldview is correct, yet despite the historically and geographically limited locus of each of the world religions, religious commitment is often promulgated as religious exclusivism, the view that only one religion is correct (one's own) and all others are mistaken. It is one thing for a religion to be distinctive, quite another for it to be exclusivist. Indeed, An-Na'im concludes that the very solidarity that religion brings to a community is exclusive, while the solidarity that human rights can bring is inclusive. While I recognize the problematic exclusivist tendencies in religion to which An-Na'im is pointing, the notion of human "rights" without the counterbalance of articulated responsibilities toward others is just as problematically exclusivist. Moreover, religious worldviews, while producing a communal solidarity in their specifics, can take a non-exclusivist outlook regarding other communities. Two non-exclusivist views of the relationships among the world religions which have been well articulated and which counter exclusivism are:

- religious inclusivism: only one world religion is fully correct, but other world religions participate in or partially reveal some of the truth of the one correct religion.
- religious pluralism: ultimately all world religions are correct, each offering a different path and partial perspective vis-à-vis the one Ultimate Reality.

To these two traditional positions, I would add another:

- henofideism: one has a faith commitment that one's own world religion is correct, while acknowledging that other world religions may be correct.[24]

Exclusivism simply does not take into account the degree to which all religious truth-claims are human constructs, subject to the limitations and fallibility of the human mind (a point which is fundamental to Abou El Fadl's analysis of Islam and human rights). For it is largely a matter of history, geography, and genetics whether one grows up as a Hindu or Sikh, Buddhist or Christian, Muslim or Bahá'í. Consequently, religious exclusivism makes a religious elite of those who have privileged knowledge, or who are socially fortunate, or who benefited from the historical serendipity of the age into which they were born. And, as is so often the case, when religious exclusivism is conjoined with the political power of the state, the result is religious egoism – the idea that what is right for a particular religious community in a society is right for all members of society. Global justice requires that humans be freed from the tyranny of religious egoism as much as from the tyranny of non-religious forms of ideological exclusivism.

Of the alternative ways to respond religiously to the conflicting truth claims of the world religions, religious exclusivism, especially in the form of religious egoism, would be actively opposed to attempts to achieve a concurrence among diverse religious and non-religious ethics. Inclusivism, pluralism, and henofideism are more conducive to the possibility of a universal religious ethic, and so the possibility of a universal ethic, and they support article 18.3 of the proposed Universal Declaration of Human

Rights by the World's Religions that "everyone has the duty to promote peace and tolerance between different religions and ideologies."

Inclusivism has become the official view within Roman Catholicism since Vatican II[25], and it might be argued that, of all the world religions, Hinduism has always been the most inherently inclusivist. Fundamentally, inclusivism supposes that there is a specific sort of religious experience and understanding of the Transcendent which is elemental to all religion (indeed, is elemental for all humans). Still, each world religion will tend to see *itself* as the culmination of the elemental apprehension of the Transcendent, as for example when the Roman Catholic theologian Karl Rahner says that the Christian has, "other things being equal, a still greater chance of salvation than someone who is merely an anonymous Christian,"[26] and this undermines the sense that religious inclusivism can be truly global. This may lend support to pluralism or henofideism. Unlike pluralists, a henofideist is not necessarily committed to the veracity of other religious worldviews than his or her own; however, while having fidelity to a single religious worldview, a henofideist, aware of other cultures and their religious perspectives, acknowledges that other religious worldviews might be correct. But in any case, once one has moved beyond exclusivism, what will matter is the shared, underlying religious point of view, the manifestation of universality in religion, and one's willingness to relate to and to treat all others equally as spirit.

Humans need to make transforming choices against self-centeredness, and to do so, they need to cultivate attitudes and habits that will eventually enable each person better to act relationally. As one avenue to this desirable end, even the secular must agree that all humans must be free to cultivate in themselves religious habits of action and learning which reflect the religious point of view. As the Universal Declaration of Human Rights by the World's Religions says in article 18.2, "everyone has the right to retain one's religion," for the pursuit of religion in a spirit of love and compassion is a universal right. Importantly, giving others the freedom to pursue religion – because one recognizes their intrinsic worth as spirit – is not only a responsibility from the religious perspective, it is, from a religious perspective, foundational to all responsibility and all rights. In spite of the dangers of any slide toward religious egoism, freedom of religion remains a fundamental human right. The free pursuit of religion has to do with not just what kind of people we want to be, but what kind of a global community we want to live in. To achieve a just global society, we need both tolerance and a shared sense of commonality, and both are strongly supported by the religious point of view. To see the spiritual potential in others, despite their differences from our own selves, is both to share our common humanity as well as to accept, and cherish, the uniqueness of other persons.

THE ROLE OF RELIGION IN RIGHTS

The twentieth century saw a great outpouring of work in secular ethics. *A Theory of Justice* by John Rawls is probably the most influential book on ethics in the twentieth century. The essence of Rawls' view is captured in the dictum "justice is fairness." As a method to eliminate prejudice and achieve objectivity in order to be fair, Rawls proposes that moral judgments should be made from behind a self-imposed "veil of ignorance." That is, he proposes that we should treat others simply as human beings, quite apart from any unique properties or special circumstances they may have.

This sounds good, but it ignores our real personhood, which is particular, not general. It ignores gender differences and, as women have long known, to be ignored as a full person, and so objectified, is worse than being recognized as the individuals we are, even if opposed. And it ignores the religious distinctiveness of each human. This is also, in part, a gender issue, for while men control religious hierarchies, often part of women's identity is caretaker of religion in the home. Moreover, if we take away the Judaism, Buddhism, Jainism, Confucianism, Christianity, and so on from our neighbors, we treat them as "its," not persons. And if we only consider justice and rights and not the relationality that the religious point of view enjoins, we will be left to deal with each other only through the rules of law. The consequences are obvious. Litigation is out of control in many Western countries. My own country, the litigious United States, certainly does not provide an ideal model for global human relations. This is where the world religions come in, for they can provide guidance, in the twenty-first century, with their various means and modes, to go beyond ego concerns to a centeredness on the personhood of others. Genuine religion offers relationality, not mere rules.

Another normative ethics which saw considerable development in the twentieth century is utilitarianism. The basic idea of morality on this view is to act so as to produce the greatest good for the greatest number. Again, *prima facie*, this secular ethics sounds good. However, minority interests are all too easily overpowered by the "great good" to the majority. In Japan only about one percent of the population is Christian. Should specifically Christian needs be legislated against if they are inconvenient or even repulsive to the majority? Or to turn the example around, should the dominant religion in the world, Christianity, with nearly two billion adherents, have more say in global society because there is a greater good for a greater number? Clearly the answer is "no" to both questions. Furthermore, unchecked utilitarianism can lead to some appalling ideas, such as Peter Singer's notorious conclusion that child infanticide could be justified on utilitarian grounds.

At the start of the First World War, the Carnegie Endowment for International Peace stated, regarding war between Greece and Bulgaria, that:

> Day after day the Bulgarians were represented in the Greek press as a race of monsters, and public feeling was roused to a pitch of chauvinism which made it inevitable that war, when it should come, should be ruthless...Deny that your enemies are men and you will treat them as vermin.[27]

This is reminiscent of Raskolnikov's characterization of the pawnbroker whom he kills in Dostoevsky's *Crime and Punishment* as a mere "louse." As Gerrie ter Haar argues in her masterfully titled "Rats, Cockroaches, and People Like Us" (chapter 5 in this volume), it is easy to violate the rights of – and even wantonly kill – those whom we do not see as persons. In place of the objectification and even verminification of others, the contribution of the world religions can be an affirmation, from the religious point of view, of the unique personhood of each and the spirituality of all. Thus, as just two examples, we find this reasoning in the Jewish and Islamic traditions, respectively:

> It was for this reason Adam was created alone: to teach you that anyone who destroys a single life, it is to be accounted to him by Scripture as if he had destroyed the whole world, and whoever preserves a single life, it is accounted to him by scripture as if he had preserved a whole world.[28]

> Why should a Muslim commit himself/herself to the rights and well-being of a fellow human being? The answer is because God has already made such a commitment when God invested so much of the God-self in each and every person. This is why the Qur'an asserts that whomever kills a fellow human being unjustly it is as if he/she has murdered all of humanity – it is as if the killer has murdered the divine sanctity and defiled the very meaning of divinity.[29]

Religion is a virtually universal and authoritative resource for humanity's understanding of morality. Thus, with respect to any purely secular human rights declaration, adherence will be limited and opposition expanded because opposition will be based not on the moral quality of the proposals but on the final authority of the proposals. As Abou El Fadl argues with respect to Islam:

> To propose secularism as a solution in order to avoid the hegemony of Shari'a, and the possibility of an abuse of power, in my view, is unacceptable. There are several reasons for this. First, given the rhetorical choice between allegiance to the Shari'a and allegiance to international human rights, quite understandably most Muslims will make the equally rhetorical decision to ally themselves to the Shari'a. Second, secularism has become an unworkable and unhelpful symbolic construct. In the Muslim world, secularism is normally associated with what is described as the Western intellectual invasion, both in the period of colonialism and post-colonialism. Furthermore, secularism has come to symbolize a misguided belief in the probity of rationalism and a sense of hostility to religion as a source of guidance in the public sphere.[30]

The logic of Abou El Fadl's point will apply equally well to all the other world religions. It is fatal for human rights declarations to ignore the moral authority (among other sources of moral authority) of religion. For as Gerrie ter Harr notes, "For most people in the world, religion is an integral part of their existence, inseparable from the social and moral order, and it defines their relations with other human beings."[31]

A secular document on human rights such as the U.N. Declaration ultimately lacks the potential moral authority and adjudicatory power of a document like the proposed Declaration on Human Rights (and, I would add, Responsibilities) by the World's Religions. The task of the latter is to draw on the authoritative power and wisdom of the world religions without diminishing or contravening either the core features of each particular religious ethic or the core goal of secular human rights projects, which are summed up by An-Na'im in the notion of "secularism:" "The key feature of secularism is its ability to safeguard the *pluralism* of political community."[32] The secular protection of pluralism against, among other dangers, religious egoism, is crucial to a just society, and so the secular must not be subservient or held captive to religious theory. But what is needed is the construction of a social ethic which takes account of *both* the secular and the religious. It is all too easy for humans to favor themselves, to give more weight to their personal circumstances, in moral questions. So it is no surprise that secularism and religion are both poor at self-regulation. Each can, though, provide a measure of accountability for the other, achieving a partnership of regulation through balance. In particular, the secular has a key role as a constructive voice against the dangers of religious egoism, and the religious can add a powerful voice to the call to other-regarding action which lies at the heart of both the religious and the moral life.

NOTES

1. Thomas Jefferson, 1776, quoted in Geoffrey Robertson, *Crimes Against Humanity: The Struggle for Global Justice* (New York: Penguin Books, 2000), p. 6.
2. Alexander Hamilton 1787, quoted in Robertson, *Crimes Against Humanity*, p. 8.
3. For a comparison, more recent and fuller articulations of rights can be found in the Indian and South African constitutions.
4. Jeremy Bentham, *Supply without Burthen or Escheat Vice Taxation* 1794, Object V.
5. Robertson, *Crimes Against Humanity*, p. 12.
6. Ibid.
7. Ibid., p. 21.
8. H.G. Wells, 1942, quoted in ibid., p. 23.
9. Ibid., p. 24.
10. Ibid., p. 27.
11. See p. 29 below.
12. See part III of this volume, esp. chap. 9.
13. In "Being Religious and Doing Ethics in a Global World," in *Ethics in the World Religions*, ed. Joseph Runzo and Nancy M. Martin (Oxford: Oneworld, 2001), p. 23, I argue that there are at least four identifiable characteristics of the moral point of view: (1) taking others into account in one's actions because one respects them as persons (benevolence); (2) the willingness to take into account how one's actions affect others by taking into account the good of everyone equally (justice or impartiality); (3) abiding by the principle of universalizability – i.e. the willingness to treat one's own actions as morally laudable or permissible or culpable only if similar acts of others in comparable circumstances would be equally laudable or permissible or culpable; and (4) the willingness to be committed to some set of normative moral principles.
14. I first argued for this in "Ethical Universality and Ethical Relativism," in *Religion and Morality*, ed. D.Z. Philips (London: Macmillan, 1996), where I defended the idea that the use of torture is always immoral.
15. See p. 305 below.
16. Margaret Farley, "Feminism and Universal Morality," in *Prospects for a Common Morality*, ed. Gene H. Outka and John P. Reeder, Jr. (Princeton: Princeton University Press, 1992), p. 182.
17. Confucius, *The Analects* (London: Penguin, 1979), p. 135.
18. Christopher Key Chapple, *Nonviolence to Animals, Earth and Self in Asian Traditions* (Albany: State University of New York Press, 1993), p. 16.

19.   Martin Buber, *I and Thou,* trans. Walter Kaufmann (New York: Scribner's, 1970), p. 59.
20.   Alan Donagan, "Common Morality and Kant's Enlightenment Project," in *Prospects for a Common Morality,* ed. Outka and Reeder, pp. 65–66.
21.   James Kellenberger, *Relationship Morality* (University Park: Pennsylvania State University Press, 1995), pp. 42 and 53.
22.   This can also be put in terms of two other features of the religious point of view which parallel the moral point of view: recognizing the spirit of everyone equally; and accepting the universalizability to others of one's own treatment of oneself as spirit.
23.   See p. 29 below.
24.   I discuss henofideism in more detail in *Global Philosophy of Religion* (Oxford: Oneworld, 2001), chap. 2.
25.   See the dogmatic constitution *Nostra Aetate* from Vatican II.
26.   Karl Rahner, *Theological Investigations,* vol. 5 (London: Darton, Longman & Todd, 1966), p. 132.
27.   Carnegie Endowment for International Peace, *Report of the International Commission to Inquire into the Causes and Conduct of the Balkans War* (1914), quoted in Jean Seaton, "The New 'Ethnic' Wars and the Media," in *The Media of Conflict,* ed. Tim Allen and Jean Seaton (London and New York: Zed Books, 1999), p. 46.
28.   Michael Fishbane, "The Image of the Human and the Rights of the Individual in Jewish Tradition," in *Human Rights and the World's Religions,* ed. Leroy S. Rouner (Notre Dame: University of Notre Dame Press, 1988), p. 19.
29.   See p. 338 below.
30.   See p. 321–322 below.
31.   See p. 80–81 below.
32.   See p. 30 below.

Plate 2 Tomb or *kramat* of Sheikh Madura, a Muslim religious leader who died whilst imprisoned on Robben Island in South Africa, erected beside a guard tower. He and many other religious and political leaders, including Nelson Mandela, were imprisoned on the island for their outspoken opposition to government policies that violated human rights, from the Dutch colonization to apartheid.

Photo: *Nancy M. Martin and Joseph Runzo*

2

THE SYNERGY *and* INTERDEPENDENCE *of* HUMAN RIGHTS, RELIGION, *and* SECULARISM

Abdullahi A. An-Na'im

With clear appreciation of the reasons for the political and social reality of tension between human rights, religion, and secularism, I will argue for synergy and interdependence of these three paradigms, rather than a choice between them. By synergy and interdependence I mean that each of the three needs the other two for fulfilling its own rationale, and sustaining its relevance and validity for its own constituency. The premise of my analysis is that a positive relationship between the three is problematic, yet it is desirable and possible to overcome the conceptual and practical difficulties of synergy and interdependence through an internal transformation within each paradigm. As explained below, the term "synergy" is used here to indicate that the possibilities of internal transformation within each paradigm are both necessary for promoting the proposed tripartite relationship, as well as being facilitated by it.

This process should be deliberately promoted for the legitimization of human rights, regulation of the role of religion in public life, and affirmation of secularism in accordance with the rationale of each of the three, as well as the practical benefits of their interdependence for individual freedom and social justice. In other words, I am concerned with these issues for their fundamental practical policy implications, rather than out of purely theoretical interest. Being from Sudan, I know that hundreds of thousands have died, and millions continue to endure untold suffering, directly because of widespread confusion over these issues. It is true that this confusion is often manipulated by hard-core ideologues or cynical politicians (such as Dr. Hassan al-Turabi, the leader of the National Islamic Front of Sudan, in my view) who may well be aware of the real issues. But I am more concerned with the general public, whose religious sentiments and apprehensions about change are being manipulated.

One can approach this discussion from a variety of perspectives, but I prefer to begin with the question of the moral or philosophical foundation of human rights because it clearly brings out the tension between the three paradigms, while emphasizing the need for and possibilities of its mediation. Article 1 of the United Nations Universal Declaration of Human Rights (U.D.H.R.) of 1948 provides: "All human beings are born free and equal in dignity and rights. They are endowed with reason and conscience and should act towards one another in a spirit of brotherhood." The omission of any specific foundation of the equality of all human beings in dignity and rights, whether religious or secular, was apparently designed to evade the issue in the interest of achieving consensus on the Declaration. But more than fifty years later, the question of the moral or philosophical foundation of human rights remains both difficult to answer and critical for the practical implementation of these rights.

Given the difficulty of agreement on a single foundation for human rights, I suggest promoting the legitimacy of, and popular support for, these rights through an overlapping consensus among multiple foundations, instead of the usual polarization of secular versus religious perspectives on this issue. Using this proposition as an entry point to a wider discussion of a creative interface between the three paradigms, I will begin with working definitions of the three terms, highlight preexisting dynamics of synergy and interdependence between the three paradigms, and discuss how that might be deliberately promoted. While insisting that synergy and interdependence between all three need to be sustained and safeguarded in all societies, I will conclude with an illustration of the importance and application of the proposed approach in the Islamic context.

WORKING DEFINITIONS AND THE FOUNDATION
OF HUMAN RIGHTS

To begin with human rights, it may be helpful to distinguish between the two senses in which this term is often used. In popular discourse, the term is frequently used to signify an intuitive understanding of the objectives or implications of historical struggles for freedom and justice in general. But as used here, the term "human rights" refers to the particular conception of individual freedom and social justice articulated in the U.D.H.R. of 1948, and more specifically specified in subsequent treaties in order to be implemented through a variety of mechanisms. In this specific sense of the term, human rights are universal claims of rights that are due to all human beings by virtue of their humanity, without distinction on such grounds as race, sex (gender), religion, language, or national origin. The key feature of human rights in this specific sense is universality, in the sense that they are rights due to all human beings, everywhere.

However, since the process by which the U.D.H.R. was drafted and adopted in 1946–1948 was not fully inclusive because the vast majority of the peoples of Africa and Asia were still suffering from European colonialism, the universality of the human rights it proclaimed was contingent on subsequent developments. It can be argued that this has already happened to some extent through the affirmation of the U.D.H.R. by newly independent African and Asian states, and their participation in the drafting and adoption of subsequent human rights treaties. But it is clear that the challenge of relevance and efficacy remains, and shall continue into the future. As emphasized below, to be relevant and legitimate in truly global terms, the concept and practice of human rights must achieve more effective implementation of economic, social, and cultural rights, and be open to possibilities of collective rights, such as a right to development and cultural self-determination. Such an evolving and dynamic conception of human rights needs both religion and secularism for mediating conflicts and tensions within the same right, as well as between different categories of rights, both individual and collective.

The working definition of religion I am proposing here focuses on what is particularly relevant to the proposed tripartite relationship with human rights and secularism, without claiming to be true of every conceivable understanding of religion or comprehensively to include all issues that might be raised regarding a particular religion. For this limited purpose, religion can be defined as a system of belief, practices, institutions, and relationships that is used by a community of believers to identify and distinguish itself from other communities. The key feature of religion in this specific sense is the exclusivity of the community of believers, as defined by its own religious faith and practice. This is not to say that it is not possible to understand some religious traditions in more inclusive terms. In fact, I am counting on that possibility for the overlapping consensus I am proposing for the universality of human rights. But common human experience indicates that adherence to any religion is exclusive of those who are not accepted as members of the community of believers. Some form or degree of at least moral, and often material, exclusion seems to be necessary for vindicating the validity of the faith of one religious community, as distinguished from that of other religious communities. In contrast, human rights, as defined here, are supposed to be intrinsically inclusive of all human beings by virtue of their humanity, and irrespective of membership in any social group.

It may be useful at this point to distinguish between the universalizing normative claims of some religions and the universality of human rights. The universal normative claims of Christianity and Islam, for instance, are a call for all human beings to accept the faith in order to benefit from its normative system as defined by the dominant doctrine of the particular faith. In contrast, the universality of human rights is supposed to represent a convergence of different traditions and be available to all human beings, regardless of religious or other social status. Whereas the former is premised on an assertion of the exclusive moral superiority of one religion, the latter is supposed to be founded on the moral equality of different religious and cultural traditions. In other words, the rationale of religious solidarity is exclusive while that of human rights is inclusive, though the full potential of the universality of the latter is still to be realized. From this perspective, the universalizing claims of liberalism or any other particular normative tradition as the exclusive foundation of human rights is as objectionable as the universalizing moral claims of some religions.

For the limited purposes of this discussion, secularism can be defined as a principle of public policy for organizing the relationship between religion and the state in a specific context. Since historical experience has shown that the exclusivity of religion tends to undermine possibilities of peaceful coexistence and solidarity among different communities of believers, secularism has evolved as the means for ensuring the possibility of pluralistic political community among different religious communities. The key feature of secularism is its ability to safeguard the pluralism of political community, subject to significant differences as to how that might be achieved in practice. In other words, I am concerned here with this particular feature of secularism, however it may be understood and applied under different regimes of government.

The problem is that the same minimal normative content that makes secularism conducive to interreligious coexistence and solidarity diminishes its capacity to support the universality of human rights without reference to another source of moral foundation. That necessary quality of secularism also fails to address the need of religious believers to express the moral implications of their faith in the public domain. In other words, secularism alone is a necessary but insufficient condition for realizing its own rationale of political stability. The proposed tripartite relationship between human rights, religion, and secularism is intended to supplement the minimal normative content of secularism as the necessary basis of national and global pluralism of political communities. This can be achieved by emphasizing a dynamic and deeply contextual understanding of secularism in each society, instead of insisting on the imposition of preconceived notions of strict separation of "church and state."

Human Rights

To briefly elaborate on these three concepts for the purposes of subsequent analysis, I would first note that the immediate antecedents and articulation of the modern concept of human rights have emerged from Western (European and American) experiences since the eighteenth century. As commonly acknowledged, however, those experiences were premised on the Enlightenment, rather than Christian or Jewish theologies, though the latter have tended to reconcile themselves with the former over time. In view of the "universalization" of the European model of the nation-state through colonialism, the basic purpose of the U.D.H.R. appears to have been to "universalize" protections of fundamental individual freedoms as safeguards against the abuse of the expansive powers of the state. While initially limited by the actual experiences of Western countries in this regard, the actual scope of rights that have emerged since 1948 is broader than what can be found under the constitutional system of any of those countries. In other words, the Western origins and immediate antecedents of human rights have already been overtaken by developments reflecting the experiences and expectations of other peoples of the world.

As universal standards that are necessary for the protection of fundamental rights against the contingencies of national politics, human rights standards are supposed to be the product of international agreement. Moreover, the claim of the international community to act as arbiter in safeguarding certain minimum standards is not plausible without the corresponding commitment of its members to encourage and support each other in the process. This is particularly critical in view of significant differences in the degree of political will, and gross differentials in institutional capacity and material resources for the implementation of these rights, in different parts of the world. Accordingly, the distinguishing features of human rights are universal recognition of the same rights and international cooperation in their implementation.

However, the present apparent consensus on international human rights standards often obscures serious cultural or ideological differences, with significant practical consequences. While problems of non-Western cultures regarding the rights of women, for example, are well known, there is little awareness of Western cultural or ideological problems regarding the true universality of human rights. From a normative point of view, economic, social, and cultural rights, such as the right to housing and education, are as fundamental as civil and political rights of freedom of belief or expression. To take a positivist view of human rights, widely ratified treaties provide for both sets of rights. Yet Western governments and public opinion alike have found it difficult to accept that economic, social, and cultural rights are human rights in the current sense of the term. In this light, it is clear that both Western and non-Western societies face the challenge of accepting the universality of some human rights within their own cultures.

Another point to note here is that agreement on international standards of human rights was only possible on the understanding that these rights are to be implemented through the agency of the state. Given prevalent understandings of national sovereignty and international relations, it was imperative for the Charter of the United Nations and the U.D.H.R. to strike a balance between the international protection of human rights, on the one hand, and respect for the domestic jurisdiction of nation-states, on the other. Thus, by universalizing certain notions of fundamental rights, the international human rights system seeks to make these rights binding under international law, while leaving application on the ground to the agency of the nation-state. The mitigation of this paradox of state self-regulation of its own human rights performance requires a clear understanding of local, national, and international actors and processes which influence the actual conduct of states in this regard, including the role of different religious communities and their view of secularism.

This understanding is necessary for diminishing what I call human rights dependency by legitimizing human rights in local cultures and generating political support for their indigenous implementation. By "human rights dependency" I am referring to the fact that international non-governmental organizations (N.G.O.s) tend to monitor violations, primarily in developing countries, and report about them in developed countries in order to prompt the governments of developed countries to pressure offending governments to protect human rights. In contrast, persons and groups in developed countries, acting on their own initiative and through local institutions, are protecting their own human rights. This approach to the international advocacy of human rights in developing countries is premised on economic, security, and political dependencies of those countries on developed countries. It is because Kenya or Egypt, for instance, is dependent on Western aid that the governments of Kenya and Egypt are sensitive to Western pressure. While it is useful to use these realities of global power relations to pressure offending governments to protect the human rights of their own people, the underlying dependencies remain, and may even be legitimized by their use in such a "noble cause." In fact, this approach assumes that the human rights paradigm is incapable of addressing structural factors and root causes of human rights violations that are overlooked, and perhaps legitimized, by the currently dominant forms of human rights advocacy.

Addressing the underlying causes of violations, in addition to providing effective remedies for individual violations as and when they occur, requires the mobilization of the maximum possible degree of political will at the local, national, and international level. The above-noted limitations of the modern human rights paradigm are unlikely to be overcome without solidarity and cooperation among different religious communities. Since this is not readily available within currently prevalent exclusive understandings of religion, human rights and secularism are needed for the internal transformation of religious doctrine, as discussed below.

Religion

The avoidance of religious perspectives since the adoption of the U.D.H.R., as noted earlier, can diminish the moral force of the purported universality of human rights. But the obvious reason for this avoidance is the exclusive nature of religious traditions. Since religion divides rather than unites human beings, the argument goes, it is better to avoid it altogether in order to find common ground for the protection of human rights among all religious believers and non-believers alike. The validity of this characterization of the basic tension between these two normative systems is enhanced, rather than diminished, by the consistency of theory and practice. The more one is a "true believer," the less likely one will be to accept non-believers as moral equals. Conversely, the more religious perspectives are excluded from human rights discourse, the less likely are believers to accept the universality of human rights.

The question is how to make an understanding of human rights equally valid and legitimate from the perspectives of the wide variety of believers, as well as non-believers, around the world. Without suggesting that religion is the only source of morality in any society, one can appreciate that those who believe that religion is a powerful foundation of the morality of a political community have as much right to that claim as those who believe in non-religious foundations. Accordingly, different foundations of human rights as an essential framework for individual freedom and social justice in the present context should in fact be seen as interdependent and mutually supportive, rather than antagonistic and exclusive of each other.

But religion is unlikely to play this role without internal transformation within the relevant religious tradition. As explained and illustrated in relation to Islam below, transformation is necessary and possible precisely because of what might be called "the secular dimension of religion." The transcendental aspect of religion is supposed to address the actual experiences of communities of believers and can only be understood in the concrete historical context and material circumstances of each religious community. In other words, competing interpretations of religious doctrine and their normative implications are bound to reflect existing human power relations within each community of believers. Human rights and secularism are critical for the fair and sustainable mediation of these competing claims within the framework of prevalent power relations of each community of believers, as well as between different communities. The consequent religious transformation, in turn, would facilitate synergy and interdependence between the religion in question, human rights, and secularism.

Secularism

As noted earlier, the basic limitation of secularism, as a social and political framework, is that appeal to it as a basis of political pluralism in diverse societies is premised on its limited view of the social good. In other words, secularism is able to unite diverse communities into one political community precisely because it makes the least moral claims on the community and its members. I am not suggesting that secularism is totally neutral from a normative point of view, as it does prescribe a certain civic ethos on the basis of some specific understanding of the person in relation to the community. Rather, my point here is that its necessarily minimalist normative content is too narrow to provide interreligious and cross-cultural foundations for the universality of human rights.

From a pragmatic or political point of view, the most serious objection to secularism as the foundation of the universality of human rights is its inability to inspire or motivate believers, who are the vast majority of the world population. In the grand sweep of human history at large, religion has been more influential than secularism as a foundation of political and social institutions. Indeed, as emphasized below, it may be necessary to seek a religious foundation or justification for the principle of secularism itself. I am not saying that a serious engagement of religion is essential for the legitimacy of both human rights and secularism everywhere, but I do believe that to be true for believers, who constitute the clear majority of people around the world.

A related concern is that secularism by itself is also unable to address any objections or reservations believers may have about any specific human rights standard or secular principle from their own religious point of view. For instance, since discrimination against women is often justified on religious grounds in many societies around the world, this source of systematic and gross violation of human rights cannot be eliminated without addressing its alleged religious rationale. Moreover, this must be done without violating freedom of religion or belief, as a fundamental human right in itself. While a purely secular discourse can be understanding and respectful of religion in general, its rebuttal of religious justifications of discrimination against women is unlikely to be convincing to, or accepted as legitimate by, believers in that religion. As discussed in the next section of this chapter, however, human rights and secularism are needed to encourage and facilitate internal transformation within religious traditions in order to overcome religious-based objections or reservations about human rights standards or secular principles.

The preceding remarks about secularism are not meant to deny the possibility of non-religious sources for the moral basis of social policy in any political community. Moreover, these remarks about the limitations of secularism as the primary or sole foundation of the universality of human rights are not intended to imply that religion is necessarily a better alternative by itself. Religion has certainly been at least as destructive as a purely secular foundation of political community throughout human history and in all parts of the world. The suggested synergy and interdependence to guard against the risks of religious as well as secular authoritarianism and oppression seeks to enhance the positive value of each of these three paradigms for its own rationale by mediating the tension between them.

The approach I propose for achieving this reconciliation is premised on a belief in the ability of human agency to promote understandings and practice of each of the three that are conducive to meaningful interdependence with the other two, as discussed in the next section. One challenge is to prevent the purported moral superiority of one religious community from diminishing the human dignity and rights of those who do not subscribe to that faith. Secularism is critical for maintaining the equal human dignity and rights of believers and non-believers alike, but its ability to play its role in political communities depends on its legitimacy to all segments of the population, including religious believers. In other words, secularism itself is unlikely to be effective in practice without religious justification for believers. Since this effort is critical for the practical utility of both human rights and secularism in the daily lives of believers, one should focus on ways of achieving it for every religion, instead of conceding that it cannot be done with one religion or another.

In terms of my analysis here, the question is how to secure the best possible conditions for human agency to achieve the necessary transformation of religious understandings for the legitimization of human rights and affirmation of secularism in each community of believers. The same applies to human rights and secularism in relation to each other and to religion, as discussed below. However, in emphasizing the centrality of human agency in promoting synergy and interdependence between these three paradigms, I am not assuming that would necessarily follow as a matter of course. Not only does the human agency of some actors tend to diminish the social and political "space" for the human agency of others to operate freely, but the outcome of the agency of every actor is also likely to be objectionable from some other point of view. Yet the human agency of some people is also capable, in my view, of countering the negative manifestations of the agency of others.

In concluding this section, I wish to emphasize that the universality of human rights can neither be assumed nor empirically verified among different cultural and religious traditions. Since the inherent and permanent diversity of the world precludes founding the universality of human rights on the normative claims of one religion or secular ideology, it is necessary to explore the possibilities of multiple foundations for the universality of human rights. This is unlikely to be readily available within existing understandings of any particular religious or secular tradition, especially in view of a dynamic and evolving conception of human rights as indicated earlier. It would therefore follow that the foundation of the universality of human rights presupposes possibilities of internal transformation within each religious and secular tradition.

Moreover, as all human societies in fact have to cope with religious and secular dimensions of daily life, any foundation for the universality of human rights must incorporate religious and secular perspectives in the same process. In any case, as explained in relation to Islam below, a sharp dichotomy between religious and secular dimensions of life is conceptually misleading and practically untenable. What is at issue is how these three paradigms relate to each other in a given context; and how to promote the possibilities of mutual cooperation among all of them at once. Drawing on the preceding discussion, I will now briefly explain the main elements of the proposed tripartite relationship, highlight some of its current expressions, and assess the prospects of promoting it further in different settings.

REALITIES AND PROSPECTS OF SYNERGY AND INTERDEPENDENCE

It seems to me that there are two main elements in the process of promoting the synergy and interdependence of human rights, religion, and secularism. First is a clear and dynamic understanding of the ways in which each side in this tripartite relationship is dependent on the other two for achieving its own objectives. This understanding should include ways in which this interdependence is already working, and how it might be deliberately improved and promoted. The second main element is a strong appreciation of the role of human agency in promoting internal transformation within each paradigm in support of greater synergy and interdependence. As discussed below, this appreciation should also include an assessment of the negative as well as positive possibilities of the specific context in which human agency is operating. I will now briefly elaborate on these two elements in relation to each other.

The interdependence of human rights, religion, and secularism outlined above, and further elaborated in this section, can be summarized as follows:

1. Human rights need religion as the most widely accepted source of moral foundation of political community, and for the mobilization of believers in particular.
2. Religion needs human rights not only to protect the human dignity and rights of believers themselves, but also to ensure freedom of belief

and practice, as well as the general development and relevance of each religion to its own adherents.

3.   Human rights need secularism for the political stability and peace among communities of believers and non-believers that are necessary for the protection of these rights.

4.   Secularism needs human rights for practical normative guidance in the daily protection of people against the abuse of the powers of the state.

5.   Secularism needs religion as the most widely accepted source of moral guidance for political community, as well as the means for satisfying the spiritual needs of believers within that community.

6.   Religion needs secularism to mediate relations between different communities within the same political space.

However reasonable or obvious these and other possible dimensions of synergy and interdependence of the three paradigms may seem, one should not expect them to be readily appreciated or acted upon without some deliberate strategies for promoting those possibilities. Since human agency is critical for the constant adaptation of human rights, religion, and secularism to changing circumstances, it should be possible to influence the direction of change within each paradigm in favor of enhancing their mutual synergy and interdependence. In other words, human agency is essential for addressing the challenge facing each paradigm to remain relevant and useful for its own purposes, which makes change inevitable for all three of them, as illustrated by the following examples.

As noted at the beginning, human rights in a general sense is the current expression of ancient struggles for social justice and human dignity. However, the specific sense of the term since the adoption of the U.D.H.R. is particularly appropriate today for organizing the extensive powers of the state over every aspect of life. Since all human societies are governed today by nation-states, certain safeguards and mechanisms have proved necessary for protecting individual rights and social justice. But the validity and sustainability of the second sense of the term is dependent on its vindication of human rights in the more general sense. In my view, the human rights paradigm has to respond effectively to the following continuing challenges if it is to achieve and maintain its legitimacy for most people around the world.

To begin with, the essence of the human rights idea is that all such entitlements should be provided as of right, and not simply as the incidental outcome of social policy, or be subject to the contingencies of the political process. People are more likely to accept the more specific sense of the term not only to the extent that it corresponds to their understanding of human rights in the general sense of social justice and human dignity, but also if it represents an added value in this regard. In other words, it is necessary for the specific sense of the term to represent effective means for realizing superior claims on the state and society at large.

By referring to human rights as "organizing" the extensive powers of the state, I am emphasizing that this paradigm includes positive obligations to implement what is commonly known as economic, social, and cultural rights, as well as "limiting" those powers in the traditional liberal sense of civil and political rights. For example, the so-called "negative" liberty of freedom of expression was traditionally understood to mean that the state should refrain from action that infringes on the right of people to express their opinions. In a more integrated sense of affirmative obligations for the state, the implementation of this human right should include the provision of education and other public facilities to enable all segments of the population at large to create and acquire knowledge and exchange information, rather than be a passive recipient. Protection of freedom of expression and provision of education are not meaningful for those who lack shelter or are ravaged by preventable or easily treatable disease. In this light, it is imperative to abandon any effort to classify human rights in different categories or set some of them as superior to others. Moreover, as emphasized earlier, this evolution in the meaning and implications of each human right is necessary for the universality of human rights to remain relevant and useful for the majority of the peoples of the world, and not only for the privileged elite.

It is also accepted by now that so-called individual human rights can only be achieved in the context of the family and community. This is clearly reflected in the text of the more recent U.N. treaties such as the Women's Convention of 1979, and Rights of the Child Convention of 1989, as well as in regional documents such as the African Charter on Human and People's Rights of 1981 and its subsequent development. Even for so-called traditional human rights, it is clear that respect for freedom of expression is dependent on contextually appropriate education that draws on the cultural traditions of the community. Language is critical for freedom of expression as well as education, yet it can hardly be conceived of in isolated individual terms. I am advocating not only transcendence of the traditional distinction between so-called civil and political rights, on the one hand,

and economic, social, and cultural rights, on the other, but also acceptance of the possibility of collective or group rights as integral to the protection of individual rights. Regarding collective rights, I should note that I am not suggesting that every claim of collective right should be accepted, but that such claims should be given serious consideration, rather than dismissed as simply inconsistent with the individual focus of human rights doctrine.

Another relevant set of issues in the human rights field relates to a broader and more dynamic understanding of the protection of human rights as the humane side of globalization. There is growing evidence that human rights have been co-opted by powerful states to further their own foreign-policy objectives and perpetuate their hegemony over developing countries. Even if this is not true yet, it is likely to happen precisely because of the moral and political power and utility of the human rights idea. But within this same dynamic of the acceleration of shrinking space and time, economic and security interdependence commonly associated with globalization can be used to redress the drastically negative consequences of these phenomena. The global and structural nature of political oppression and economic deprivation call for global strategies of response that are facilitated by the same mechanisms and technologies of global integration.

The preceding remarks are not meant to suggest that human rights as such must be the answer to all problems of differential power relations, whether locally or beyond. Rather, the point is that human rights need to be "owned" by different peoples around the world, instead of being perceived as simply another facet of Western hegemony. In other words, for the human rights idea to remain useful for its intended purposes of liberation and justice at all levels throughout the world, it must be accepted as relevant and meaningful for the needs and expectations of all persons and groups. This would clearly suggest that legitimizing human rights in local cultures and religious traditions is a matter of vital importance for the survival and future development of the human rights paradigm itself. Given the internal transformation indicated below, religion can also provide the moral under-pinnings of dynamic development of the idea to address emerging issues in different settings. Secularism contributes to the political stability and communal security that provide the practical context for negotiating the relationship between human rights and religion in each setting.

Shifting now to the *religion* side of the relationship, I would strongly emphasize that internal transformation is critical for the very survival of religious traditions, as well as for the legitimacy of religious experience. At a more fundamental level, every orthodox precept or view that believers take for granted today started as a heresy from the perspective of another orthodox doctrine, and may well continue to be considered as such by some believers in the same religion. In everyday life, without such human rights as freedom of belief and expression, there will be no possibility of growth and development within the existing doctrine of any religion. This same need is served by secularism as a principle of public policy for ensuring that an authoritarian religious group taking control of the state will not threaten the essential interests of any segment of the population.

The main difficulty here is not the possibility of theoretical development of liberal or liberation theology within the framework of the major religions of the world. Rather, the problem is that issues of authority and representation often frustrate the propagation of such views for wider support among believers. If a community defines itself to the exclusion of others, it is unlikely to listen to outsiders defining or contesting its own religious doctrine, or its normative and behavioral precepts. This is, of course, a constant problem with religious communities throughout history, as critical voices always risk being de-legitimized by attacks on their so-called religious credentials. For instance, Muslims are unlikely to take seriously the advocacy of Islamic reform by a non-Muslim, or a Muslim who is perceived to be a heretic or apostate for going too far in his or her critique of prevalent understandings of Islam.

The dilemma facing religious reformers is therefore how to retain credibility as internal agents of change, while being critical of the beliefs and practices of their own community of believers. This dilemma is particularly sharp when such critique is believed to be serving the hegemony of external powers. The more a religious community feels threatened by internal instability or external domination, the less likely it is to be tolerant of religious dissent. In order to discredit the dissenting person's views, questions are raised about his or her personal piety and authority to represent the authentic voice of the community. Moreover, the defense of dissidents by external forces is often taken as proof that they are agents of foreign powers or cultures intent on undermining the community of believers from within. This would tend to limit the utility of both human rights and secularism in protecting the rights of religious dissidents without a religious justification for these two paradigms.

The role of human agency has always been contested, especially in relation to the divine, perhaps precisely because of the centrality of that role for the possibilities of reinterpretation and reform. While this is also true of secular ideologies, as illustrated by recent experience with Marxism or various forms of nationalism, it is probably more problematic in religious discourse because of the transcendental nature of most religious doctrine. One way of minimizing the negative impact of these tendencies on the possibilities of internal transformation is to emphasize the social and political implications of religious doctrine for the everyday lives of persons and communities. Since an exclusively religious frame of reference for assessing those implications is likely to simply reinforce the orthodox view, human rights and secularism can provide some commonly agreed criteria for that purpose. That is to say, dissidents can point to international consensus on the universality of human rights and the experiences of other societies with secularism in support of their social and political critique of religious chauvinism. In contrast, if they rely on what is perceived to be an external justification for an "innovation," that will be rejected as "unauthentic."

The obvious benefit of human rights and secularism in this context is that they ensure the "space" for human agency of minority voices to compete for achieving authority and acceptance on their own merits, instead of being suppressed simply because they disagree with the prevailing view. But the space thereby created or secured should also be conducive to overcoming the problematic of the so-called insider–outside dichotomy. It is true, in my view, that the legitimate importance of this divide is often exaggerated. Instead of assessing a person's credibility by the arbitrary divide of nominal membership of a community of believers, which is often more a matter of "accident of birth" than genuine personal choice, the criteria should be a person's understanding of and empathy with the beliefs and concerns of that community. But since this dichotomy remains real for most people, and may indeed have some justification in certain settings, human rights and secularism are needed as viable structural means for securing the right of dissent within any community, rather than simply appealing for toleration of dissent.

This protection would be particularly important when there is need for a fundamental paradigm shift in religious discourse through human agency without necessarily claiming to have received new revelation or starting a new religion. As discussed in relation to Islam in the next section, this can happen through a contextual critique of the basic assumptions and methodology of current orthodox doctrines within the particular religious tradition. Such an approach may be relevant to other scriptural religions, Christianity and Judaism, but some parallel analysis can probably apply to other religions. The point is that if and when a paradigm shift or its equivalent is needed, it would be emerging within the framework of the religion in question, rather than through seeking to "transplant" ideas from a different religious or secular tradition. But that is unlikely to happen without some normative guidance and institutional safeguards, which can be provided by human rights and secularism.

An apparent problem here is how can the normative guidance of the religion in question be given, when the community of believers rejects its own reformers as heretics for suggesting a paradigm shift in support of human rights and secularism within their own community? The way out of this paradox, I suggest, is in the synergy between these three concepts and their dynamic interaction in practice. For instance, as I will show in the next section, it would be possible for Muslim advocates of human rights and secularism to draw on the moral guidance of Islam, regardless of strong opposition by the proponents of orthodoxy, through the application of these principles. In doing so, they could gradually "win over" more Muslims to their position, thereby enhancing their credibility among the community, which would in turn be conducive to persuading other Muslims. This process would be facilitated, I believe, by mounting appreciation of the practical benefits of human rights and secularism in the modern context of Islamic communities.

As noted earlier, however, the ability of secularism to protect the "space" for human agency to operate more freely in religious discourse is dependent on its minimal normative content. On the positive side, this means that secularism would preclude a specific understanding of religious doctrine from being enforced as official state policy. This is conducive for internal religious transformation because it defines the outcome in more acceptable terms. Believers are less threatened by unorthodox views that are not forced on them through the organs of the state, while the population at large is reassured that public policy is determined through a more inclusive political process. Since people are more likely to consider accepting a point of view if they are not forced to live with the consequences of their choice, novel ideas have a better chance of being considered seriously on their own merit, as long as they are not made into official state policy. This indicates that what is known as "separation of church and state" (or religion and politics) is necessary, though insufficient.

But to play this constructive role in national politics, secularism needs the normative guidance of human rights and the moral justification of religion. The importance of human rights standards is obvious because secularism by itself may not be enough for safeguarding individual freedoms and social justice, as illustrated by recent experiences with totalitarian secular regimes, from Nazi Germany to the Marxism-Leninism of the Soviet Union and beyond. What is not sufficiently appreciated, in my view, is the importance of a religious justification and rationale for secularism. While the material conditions of coexistence may force a level of religious tolerance and diversity, this is likely to be seen as temporary political expediency by believers unless they are also able to accept that as at least consistent with their religious doctrine. Thus, as noted earlier, sustained secularism needs a religious justification for believers. This is not as difficult as it may seem because secularism and religion are in fact fundamentally overlapping and interacting. I will now focus on this particular dimension of synergy and interdependence in relation to the supposedly "hard case" of Islam in the next section, while insisting that similar analysis needs to be applied to other religious as well as secular ideologies.

SYNERGY AND INTERDEPENDENCE IN THE ISLAMIC CONTEXT

To illustrate the application of the above analysis in the Islamic context, I will focus on two main aspects of the possibility of religious transformation: a theological argument for change; and the political and social context within which that change may be realized in practice. On the theological side, it is necessary first to recognize and understand the role of human agency through an exegesis of the Qur'an and Sunna (traditions of the Prophet) in a historical context. Regarding the political and social context of that transformation, secularism secures the space for that debate to happen in a peaceful and orderly manner, while human rights provides a frame of reference for the organization of public and private life within the now universal model of the nation-state. Wide recognition and understanding of the centrality of human agency in Islamic discourse is critical for appreciating that secularism is in fact integral to religion, rather than opposed to it, and for accepting human rights as a framework for internal transformation of Islamic doctrine and practice. But for either of the two to play its role, secularism and human rights themselves must be open to their own internal transformations in response to various challenges in different contexts, as outlined earlier.

To begin with, I wish to emphasize two caveats about the role of religion in Islamic communities today. First, while many Muslims may claim that Islam is definitive in their private and communal lives, it is not the sole determinant of the behavior of Muslims or the basis of social and political organizations, even in purportedly Islamic states such as Iran, Pakistan, Saudi Arabia, and Sudan. In fact, some Islamic communities may have more in common with non-Islamic communities that share their ethnic and cultural affiliations, historical experiences, economic resources, political and security concerns, and so forth than with other Islamic communities in a drastically different context. In other words, Muslims' understanding and practice of Islam is conditioned by those factors, rather than simply reflecting an abstract, purely divine conception of the religion.

Second, there has always been significant diversity of theology/jurisprudential views and political opinion and practice within and between Islamic communities. Profound political and theological differences have divided Muslims from the beginning in the Arabia of the seventh century, resulting in a series of civil wars within a few decades of the Prophet's death in 632 CE. Significant disagreements over the interpretation and implementation of Islamic doctrine have already resulted in the emergence of distinctive religious factions and different schools of jurisprudence (*madhhab*, pl. *madhahib*), as well as wide differences of opinion within the same school. This diversity of views and practice is likely to become more intensified and widespread under modern conditions of education and communication. As more Muslim men and women are educated enough to know and consider the Qur'an, Sunna, and Islamic history for themselves, and communicate with others in different parts of the world about theological and political issues of common concern, there are more opportunities for disagreement as well as agreement. Muslim scholars and communities at large routinely cite this diversity of opinions and beliefs as a positive feature of their faith.

Indeed, disagreement is logically integral to the legitimacy and validity of religious experience itself because human beings cannot truly and honestly believe unless they are also able to disbelieve and/or change their view of the meaning and implications of their beliefs. This proposition may sound like a modern liberal notion, but it is in fact directly emphasized in 114 verses of the Qur'an and rooted in Islamic theological and philosophical discourse since the eighth century CE. Verse 18 of chapter 29, for example, reads: "Tell them that Truth is revealed from God, and let those who wish to believe, believe and those who wish to disbelieve disbelieve." But as I have discussed elsewhere, the real issue is the "framework of interpretation," and not simply the availability of texts of Qur'an and Sunna that can be understood one way or another. In other words, it is human agency that determines which texts are relevant to the issue at hand, and how they should be interpreted. Appreciating that whatever role Islam may play in the life of a Muslim community today is necessarily based on a specific understanding of the religion, in contrast to other understandings, supports the religious legitimacy of articulating competing interpretations.

In light of these two caveats, Islamic communities need to examine the relationship between their understandings and practice of Islam, on the one hand, and human rights and secularism, on the other. As already indicated, there is a theological and a political dimension to internal debates about these relationships. On the theological side, while such debates need to occur within an internal frame of reference (Qur'an and Sunna), human agency has always been central to Muslims' understanding and practice of Islam. Muslims believe that the Qur'an is the literal and final word of God, and Sunna is the second divinely inspired source of Islam. But the Qur'an and Sunna have no meaning and relevance in the daily life of individual believers and their communities except through human understanding and behavior. The Qur'an was revealed in Arabic, which is a human language that evolved in its own specific historical context, and many normative parts of the Qur'an were addressing specific situations in Mecca and Medina when they were conveyed by the Prophet. Sunna had to respond to the immediate issues and concerns that emerged in that context, in addition to any broader implications it may have. It is therefore clear that human agency was integral to the process of revelation, interpretation, and practice from the very beginning of Islam in the seventh century. In any case, the Qur'an and Sunna cannot be understood and applied at a given time and place, except by human beings who share the same basic qualities, and are influenced by the same concerns, as human beings everywhere.

From this perspective, a sharp distinction between the religious and the secular is misleading. Religious precepts necessarily respond to the secular concerns of human beings and have practical relevance only because those responses are believed to be practically useful by the people they are addressing and useful for their secular concerns. In other words, religious doctrine is necessarily implicated in the secular, and the secular is perceived by believers to be "governed" by religious doctrine. Muslims who find this proposition disturbing tend to think that it undermines the "divinity" of the sources of Islam. But that apprehension fails to appreciate that the Qur'an and Sunna are intended for human imperfection, and not simply as manifestations of the divine in the abstract. This point is critical for the theological basis of the relationship between Islam and both human rights and secularism.

The political side of internal discourses about this relationship relates to the historical context of the people concerned. Their ability to understand and appreciate what is proposed about the meaning and relevance of their faith to their daily lives is conditioned by their perception of their own situation. A reformer's ability to gain the confidence of a constituency, and authority among its members, depends on his or her understanding of all the complexity of their history and immediate context, concerns, and aspirations. Relevant questions include: Whose interests are undermined or promoted by one interpretation or another? What personal or psychological as well as broader political, economic, and sociological factors influence people's understanding (or willingness or ability to understand) the Qur'an? What is the influence of broader geo-political or security concerns on a community's ability or willingness to be open to challenge to its basic moral and metaphysical precepts?

It may be helpful at this stage to focus briefly on the question of the relationship between Islam and secularism in order to question the commonly presumed incompatibility between the two. As indicated above, there are theological and political/contextual dimensions to this issue. But it should first be emphasized that the confusion is definitional and terminological as well as substantive. This does not mean that the issue is not real and serious, especially in view of its drastic practical consequences. Rather, the point is that one needs to begin by clarifying questions of definition and terminology in order to frame the substantive side of the issue in more precise terms.

The main problem on the definition side, in my view, is the tendency to limit secularism to the experiences of West European and North American countries with Christianity since the eighteenth century. Whether viewed as "separation of church and state" or "disestablishment of religion," such definitions are obviously specific to certain situations and do not address the continuing social and political role of religion in public life. It is also problematic to equate secularism with the diminishing of the influence of religion in general. For example, Ernest Gellner said: "One of the best known and most widely held ideas in the social sciences is the secularization thesis: in industrial and industrializing societies, the influence of religion diminishes... One thing, however, is clear: the secularization thesis does not apply to Islam."[1] Since that could not possibly mean that religion has no influence whatever in any society, as that is obviously false, the question becomes what sort of influence, and how is it diminishing? From this perspective, I suggest that secularism should be understood in terms of the type of relationship between religion and the state, rather than a specific way in which that relationship has evolved in one society or another. I would also emphasize that the form that relationship should take in pluralistic societies has to be the product of organic development over time and be accepted as legitimate by the population at large, instead of expecting it to change immediately and drastically by constitutional enactment or political rhetoric.

As a matter of terminology that is relevant to this deeply contextual approach, it should be noted that the term "secularism" in its West European and North American sense has come to Africa and Asia in the suspect company of colonialism. For the Islamic societies in particular, this term is commonly associated with militantly anti-religious attitudes of the French Revolution, in relation to Christianity in particular. Nevertheless, this term can be used in relation to experiences of African and Asian societies, provided it is understood and applied in the specific context of each society, rather than being a feature of liberal political or constitutional transplant. This view of secularism, I believe, will redress much of the apprehension about the concept as a tool of Western imperialism, thereby facilitating possibilities of internal transformation to promote the proposed synergy and interdependence with human rights and religion.

Regarding the substantive issue, the most compelling argument for an Islamic rationale for secularism is its necessity for pluralistic nation-states, and the legitimacy of individual and communal religious experience, as well as the possibilities of internal transformation, as explained earlier. It is commonly claimed that Islam mandates the establishment of an "Islamic state" which will implement and enforce Shari'a (the normative system of Islam) as the law of the land. But in my view, the notion of an Islamic state is a contradiction in terms because Shari'a ceases to be the normative system of Islam by the very act of enacting it as the law to be enforced by the state. Since there is so much diversity of opinion among Islamic schools of thought and scholars, as noted earlier, any enactment of Shari'a principles as law would have to select some opinions over others, thereby denying believers their freedom of choice among equally legitimate competing opinions. Moreover, there is neither a historical precedent of an Islamic state to be followed, nor is such a state practically viable today. As the most avowed advocate of an Islamic state today would concede, there has never been such a state throughout Muslim history, since that of the Prophet in Medina was too exceptional to be practically useful as a model to be applied today. The implementation of Shari'a as the official state law is also untenable in economic and political terms for the modern nation-state in its global economic and political context.

The preceding analysis can be illustrated by debates about the status of Islamic family law, commonly known as Muslim personal law (M.P.L.) in many Islamic communities, both as majorities and minorities of their countries. While most countries, including many with a predominantly Muslim population, have opted for constitutional regimes that seek to uphold the fundamental human rights of women, those societies continue to struggle with how to reconcile that commitment with an equal commitment to communal cultural self-determination. For Muslims, even where they constitute a minority of the population, as in India, the enforcement of M.P.L. by the state is seen as critical for the cultural survival of their communities. But the problem is that M.P.L., as currently understood and applied by the state in some forty Muslim-majority countries around the world, and informally practiced by Muslim communities elsewhere, clearly discriminates against women. Consequently, the question is how to protect the individual human rights of women, while respecting communal demands for cultural self-determination. Even if the state is able and willing to uphold the human rights of women, how can that be done without presenting Muslim women with a tragic choice between their individual rights and the communal integrity of their communities?

Applying the proposed tripartite relationship, I would suggest the following strategy for mediating this conflict. Since upholding a commitment to the human rights of women in this regard does not happen in a vacuum, there is need for an internal discourse whereby Muslims can be persuaded to accept equality for women as consistent with their religious beliefs. This internal discourse is also necessary for negotiating the limits and implications of freedom of religion and belief as a human right. While both the universality of human rights and the principle of secularism are essential for protecting the necessary space for this discourse to take place, neither can be understood outside the concrete historical context of the community in question, and its relationship to other communities.

I opened this chapter by proposing that there should be synergy and interdependence between human rights, religion, and secularism, instead of a choice between them. But there is a choice in another sense after all, namely, whether or not to pursue the possibilities of mediating the tension between these three paradigms. In other words, I am urging scholars and policy makers to opt for synergy and interdependence rather than dichotomy and incompatibility between these paradigms because both choices are theoretically possible and practically available. However plausible an approach to mediation may be, whether the one I outlined above or any other, it is ultimately a human choice whether or not to adopt and implement it in practice.

NOTES

1. Ernest Gellner, "Foreword," in *Islam, Globalization and Postmodernity*, ed. Akbar S. Ahmed and Hastings Donnan (London and New York: Routledge, 1994), p. xi.

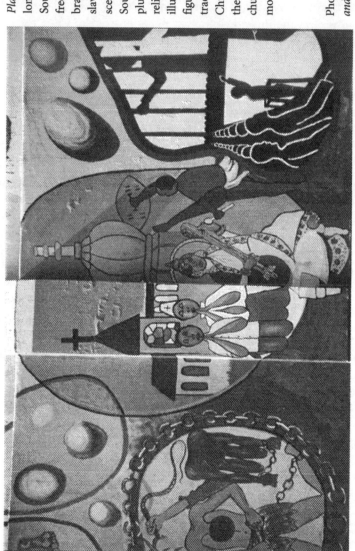

Plate 3 Section of a block-long mural in Durban, South Africa, portraying freedom of religion. Here, bracketed between a black slave being punished and a scene in a jail, the new South African vision of a pluralistic and multi-religious society is illustrated with a Zulu figure, a Hindu woman in traditional dress, and two Christians praying, while the skyline shows both a church steeple and a mosque.

Photo: *Nancy M. Martin and Joseph Runzo*

3

FAITH, FAITHS, *and the* FUTURE: THE FIRST TWO LIMBS *of* YOGA

Arindam Chakrabarti

> By the luminous sparks of speech, Brahman who alone knows Brahman, is appearing (in many forms) within his own self as if in a dream. Whoever apprehends however they have experienced that Brahman, through the meanings of words such as "This," "That," "Myself," let them apprehend that.[1]

Yogavasishtha, Utpatti 3.1

> If his works be good, he is faithful, however much his doctrines may differ from those of the rest of the faithful: if his works be evil, though he may verbally conform, he is unfaithful.

Benedict de Spinoza, *Tractatus Theologico-Politicus XIV*

HOPE FOR AN UNSCIENTIFIC POSTSCRIPT

An influential school of classical Hindu hermeneutics takes the whole meaning of a Vedic utterance such as "The unsharing eater incurs only sin" (*Rig Veda* X:117) to consist in its action-prompting imperative force. To have faith in such an utterance is not to have an idle belief that it corresponds with reality. To have faith in it is to will to act according to it – in this case, to be ready to share one's food and wealth with needy others.

But besides the purely categorical moral force, the concept of faith, or the Upanishadic notion of *shraddha*, also requires that faith should stir the heart with an assurance about the future: that non-attached performance of virtuous actions would eventually lead either to heavenly happiness or to blissful freedom, or to a cessation of suffering unimaginable by secular pleasure-seeking or power-thirst. This "hope," as Kant calls it, is non-scientific. It springs from the heart's demand that the universe could not be ethically unseeing or unjust.

Such a claim finds no evidential support in the naturalistic history of human lives and no *a priori* rational justification from the very concept of a faithful virtuous action. It is neither historically improbable nor logically impossible that the piously virtuous person would only lose and suffer like Job until the bitter end, while the technologically prudent, morally unscrupulous person would thrive. It is the mark of tradition-rooted faith that it flouts such scientific evidence or logic and stands by the heart's certitude that in the final future, genuine goodness will prevail and dharma will bring joy and freedom from misery.

Scientific empiricism is not the only enemy of such faith. The fact of a conflicting plurality of faiths, made glaring by recent technological and economic globalization coupled with the erosion of tradition-rooted hearts, makes it hard, at the present time, to listen lovingly to the voice of any single faith. Exclusivist zealotry, the bitter cultural aftertaste of a proselytizing past, religious nationalism, burning missionaries and razing mosques in a spirit of retaliative revivalism – such ugly faces of so-called faith turn the already slackening hearts against all faiths. Since there is no trans-traditional basis for a choice between them, and all supply enough arguments against each other, the historically aware, rational faith-choosers simply give up!

In this chapter I wish to suggest some ways in which we can try to use the first two moral limbs of the eight-limbed Yoga of Patanjali as a basis for a future pluralistic synthesis of faiths. A synthesis, of course, is not a corporate merger. Neither is it a peaceful coexistence in mutual indifference and incomprehension. It is an acceptance – even a celebration – of divergent philosophical and social orientations with a moral overlap at the bottom and a supra-rational (mystical) experimental overlap at the top. My hope that such a synthesized co-flourishing of many faiths will happen on earth is itself an article of faith. Without this hope I cannot practice that respect for other religions that my religion propels my heart to practice.

THE FUTURE AS AN OBJECT OF FAITH

Sutras 16, 17, 25, and 27 of Patanjali's *Yogasutras* state the four items on Yoga's therapeutic agenda: the malady, its cause, the means to its elimination, and the state after its elimination. The ill that ought to be eliminated is described with brilliant brevity in sutra 16: "Future suffering ought to be eliminated" (*heyman duhkham anagatam*). But "ought" implies "can." Therefore the practitioner of Yoga must have faith that such a sufferingless state can be attained in the future. His or her soul has suffered the agonies of repeated births, agings, and deaths for innumerable lives. So past experience inductively teaches the practitioner that the future life is likely to be full of suffering too. Yet he or she must hope that the desire to be free from pain, which is contained in the very experience of pain, cannot be in vain. Since pain must go, it must be the case that one day the practitioner will isolate him- or herself from this three-stranded tangle of pleasure, pain, and torpor and be a pure, uninvolved witness of these natural transformations.

The future is an object of wish, will, and faith. We wait and plan for, worry about, fear, dream, expect, imagine, and anticipate the future, but we never quite *see* it. The reason for this has been cautiously stated by K.C. Bhattacharya: the present is known only as beginning, never as ending.[2] Yet the future lies at that unseeable ending of the present. For a crass empiricist, Charvaka, for whom seeing alone is believing, there simply is no future to believe in.[3] Yet even the crass empiricist has desires and aspirations. Faithless wishing is at best a form of greedy gambling. While faith (that x will come to pass) without will or endeavor (to bring x about) can be a lazy pretense of certitude and surrender, faithless willing leads either to suicidal desperation or to demonic manipulativeness running amok with an incorrigible illusion of making history.

Faith alone nurtures the practical belief that truth will triumph and lies will lose. The belief that wherever there is dharma there is victory is not a piece of C.N.N. news. It can never be proven by empirical or logical reasoning. It is an article of faith nourished by the moral ardor of the heart (*shraddham hridayyaya akutya* – Rig Veda X:151, 4). Without this faith, our collective future is either a set of private fantasies or a dark inevitability of a common doom.

One of the ironies of the present times is that while human beings are obsessed with the future – in their greed for growth, dreams for newer technological wonders, political utopias, and fears of global ecological disasters – they also seem to be proudly bereft of faith. As speedy information-gatherers, the twentieth-century educated elite lives under the gloom of futurelessness, of not seeing where one is headed, not knowing what to want next, ready to wait and see, or – equally possible – wait and not see. The fear of being labeled a "gullible fanatic," a "blind believer," or an "illogical crank" haunts all post-Enlightenment human pursuits.

Yet the future is not given to observation and experiment. Predictive inferences, like weather reports, give probabilities. But in order for unwavering actions to be undertaken, we need more than comparisons of likelihood. We need the leap or plunge of faith that what one is striving for will come to pass because it morally must. Every choice entails a sacrifice. Choosing the razor's edge of the life of Yoga means giving up all the natural hedonism, the wonderful pleasures of an extrovert life.

But what if one never arrives at the promised state of Brahma-nirvana? When Arjuna voices the most common human anxiety, asking "What if, in midway, not having arrived at the goal, torn from both ends, the pursuer of the moral-spiritual path to Brahman, just perishes like a stray cloud?" (*Bhagavad Gita* VI:38), Krishna has to restore his faith in no uncertain terms, addressing his friend filially as "my child" (*tata*): "Partha! Neither here on earth nor hereafter can such a seeker perish. The doer of good, my child, never ends up in a bad way" (*na hi kalyanakrit kashchit durgatim tata gacchhati*) (*Bhagavad Gita* VI:38). Yet not all hearts warm up to such divine assurance.

The great book of human life, the epic *Mahabharata*, even after its bleakly happy ending, addresses us, at it were, with a touch of bitter disappointment in its unbelieving audience: "Raising my hands, here I cry out, but no one listens to me: From virtue (*dharma*) eventually come both Pleasure (*kama*) and Wealth (*artha*), so why not practice that?"[4] Dharma, of course, does not teach us how to have fun or get rich now or in the future, but teaches us how we ought to behave in order to become worthy of happiness and success. Faith falters at the sight of unworthy, unvirtuous people getting not only richer but sometimes even happier while the unilateral observer of dharmic duties either waits in line or faces ruin.

Harrassed, wronged, and enraged, Draupadi pours sarcasm on a pacifist pious son-of-dharma: "Dharma, I am told, protects all those kings who observe it, except you whom it does not seem to protect!"[5] So she argues that *now* is not the time to forgive or forbear; it is rather the time to take revenge and wage a war. And the war happens.

Projecting a Draupadi-like image of harassed Hinduhood, the "present" times have been described as the time for a violent reclamation of India's "Vedic" heritage, for quite a few decades by some. My conjecture is that such call for action on behalf of a "faith" is actually prompted by a loss of faith in dharma. It is a modernistic response to the worldwide web of impatience and aggressive desire for exclusive control and market success.

Indeed, the *Mahabharata* dictum that Draupadi was sarcastically alluding to – *dharmo rakshati rakshitah* (which is used in the logo of a

World Hindu Council) – does not mean that dharma can save us only when we protect it from foreign attacks. It means that if we keep morally faithful in our own lives to our own dharmic duties, then dharma takes care of our own futures. Apart from the misinterpretation of dharma in that dictum as a particular religion, the second occurrence of the verb *raksha* ("protect"/"save") in the *Mahabharata* means "observe or practice." It does not mean "defend, spread, or fortify." Unfortunately the political fever that ensues from regarding Hinduism as an endangered culture needing all the modern aggressive product-promoting marketing techniques to "protect" it from extinction or pollution is, like many forms of aggression, a symptom of insecurity rather than conviction and leaves little time, patience, and contemplative quiet for the actual practice of friendship, compassion, elation, and indifference, of non-injury, truthfulness, non-theft, and control of the passions – the real heart of *dharma-raksha!*

These are the negative and positive virtues that constitute the first two limbs of Yoga that I shall talk about in the next section. But let me spend a bit more time diagnosing the complex phenomenon of morally shaky faith campaigning for religious solidarity. There were very good psycho-social reasons for Draupadi's loss of faith and her impatience. She had gone through too much. She could not wait for the indefinite future when the righteousness of her husbands would bear fruit and the depravity of Dury-odhana and his brothers would karmically ripen into their total ruin. Krishna saw the truth but, like Tolstoy's God, waited. The dark testing night of exile and humiliation did not seem to be ending. Draupadi wanted to will the future of power and prestige that she wished for, rather than have faith that it would come in some future heaven.

There is a common ten-point definition of universal dharma in Sanskrit, which starts with the virtue of patience (*dhriti*). This is forbearance, the ability to wait that one is supposed to learn from Mother Earth. Sita was the daughter of this Earth, the goddess of patience, so she bore a lot. But Draupadi was no Sita. She was born from the sacrificial fire. Her speech was fiery, and she admired the speed with which Arjuna's arrow or Bhima's fists flew. She hated the philosophy of non-violence that Yudhishthira preached with long-winded lectures quoting moral legends from the past. Now, there is some connection between love of speed and egotism.

The last hundred years, it is often remarked, have witnessed a tremendous revolution in speed. Along with unthinkable technological advances enabling fast travel, fast communication across continents, and swift massacre of as large a number of lives as possible, acquiring merchandise through the Internet has made instantaneous superfluous buying seem like a basic survival need, if not a fundamental human right. Being totally oblivious of the past and having little patience for the future, the economically liberated person is typically distrustful of *other* times! Now, distrust of other times except the present must be closely related to distrust of other minds or other people. A society, drunk with the latest communication technology, cannot spare much time for learning about its own past, let alone performing rituals for ancestors. Similarly, a community wishing to "develop" fast cannot afford to think of leaving enough natural resources for the future.

"Two processes," says Georg Simmel in his *Philosophy of Money*, "that are endemic to the heights of a money-culture [are] cynicism and a blasé attitude."[6] Cynicism is manifested in the disparagement of all old values. Simmel's description written a hundred years back seems to fit the attitude of the young, successful e-business millionaires of today.

> The nurseries of cynicism are those places where money is available in huge quantities and changes owners easily. The more one discovers that honor and conviction, talent and virtue, beauty and salvation of the soul are exchanged against money...the more a mocking and frivolous attitude will develop in relation to these higher values that are for sale for the same kind of value as groceries and that also command "market price."[7]

Such cynicism, in its turn, leads to what Simmel calls the "blasé attitude" which results in an incapacity to be stimulated by the very objects of enjoyment that one too easily acquires. Homes and hotels need to be more and more luxurious; horror movies or danger-sports have to be scarier and scarier until everything feels dull and boring; "out of this emerges the craving today for excitement, for extreme impressions, for the greatest speed in its change...by the quantitative exaggeration of its content."[8]

All this cloying love of money and speed is somehow deeply connected with a shameless celebration of selfishness. In a recent issue of a popular American Sunday magazine, the last millennium has been termed "The Me-Millennium." In Indian society this epidemic of egotism has taken the form of a general pessimism about our collective future, a fraudulent glorification of a fabricated past, leading to the shameless mad pursuit of personal financial gain – a sort of ideological switch from Gandhi to Ayn Rand! Though this can be packaged positively as human beings' journey towards greater individualism, in the recent past this tendency no longer to depend on any supra-mundane power or to rely on nature's whims but to take personal control of one's own life has shown its ugly negative face precisely through this loss of faith in the Other: the divine Other, the species-other, the religious or cultural other, and indeed even the individual other – one's neighbor. This faithless hubris often expresses itself in slogans like "I have confidence in ME"!

Blasting Vedic chants and Qur'anic prayers simultaneously through loudspeakers from temples and mosques or practicing one universal spiritual Esperanto of an eclectic religion will not cure this disease. Discovering an underlying ethical common ground across the world religions and practicing those virtues with support from one's faith in one's own chosen or inherited tradition could be our only hope of remedy.

YAMA AND *NIYAMA* AND *AHIMSA* AS THEIR CENTER

In the first section I suggested that increased knowledge of and contact with many conflicting traditions and religious faiths can generate despair about the possibility of finding any shared ethic, let alone a common theology or ontology across these traditions. Now, one aspect of Yoga has of course begun to seep into mainstream Western life – that is, Yoga as a technique for bodily health and healing and psychological relaxation or efficiency-increasing focusing habits. From the point of view of classical Patanjala Yoga, however, to start with postures and breathing techniques – *asana* and *pranayama* – or with concentration and meditation – *dharana* and *dhyana* – would be to skip the first two rather vital limbs of Yoga. It is these two sets of moral and spiritual prerequisites – *yama* and *niyama* – that I want to speak about as my proposed trans-traditional bridge across the faiths.

To list them as they occur in Patanjali's text, *yamas,* the negative virtues of abstention, are non-injury, truthfulness, non-stealing, sexual self-control, and non-acquisitiveness. *Niyamas,* the positive virtues, are cleanliness, contentment, austerity, studiousness, and meditation on God or the Omniscient Special Person.

All other virtues are said to flow from or serve to support the first one – non-injury. Even non-greediness follows from the will to be non-violent. Those who nowadays demand "intellectual property rights" for their "own" ideas and wish to make money by selling technological and scientific "knowledge" take the typically unsharing violence of the intellectually insecure to be the default position of all inventors and knowledge seekers! The *Yoga Bhashya* commentary attributed to Vyasa tries to show how non-violence would be incompatible with hoarding or suppressing true information or with deliberate prevarication or with the telling of hurtful truths. From that same central virtue of non-injury also flows the need to respect others' faith.

From the Vedic announcement that "One is the Real, but inspired seers describe It in many different ways" through the Jaina philosophy of alternative true views, this faith in plurality without rivalry of faiths seems to have flourished in India, until partition riots and inter-communal rapes mocked and mauled Gandhi's chant "Ishwara Allah tera nam" (literally, "'Ishwara' and 'Allah' are both your names, O Lord!"). This last decline of hope has now marked religious faith itself as a destructive rather than constructive force, because blind faith, apparently, has too often led to mass conversion, genocide, communal revenge spirals, and the politics of hate. In this short chapter I cannot address the hard and complex issue of choice of faith from among those various faiths that a multicultural society seems to open up to our future choice-loving children. I am not even sure that faith can be freely "rationally" chosen like breakfast cereals. Any "shopper's guide" to the multicultural market of faiths which I see makes me uncomfortable and suspicious. I am only concerned with the need to have faith in general in one's own tradition's ethical ideals and the necessity of having a hopeful heart, in spite of an unbelieving brain. But I do want to make three quick points about conflict of faiths and its alleged potential for violence.

First, as I have already remarked above, it is not faith but lack of faith that usually turns a community violent. If Hindus really believed that Rama or Shiva is omnipotent and omnipresent, then they would not have taken up arms or microphones to protect Rama or mimic past usurpers of Hindu sacred spaces in trying to rehabilitate Rama. Swami Vivekananda was told something to this effect by the divine Mother when he thought to himself, amidst the ruins of Khir Bhavani Temple in Kashmir, that had he been alive at the time he would have protected the original temple from Muslim invaders.

Second, faith – at least of a more festive, inclusive, and diversity-celebrating kind – has been a source of tolerance and syncretism rather than separatism. Devout Muslims have sung "Hari Om tat Sat" or "Vande nanda kumaram,"[9] while Hindus have worshiped in *dargahs* (tombs) of great *pirs*, and Hindus and Sikhs have visited Hemkund and Badrinath together in busloads for many, many years. Analyzing the potentials of popular faith as a means of preserving a rooted religious but non-sectarian public culture, Rustom Bharucha ends his searching critique of modern Indian secularism with these remarks: "Secularists have a lot to learn from the idioms of tolerance embedded in every religious faith."[10] As Ashis Nandy rightly points out, one can hope that "the state-systems in south Asia may learn something about religious tolerance from everyday Hinduism, Islam, Buddhism, and Sikhism."[11]

It is only Hindusim and Islam with state-making ambitions that generate hatred. Elements such as pollution taboos about food in Hinduism and anti-idolatry animus in Christianity and Islam can create tensions between the communities. But poets such as Kazi Nazrul Islam, who are proud to be Muslim devotees of Mother Kali, or social reformers such as Brahmabandhav Upadhyaya, who roam around in ochre robes with crucifix-necklaces as Catholic Vendantins, prove that the actual practice of these faiths leaves enough room for wonderfully gray areas in their borders.

Third, it is not just politicization of religions that makes faith wear a mask of hate. Intellectual and rational reflections on religious experience that give rise to theologies also impose upon faiths their rigidly drawn doctrinal boundaries. Now, in every other sphere of social action and policy determination, debate and argumentation are excellent dialogical tools for an open society. But spiritual or mystical experiences are better communicated through poetry, music, and direct human interaction than through philosophical systematizations. When we try to examine the ecumenical claims logically, they seem to suffer from some such mistakes as the illicit "quantifier shift" from "All religions believe in some (at least one) ineffable real" to "There is one ineffable real that all religions believe in."

But somehow, I cannot forget that I have seen with my own eyes one Hindu theistic "soul-believing" saintly person communicating and communing with another world-famous Buddhist atheistic "no-soulist" saintly person like two intimate spiritual colleagues, and claiming to have attained commensurable levels of spiritual self-realization! Thus, while Ramakrishna and Keshab Chandra Sen would sing and meditate together, the Hindu and Brahmo pundits may be fighting about the permissibility of worshiping God in idols. Philosophical attempts to find the universal spiritual core of conflicting creeds are usually looked upon with great suspicion by theologians and philosophers of each creed.

"The Real is one, but the sages speak of it in different ways." That is perhaps the most oft-quoted utterance from the *Rig Veda*. It sounds ironic, and open to more than one correct way of envisioning the ultimate. But the *Yajurveda* records an ecstatic announcement by a seer, "I have known that Great Person of the color of the sun, who lies beyond all darkness, knowing whom alone one attains deathlessness. *There is no other way to cross over!*"[12] That sounds exclusivist. Is the certitude of faith (especially when it is supported by direct mystical experience of the object of faith) compatible with a pluralistic open-mindedness about equally valuable alternative visions or faiths?

Faith is supposed to bring a certain fervor of non-rational certitude which seems incompatible with a plurality of alternatives. Is not alternation the typical form that doubt rather than certitude takes? And yet we have in front of us a multitude of faiths, each claiming a time-tested tradition of direct mystical experience that leaves no room for doubt! Faith can cope with science and materialistic consumerism – two of its current global enemies – but how can it deal with other faiths which often clearly contradict its own creeds?

A recent Sanskrit monograph by Professor Govinda Chandra Pande called *Ekam Sad Vipra Bahudha Vadanti* ("Reality is One, but the Sages Speak of it by Many Descriptions") is an astute and responsible attempt at defending an appeal to direct spiritual experience as the shared epistemology of all the world's great religions.[13] This tiny but intricately argued book shows how different social and environmental conditions cause a basically unificatory non-dualistic religious experience to be interpreted into incompatible ontologies and religious dogmas at different historical junctures. Now, once again, it is easy to detect an Advaitic bias in Pande's categorization of the core experience! After all, Pande's book is meant for intellectuals. But one has seen less dispute between Buddhist, Sikh, Hindu, and Sufi saints than one has seen between Buddhist, Hindu, Sikh, Muslim, and Christian theologians and philosophers. So perhaps we need what Philip Quinn has called "thinner theologies"![14]

This last point should not mislead us into a general denunciation of rational philosophical discourse and a promotion only of hymn chanting and mass meditation camps (although I do think *kirtans* and devotional music have had and always will have a major role to play in bringing out the integrative rather than divisive side of faiths). Indian religions have had the richest traditions of uncensored philosophical debates which have kept even the common illiterate masses always aware of the falsifiability of religious theories. A hearty debate between priests and scholars has been almost a festive part of a social spectacle in India since the court of Janaka, as described by *Brihadaranyaka Upanishad*. The fact that each of these religions diversifies into plural interpretations of its own central revelatory text is a great blessing. The practice of social and intellectual non-injury towards a dualist Vendantin on the part of a non-dualist one, the practice by Catholics of respect towards Protestants, the Shia practice of respecting a Sufi in spite of doctrinal difference – all these practices of intra-religious pluralism should help the Hindu, Christian, or Muslim to respect each other, knowing that Hindus themselves, for instance, come in widely unlikely shapes! This variety of faces of truth should not confuse the Hindu or slacken him or her in his or her personal variety of faith.

Even the *Rig Veda* celebrates the spirit of questioning and debate.[15] A healthy dose of skepticism keeps the sage Dirghatamas, the seer of that syncretic hymn, ready for the spiritual awakening after that dark night of unknowing that his name – "long" + "darkness" – suggests. Such a doubting, debating honest inquiry is quite compatible with the simple moral faith that keeps us hoping that "there must be a truth behind all these faces!" The not knowing goes on in the intellect while the assurance that one shall know directly one day possesses the heart. And "With the heart alone one knows the Truth, it is in the heart that Truth gets firmly established."[16]

The Sanskrit word for faith, *shraddha*, is etymologically connected with the English word "cardiac." *Srat* means the heart. In faith the heart finds its resting place. A mere intellectual heartless existence is bound to be wedded to skepticism and conflict. Bertrand Russell was plagued by such pure intellectualism and its attendant faithlessness all his life, until he claimed to have found solace in romantic personal love.

Humans cannot live by skepticism and relativism alone. "This human person is made of faith, you are what you have faith in," says the first epigraph I have lifted from the *Bhagavad Gita.* Faith is particularly crucial as an epistemic constituent of that attitude toward the future which we call "lovingly looking forward to, without rational or empirical ground of expectation."

In his *On Faith in Things Unseen,* St. Augustine writes:

> Verily, out of your heart you believe in a heart that is not yours, and you place faith where you do not focus the glance of either your body or your mind. You discern your friend's countenance by means of your body...but your friend's faith is not appreciated by you, unless there is in you a reciprocating faith, by which you may believe what you do not see in him.[17]

St. Augustine gives two excellent arguments for the indispensability of faith in this sense. First, without such reasonless faith human relations would break down. Children would not recognize or depend upon parents because there is no evidence for most of us that these are our parents, and no guarantee that they will take care of us. Friends without faith would not trust each other because friendship can only be felt by faith.

Second, the search for a knowledgeable teacher (since I find myself in a state of ignorance) requires that we unknowingly trust someone, on pain of a vicious cycle of needing to know what this teacher knows, etc.:

> For how will we fools be able to find a wise man?... the fool does not know wisdom and not knowing it cannot recognize it elsewhere...For this immense difficulty in our search for religion, then only God can supply the remedy. And unless we believe (without knowing with reason) that he exists and assists human souls we ought not even look for the true religion itself.[18]

Such a paradox did not threaten young Nachiketas (whose name meant, with humility, "one who does not know") when faith possessed him (*shraddha avivesa – Katha Upanishad* 1:2). When Nachiketas asked him this question "Is there life after death or not, since some say there is and some say there is not?", Death tried his best to dodge the question, but Nachiketas, although he had an exceptional doubt about the nature of the soul, had unflinching faith that Death knew the answer to his question and that he would not go back without that answer. But how did Nachiketas gain such faith? Well, he detected bad faith in his father, Vajasravas. Vajasravas was pompously performing an all-giving sacrifice. But he was not actually giving all he had; he was giving out old cows which could no longer breed or give milk, or even chew grass any more. Nachiketas sensed that father was outwardly religious but faithless. Had he really been giving away all he had, he should have been giving away his son (Nachiketas himself), one of his most precious possessions. So with simple faith he asked his father, "To whom are you giving me?" When the father felt pestered by the son's persistent query, he yelled at him, "I give you to Death." So, to Death he went.

The syndrome that plagues Indian society now, as it faces technological globalization and is already wallowing in economic liberalization, is not lack of religious zeal. Hindu temples inside and outside India are thriving as much as ever, and garish religious television programs are endlessly popular. Gurus and priests carry cell-phones, ashrams have web-pages, and to crown it all, successful politics is, more than ever before since independence, unabashedly religious. Yet somewhere there is a deep dearth of faith in all this religious regeneration. It is as an antidote to this faithless religiosity that I mainly wished to refocus attention on the ethical prerequisites of Patanjali's Yoga which is supposed to be one of the more ecumenically globalized parts of the Hindu traditions. I think the proudly Hindu part of Indian society is suffering from what I would like to call the "Vajasravas syndrome." We are giving our speeches and our Sunday morning T.V. watching and our N.R.I. (non-resident Indian) excess income charities to the cause of Hindu revival, but we are keeping our children for education in English-medium schools and Americanized I.I.T. (Indian Institutes of Technology[19]) education, eventually packing them off to the States. Very soon our frankly un-understanding children will detect this lack of faith in us. Let us hope that pure faith possesses their pure hearts, too, and that they get their direct lesson from dharma without having to wait many nights at the door of Death!

A FRIVOLOUS ALLEGORY OF THE OCEAN AND ITS VIEWERS

Let me try to explain the positive proposal I am making by the following modern parable. There was once upon a very recent time a disagreement among the various tourists staying in a Waikiki hotel by the oceanside in Honolulu. Reverend Planta Tinga from Uganda said, "Different windows offer different views. What I see from my window is the best view of the real ocean. It may sound rude, but let's face the truth – all those other windows offer false, partial, virtual, or distorted views."

Mr. Rortihiro from Tokyo responded: "Different windows offer different views. Each view is correct because there is no ocean out there. There are just these windows and those views!"

Mr. Hickman Khan from Abu Dhabi said, "Different windows offer different views, and they are all views of one and the same ocean. But the real ocean is not seen through any of these windows. Indeed no one has ever seen it!"

But Mrs. Viveka Chuda Mani from Sri Lanka said, "Different windows offer different views of the real ocean. All those views lead to the ocean. But only from my window can you appreciate the fact that all windows offer such equally good views of the ocean."

There was one tourist among them who introduced himself as a San Francisco syncretist who was really good at smelling people's spiritual aromatic auras. His name was Mr. Hash Brown. He said, "Windows are great! I would really like to combine all the views and get the most comprehensive panoramic 'experience' of the transcendental ocean! But that keeps me so busy window-hopping that, frankly enough, I have very little time to sit and gaze through any one window, and when I do, I find the ocean a bit boring!"

Hearing all this, Mr. Abhi Nav Gupta, who was reading a book of poems, sighed and said, "Different windows indeed offer different good views of the ocean. I firmly believe that the ocean is just as it looks from my window. When two viewers from two different windows both go for a swim, the ocean that looked so very different feels pretty much the same to both of them. But of course how can one *say* how the ocean *feels*? But once again when back in my room, while describing my experience I would naturally use the framework of *my* window to describe it and you would use yours! I told you I really love the view from my window! But what is the point in wasting time talking? Let's all go for a swim!" My sympathies, let me confess, lie with Mr. Gupta!

RESPECTING WITHOUT EMBRACING

Let me end with a charming story about unflinching devotion to one's own chosen deity (*ishtanishtha*). Tulsidas, a devotee of Rama, received a letter from a great scholar of the Hindu scriptures. The letter said: "Lord Rama, whom you worship, according to the scriptures, is only one sixteenth of an incarnation of Lord Krishna. Isn't it time you switched your allegiance to the real Supreme God?" Tulsidas wrote back: " I am really grateful to you for strengthening my faith. I surrendered my heart eternally at the feet of dear Lord Rama, knowing just that he was this human son of King Dasharatha. Now that you have informed me that he is also one sixteenth of a divine incarnation, my reverence for Rama has been ever so enhanced." Was Tulsidas showing disrespect towards Krishna?

NOTES

1. *vaghabhir brahmavid brahma bhati svappa ivatmani*
   vad idam tat svasabdarthsir yo yad vetti sa vettu tat.
2. K.C. Bhattacharya, *Studies in Philosophy* (Delhi: Motilal Banarsidass, 1983), pp. 635–642.
3. See "Charvakadarshanam" in any translation of *Sarvadarshanasamgraha* by Madhavacharya, especially the doctrine of perception alone as reliable knowledge source, and a crude presentist metaphysics.
4. *Mahabharata*, XVIII, chapter 5, verse 62.
5. *Mahabharata*, III, chapter 30, verse 8.
6. Georg Simmel, *Philosophy of Money,* 2nd ed. (London: Routledge, 1990), p. 225.
7. Ibid., p. 256.
8. Ibid., p. 257.

9. "That Being is Om." or "Praise to Nanda's son." The particle "Om" in Sanskrit means "yes," and Nanda is Krishna's adoptive father.

10. Rustom Bharucha, *The Question of Faith* (Calcutta: Orient Longman, 1993).

11. Ashis Nandy, quoted in ibid.

12. *Shwetashvatara Upanishad,* III:8.

13. Govinda Chandra Pande, *Ekam Sad Vipra Bahudha Vadanti* (Varanasi: Sampurnananda Sanskrit University, 1997).

14. *The Philosophical Challenge of Religious Diversity,* eds. Philip Quinn and Kevin Meeker (New York: Oxford University Press, 2000), pp. 226–243.

15. *Rig Veda,* mandala VIII/chapter 10/ hymn 101/ verse 4: "Save us from those evil ones who do not question, do not offer oblations to the fire and do not revel in public discourse (*samvad*)."

16. *Brihadaranyaka Upanishad* III:9, 23.

17. St. Augustine, *On Faith in Things Unseen,* 2.

18. St. Augustine, *Advantage of Believing* 13, 28.

19. The I.T.T. is one of the premier institutions for training high-profile engineers and scientists, modeled after M.I.T. and Caltech and the greatest exporters of Indian computer scientists to America.

Plate 4 Two South Africans, passing each other on the streets of Durban in front of a mural that proclaims freedom of association and freedom of assembly in the new post-apartheid South Africa.

Photo: *Nancy M. Martin and Joseph Runzo*

4

THE RELIGIOUS PERSPECTIVE: DIGNITY *as a* FOUNDATION *for* HUMAN RIGHTS DISCOURSE

Arvind Sharma

I begin, like the song of Wordsworth's solitary reaper, with "old unhappy far off things and battles long ago," as long ago as the time of Alexander the Great. It might not seem exactly auspicious, and in fact even outright unpromising, to commence a discussion of human rights with an incident in the life of Alexander the Great. Perverse you may think I am, but this is exactly what I intend to do. The West, of course, looks upon Alexander as a great conqueror, but many in the East look upon him as no more than another egregious violator of human rights. A widely read book on Indian history offers the following assessment of Alexander's invasion of India:

> The general Indian position with reference to the Macedonian invasion is well expressed by Matthew Arnold: "She let the legions thunder And plunged in Thought again." The only permanent result of Alexander's campaign was that it opened up communication between Greece and India and paved the way for a more intimate intercourse between the two. And this was achieved at the cost of untold sufferings inflicted upon India – massacre, rapine and plunder on a scale till then without a precedent in her annals. In spite of the halo of romance that Greek writers have woven round the name of Alexander, the historian of India can regard him only as the precursor of these recognized scourges of mankind.[1]

Although these scourges detract from, rather than add, to human dignity, nevertheless I would like to propose that Alexander's invasion might help us advance our discussion of human dignity, on the basis of a conversation he had with an Indian king the Greek sources call Porus, whom he defeated in a famous battle at the Hydaspes in 326 BCE. It is a battle studied even now at West Point and Sandhurst for the brilliant strategy employed therein by Alexander. We are, however, more concerned with what followed! After Porus had lost the battle and was captured:

> Alexander rode in front of the line with a few of the Companions to meet Porus; and stopping his horse, he admired his handsome figure and his stature, which reached somewhat above five cubits. He was also surprised that he did not seem to be cowed in spirit, but advanced to meet him as one brave man would meet another brave man, after having gallantly struggled in defence of his own kingdom against another king. Then indeed Alexander was the first to speak, bidding him say what treatment he would like to receive. The story goes that Porus replied: "Treat me, O Alexander, in a kingly way!" Alexander, being pleased at the expression, said: "For my own sake, O Porus, thou shalt be thus treated; but for thy own sake, do thou demand what is pleasing to thee!" But Porus said that everything was included in that. Alexander, being still more pleased at this remark, not only granted him the rule over his own Indians, but also added another country to that which he had before, of larger extent than the former. Thus he treated the brave man in a kingly way, and from that time found him faithful in all things.[2]

Please keep the crucial elements of the conversation in mind. To paraphrase, Alexander said to Porus, "How do you wish to be treated?" Porus responded to Alexander, "As a king treats a king." Alexander then said to Porus, "Elaborate." And Porus replied to Alexander, "When I said as a king treats a king, everything was contained in that." We have there, I dare say, an example of regal dignity. But we live in more democratic times and perhaps that dignity which was once the preserve of kings may now be the possession not just of kings but of commoners as well.

Imagine now a situation in which a dissident is at the mercy of his torturer and the torturer were to ask (in dark jest perhaps), "Now how do you wish to be treated?", both knowing full well that the torturer had the power of life and death over the dissident. And the dissident were to say, "As a human being should treat another human being." And the torturer were to reply, "Elaborate your point." And the dissident were to say, "When I said treat me as a human being should treat another human being, everything was contained in that." I invite you to regard this statement as an expression of human dignity and now join me in exploring it from a religious perspective.

RELIGION AND RIGHTS, DIGNITY, AND DUTY

Several approaches could be brought to bear on the relationship between religion and human rights – a relationship which could be evaluated either positively or negatively, or, more comprehensively and analytically, as including both the possibilities. In this chapter I shall take a *prima facie* positive view of this relationship. I therefore begin by raising the question of how religion might be used as a positive resource in human rights discourse.

In framing this question, I have deliberately used the word "religion" in the singular. So the question I ask is not "In what way can religion*s* be used as a positive resource in human rights discourse?" Nor is my question identical with a similar question which one hears raised these days: "In what ways can *world religions* be used as a positive resource for human rights?" Both of these are rewarding questions. But these are not the questions I ask now. The question I ask now is this. In what way can *religion*, in the singular, be used positively in thinking about human rights?

In my attempt to answer this question, I will now try to identify a feature of religion or religious experience in general, which I have found helpful in trying to think about this topic. It is this. Somehow or other, religion links us and the world we live in with the transcendent – to something beyond us. Some have even argued that it is this transcendental dimension of religion that enables us to distinguish religion from ideology. Whether this is so, or what that transcendent is, or even if it is are questions of immense importance but need not detain us here. I would like to focus on this transcendental linkage alone for the time being, for it seems to me to offer an important clue regarding how we might wish to think about human rights from a religious perspective.

Human rights discourse is at present largely juristic in its orientation. It primarily belongs to the realm of law, though not divorced from considerations of morality. This raises the following question in my mind. Given the way in which human rights discourse has come to dominate normative thinking in the public domain, are human rights strong enough as a concept to bear the heavy weight we are placing on them? For if they are primarily a juristic concept – and you may wish to challenge me on this – then what the law gives, the law can take away, like the Lord. A society based solely on law is better – but perhaps only marginally better – than a society without it. In one the letter of the law might kill, if lawlessness kills in the other. Let me put the matter another way. Suppose the U.N. collapses tomorrow and the Universal Declaration of Human Rights becomes a dead letter. Could it then mean that as human beings we have now ceased to possess human rights? I sense a danger lurking here, the danger of aspiration becoming overly identified with an expression, a manifestation, of that aspiration, to the point that if the manifestation is compromised, the aspiration itself may run the risk of being lost hold of, or at least lost sight of.

It is here that I see merit in introducing a transcendental dimension to the discourse. Such a transcendental dimension pervades religious discourse. At the most abstract level, the reality always transcends any manifestation of reality. At a theistic level, God transcends the universe. At a more concrete level, a religious tradition possesses a quality which exceeds or transcends its contents. I do not wish to be misunderstood. I am not trying to smuggle religion in through the back door. What I *am* trying to do is to take into account the phenomenon described by Professor Charles Taylor as the suppression of ontology in modern pluralist and relativist culture. Let us, for instance, in pursuit of a firmer anchor for the concept of human rights, ask the question of what a human being's humanity consists of.

Several answers are possible, answers on which even reasonable people might differ, to say nothing of unreasonable people. The answers that have been offered to this question, in my view, either go too far or do not go far enough. It is tempting to anchor human rights, for instance, in religious or moral discourse. However, religions are characterized by ontological differences, and the search for moral universals is beset by various problems so that to look for a religious or moral anchor, in my view, compounds the problem. On the other hand, to place complete confidence in a merely legal conception of human rights alone, as complete and secure by itself, seems to me to leave too much in the hands of law. Even at a less elevated level, law cannot always be relied on even to secure justice in everyday life, without its ongoing and continuous scrutiny as a means of securing it.

If you are willing to come along with me this far, then, what we need is something less heavenly or lofty than religion or morality, but also less earth-bound or down-to-earth than just law. It is here that I offer my suggestion – not a novel one, I am afraid, but one which should be revisited – that human rights be anchored in human dignity, not in God or morality or merely law but in the concept of human dignity.

Before proceeding further I must point out that human dignity as a concept can be related to human rights in at least three ways.

1.   Human dignity can be regarded as the product of the successful assertion of human rights.
2.   Human dignity could be regarded as a partner-concept of human rights. One could then say, for instance, that participation in the political process enhances both human dignity and human rights.

3. One could also regard human dignity as the source of human rights
    and consider human rights as flowing from human dignity. When one
    is operating with such evocative words as human dignity and human
    rights, which themselves possess multiple vectors of meaning, it
    should not come as a surprise that the relationship between them may
    be amenable to different patterns.

To clarify my own position, therefore, I would now like to propose my own
model which links the three concepts of human dignity, human rights, and
human duties in a specific way. This model emphasizes the last of the three
ways in which the two concepts of human dignity and human rights may
be related, namely, human dignity as a source of human rights.

I take my cue from Aristotle's dictum that dignity does not consist in
our receiving honors but in our consciousness that we deserve them. If we
replace the word "honors" by "rights" here, then human dignity may be said
to consist in our consciousness that we possess and deserve to possess
human rights, even when they are denied to us. This consciousness is coterminous with our consciousness of being a human being. Lest one feel that
this involves splitting a particularly fine conceptual hair with little practical
consequence, imagine a black rights activist in chains; she may have been
deprived of her rights, but she is capable of experiencing and displaying
human dignity. This was confirmed by something I read recently:

> It is worth noting that much of the moral force of the civil-rights era of the
> early 1960's was achieved by blacks in the South – who, through the dignity
> and restraint of their personal behaviour in the face of segregation's indig-
> nities, managed to transcend and shame – and ultimately defeat – a system
> designed to humiliate them.[3]

Once this interiority of human dignity is recognized as a psychic
component of our make-up as a human being, which is independent of
human rights but of which human rights constitute one particular recognition, then the entire model may be presented as follows.

Human dignity inheres in all human beings qua human beings. Human
rights constitute one expression of it. Human dignity is a quality which is
always present in but is also more than and above its various expressions.
Thus human dignity has to do with dignity which inheres in oneself as a
human being and possesses a dimension of interiority as it relates to one's
self-perception. The external recognition of this dignity by another constitutes the basis of human rights. Respecting them then devolves on the other
party as its duty. In this way, human dignity, human rights, and human

duty become intertwined in a web of relationships. Take two human beings, A and B. Both possess human dignity within themselves in their awareness that they are human beings. B's recognition of this human dignity of A gives rise to A's human rights, which it is B's duty to respect. Similarly, it is A's duty to respect B's human rights, which flow from B's human dignity.

What have we accomplished through this exercise? Let me demonstrate the outcome in terms of beneficiaries and obligors with the help of a classification I owe to Brian Lepard. In case 1 the beneficiary is an infant, the obligor its mother. Let us now progressively enlarge the category. In case 2 the beneficiaries are children, the obligors parents. In case 3 the beneficiaries are citizens, the obligor the state. In case 4 the beneficiaries are all human beings, the obligors all human beings, through the rights–duty interface among them generated by the concept of human dignity.

It has been pointed out to me[4] that the same argument could be made in the parallel idiom of duties rather than rights. Take infants and mothers. The infant has a right to the mother's care, but once the infant grows up and the mother grows old, it becomes the grown-up infant's duty to take care of the mother. Again: children have rights vis-à-vis parents. But it is the duty of grown-up children to take care of their old parents. Again: citizens have rights against the state in normal times; in critical times it becomes the duty of the citizens even through conscription to protect the state. Finally, if all human beings have rights in relation to other human beings, the same holds true of duties.

THE CONTRIBUTION OF HUMAN DIGNITY TO HUMAN RIGHTS DISCOURSE

Now that an outline of human rights discourse as modeled on human dignity has been presented, one is brought face to face with the inevitable question of how this privileging of human dignity contributes to human rights discourse, if at all. An obvious advantage is the way in which the concept of human dignity allows one to intermesh rights and duties. Another less obvious, but equally clear-cut, advantage may lie in the fact that the concept of human dignity is similarly able to connect several generations of human rights discourse, those consisting of first-generation civil and political rights; second-generation social, cultural, and economic rights; and third-generation environmental and developmental rights.[5] These are also sometimes referred to as distinct families of rights.[6] One could venture the opinion, from the perspective of human dignity, that while the first-generation rights – or more precisely those norms therein which relate to physical and civil security (for example, no torture, slavery, etc.)[7] recognize human dignity; the rest enhance or enlarge it. Or one might say that the first-generation rights treat human dignity as a noun, and those of the succeeding generations treat it as a verb. That said, allow me to make three more points.

First, the rise of human rights discourse in the West is closely associated with the rise of liberal secular thought. The secular location of this thought has not prevented scholars from wondering whether it might not be capable of a religious extension. As Ninian Smart and Shivesh Thakur have pointed out:

> An intriguing question arises as to whether differing cultures can arrive at a similar conclusion about rights by rather different routes – some via explicit philosophizing, as with Locke, Kant and others in the West; others by contemplating religious texts and duties (as...the *Mimamsa* and *Gita*); others again by exploiting ideas of ritual and performative behaviours towards others (e.g. *li* in China as a source of rights). It would be a happy outcome if so: since it would allow a confluence model of world society to establish itself – differing civilisations like so many rivers coming together, like the reverse of a delta.[8]

This creates room for suggesting that the idea of human dignity might enable one to build a bridge from the secular to the religious realm.

For instance, Louis Henkin begins by claiming an exclusively secular provenance for human dignity when he writes:

> The human rights idea and ideology begin with an *ur* value or principle (derived perhaps from Immanuel Kant), the principle of *human dignity*. Human rights discourse has rooted itself in human dignity and finds its complete justification in that idea. The content of human rights is defined by what is required by human dignity – nothing less, perhaps nothing more.[9]

But he is careful to add parenthetically: "Some advocates of human rights may derive their commitment to human dignity from religious ideas or assumptions – for example, from the creation of persons by God in the image of God – but the human rights idea itself does not posit any religious basis for human dignity."[10] The point, however, was destined to break out of the parenthetical cage as well, for Henkin himself goes on to say later on in the same essay:

Indeed some religions have begun to claim to be the source and the foundation, the progenitors, of the human rights idea, of the idea of human dignity that underlies it, of the commitment to justice that pervades it, of the bulk of its content. They have come to see human rights as natural rights rooted in natural law, natural law religiously inspired. The ancestors of the human rights idea, we are reminded, were religious Christians (Locke, Kant) – or at least deists (Jefferson). Religions have begun to welcome, and claim, human dignity as a religious principle implicit in teachings concerning the *imago dei*, the fatherhood of God, the responsibility for the neighbor. They have claimed as their own the concept of justice and its specifics: criminal justice, distributive justice, justice as fairness; some religions include economic and social rights as religious obligations. The law of some religions has provided ingredients for particular human rights: for example, the right of privacy.[11]

Second, the concept of human dignity allows one to clarify the concept of human rights. Allow me to explain how. The concept of universal human rights – famously enshrined in the Universal Declaration of Human Rights – suffers from a subtle ambiguity, which pertains to the relationship between the concepts of the individual and the universal. Often the two words are used interchangeably; but a significant, if subtle, difference also characterizes them. For instance, three statements can be made of an individual, any individual, such as you or I: (1) that an individual is like no other, that in some sense we all possess a unique identity; (2) that an individual is like some others – that is to say, we possess a group identity as citizens of a particular nation or as belonging to a class, such as of academics, for instance; and (3) that an individual is like all others – that is to say, we possess an identity coterminous with all human beings, as possessing a mind and body, etc. It is only in this third sense that the individual and the universal overlap. If in some people's minds the concept of human rights has been exclusively identified, or in their opinion should be exclusively identified, with the third sense, this may explain the sense of unease some people might feel when women's rights, etc., are considered human rights.

Being human, however, involves all these three dimensions, and thus the juxtaposition of the words "human" and "universal" creates an ambiguity. As being human involves all these three dimensions, the concept of human dignity would also embrace all the three dimensions, and enables us to understand the word "universal" in an extended sense, as embracing individual and group differences (since such differences characterize all human beings also) beyond their similarity in possessing in common what characterizes all human beings.

Third, the concept might also help us understand the relationship between religion and human rights better. For instance, Louis Henkin writes, "The human rights ideology, though it has not wholly outlawed capital punishment, clearly aims at its abolition because it derogates from human dignity the dignity of the person executed, as well as the dignity of the members of the society that executes."[12] He then adds parenthetically, "It does not accept the argument that the human dignity of the victims of crime requires or justifies capital punishment."[13] Now, it is precisely in terms of the human dignity of the victims and of the members of the victims' families that an argument in support of capital punishment will be mounted by those who should wish to challenge human rights ideology on this point, as for instance, the supporters of the provision of blood-compensation in Islamic law[14] – a practice which seems so recalcitrant to empathetic analysis at the first blush, until viewed in terms of the human dignity of the various parties involved, and especially of the victims' relatives.

CONCLUSION

In conclusion, it seems to me that the model of human dignity, human rights, and human duties, which I have outlined, perhaps enables us to engage issues of human rights in a new way. It does not follow from this, however, that it solves all the problems associated with that discourse. To the extent that it enables us to come to grips with the issues more cogently, it may help toward achieving their resolution, but whether such a resolution is achieved or not depends on the case. Helping understand a problem better is not the same as solving it. There is all the difference in the world between the elucidation of a problem and its solution, but one may not disdain a better understanding of the problem even if no solution might be yet forthcoming – especially if the probability of reaching one may be enhanced by such an improved understanding.

In this spirit one might say that the concept of human dignity enables us to understand statements such as the following. It can be affirmed that human rights are universal, but it is much more difficult to assert a universal standard of justice in upholding them.[15] This remark was prompted by what Archbishop Tutu said during a visit to Edmonton, Canada, in his capacity as chairman of the Truth and Reconciliation Commission in South Africa.

In Edmonton, Archbishop Tutu told a story of four men who had murdered young people in a small town. They appeared before his commission in the same town in a crowded hall before the very people whose relatives had been lost. They admitted their guilt. They expressed their remorse. They asked for forgiveness.

It was a hot night. The hall had been filled with anger and passion. After some moments of silence, the crowd broke into applause and the guilty men wept. God was in the room that night, said Archbishop Tutu.[16]

I do not wish to comment on the case but would like to raise the following question. Dignity may well have been present in the room. Could it also be said that humanity was present in the room? Were both divinity and humanity present in full measure, in some Christological way? Or, could it be further asked in exactly what way was human dignity present in the room? Had the human dignity of all been upheld, or had the human dignity of the victims been compromised, as some allege? I must leave the answer in your hands.

NOTES

1. Radha Kumud Mookherji, "Foreign Invasions," in *The Age of Imperial Unity*, ed. R.C. Majumdar (Bombay: Bharatiya Vidya Bhavan, 1951), p. 53.
2. R.C. Majumdar, *The Classical Accounts of India* (Calcutta: Firma KLM Private Ltd., 1981), pp. 42–43.
3. *The Gazette*, Montreal, October 4, 1998, p. C6.
4. I owe this insight to Marie Royer.
5. John Witte, Jr., "Law, Religion, and Human Rights," *Columbia Human Rights Law Review*, 28, 1 (Fall 1996), p. 13.
6. Gregory Baum, "Human Rights: An Ethical Perspective," *The Ecumenist* (May/June 1994), p. 65.
7. Sumner B. Twiss, "Moral Grounds and Plural Cultures: Interpreting Human Rights in the International Community," *Journal of Religious Ethics*, 26, 2 (Fall 1998), p. 272.
8. Ninian Smart and Shivesh Thakur, "Introduction" in *Ethical and Political Dilemmas of Modern India*, eds, Smart and Thakur (New York: St. Martin's Press, 1993), p. xi.
9. Louis Henkin, "Religion, Religions and Human Rights," *Journal of Religious Ethics*, 26, 2 (Fall 1981), p. 232.
10. Ibid.
11. Ibid., p. 236.
12. Ibid.
13. Ibid.
14. Ibid.
15. William Thorsell, "Whose Justice is it?", *The Globe and Mail*, Toronto, January 9, 1999, p. D6.
16. Ibid.

Part II

BEING HUMAN AND HAVING RIGHTS

Plate 5 Section of a block-long mural in Durban, South Africa, illustrating the many human rights which are found in the new, post-apartheid South African constitution. A pass book used to identify each citizen in the apartheid era in order to restrict the different "classes" of people is set among the new proclamation of the "rights of arrested, detained and accused persons," "freedom of religion and belief," "freedom of expression," "freedom from slavery," and "freedom of movement."

Photo: *Nancy M. Martin and Joseph Runzo*

5

RATS, COCKROACHES, *and* PEOPLE *like* US: VIEWS *of* HUMANITY *and* HUMAN RIGHTS

Gerrie ter Haar

Many people appear to believe that there are a growing number of religious conflicts in the world, particularly since the end of the Cold War. On closer examination, however, it seems that the number of conflicts of the type which are today often labeled "ethnic" or "religious" has in fact been growing since the 1950s.[1] Many such conflicts were already detectable in the period of the Cold War, but at that time they were usually interpreted within a framework of East–West relations.

There has, without doubt, been a change in the patterns of violent conflict in the world since the end of the Cold War, but above all there has been a massive shift in perceptions. Among the world's recent conflicts which are now seen as largely or primarily religious in nature are, for example, Bosnia, Algeria, Kashmir, Chechnya, Indonesia. This development is one reason for a growing interest in religion in relation to human rights, a subject which, it may even be argued, has been one of the main features of the human rights debate in recent years.[2] Many people in the West, where secular politics are considered the norm, seem to have come to the conclusion that religion is all too often a negative aspect of human culture, that it divides people rather than unites them. As a result, there exists a widely held belief today that religion is responsible for abuses of human rights more often than it is a factor in their protection.

This contrasts rather sharply with the period before the 1990s, when academics as well as policy makers often failed to appreciate the significance of religion in the political realm because of an undiscriminating belief in the inevitability of secularization. We may now see that secular pressures often in fact strengthen religious belief.[3] The emergence of a worldwide vibrant political Islam may be considered as one telling example; similar tendencies toward a return to the fundamentals of faith can also be discerned within other major religious traditions.[4]

SOME VIEWS OF HUMAN RIGHTS

Until the last years of the twentieth century, secularism appeared to political elites throughout the world to be an unstoppable force, and human rights to be very largely a matter of legislation. Hence, in the academic field, the debate on human rights, including in matters concerning religion, has been dominated by experts on international law and other jurists. On occasion, theologians and scholars of religion have also added their voices, but without developing any systematic analysis of the relationship between religion and human rights. Systematic thought has been more forthcoming from ethical philosophers, both in the Western and non-Western worlds.[5] A contribution from this quarter is hardly surprising considering that the moral dimension of human activity is of central concern to the human rights debate.

Nowhere do these remarks apply with greater pertinence than in discussion of the United Nations Universal Declaration of Human Rights of 1948. This is now often interpreted primarily as a legal document, and no doubt for this reason has received most attention from scholars working within the field of law. In retrospect, more than fifty years after the Declaration, it is becoming clear that legal instruments are not enough if human rights are to be firmly grounded in different cultures, for people's understanding of human rights is informed by their own worldviews and cosmologies. It is plain that in many countries human rights ideology finds its theoretical justification in religion. The human rights concept as expressed in the United Nations Universal Declaration is at root a secular idea, yet it seems that of all the cultural factors that affect views of humanity and human rights in different parts of the world, none is more important than religion. As a consequence of such different viewpoints, today a number of other human rights declarations exist which reflect the particular worldview of their designers.[6] Although the emergence of alternative declarations has often been politically inspired, the fact that the Universal Declaration conceives human rights in a purely secular mode is nevertheless a matter of genuine concern for many otherwise sympathetic observers, notably outside the Western world.[7]

Clearly, if we wish for a successful inculturation of human rights, we must give serious thought to the role played by religion.[8] For most people in the world, religion is an integral part of their existence, inseparable from the social and moral order, and it defines their relations with other human beings. If relations between human beings are central to the concept of human rights, it becomes important to consider whether, in any given society, these relations have been informed by a religious worldview or whether the philosophical basis is a secular one. In the case of the former, believers often feel that the way in which they perceive the world does not find sufficient recognition in the United Nations Universal Declaration. We may say, with hindsight, that the Universal Declaration is itself a product of the secular developments that I referred to earlier.

The phrase "human rights," after all, implies two separate concepts: the existence of human beings and the assertion that they have inalienable rights. Scholarly debate on the Universal Declaration invariably turns upon the nature of these rights and ways of applying them, without questioning the notion of a human being. That is, in addressing the fundamental question of a human's rights and the universal application of these, the Declaration takes it for granted that we all agree upon what precisely *is* a human being. The question regarding the actual nature of a human being is in many cases deemed to be a metaphysical one, and is therefore often expressed in religion. To avoid any misunderstanding, I am not arguing that there is anything fundamentally flawed in the Universal Declaration; what I am saying is that in view of what we know now, one may consider that perhaps it is simply not explicit enough in certain areas. In the view of many, it lacks a profound view of what a human being is.

Interestingly, the same point has recently been made by Václav Havel, when he asked why human beings have the prerogative to enjoy human rights. The answer he has advanced resembles that of many non-Western critics. "I am convinced," he states, "that the deepest roots of what we now call human rights lie somewhere beyond us, and above us; somewhere deeper than the world of human covenants – a realm that I would, for simplicity's sake, describe as metaphysical."[9] One viable way, in his view, out of the problems that may arise from a difference in worldview over the interpretation of human rights is placing emphasis on their spiritual source. We should make an effort, he argues, to highlight the spiritual dimension and spiritual origin of the values guarded by the United Nations and translate this into the Organization's practical activities.[10] Whatever our personal views on this may be, it seems evident that present circumstances require a rethinking of the relationship between religion and human rights. This is necessary in order to address some of the changes that have taken place in recent decades and which have shed new light on the role of religion in human rights matters.

Consideration of the place of religion in the social and political circumstances of today's world raises a number of important questions, not all of which can be discussed here and now. I will limit myself to discussing only those three points that I believe need our most urgent scholarly attention. I will begin with the most widely recognized of the debates raised by notions of globalization in regard to human rights, namely the issue of cultural relativism. Second, I will review the relationship between religion and culture, which, in my view, takes the inquiry further. Finally, I will conclude with what seems to me to lie at the heart of the matter, namely the way in which many of the world's people conceive of a human being in partly spiritual terms. The third and last of these points is particularly important since the question of human rights is bound up with a given society's fundamental view of what one author refers to as "what sort of thing a human being is."[11] This really is a consideration of the elements that separate human beings from other categories and by virtue of which they may enjoy certain rights.

CULTURAL RELATIVISM

The task of providing a common moral language for all humanity is fraught with difficulties. The central paradox here is that achieving such a goal requires the prior development of an indigenous human rights language within the various moral traditions of the world.[12] Given the state of affairs in the world today, there is increasing doubt as to whether a worldwide consensus on human rights can ever be achieved. In a controversial essay published in 1993, Samuel Huntington suggested that certain differences between peoples and populations can never be bridged.[13] His argument is that there is a fundamental incompatibility between different types of civilization, whose traditions have been shaped over centuries. The most important source of conflict in the world today, in his view, is not ideological or economic but cultural. According to Huntington, we are experiencing a clash of civilizations in the world, in which religion plays a major role. Since there is no prospect of unity being created out of the world's cultural diversity, he proposes that the Western world should accept that these cultural "fault lines" exist. Western countries should therefore rather strive for unity within their own cultural field and cooperate primarily with those whose cultures are closest to their own.

Huntington's line of thought, which has been influential though much criticized,[14] is at odds with the vision of the United Nations Universal

Declaration, which maintains that there are certain values which are shared by all peoples.[15] Huntington's outlook, however, stands in a long tradition. I may cite, for example, the precedent offered by the American Anthropological Society which in 1947 opposed the adoption of a Universal Declaration of Human Rights on the grounds that individual cultures had their own standards and values, and later accused the drafters of ethnocentrism.[16] American anthropologists of fifty years ago, like Samuel Huntington today, found it hard to believe that human beings may find ways to transcend their cultural divides. Rather than the cultural fault lines identified by Huntington, the vision embodied in the Universal Declaration acknowledges the existence of a cultural weave underlying a common human pattern. If we accept this to be so, it means that in human rights thinking the human, and not culture, is the fundamental category.[17] Such matters are ultimately a matter of faith, which is why belief in the universality of human rights is sometimes referred to as a secular religion.

In view of this type of culturalist critique, it is important to remind ourselves that the Universal Declaration was the work of a team of both Western and non-Western drafters, standing in different religious traditions. The core group of eight drafters comprised representatives from Australia, Chile, China, France, Lebanon, the former Soviet Union, the United Kingdom, and the United States.[18] In the final phase, only eight of the fifty-eight states involved in the process decided to abstain from voting on adoption of the Declaration, including South Africa, the Soviet Union, and Saudi Arabia.[19] It is significant that none of the dissenters voted against the Declaration.

The drafters of this document clearly considered how to make a universal appeal to people of different cultures, for their aim was to communicate a vision to ordinary people, men and women from all walks of life in all parts of the world. Such a vision has great mobilizing power, which is precisely what governments and others wielding political power often fear in the United Nations Universal Declaration. Its claim to universality, I would argue, lies much more in its conviction that it can be shared by all people, whoever and wherever they are, than in the likelihood that its principles will actually be respected by political elites. The principal aim of the Declaration was thus an educational one: every person was to be aware of certain fundamental values in order to prevent a repeat of the horrors that had occurred during the Second World War with its 50 million dead, only months before the Declaration was drafted.

In his book *Modernity and the Holocaust* the sociologist Zygmunt Bauman has argued that the atrocities of the Second World War were made possible by the systematic repression of the moral dimension of people's acts in modern industrial society.[20] If this is so, it is all the more disturbing because "modernity," as it is often referred to,[21] has today made inroads in all societies worldwide. The globalization of life that has accompanied modernity has given a new impulse to the debate on universalism versus particularism in human rights. The argument in favor of universality may be strengthened by the observation that in a globalized world, norms and values are likely to be influenced by the process of globalization.

On the other hand, it is increasingly argued outside the Western world, by politicians especially, that globalization threatens the specific identity of individual societies. Every country therefore (or so it is argued) should be allowed to develop its own particular philosophy of human rights, based on its own cultural values. In many cases this is explicitly related to the religious morality of a particular culture or society. The Islamic Declaration on Human Rights is one example. Another is the Bangkok Declaration, drafted in the early 1990s by some forty states from the Asian and Pacific region, which made a plea to consider "the significance of national and regional particularities and various historical, cultural and religious backgrounds" in interpreting and applying human rights.[22] Culture-related values, however, as feminist writers especially have pointed out, can be very oppressive for social and religious minorities inasmuch as they tend to deny cultural and religious diversity within a given society.[23]

It is notable that a related debate has arisen in Western societies, such as Europe and North America, in the form of the heated issue of multiculturalism. The argument here turns upon the degree to which our societies should encourage minority groups to nurture specific cultural and religious identities. Inherent in this is a perception similar to that of the Islamic and Asian activists whom I have just mentioned: namely, that certain groups of people are so different from us as to require different treatment, in conformity with those norms and values that are deemed to be their own. Some influential analysts, including Kwame Anthony Appiah and Michael Ignatieff, have labeled this view the "narcissism of minor difference."[24] Labeling people as "not like us" always concerns matters of identity – who are we and who are they? The merits of the argument must be examined case by case. For example, I have argued elsewhere in regard to African immigrants in Europe that it is often Europeans, and not Africans themselves, who insist on the need for Africans to develop their own (i.e. African) identity. In effect such an argument becomes a mechanism of exclusion, a discourse which contributes to the defense of Fortress Europe.[25]

Perceptions of human difference are inseparable from perceptions of identity. Whether we are discussing human rights in the international arena or group rights within multicultural societies, it is of crucial importance to establish who is the agent in defining people's identities. Who precisely is advocating a position of exception, and for whom? Often, it is not the victims but the violators of human rights who use a relativist argument against the principle of universality.[26] One instance is that of the late President Mobutu of Zaire, who argued that his country should be exempt from international norms on the grounds that Zaireans had their own authentic way of doing things. Conversely, relatively powerless indigenous groups may seek to protect their communal rights by invoking universal values and associating themselves with global movements.[27]

Any claim to exception of the sort I have described carries a risk of political manipulation. This includes claims made on religious grounds. The political manipulation of religion has been evident, for example, in the last Balkan wars, notably in forging a link between religion and nationalism. Religious identities there gained an overriding importance in recent years as a result of the extreme violence of the conflict. It has been argued that it is not religion, but a "politics of identity," which turned minor differences into major divides and set different believers against each other.[28] This may equally prove true of situations of conflict between religious groups in other parts of the world where people previously lived in relative harmony.

Conflict is often exacerbated when religion becomes a tool in the hands of politicians or political interest groups and is thus used to create, maintain, or strengthen a factional position. It is the political manipulation of religion that causes secularists to mistrust religiously inspired arguments about human rights. Indeed, there can be no doubt that religion may easily be associated with the violation of human rights. But this observation is not sufficient to disqualify religious belief as an instrument for the propagation and protection of human rights.

In some countries it is argued that the secular ideology of the state is itself a root cause of, and not the solution to, religious violence, because it fails to take account of the religious values of citizens. This is the case in India, for example, where some thoughtful scholars advocate the creation of a state based on the original Hindu tradition of religious tolerance.[29] The fact is that in any society where a substantial number of people profess religious belief, religion has a role to play in protecting human rights, just as it can have a role in violating them.

In other words, we should not deny the legitimacy of various societies developing their own methods for solving problems of human rights.[30] In fact, sensitivity to cultural diversity is, in my view, a precondition for the successful inculturation of human rights. But cultural sensitivity – an open-mindedness about the potentials of unfamiliar cultures – is not the same as cultural relativism. Whereas the former makes possible a process of dialogue which can be mutually enriching, the latter leads to a separate development of human rights.

RELIGION AND CULTURE

The tendency to emphasize differences between cultures rather than to focus on what may bind them leads to some important philosophical questions. The most pressing of these is perhaps, in view of our subject, the question whether cultural particularism breeds moral particularism. In other words, if we adhere to the primacy of cultural diversity, on the grounds that there exists a range of specific cultural identities, can we at the same time uphold the existence of moral standards which override a particular cultural tradition, such as those embedded in the United Nations Universal Declaration of Human Rights? If not, the only logical alternative is to believe that each culturally defined entity should adopt its own separate human rights standards.

This, we may note, is the logical corollary of both Huntington's argument about cultural difference and of the more extreme advocates of multiculturalism within Western societies. This is an unappealing prospect, in my view. Rather, we should aim to develop global moral connections, asking ourselves what moral relationships a global culture creates. This has also been suggested by Michael Ignatieff, who calls for a type of involvement which will be "a crucial new feature of the modern moral imagination."[31] Since religion is the idiom in which many people express their views about the world, it will need to be part of such a moral imagination.

I should say at this juncture that the conventional Western idea of what religion is, and the way we apply this to the issue of human rights, has been much influenced by Western monotheism.[32] The term "world religions" was often applied only to religions based on a written authority, notably Christianity and Islam. Scholars and others often contrast these so-called "world religions" with so-called "ethnic religions," usually meaning in effect religions that have no sacred book but which are based on oral traditions. In such a classification, "ethnic religions" are connected to a specific ethnic group or "tribe" and its culture. Such notions were coined during colonial

times by the West in regard to people "not like us," and are intrinsically connected to concepts of race. In our time, the concept of ethnicity has come
to replace the nineteenth-century concept of race in the definition of perceived differences between human populations.[33] The main attraction of
using the term "ethnic" appears to lie in its usefulness in the process of
"othering," that is in distinguishing systematically between "us" and
"them."[34] In the same vein, even when the definition of "world religions" is
expanded to include traditions that are open to all peoples and conscious
of a universal vocation, they are defined in contrast to so-called "ethnic religions" which are viewed as innate, static, and closed.[35]

This view, although conventional, is today in dire need of revision, not
only because it is not congruent with observable facts, but also because it
gives comfort to cultural relativists. "World" or "universal" religions have
developed firm roots in local cultures around the world as a consequence
of modern processes of globalization. An unprecedented diversity has
arisen within these religions, which is evidenced by popular forms of religious expression. In such cases, interpretation of scripture is increasingly
adapted to the local context of the believers. At the same time, a movement
has taken place in the opposite sense, as so-called "ethnic" or "tribal" religions are increasingly taking on universal characteristics. This is so, for
example, with African traditional religions, which can be found in various
parts of the world.[36] Formerly this was a consequence of the transatlantic
slave trade; today African religious traditions have traveled overseas
through the international migration that is a hallmark of modern globalization. Yoruba religion is now more flourishing in New York than in Lagos.
Muslim brotherhoods are making converts in Chicago and are firmly established in southern Europe. There are churches founded by Africans which
have now become international.[37] Processes of inculturation and contextu-
alization have caused so-called world religions and ethnic religions to
resemble each other more closely in structure. Both have become grounded
in the particular culture where they are being practiced, all over the world.

These dynamics of change need to be considered in any up-to-date
analysis of the relationship between religion and human rights. Only then
can we aim to make the global moral connections that are needed if basic
human rights are to be upheld worldwide.

BEING HUMAN

If anything can be said about the great diversity of religions in the world, it
is that they all perceive good and evil to be part of the human condition.

They concern themselves with exploring the nature of these qualities, the relationship between them, and methods of keeping these two forces under control. "The wise man," states the Moroccan sociologist Muhammad Guessous, commenting on what his fellow-countrymen believe to be the essence of a human being, "is the man who does not expect good things in this life but who takes precautions to minimize the evil."[38]

To minimize evil, Guessous observes, Moroccans believe that a person needs to do two things: to work hard and to worship. *Ora et labora*, others might say. Many religious traditions recognize the need to worship in order to minimize "evil" broadly defined, meaning everything that is seen as reducing the quality of human life, including illness, poverty, and death. A predominance of religious believers are ultimately aware that successful living is dependent on their relationship with an invisible world, which they believe to be inhabited by spiritual forces that can make their presence felt in the visible world. Religious practice, therefore, consists, in many cases, of a skillful manipulation of these unseen forces in order to manage the good and evil humans experience in their lives.

All societies have some concept of evil, and of the way in which human beings are implicated. In many societies such ideas are expressed through discourses of religion. Accusations of witchcraft, for example, are one way in which people may express the notion that evil can take on a human form.[39] The belief in witchcraft is a popular one, in the sense that it is widely held, notably but not only in Africa. It expresses an essentially religious idea about human nature, which may find a different expression in other cultures. For, even where religion has been abandoned as an explanatory model, secular ideologies have emerged which deal with the same question of how to manage and ward off manifestations of evil.

Both religious and secular ideologies tend to ascribe evil notably to those who are not considered people "like us." Both types of ideology have shown a capacity to destroy the lives of others by placing them outside the category of humans. The way in which this happens may differ, but in all cases it implies some form of disqualification as a person. In 1914, the Carnegie Endowment for International Peace observed in relation to a war between Greece and Bulgaria that "Day after day the Bulgarians were represented in the Greek press as a race of monsters, and public feeling was roused to a pitch of chauvinism which made it inevitable that war, when it should come, should be ruthless…Deny that your enemies are men and you will treat them as vermin."[40] Something similar happened during the Second World War, when whole groups were described as not fully human, not "people like us." Anti-Arab pogroms in 1950s Algeria were known to French settlers as *ratonnades,* or "rat-hunts." In preparation for the 1994 genocide in Rwanda, the organs of state and mass communication consistently conveyed the message that part of the population were actually "cockroaches."[41]

Examples from all parts of the world indicate how effective and how lethal dehumanizing is as a mechanism of exclusion. It denies humanity to a person or a group. It is one extreme of the process of "othering," or the constitution of a primal opposition between "us" and "them." Nevertheless, it is necessary to recall, this is a process which takes place permanently in less radical forms in all societies. It is for that reason that minority groups are everywhere in a vulnerable position. When their otherness becomes justified by an ideology either religious or secular, they risk different treatment on the grounds that they *are,* after all, different. Hence, they may be deemed to have fewer rights than people "like us," or even no rights at all.

This clearly has major implications for human rights, which are claims that individuals are entitled to make simply by virtue of their status as human beings. It raises a question not so much about the nature of rights as about the nature of humanity. In any particular culture or society, what do people think constitutes a human being? And who is therefore qualified to claim human rights? In most cases, the answer is to be found in the belief system of people. These questions are fundamental for understanding the relationship between religion and human rights.

In many cultures, people attach overwhelming importance to the spiritual dimension of a person, believing that it is this that defines him or her as possessing a truly human identity.[42] In other cases, human identity is not considered a fixed category, but something fluid. In some forest countries of West Africa, for example, it is widely believed that people closely resemble certain animals, including leopards and chimpanzees, and may even take on some of their characteristics.[43] Similar examples can be found all over the world. New Zealand, for example, recently became the first country to recognize in law the status of the great apes as humans' closest relatives. This step was taken on the basis of scientific evidence that the great apes share not only our genes but also basic human traits such as self-awareness and intelligence.[44]

Societies, moreover, hold different views about the precise point at which true human life may be identified, and when it ceases. In some cultures, very young children may be lawfully killed on the grounds that they are not, or not yet, really human. A similar debate on the definition of humanity takes place in Western societies today, in relation to such questions as abortion, euthanasia, and gene technology. In many places, theologians or other religious specialists decide upon such matters. In Western society, questions such as these are now largely referred to experts in medical ethics. By replacing the theologians, they have become the secular moralists of our time.

Let me summarize my argument at this point. The profound changes that the world is experiencing today impel us to examine religion anew, as one of the agents of social change. Present circumstances, I have argued, require a reconsideration of the relationship between religion and human rights. Religion, or religious belief, I suggest, while often seen as a root cause of violent conflict, is in fact a particular expression of human sentiments and ideas which are also present in secular cultures. In most cases the outbreak of violence cannot be ascribed to the nature of religious belief as such since, like all human institutions, religion can be used for either constructive or destructive purposes. Its resources can be applied both for the protection of human rights and for their violation. The challenge is to try and exploit the positive resources which are present in virtually all religions.

So far, little use has been made by human rights promoters of the world's religious and spiritual resources.[45] An intelligent use of religious resources requires and presupposes a serious consideration of religion as an important factor in people's lives. In this one respect, we can agree with Huntington, when he concluded his somber analysis with a call to develop a more profound understanding of the basic religious and philosophical assumptions underlying what he describes as "other civilizations."[46]

I have further argued that globalization contains, almost inevitably, a tendency towards the globalization of moral ideas in connection with human rights, whether these ideas are based on a religious or secular ideology. Consequently, cultural relativism, which demands a position of exception, is becoming an increasingly untenable stance. At the same time, it must be clear that universalizing human rights is not the same as Westernizing human rights. For the inculturation of human rights must be a two-way process, in which Western proponents of human rights learn and accept that certain values derived from a culture which is originally not theirs may actually be of use to them too. These may include religious values.

Finally, given the fact that human rights are claims that people are entitled to make simply because of being human, I have emphasized the importance for all of us, in and outside the Western world, of considering the fundamental question that underlies all human rights thought: what is a human being? This is necessary if we are to develop a proper under-standing of the process which begins with labeling people as different from us, and which can lead, through excesses of language, to the grossest viola-tion of human rights. The same question draws us toward ideas about good and evil which are prominent in many religions in the world and which to a greater or lesser extent guide people's actions toward others and thus have a bearing on human rights.

NOTES

This article is a revised version of the inaugural address delivered on April 13, 2000 at the Institute of Social Studies (ISS) in The Hague (Netherlands) to inaugurate the new Chair in Religion, Human Rights, and Social Change. The original version was published by the ISS.

1. *The Media of Conflict: War Reporting and Representations of Ethnic Vio-lence,* eds. Tim Allen and Jean Seaton (London and New York: Zed Books, 1999), pp. 11–42, esp. p. 22.

2. A wealth of literature has been produced during the last ten years, which in various ways introduces religion as a critical factor in human rights matters, not only in relation to conflict. Cf. David Little, "Rethinking Human Rights: A Review Essay on Religion, Relativism and Other Matters," *Journal of Religious Ethics,* 27, 1 (1999), pp. 151–177.

3. Ibid., p. 155. Cf. also Jeff Haynes, *Religion in Global Politics* (London and New York: Longman, 1998).

4. For a recent analysis of political Islam, see *Political Islam: Revolution, Radicalism, or Reform?,* ed. John L. Esposito (Boulder and London: Lynne Riener, 1997). For a general overview and analysis of fundamentalism in different religious traditions in the world, see the five volumes that have emerged from the Fundamentalism Project carried out by the University of Chicago under the leadership of Martin E. Marty and R. Scott Appleby, eds. See notably volume 1: *Accounting for Fundamentalisms: The Dynamic Character of Movements* (Chicago and London: University of Chicago Press, 1994). See also *The Freedom to do God's Will: Religious Fundamentalism and Social Change,* eds. Gerrie te Haar and James J. Busuttil (London and New York: Routledge, 2003).

5. One leading example is the *Journal of Religious Ethics,* published in the United States. See notably the special issue on human rights, vol. 26, no. 2, 1998.

6. Notably the Cairo Declaration on Human Rights in Islam of 1993, which has been adopted by some fifty member states of the Organization of the Islamic Conference (O.I.C.). Earlier, in 1981, a Universal Islamic Decla-ration of Human Rights (U.I.D.H.R.) was drafted under the auspices of the Islamic Council, a London-based organization affiliated with the

Muslim World League. Apart from these, there are various documents concerning Islamic human rights policy. More recently, a debate has emerged on Asian values in human rights, which resulted in the so-called Bangkok Declaration. This declaration was drafted at a regional preparatory meeting in Bangkok prior to the Second World Conference on Human Rights in Vienna in 1993.

7.   This became clear, for example, during the recent meeting of the Parliament of the World's Religions in Cape Town in December 1999, which contained a number of panels on religion and human rights.

8.   Many observers have commented on the need for the inculturation of human rights. Some examples are: *Human Rights in Cross-Cultural Perspective*, ed. Abdullahi Ahmed An-Na'im (Philadelphia: University of Pennsylvania Press, 1992); David Little, John Kelsay, and Abulaziz Sachedina, *Human Rights and the Conflict of Cultures* (Columbia: University of South Carolina Press, 1988); and *Human Rights and Cultural Diversity: Europe, Arabic-Islamic World, Africa, China*, ed. Wolfgang Schmale (Goldbach: Keip, 1993). More specifically on the role of religion, see for example: *Religious Diversity and Human Rights*, eds. Irene Bloom, J. Paul Martin, and Wayne L. Proudfoot (New York: Columbia University Press, 1996); *Religion and Human Rights*, eds. John Kelsay and Sumner B. Twiss (New York: The Project on Religion and Human Rights, 1995); *Religious Human Rights in Global Perspective: Religious Perspectives*, ed. John Witte and John van de Vyver (The Hague: Kluwer, 1996). For a historical and comparative perspective, see also *The Universal Declaration of Human Rights: Fifty Years and Beyond*, eds. Yael Danieli, Elsa Stamatopoulos, and Clarence J. Dias (Amityville, NY: Baywood Publishing Company, 1999).

9.   Václav Havel, in *The Universal Declaration of Human Rights*, ed. Danieli et al., p. 332.

10.   Ibid., pp. 333–334.

11.   Robert Thurman, "Human Rights and Human Responsibilities: Buddhist Views on Individualism and Altruism," in *Religious Diversity and Human Rights*, ed. Bloom et al., p. 90.

12.   James Turner Johnson, "Human Rights and Violence in Contemporary Context," *Journal of Religious Ethics*, 26, 2 (1998), p. 326.

13.   Samuel P. Huntington, "The Clash of Civilizations?" *Foreign Affairs*, 72, 3 (1993), pp. 22–49. The argument was further elaborated in his book *The Clash of Civilizations and the Remaking of World Order* (New York: Simon & Schuster, 1996).

14.   See later issues of *Foreign Affairs*, notably vol. 72, no. 4.

15.   Many of these, incidentally, are considered to be present in most, if not all, religions. This is a view commonly held, in any case, by religious believers themselves, as well as by those who have been writing specifically on the subject of religion and human rights.

16. See Johannes Morsink, "Introduction: The Declaration at Fifty," in Johannes Morsink, *The Universal Declaration of Human Rights: Origins, Drafting and Intent* (Philadelphia: University of Pennsylvania Press, 1999).

17. Cf. Irene Bloom, "Religious Diversity and Human Rights: An Introduction," in *Religious Diversity and Human Rights*, ed. Bloom et al., pp. 1–11, esp. pp. 2–3.

18. When we look at the composition of the General Assembly, we see that of the fifty-eight national representatives thirty-seven, i.e. a majority, stood in the Judeo-Christian tradition, eleven in the Islamic, six in the Marxist, and four in the Buddhist tradition. There was, however, a notable under-representation from Asia and Africa. For a detailed record, see Morsink, *The Universal Declaration of Human Rights*, chap. 1, "The Drafting Process Explained."

19. Ibid., pp. 21–27. We should mention here the significant influence of some Muslim drafters, and also the strong influence of notably Latin American socialists, to whom we owe the inclusion of social, economic, and cultural rights in the Declaration.

20. Zygmunt Bauman, *Modernity and the Holocaust* (Cambridge: Polity Press, 1989).

21. Theorists of globalization make a distinction between the first and the second modernity. Whereas in the first modernity there was an equation of state, society, and identity, in the second modernity this equation is undermined by new developments inherent in the processes of globalization. The most important dimensions of globalization are considered to be communications technology, ecology, economics, work organization, culture, and civil society. See Ulrich Beck, *What is Globalization?* (Cambridge: Polity Press, 2000), esp. p. 19.

22. Quoted in Little, "Rethinking Human Rights," p. 153.

23. See e.g. Harriet Samuel's discussion of this in her article, "Hong Kong on Women, Asian Values, and the Law," *Human Rights Quarterly*, 21, 3 (1999), pp. 707–734.

24. See Michael Ignatieff, *The Warrior's Honor: Ethnic War and the Modern Conscience* (New York: Henry Holt & Co., 1997), p. 54. See also Kwame Anthony Appiah in an interview with *de Volkskrant* on 23 October 1999 commenting on his essay "Color Conscious: the Political Morality of Race."

25. Gerrie ter Haar, *Halfway to Paradise: African Christians in Europe* (Cardiff: Cardiff Academic Press, 1998). Also published in 2001 in an African edition under the title *African Christians in Europe* (Nairobi: Acton Publishers).

26. As Jackie Selebi, then Director-General of the South African Department of Foreign Affairs, pointed out at a ceremony in Geneva on August 12, 1998 when he received a human rights award.

27.   One interesting example has been recorded by Sally Engle Merry, "Legal Pluralism and Transnational Culture: The *Ka Ho'okolokolonui Kanaka Maoli* Tribunal, Hawai'i, 1993," in *Human Rights, Culture and Context: Anthropological Perspectives*, ed. Richard A. Wilson (London and Chicago: Pluto Press, 1997), pp. 28–48.

28.   Ger Duyzings, *Religion and the Politics of Identity in Kosovo* (London: Hurst & Co., 1999).

29.   Cf. Dick Kooijman, "Religieuze tolerantie en seculiere staat in India," *Wereld en Zending*, 28, 2 (1999), pp. 97–106. One leading intellectual advocating this point of view is the social psychologist Ashis Nandy; see notably his essay "The Politics of Secularism and the Recovery of Religious Tolerance," in *Mirrors of Violence: Communities, Riots and Survivors in South Asia*, ed. Veena Das (Delhi: Oxford University Press, 1992).

30.   We may quote in this connection Richard A. Wilson, who states that "It is possible to have contextualisation without relativisation, since one can keep open the possibility, and in the dying embers of the twentieth century, the likelihood, that contexts are interlinked through a variety of processes." Just because a cultural form is global, he argues, it does not mean that everyone relates to it in the same way ("Human Rights, Culture and Context: An Introduction," in *Human Rights, Culture and Context*, ed. Wilson, p. 12).

31.   Ignatieff, *The Warrior's Honor*, pp. 5, 98.

32.   For a scholarly and critical analysis of the term "religion" in different historical and social contexts, see *The Pragmatics of Defining Religion: Contexts, Concepts and Contests*, eds. Jan G. Platvoet and Arie L. Molendijk (Leiden: Brill, 1999); notably the epilogue by Platvoet, "Contexts, Concepts and Contests: Towards a Pragmatics of Defining Religion," pp. 463–516.

33.   In his book *Race and Ethnicity in Modern Britain* (Oxford: Oxford University Press, 1995), the sociologist David Mason provides analytical insight into the mechanisms involved in this process, drawing attention to the important distinction between difference and diversity.

34.   See, for example, the critical comments made by Teresia Hinga in a short essay, "Inculturation and the Otherness of Africans: Some Reflections," in a volume about the perceived otherness of Africa, *Inculturation: Abide by the Otherness of Africa and Africans*, ed. Peter Turkson and Frans Wijsen (Kampen: Kok, 1994), pp. 10–18.

35.   In some cases, world religions have proved to be a colonial invention. This is the case with Hinduism, which was constructed by the British in the nineteenth century as a unitary national religion, a process which some have described as the "semitification" of Hinduism in the modern era. There are also scholars who argue that being Hindu has no religious connotation whatsoever. See Richard King, "Orientalism and the Modern Myth of 'Hinduism'," *Numen*, 46, 2 (1999), pp. 146–185.

36. Universalization is only one remarkable tendency in the current process of revitalization of African traditional religions. See Rosalind Hackett, "Revitalization in African Traditional Religion," in *African Traditional Religions in Contemporary Society,* ed. Jacob K. Olupona (New York: Paragon House, 1991), pp. 135–149.

37. Ter Haar, *Halfway to Paradise.*

38. Quoted in Kevin Dwyer, *Arab Voices: The Human Rights Debate in the Middle East* (London: Routledge, 1991), p. 119.

39. A point in case is present-day South Africa, where in certain parts of the country witchcraft accusations have become so frequent that the national government has set up various organs to try and tackle what has become a grave social problem which has led in recent years to the violent deaths of hundreds of people. Under the umbrella of SANPAD, the South Africa–Netherlands Programme on Alternatives in Development sponsored by the Dutch government, a research program has been developed with the title "Crossing Witchcraft Barriers in South Africa." An interim report was published in 2000. A final publication was due in 2003 under the title "Crossing Witchcraft Barriers in South Africa: Exploring Causes and Solutions to Witchcraft Accusations."

40. Carnegie Endowment for International Peace, *Report of the International Commission to Inquire into the Causes and Conduct of the Balkan Wars* (1914), quoted by Jean Seaton, "The New 'Ethnic' Wars and the Media," in *The Media of Conflict,* ed. Allen and Seaton, p. 46.

41. See Alison Des Forges, *Leave None to Tell the Story: Genocide in Rwanda* (New York: Human Rights Watch, 1999).

42. Among the Akan in Ghana and the Yoruba in Nigeria, for example, the spiritual dimension of a person is deemed an essential part of the human condition. We find similar ideas in all parts of the world, where the human world and the spirit world are believed to be interrelated in a way that has become uncommon in the West.

43. Paul Richards, "Local Understandings of Primates and Evolution: Some Mende Beliefs Concerning Chimpanzees," in *Ape, Man, Apeman: Changing Views Since 1600,* eds. R. Corbey and B. Theunissen (Leiden: Dept. of Prehistory, Leiden University, 1995), pp. 265–273. See also Stephen Ellis, *The Mask of Anarchy: The Destruction of Liberia and the Religious Dimension of an African Civil War* (London: Hurst & Co., 1999), esp. pp. 220–280.

44. "New Zealand Gives Human Rights to Great Apes," *Noseweek,* 28 (Dec. 1999/Jan. 2000), p. 12.

45. One notable exception is the Parliament of the World's Religions, which gathers men and women from religious and spiritual traditions all over the world to discuss issues of common concern.

46. Huntington, "The Clash of Civilizations?", p. 49.

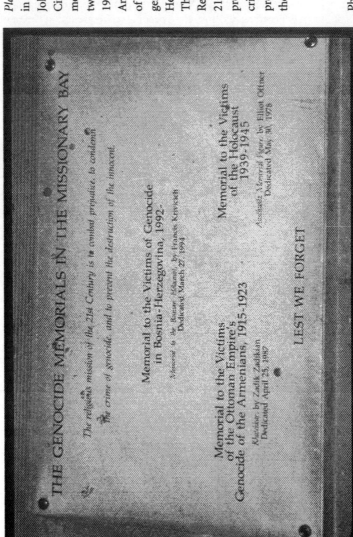

Plate 6 Genocide memorial in the missionary bay of St. John's Cathedral, New York City, commemorating three moral tragedies of the twentieth century: the 1915–1923 genocide of the Armenians, the Holocaust of 1939–1945, and the genocide of Bosnia-Herzegovina in the 1990s. The plaque reads, "The Religious Mission of the 21st Century is to combat prejudice, to condemn the crime of genocide, and to prevent the destruction of the innocent."

Photo: *Joseph Runzo*

6

HUMANITARIAN INTERVENTION, INTERNATIONAL LAW, *and the* WORLD RELIGIONS

Brian D. Lepard

In this chapter I will argue that evolving international law, particularly international human rights law, endorses certain fundamental ethical principles of relevance to the problem of military intervention with humanitarian aims, or "humanitarian intervention." These principles are logically related to a principle of "unity in diversity." I will also demonstrate, briefly, that selected passages from the revered moral texts of various world religions and philosophies may be interpreted to support these ethical principles. These fundamental ethical principles, in turn, can help resolve certain legal problems relating to humanitarian intervention. I will touch very briefly on two of these legal problems in this chapter.[1]

THE U.N. CHARTER AND HUMANITARIAN INTERVENTION

We find in the U.N. Charter a tension among norms aimed at preventing war, implementing a system of collective security, safeguarding state autonomy and sovereignty, protecting human rights within states, and supporting collective decision making among states. All of these concerns relate to the problem of humanitarian intervention, but the Charter nowhere addresses the issue of humanitarian intervention specifically.

A number of provisions of the Charter potentially relate to humanitarian intervention, however. First, article 1.1 states that one purpose of the U.N. is to maintain international peace and security, and to that end, "to take effective collective measures for the prevention and removal of threats to the peace, and for the suppression of acts of aggression or other breaches of the peace." It also indicates that a purpose of the U.N. is to bring about the settlement of international disputes by peaceful means.

Article 1.2 affirms that another purpose of the U.N. is to "develop friendly relations among nations based on respect for the principle of equal rights and self-determination of peoples," thus implying respect for state sovereignty. Indeed, article 2.1 affirms that the organization "is based on the principle of the sovereign equality of all its Members," and article 2.7 provides that nothing in the Charter shall authorize the U.N. "to intervene in matters which are essentially within the domestic jurisdiction of any state... but this principle shall not prejudice the application of enforcement measures under Chapter VII."

At the same time, article 1.3 of the Charter states that one of the purposes of the U.N. is to achieve international cooperation "in promoting and encouraging respect for human rights and for fundamental freedoms for all without distinction as to race, sex, language, or religion." And articles 55 and 56 impose obligations on U.N. member states to take "joint and separate action in cooperation with the Organization" for the achievement of this purpose, among others.

Chapter VII of the Charter, including article 39, empowers the Security Council to adopt economic or military measures in response to a "threat to the peace, breach of the peace, or act of aggression." Under article 41 the Council can adopt non-military enforcement measures, including economic sanctions, and under article 42 it can take such military action "as may be necessary to maintain or restore international peace and security" if it judges that non-military measures have been, or would be, inadequate. In practice, the Cold War stymied the Council's ability to undertake or authorize collective enforcement action, with only a few exceptions. Instead, the U.N. developed and emphasized the concept of peacekeeping, in which troops are placed on the ground only with the consent of the parties, force is not to be used except in self-defense, and the troops must act impartially.[2]

In keeping with the Charter's attempt to legitimize only the collective use of force under the direction of the Security Council, article 2.4 provides that "all Members shall refrain in their international relations from the threat or use of force against the territorial integrity or political independence of any state, or in any other manner inconsistent with the Purposes of the United Nations." However, the Charter does permit the use of force in individual or collective self-defense of a state against an armed attack.[3]

The above-mentioned Charter provisions reflect conflicting norms and values and therefore raise various problems of interpretation. In particular, they elicit questions such as the following.

1. How should the protection of state sovereignty be balanced with a concern for universal human rights? In Security Council decision making under the Charter, which should take priority, concern for the independence of states or for the human rights of the individual?

2. Is it appropriate for the Security Council to authorize the use of force under chapter VII of the Charter to attempt to thwart gross human rights violations, especially when the Charter does not explicitly contemplate such uses of force? Or is it better to rely on traditional peacekeeping, in which peacekeeping troops can only use force in strict self-defense? Is there some obligation on the part of member states to help human rights victims, if necessary through military means?

Recent events in Somalia, Bosnia, Rwanda, Haiti, Kosovo, East Timor, and Afghanistan, among others, and the U.N.'s response to them, have brought new attention to these legal issues. Moreover, these questions have salient ethical dimensions.

How do we resolve these problems of Charter interpretation, especially where they involve ethical considerations that are inextricably interwoven with legal issues? International law, as a discipline, has developed rules for interpreting treaties like the U.N. Charter.[4] These rules generally focus on the "ordinary meaning" of the text, along with subsequent agreements among the parties as to the meaning of the words. When these strategies still leave the meaning unclear, they allow resort to the drafting history of the relevant treaty.[5] Unfortunately, these approaches do not provide much guidance on the above problems. Some legal scholars, and courts, have advocated an interpretive approach to treaties like the U.N. Charter that looks to the overall "purpose" of the treaty.[6] The problem with such an approach is that the Charter expresses conflicting purposes, including the protection of state sovereignty and the promotion of human rights, which have to be reconciled.

In view of these deficiencies of traditional approaches to Charter interpretation, certain legal scholars have maintained, and rightly so, that international lawyers and policy makers must seek some outside source of philosophical guidance to aid them in resolving these difficult problems of legal interpretation. They have turned to the theories of particular Western

philosophers, such as Kant.[7] In this chapter I build on these laudable innovations. In particular, it seems appropriate, in a multicultural world, to
develop an approach to humanitarian intervention and international law
that turns for ethical insight both to contemporary international legal texts
themselves, which increasingly reflect agreement of the world's governments on certain broad ethical principles, and to the teachings of the world
religions and philosophies. The vast majority of governments and people in
the world today look either to these legal texts, or to these religions and
philosophies, for a practical moral compass.

I will argue that contemporary international legal texts articulate
certain ethical principles that are logically related to a primary ethical principle of the unity of the human family alongside a respect for individual
and social diversity – or what I will refer to as a principle of "unity in
diversity." Moreover, certain passages from the revered moral texts of seven
world religions and philosophies may be interpreted to support these principles. These passages reveal at the least the *potential* for agreement on
fundamental ethical principles related to a principle of unity in diversity.

These ethical principles can help us to make progress in reconciling the
competing norms and values evidenced in the U.N. Charter relating to
humanitarian intervention. They can pave the way for better interpretation
of the Charter as a legal instrument, and also better policy making,
although they cannot provide clear-cut solutions or avoid challenging
moral choices.

SELECTED PASSAGES FROM CONTEMPORARY INTERNATIONAL
LEGAL TEXTS AND FROM REVERED MORAL TEXTS

In this section I will identify a very limited number of examples of textual
support in international treaties and declarations and in revered moral
texts for certain ethical principles in international law that are related to a
fundamental principle of unity in diversity.[8] For the purposes of this
chapter I have chosen to place relatively greater emphasis on passages from
revered moral texts. I have concentrated on selected texts of those world
religions and philosophies with the most widely represented membership
in different countries around the globe according to a frequently cited
survey. These religions and philosophies are, in descending order of global
representation: Christianity (238 countries), the Bahá'í Faith (221 countries), Islam (208 countries), Judaism (138 countries), Buddhism (128
countries), Hinduism (114 countries), and Confucianism and Chinese

"folk-religions" (91 countries).[9] I mention textual references in the approximate chronological order of the religious and philosophical systems of which they form a part.

I will focus here only on a few relevant ethical principles, namely

1.   the principle of unity in diversity, as described above;
2.   the principle of equal human dignity and human rights;
3.   strong moral obligations to assist others in need, regardless of their race, ethnicity, or religion, as emphasized in many of the articles in the Universal Declaration of Human Rights by the World Religions, especially article 6, paragraph 2, and article 29, and the permissibility, in extreme cases, of the threat or use of force for the limited purpose of rescuing victims of human rights abuses; and
4.   the importance of open-minded consultation on difficult moral and policy issues as a means of arriving at agreement on a policy that best implements relevant ethical principles.

Unity in Diversity

A number of contemporary international legal texts articulate a preeminent ethical principle of the unity of the human family. For example, the Universal Declaration of Human Rights, adopted by the U.N. General Assembly in 1948, emphasizes the importance of "recognition of the inherent dignity and of the equal and inalienable rights of *all members of the human family*."[10] Further, it asserts that all human beings "are endowed with reason and conscience and should act towards one another *in a spirit of brotherhood*."[11] And the Millennium Declaration adopted by the U.N. General Assembly in September 2000 states that the United Nations is "the indispensable common house of the *entire human family*."[12]

At the same time that international legal texts emphasize this familial metaphor, they stress the value of individual and group diversity. For example, the Millennium Declaration refers to "our common humanity in all its diversity." And it affirms that "differences within and between societies should be neither feared nor repressed, but cherished as a precious asset of humanity."[13]

Support for such a principle of "unity in diversity" may also be found in selected passages from revered moral texts. Thus, the *Bhagavad Gita* contains the instruction that one is to treat all human beings, whether Brahmin or outcaste, and all animals, with the same respect: "In a knowledge-and-cultivation-perfected Brahman, a cow, an elephant, And in a mere dog, and an outcaste, the wise see the same thing" (V: 18).[14] This equal respect requires an equal concern for all human beings: "Brahman-nirvana is won by the seers… Who delight in the welfare of all beings" (V: 25). The Hindu philosopher, scholar, and statesman Sarvepalli Radhakrishnan (1888–1975) believed that the *Gita* called for world brotherhood and sisterhood and an attitude "which sees all human beings as one family."[15]

According to the Hebrew scriptures, "Have we not all one Father? Did not one God create us?" (Mal. 2: 10).[16] The books of the later prophets often portray Israel as one of many nations created by God. For example, Amos affirms: "To Me, O Israelites, you are just like the Ethiopians – declares the Lord. True, I brought Israel up from the land of Egypt, but also the Philistines from Caphtor and the Arameans from Kir" (Amos 9:7).

Buddhist scriptures recount that the Buddha stated: "It is for the weal of the world that a Buddha has won enlightenment, and the welfare of all that lives has been his aim."[17] The Buddha taught that one should empathize with others and care for them with the same love that a mother shows for her only child: "Even as a mother watches over and protects her child, her only child, so with a boundless mind should one cherish all living beings, radiating friendliness over the entire world, above, below, and all around without limit. So let him cultivate a boundless good will towards the entire world, uncramped, free from ill-will or enmity."[18] Buddhist scriptures indicate that while a healthy national pride is legitimate,[19] it should not be excessive or blind one to the faults of one's country: "If you should hit on the idea that this or that country is safe, prosperous, or fortunate, give it up, my friend, and do not entertain it in any way; for you ought to know that the world everywhere is ablaze with the fires of some faults or others."[20]

Confucius' teachings enjoin all human beings to regard one another as brothers. In the *Analects* one of Confucius' disciples counseled another: "If a gentleman is assiduous and omits nothing, is respectful to others and displays decorum, then within the Four Seas, all are his brothers. Why should a gentleman worry that he has no brothers?" (*Analects* 12:5).[21] Mencius taught that the carrying out by a prince of his kindness of heart "will suffice for the love and protection of all within the four seas," and that if a prince should fail to carry out such kindness to all, then "he will not be able to protect his wife and children."[22] He thus identified an organic relationship between protection of one's kin and kindness toward all humanity.

Jesus taught that one should love one's neighbor as oneself. When a lawyer asked him who a "neighbor" is, Jesus told the story of the Good Samaritan. The Good Samaritan, when he saw a man who had been beaten and stripped by robbers, took pity on him, bandaged his wounds, and brought him to an inn (Luke 10:25–37).[23] Jesus stated that the Good Samaritan, by caring for the man, became his "neighbor." The story suggests that ethically all individuals ought to act toward others as "neighbors." Moreover, Jesus affirmed that all human beings are children of God: "And call no one your father on earth, for you have one Father – the one in heaven" (Matt. 23:9).

Many teachings of the Qur'an are also humanity-oriented and center on the principle of the oneness of the human family.[24] For example, the Qur'an states that all human beings were created by one God, which confers on them a fundamental dignity as children of God: "We have honoured the Children of Adam and carried them on land and sea, and provided them with good things, and preferred them greatly over many of those We created" (17:72).[25] And it affirms: "Mankind, fear your Lord, who created you of a single soul" (4:1). According to one *hadith,* the "whole universe is the family of Allah," and to another, human beings are as "alike as the teeth of a comb."[26] The Qur'an encourages the diverse peoples of the earth to associate with one another in harmony: "O mankind, We have created you male and female, and appointed you races and tribes, that you may know one another. Surely the noblest among you in the sight of God is the most godfearing of you" (49:13). The Qur'an affirms, in fact, that one of the signs of God is the creation of "the variety of your tongues and hues" (30:21).

Bahá'u'lláh, the Prophet-Founder of the Bahá'í Faith, exhorted all human beings to see themselves as members of one human family and one spiritual country: "It is not for him to pride himself who loveth his own country, but rather for him who loveth the whole world. The earth is but one country, and mankind its citizens."[27] But such world citizenship does not exclude love of one's nation. In the words of Shoghi Effendi, the Guardian of the Bahá'í Faith, the principle of the oneness of humankind taught by Bahá'u'lláh "can conflict with no legitimate allegiances, nor can it undermine essential loyalties. Its purpose is neither to stifle the flame of a sane and intelligent patriotism in men's hearts, nor to abolish the system of national autonomy so essential if the evils of excessive centralization are to be avoided."[28]

All of the above quotations reflect not only the principle of the unity of the human family, but also the centrality of human dignity, which is supportive of modern-day human rights concepts. The concept of equal human dignity and equal human rights follows from that of unity in diversity. In this connection, the Universal Declaration of Human Rights affirms that all human beings "are born free and equal in dignity and rights."[29] Certain passages from the world's revered moral texts, including those mentioned above, may also be interpreted to support this principle.[30]

The Obligation to Assist Others in Need, Potentially Through the Threat or Use of Force

Contemporary international law does not explicitly identify a moral obligation to help others in need, potentially through the threat or use of force. However, such an ethical obligation follows from the strong ethical principle of the unity of the human family, which implies the existence of salient obligations to rescue other family members in distress, in tandem with the ethical principle of equal human dignity, which implies the importance of a concern for the dignity and human rights of all other members of the human family. Moreover, international legal texts do not completely renounce all threats or uses of force, but suggest, as we saw earlier, that they ought to be internationally sanctioned and limited to certain legitimate ethical ends. The U.N. Charter declares in its preamble, for example, that one of its purposes is to ensure, "by the acceptance of principles and the institution of methods, that armed force shall not be used, save in the common interest."

Many passages from the revered moral texts of the seven world religions and philosophies I have considered emphasize such an ethical obligation to assist others in need. In addition, many of them indicate or imply that such an obligation may have to be carried out by the threat or use of force as a last resort.

For example, the *Bhagavad Gita* promotes the cultivation of virtues involving care and concern for others, such as generosity and unselfishness, compassion toward creatures, harmlessness (*ahimsa*), gentleness, and the non-use of force (see, for example, XII:13–20, XIII:7, XVI:1–3, XVIII:51–53). The *Gita* stresses the merits of non-violence, and condemns those who take pride in slaying others (see XVI:9–16). At the same time, the poetic setting of the *Gita* is a battle between Arjuna and an opposing army composed of members of a branch of Arjuna's family that has illegitimately gained control of the kingdom.[31] Krishna instructs Arjuna to fight as a warrior, because that is his caste duty (see II:18). Krishna's instruction might be interpreted to suggest that violence may sometimes be required to maintain social order or secure justice, but must be employed impartially, without personal animosity, and only as an absolute last resort. Such an interpretation, in combination with the recognition of duties to promote the well-being of others, might support the concept of humanitarian intervention.

Turning to the Hebrew scriptures, the Torah's most important ethical teaching, according to Judaic scholars, is to "love your fellow as yourself" (Lev. 19:18). In keeping with this principle, there is biblical and rabbinical authority for the use of force, within strict limits, to save those who are persecuted or in need. For example, according to a verse in Psalms: "Judge the wretched and the orphan, vindicate the lowly and the poor, rescue the wretched and the needy; save them from the hand of the wicked" (Ps. 82: 3–4). Kings must save those who cry out and have no helper (Ps. 72:12). Individuals cannot claim ignorance as an excuse for failing to come to the rescue of those threatened with slaughter: "If you refrained from rescuing those taken off to death, Those condemned to slaughter – If you say, 'We knew nothing of it,' Surely He who fathoms hearts will discern [the truth], He who watches over your life will know it, And He will pay each man as he deserves" (Prov. 24:11–12).

According to Buddhist scriptures, one must serve others with compassion: "Not to be helpful to others, Not to give to those in need, This is the fruit of Samsara [the world of birth and death]. Better than this is to renounce the idea of a self."[32] On the problem of the use of force, Buddhist scriptures indicate that the Buddha affirmed: "All warfare in which man tries to slay his brother is lamentable, but he does not teach that those who go to war in a righteous cause after having exhausted all means to preserve the peace are blameworthy. He must be blamed who is the cause of war."[33] According to one scholar, Buddhism's social teaching is thus "not an absolute pacifism, but a philosophical ethic, making for peace, moderation, and magnanimity."[34] It appears to leave open the possibility of humanitarian intervention.

Confucius advocated a principle of reciprocity – effectively the Golden Rule. One of Confucius' disciples asked, "is there one saying that one can put in practice in all circumstances?" Confucius replied: "That would be empathy, would it not? What he himself does not want, let him not do it to others" (*Analects* 15:24). Confucius also taught the principle of *ren*, which evolved into a civilian concept similar to "benevolence" or "humaneness."[35] In keeping with such a principle, one contemporary scholar has taken the position that "Confucians would approve the use of force by one state against another state for the protection against abusive rule in the latter if properly carried out."[36] For example, the works of Mencius state that the ruler of Qi invaded the state of Yan, whose ruler was "tyrannizing over his people." The people approved of the intervention at first. Mencius said he would sanction the annexation of Yan to Qi if the people of Yan would be pleased with it. But the ruler of Qi himself murdered and imprisoned the people of Yan. Mencius counseled the ruler of Qi to designate a new ruler of Yan after consulting with the people of Yan, and then to leave Yan. Mencius accordingly emphasized that such an intervention on humanitarian grounds must not make the condition of the people worse.[37]

Many of the central moral teachings of Christianity are conveyed in Jesus' "Sermon on the Mount." One of these is the Christian version of the Golden Rule: "In everything do to others as you would have them do to you; for this is the law and the prophets" (Matt. 7:12). The parable of the Good Samaritan, too, indicates that there is a strong moral duty to provide some kind of assistance to victims of human rights violations. Christian theologians have adopted different approaches, however, to the problem of reconciling a principle of non-violence with the principles of Good Samaritanism, Christian love, and the Golden Rule in cases where force appears to be necessary to rescue one in need or under attack. Some theologians have emphasized an absolute moral duty of non-violent resistance.[38] Others, such as Paul Ramsey, have argued that the compelling moral obligation to defend the innocent may in some cases justify the threat or use of force, in keeping with the just war tradition within Christianity.[39]

The Qur'an prescribes humanitarian care and charity toward others, including foreigners: "Be kind to... the neighbor who is of kin, and to the neighbor who is a stranger" (4:41). On the specific issue of humanitarian intervention, there is a passage in the Qur'an that may be interpreted to permit, and call for, the use of force to defend victims of human rights violations: "How is it with you, that you do not fight in the way of God, and for the men, women, and children who, being abased, say, 'Our Lord, bring us forth from this city whose people are evildoers, and appoint to us a protector from Thee, and appoint to us from Thee a helper'?" (4:77).[40] A number of scholars have concluded, therefore, that there is an Islamic ethic of humanitarian intervention.[41]

Turning to the Bahá'í Faith, the Bahá'í writings emphasize duties to protect the rights of others and defend them against tyranny and oppression. For example, Bahá'u'lláh counseled every human being to be "an upholder and defender of the victim of oppression."[42] At least one passage from the writings of Bahá'u'lláh might be interpreted to endorse collective military intervention to prevent oppression and extreme human rights violations. Bahá'u'lláh appealed to all kings and rulers not only to undertake joint action in support of a system of collective security, but also to unite to "shield mankind from the onslaught of tyranny."[43]

Open-Minded Consultation as a Means of Problem Solving

Finally, contemporary international legal texts emphasize the importance of open-minded consultation among governments and peoples in peacefully solving, if at all possible, the difficult problems faced by the international community. The purpose of such consultation is to reach a consensus on solutions to common problems, and then to implement the agreed solutions through cooperative efforts. It thus reflects and flows from the principle of unity in diversity.

The U.N. Charter proclaims in this connection that one of the U.N.'s fundamental purposes is to achieve "international co-operation in solving international problems," including, we have seen, in promoting and encouraging respect for human rights. And according to the Charter the U.N. is to serve as "a centre for harmonizing the actions of nations in the attainment of these common ends."[44]

Many passages from the revered texts of the seven world religions and philosophies I have considered endorse such an ethical principle of open-minded consultation. For example, among the virtues praised in the *Bhagavad Gita* are those consistent with consultation, including the pursuit of truth, restraint in speech, and abstention from backbiting (see, for example, XII:19, XVI:2, XVIII:52). A principle of consultation is also found in the Judaic tradition. Proverbs declares, for example, that "plans are foiled for want of counsel, But they succeed through many advisers" (Prov. 15:22). Kings are wise to consider various points of view: "Koheleth... listened to and tested the soundness of many maxims" (Eccles. 12:9).

According to Buddhist scriptures, the Buddha emphasized the importance of being open to other perspectives. He opposed religious dissension and arguments based on exclusive claims to a sole "truth."[45] He recounted the parable of the blind men and the elephant, which may be interpreted as illustrating that there are many aspects of truth and that humble consultation is required to perceive these many dimensions of truth.[46] And Confucius stressed that the search for truth must include consultation with, and learning from, others with a humble attitude: "When I am walking in a group of three people, there will surely be a teacher for me among them. I pick out the good parts and follow them; the bad parts, and change them" (*Analects* 7:22).

A number of passages from the New Testament endorse a process of consultation among believers, in which each expresses his or her own views while considering thoughtfully the views of the others and seeking to learn from them. For example, St. Paul said:

> When you come together, each one has a hymn, a lesson, a revelation, a tongue, or an interpretation... Let two or three prophets speak, and let the others weigh what is said. If a revelation is made to someone else sitting nearby, let the first person be silent. For you can all prophesy one by one, so that all may learn and all be encouraged. (1 Cor. 14:26, 29–31)

There are verses in the Qur'an that endorse a principle of consultation. For example, the Qur'an affirms, "take counsel with them in the affair; and when thou art resolved, put thy trust in God" (3:153).[47] And a *hadith* recounts that the Prophet replied as follows to a question about how a problem should be resolved after his passing that neither he nor the Qur'an had addressed: "Get together amongst my followers and place the matter before them for consultation. Do not make decisions on the opinions of any single person."[48]

The Bahá'í writings also strongly emphasize the importance of sincere consultation among individuals and all social institutions as a means of finding the truth and discovering solutions to practical and moral problems. Bahá'u'lláh stated: "Take ye counsel together in all matters, inasmuch as consultation is the lamp of guidance which leadeth the way, and is the bestower of understanding."[49] According to 'Abdu'l-Bahá, son of Bahá'u'lláh, "consultation must have for its object the investigation of truth. He who expresses an opinion should not voice it as correct and right but set it forth as a contribution to the consensus of opinion, for the light of reality becomes apparent when two opinions coincide."[50]

APPLICATION OF THE ABOVE-MENTIONED PRINCIPLES TO CERTAIN PROBLEMS OF U.N. HUMANITARIAN INTERVENTION

How can these ethical principles evident in contemporary international law, consistent with a preeminent principle of unity in diversity, and supported by selected passages from revered moral texts, help resolve the above-mentioned problems of interpreting the U.N. Charter's provisions relating to humanitarian intervention? They suggest certain preliminary conclusions, which can be only very briefly stated here.

First, on the problem of balancing sovereignty with human rights, the above principles suggest that while respect for sovereignty is important because of the moral legitimacy of nations and allegiances to them, it must be limited by the universal dignity to which all human beings are entitled as members of a single human family. So "sovereignty" cannot be used as a shield to prevent outside inquiry about human rights violations, or to excuse such violations. Indeed, the principle of the unity of the human family indicates that human beings have a duty to look after the welfare of citizens of other states. The Security Council should take account of these principles in exercising its discretionary authority under the Charter.

Second, on the problem of whether it is appropriate for the Security Council to authorize the use of force to attempt to prevent or stop gross human rights violations, a number of points can be made. Above all, the ethical principles supported by international legal texts and revered moral texts reviewed above suggest that there is an important role both for traditional peacekeeping forces and for more robust military intervention in extreme cases, and that the U.N. Charter should be interpreted, to the extent possible under established principles of treaty interpretation, to permit such intervention pursuant to chapter VII under the guidance of the Security Council in appropriate circumstances. These ethical principles call for recognition of at least a moral obligation on the part of the U.N. and its member states to take some reasonable action in response to gross human rights violations, which may include military action. At the same time, the principles of consultation and of unity in diversity strongly indicate the importance of open-minded consultation among U.N. member states, and particularly members of the Security Council, about the morally complex issue of whether and when the use of force is the most appropriate response to human rights violations. It is clearly a response that should be adopted only as a last recourse.

CONCLUSION

I have suggested that ethical principles, supported, directly or indirectly, by contemporary international law, and logically related to a primary principle of unity in diversity, can provide helpful guidance in interpreting the provisions of the U.N. Charter relevant to humanitarian intervention and in helping to reconcile competing norms and values in the Charter. I have also suggested that certain passages from the world's revered moral texts can be interpreted to support these principles. Through the efforts of statesmen and stateswomen to interpret and reform international law in light of these principles, we may in the near future witness important steps toward improving the world community's capacities for collective humanitarian intervention.

NOTES

1. This chapter incorporates ideas developed in much more detail in my book *Rethinking Humanitarian Intervention: A Fresh Legal Approach Based on Fundamental Ethical Principles in International Law and World Religions* (University Park: Pennsylvania State University Press, 2002). I wish to express my appreciation for the comments of Peter Terry.

2. These principles were originally formulated by Secretary-General Dag Hammarskjöld when the U.N. Emergency Force in the Sinai was deployed in 1956. See, e.g., *Second and Final Report of the Secretary-General on the Plan for an Emergency UN Force*, U.N. Doc. A/3302 (1956), paragraphs 4–12.

3. See U.N. Charter, article 51.

4. See generally, e.g., the Vienna Convention on the Law of Treaties, U.N. Doc. A/CONF.39/27 (1969), articles 31–33; Sir Ian Sinclair, *The Vienna Convention on the Law of Treaties*, 2nd ed. (Manchester: Manchester University Press, 1984), pp. 114–158.

5. See Vienna Convention, articles 31–32.

6. See, e.g., Sinclair, *The Vienna Convention*, pp. 130–135 (describing "teleological" approaches to treaty interpretation).

7. See, e.g., Fernando R. Tesón, *Humanitarian Intervention: An Inquiry into Law and Morality*, 2nd edn (Irvington-on-Hudson: Transnational Publishers, Inc., 1997).

8. For a fuller exploration of textual support for these ethical principles in contemporary international law and in revered moral texts, see my book. There are, of course, many scriptural passages that may be interpreted to oppose these principles, which I do not discuss here. For a more rigorous analysis of the ethical teachings of various religions of relevance to human rights, see, e.g., *Religious Diversity and Human Rights*, ed. Irene Bloom, J. Paul Martin, and Wayne L. Proudfoot (New York: Columbia University Press, 1996), as well as the other chapters in this volume.

9. "Worldwide Adherents of All Religions by Six Continental Areas, Mid-1998," in "Religion: World Religious Statistics," in *1999 Britannica Book of the Year* (Chicago: Encyclopaedia Britannica, Inc., 1999), p. 315. These figures are best regarded as approximations. The figure for Confucianism and Chinese folk-religions is the higher of the separate figures for Confucianism (15 countries) and Chinese folk-religions (91 countries).

10. Universal Declaration of Human Rights, G.A. Res. 217A (1948), Preamble (emphasis added).

11. Ibid., article 1 (emphasis added).

12. Millennium Declaration, G.A. Res. 55/2 (2000), paragraph 32 (emphasis added).

13. Ibid., paragraphs 5–6.

14. All quotations from or citations of the *Bhagavad Gita* are from the translation by Franklin Edgerton. See Franklin Edgerton, trans. and interp., *The Bhagavad Gita* (Cambridge, MA: Harvard University Press, 1972).

15. Robert N. Minor, "The *Bhagavadgita* in Radhakrishnan's Apologetics," in *Modern Indian Interpreters of the Bhagavadgita,* ed. Robert N. Minor (Albany: State University of New York Press, 1986), p. 167.

16. All quotations from or citations of the Hebrew scriptures are from *Tanakh: A New Translation of the Holy Scriptures According to the Traditional Hebrew Text* (Philadelphia: Jewish Publication Society, 1985).

17. Edward Conze, trans., *Buddhist Scriptures* (London: Penguin Books, 1959), p. 55.

18. Ibid., p. 186.

19. See Padmasiri de Silva, "The Concept of Equality in the Theravada Buddhist Tradition," in *Equality and the Religious Traditions of Asia,* ed. R. Siriwardena (New York: St. Martin's Press, 1987), p. 89.

20. Conze, trans., *Buddhist Scriptures,* p. 111.

21. All quotations from or citations of the *Analects* are from the translation by E. Bruce Brooks and A. Taeko Brooks. See E. Bruce Brooks and A. Taeko Brooks, trans., *The Original Analects: Sayings of Confucius and his Successors* (New York: Columbia University Press, 1998).

22. James Legge, *The Chinese Classics: The Works of Mencius* (Hong Kong: Hong Kong University Press, 1960), vol. 2, bk. I, pt. I, ch. VII, paragraph 12, at p. 143.

23 All quotations from or citations of the New Testament are from the New Revised Standard Version of the Bible. See *The Holy Bible Containing the Old and New Testaments: New Revised Standard Version* (New York: Oxford University Press, 1989).

24. On the principle of the oneness of humankind in Islam, see generally C.G. Weeramantry, *Islamic Jurisprudence: An International Perspective* (New York: St. Martin's Press, 1988), p. 133.

25. All quotations from or citations of the Qur'an are from the translation by A.J. Arberry. See A.J. Arberry, trans., *The Koran Interpreted* (New York: Touchstone, 1955).

26. Quoted in Weeramantry, *Islamic Jurisprudence,* p. 133.

27. Bahá'u'lláh, *Gleanings from the Writings of Bahá'u'lláh,* trans. Shoghi Effendi, 2nd rev. ed. (Wilmette: Bahá'í Publishing Trust, 1976), p. 250.

28. Shoghi Effendi, *The World Order of Bahá'u'lláh: Selected Letters by Shoghi Effendi* (Wilmette: Bahá'í Publishing Trust, 1974), p. 41.

29. Universal Declaration, article 1.

30. See my book for more detailed references.

31. See, e.g., Robert N. Minor, *Bhagavad-Gita: An Exegetical Commentary* (Columbia, MO: South Asia Books, 1982), pp. xxii–xxiv.

32. Conze, trans., *Buddhist Scriptures,* p. 180.

33.   Paul Carus, *The Gospel of Buddha* (Chicago: Open Court Publishing Co., 1915), p. 149.

34.   Norman Bentwich, *The Religious Foundations of Internationalism: A Study in International Relations through the Ages,* 2nd ed. (New York: The Bloch Publishing Co., 1959), p. 187.

35.   See, e.g., Brooks and Brooks, trans., *The Original Analects,* pp. 19, 93.

36.   Frederick Tse-Shyang Chen, "The Confucian View of World Order," in *Religion and International Law,* eds. Mark W. Janis and Carolyn Evans (The Hague: Martinus Nijhoff Publishers, 1999), p. 35.

37.   See Legge, *The Works of Mencius,* bk. I, pt. II, ch. X–XI, at pp. 169–172.

38.   See, e.g., Dale Aukerman, "The Scandal of Defenselessness," quoted in John H. Yoder, *What Would You Do? A Serious Answer to a Standard Question* (Scottdale, PA: Herald Press, 1983), pp. 75–77.

39.   See, e.g., Paul Ramsey, *The Just War: Force and Political Responsibility* (New York: Charles Scribner's Sons, 1968), pp. 500–503.

40.   On obligations to come to the defense of others in Islam, see, e.g., Weeramantry, *Islamic Jurisprudence,* pp. 83–85.

41.   See, e.g., Sohail H. Hashmi, "Is There an Islamic Ethic of Humanitarian Intervention?", *Ethics and International Affairs,* 7 (1993), pp. 55–73.

42.   Bahá'u'lláh, *Gleanings,* p. 285.

43.   Ibid., p. 249.

44.   U.N. Charter, article 1, paragraphs 3–4.

45.   See the passages reproduced in *The Teachings of the Compassionate Buddha: Early Discourses, the Dhammapada and Later Basic Writings,* ed. E.A. Burtt (New York: Mentor Books, 1982), pp. 36–39.

46.   See F.L. Woodward, trans., *Some Sayings of the Buddha According to the Pali Canon* (London: Oxford University Press, 1973), pp. 190–192.

47.   See also 42:36 ("their affair being counsel between them"). On the principle of consultation in Islam, see Fazlur Rahman, *Major Themes of the Qur'an* (Minneapolis: Bibliotheca Islamica, 1980), pp. 43–44.

48.   Quoted in Weeramantry, *Islamic Jurisprudence,* p. 92.

49.   Bahá'u'lláh, *Tablets of Bahá'u'lláh Revealed after the Kitáb-i-Aqdas,* trans. Habib Taherzadeh (Haifa: Bahá'í World Centre, 1978), p. 168.

50.   'Abdu'l-Bahá, *The Promulgation of Universal Peace: Talks Delivered by 'Abdu'l-Bahá During his Visit to the United States and Canada in 1912,* comp. Howard MacNutt, 2nd ed. (Wilmette: Bahá'í Publishing Trust, 1982), p. 72.

Plate 7 Stained-glass window designed by John Piper (1903–1992) which adorns the sanctuary of the twelfth-century Norman church (1170–1180) in the village of Iffley, just outside Oxford, in England. Portraying a host of creatures on the Tree of Life, the banner in the lower panel reads, "Let man and beast appear before Him and magnify His name together."
Photo: *Nancy M. Martin*

7

HUMAN RIGHTS, ENVIRONMENTAL RIGHTS, *and* RELIGION

James Kellenberger

The preamble of the United Nations Universal Declaration of Human Rights begins: "Whereas recognition of the inherent dignity and inalienable rights of all members of the human family is the foundation of freedom, justice and peace in the world..." I wish to start with an acceptance of the concept of human rights embodied in this claim, for I believe that it is essentially correct. Perhaps the claim that the recognition of human rights is the foundation of freedom, justice, and peace is also correct. However, my interest is in the concept of rights used in this element of the preamble, the way rights are being thought of in it.

In what follows I shall address four concerns. First, I want to bring into relief several features of the essentially correct concept of rights used in the United Nations statement and to note how other notions of rights do not share these features. Second, I shall try to show how relationships are foundational to and provide an understanding of human rights when human rights are understood in terms of the concept used in the United Nations Declaration. Third, I shall bring out the analogy between human rights and environmental rights. Finally, I shall consider whether rights, environmental rights in particular, can be accommodated by the Judaic and Christian religious traditions.

THE CONCEPT OF HUMAN RIGHTS IN THE UNITED NATIONS DECLARATION

What are the salient features of human rights in the concept of rights used by the United Nations in its Declaration? The first thing to be noted is that such rights are moral rights, not legal rights. They are not legal rights because they do not exist by virtue of some legal instrument or proclamation; they are not created by the action of a legal body, in particular they are not created by the action of the United Nations in declaring them. These rights are rights the violation of which is a moral fault or failing; thus, even if no legal jurisdiction in the world would or could prosecute a violator, even if there were no legal fault, there would be a moral fault. Of course the rights named by the United Nations Declaration may become legal rights as well; they could become legal rights with standing in international law by virtue of some binding action by the members of the United Nations, or they could become legal rights in a country by virtue of the action of a country's lawmaking body. But this does not affect their underlying status as moral rights in the conception before us.

Correlated with this first feature is a second feature. Human rights are recognized; they are not created. They are acknowledged; they are not invented. In declaring the universal rights of human beings, the United Nations, in its own understanding, went on record as recognizing rights that persons have by virtue of being human beings, independently of the pronouncements of any governmental body or organization. This feature entails that if a human right exists, it exists whether or not it is acknowledged, and may be violated even though that violation is not acknowledged or recognized.

That human rights are or can be recognized means, third, that rights in the conception before us are real in the sense that they are not fictions. The concept of human rights embodied in the United Nations Universal Declaration, then, stands opposed to conceptions of human rights that (1) make them merely legal rights; (2) present them as being created or invented; or (3) regard them as fictions. Opposing conceptions of human rights that embrace one or more of these three elements of course exist and have their proponents. The moral philosopher Alasdair MacIntyre, for instance, regards human rights as "fictions," as "moral fictions," as he says.[1] And the political theorist Jack Donnelly believes that human rights were invented at a certain point in the history of moral thinking and need. We shall take a closer look at Donnelly's view shortly.

Just here, though, we ought to acknowledge two related concerns that some have with a moral focus on rights. Our pursuing these two concerns will bring into relief two further features that may be taken to be features of rights in the conception used by the United Nations, but in fact are not features of that conception. The first of these related concerns is with an "ethic of rights" that makes rights morally "basic." This ethic regards as paradigmatic moral deliberation the impartial weighing of rights and rights claims in the light of general principles of justice. One critic of such an ethic, Iris Young, has observed that an "'ethic of rights' corresponds poorly to the social relations typical of family and personal life," though she allows that it may fit better "in the impersonal public contexts of law, bureaucracy and the regulation of economic competition."[2]

The second concern, voiced by several, is with the "atomistic" self.[3] This concern is with a picture of the human moral situation that portrays individuals as "atoms" who are unconnected strangers with no sense of close personal relationships, who morally interact exclusively or mainly by pursuing their individual interests through claiming their rights, and by adjudicating rights claims.

We may well be concerned about and reject the atomistic picture of human morality along with the connected idea that morality is an ethic of rights whereby rights are the basis of all morality. For the atomistic picture of morality wrongly denies those dimensions of our moral lives that are created by our connectedness to others, and an ethic of rights wrongly makes rights and the weighing of competing rights the basis of all of morality. However, we should be clear that to reject the atomistic picture as a spurious picture of morality, and to reject the idea that morality is an ethic of rights whereby rights are basic, as I think we should do, we need not and should not reject either of the following: (1) that human beings have moral rights, which they have by virtue of being human persons; and (2) that these rights are open to our recognition. To put it another way, neither the atomistic moral picture nor an ethic of rights is a feature of or necessitated by the United Nations conception of rights; and thus we need not reject rights in the conception used in the United Nations Declaration in order to reject both the atomistic moral picture and an ethic of rights.

HUMAN RIGHTS AND RELATIONSHIPS

If rights are not morally basic, what is? I suggest that relationships between persons are basic to morality. If this is so, then of course relationships are basic to moral rights. One fundamental relationship in particular is basic to human rights. This is the relationship we as persons have to all persons – not by virtue of marriage, parenthood, friendship, citizenship, or ethnic identity – but simply by virtue of being persons. Let us call it the "person–person relationship".

We as individuals have many familiar relationships that we have no trouble identifying as "personal" relationships, such as friendships and child–parent relationships. However, many relationships between persons are not of this close personal character, such as our relationship to others in our community and in our nation. The person–person relationship is like those just mentioned in the respect that it holds between us and others whom we may not know personally. As a relationship involving all persons, and that each person has to each person, by virtue of nothing more than being a person, this relationship extends to persons unseen by us and whom we will never meet.

Relationships between persons, like the marital relationship and relationships of friendship, can be lived up to or violated. As the marital relationship is violated when its requirement of marital fidelity is not kept, so the person–person relationship can be violated when its requirements are not met. The central requirement of the person–person relationship is that we treat persons as persons. We violate this relationship, as it exists between us and some other persons, when we fail to treat them with the kind of respect that persons deserve as persons.

Not treating persons as they deserve can of course take many forms. We can violate the person–person relationship in our close personal relationships, as when we fail to treat persons close to us as they should be treated as persons. We can also violate this relationship in our general relationships; thus we violate the person–person relationship when we fail to keep the general obligation not to harm others and when we fail to observe the general obligation to be just in our dealings with others.

How does what I am calling the person–person relationship underlie and explain human rights? In accord with the concept embodied in the United Nations Declaration, human rights are the rights human persons have as persons. They are general rights (holding for human beings generally), and they are moral rights (in that they are not bestowed or created by a legal document or by legal action). The basic human right is the right to be treated as a person. Understood one way, the source of this basic human right is the inherent worth persons have by virtue of being persons (the "dignity" of persons, as it is sometimes put; the United Nations Universal Declaration speaks of the dignity of human beings). The inherent worth of persons is the source of the basic right to be treated as a person in the sense that it is a requirement of the right – that is, the right to be treated as a person is the right to be treated in accord with the inherent worth one has as a person. Understood another way, the source of the basic human right to be treated as a person is the fundamental relationship that involves all persons simply by virtue of their being persons, the person–person relationship. It is this fundamental relationship that is violated when persons are *not* treated as persons and is respected when they *are* treated as person.

Persons have whatever other human rights there are, again, by virtue of their status as persons; and when these other human rights are not respected, again, the person–person relationship is violated. In this way the person–person relationship is a broad test for human rights and explains not only the basic human right to be treated as a person but whatever other human rights there are as well. Thus, if there is a human right to liberty (as affirmed in art. 3 of the Universal Declaration), this is because a denial of liberty would violate the person–person relationship to those denied liberty. Similarly, if there is a human right to own property or to religious belief and practice, or to freedom of expression, or to education (art. 17, 18, 19, and 26 of the Universal Declaration), it is because their denial would violate the person–person relationship. If there is a human right to share in the natural resources of the world, and future generations share in this right, that is because those persons are also in the person–person relationship with us.

Many secondary human rights can be given up, as when I give away my property or voluntarily present myself to the authorities to be interned for my own safety. And there can be times when certain human rights must be taken away or overruled, as when a psychotic individual, dangerous to himself and to others, is confined. In these cases the test of the person–person relationship remains in place: when I renounce my right to my property or present myself for internment or when we confine the psychotic, the person–person relationship must not be violated. The primary human right to be treated as a person is truly inalienable for persons, since it exists simply by virtue of one's being a person (and one's participation in the person–person relationship thereby).[4]

These reflections on the person–person relationship speak to the questions: Are there human rights? What are they? And who has them? The form of particular human rights is another matter. The form of respecting various human rights can be importantly determined by other relationships. For instance, the right to own property, the right to religious belief and practice, and even the basic right to be treated as a person may be determined by other relationships, which are themselves partially culturally defined. Thus what counts as private property may to a great extent be culturally determined. If there is a strong commons tradition, then grazing land may not be open to private ownership, and in the traditional society of the Oglala Sioux, while food, clothing, and livestock could be owned, the land upon which they hunted could not be. The right to religious belief and practice may in the cultural setting of the Native American Church extend to the ritualistic taking of peyote – in contrast to that right's entailment in, say, a moderately high Episcopal church setting. Thus the person–person relationship explains the existence of human rights transcending cultural restrictions, while the requirements of other relationships, themselves partially molded by societal factors, explain the culture-dependent aspect of human rights.

If rights derive from relationships, they are not a matter of human invention or creation. Legal rights may be, but moral rights are not. Human rights, as the Universal Declaration says, are recognized; they are not created and bestowed; and relationships explain how human rights can be recognized. Donnelly says, however, that the "human rights approach to human dignity... was first developed in... the early modern period [in] seventeenth-century England." For him, the "West" invented human rights.[5] Why, asks Donnelly, were there no human rights in non-Western societies or in Western societies before the seventeenth century? Because, he says, "prior to the creation of capitalist market economies and modern nation states... the particular violations of human dignity that [human rights] seek to prevent either did not exist or were not widely perceived to be central social problems."[6] Alternatively, human rights, or basic human rights, existed prior to this time, but were articulated in a forceful way only in the seventeenth century. It is true that certain human rights of definite focus require a reference to certain "institutions": thus if there is a right to vote, that right will require a political institution that accommodates voting. And if there is a right to nationality, that right will require nation-states. However, the right to liberty does not require any political institution. And the most fundamental human right of all, the right to be treated as a person, has no institutional requirement.

ENVIRONMENTAL RIGHTS

If what I have said so far is correct, relationships, and the person–person relationship in particular, are basic to human rights. What about environmental rights? Are there environmental rights? What are they? What beings have them? Once again I believe that reflecting on relationships involving persons will shed light on these questions.

By "environmental rights" I mean whatever moral rights non-human environmental beings may have. Thus I understand the category of environmental rights to cover what are called "animal rights," the rights of non-human animals, as well as the rights of non-sentient environmental beings, such as plants, forests, mountain ranges, wetlands, deserts, species of plants and animals, and the environment as a whole.

When we go from human rights to environmental rights, we have taken a conceptual step. It is a step, I think, and not a leap. The reason I say this is because most of us have a pretheoretical appreciation of at least some obligations toward at least some environmental beings: most of us, for instance, would recognize an obligation not to cause gratuitous pain to an animal. This recognition brings us very nearly to the point of acknowledging the right of animals not to have pain needlessly inflicted upon them, and I think that many of us do pretheoretically acknowledge this right. Nevertheless, while I think that we can meaningfully speak of environmental rights and coherently consider what they are, I must concede that others have expressed reservations about the idea of environmental rights or certain classes of environmental rights.

Peter Singer, for instance, argues for "a new ethical status of animals" on the basis of equal treatment, but he does not do so on the basis of the moral rights of animals. Singer is suspicious of the idea of animals' moral rights, but that is because he is suspicious of the idea of moral rights itself, even in its application to human persons. Proceeding from a strongly utilitarian orientation, which looks to the maximization of good effects for moral justification, he quotes with sympathy Jeremy Bentham's comment that "natural rights" are "nonsense," and "imprescriptible rights" are "nonsense upon stilts."[7] Tom Regan, by way of contrast, has defended the moral rights of animals – rights that would make claims upon human moral agents, but he expressed misgivings about attributing moral rights to environmental entities that are collections, like forests or ecosystems, as opposed to individuals, which are, he allowed, "paradigmatic right-holders."[8]

In the United Nations Declaration the rights spoken of are human rights, the moral rights of human persons. Such rights, of course, are those of human beings, not those of non-human animals and not those of natural entities. Those who possess such human rights typically have responsibilities to respect the rights of other persons, and those who have such rights are individuals. These features of rights, however, though strongly associated with human rights, need not be regarded as essential to the idea of moral rights. If human infants have rights, then, since infants do not have moral responsibility for their actions, there is among human beings a precedent for having rights without having obligations; and if there are "group rights" – rights of groups of persons – then, again, in the realm of human persons there are rights that are not individual rights. It seems, then, that we can, without exceeding the concept, coherently attribute moral rights to non-human beings and even to collectives like forests or mountain ranges.

Allowing that the idea of environmental rights is coherent allows only that we may without confusion speak of possible environmental rights. What might such rights be? And what would establish that there are such rights? As with human rights, I suggest that relationships provide a foundation for environmental rights. Relationships between us human persons and animals and other environmental entities underlie and explain whatever environmental rights there are. Just as the fundamental person– person relationship that persons have to persons requires us to respect the worth of persons by treating persons as persons, so we should allow there is a fundamental relationship that we have to the natural beings of the environment that requires us to respect their worth as natural beings.

Precisely what this respect requires may be open to some question, as it is open to question what respecting the worth of persons requires in many instances. That is, just as there may be questions about what human rights there are and what they require of us, so there can be questions about what environmental rights there are and what they require of us. In the case of the environment there is of course the further question of which rights which entities have. The rights that forests have may be different from certain rights that sentient beings in the environment have. However, if our fundamental relationship to persons requires us never to disregard the worth that persons have as persons, our fundamental relationship to the environment requires us never to disregard the worth of natural beings. If persons have a right to be treated as persons, natural entities have a right to have their integrity respected. And the broad test for our violating the rights of any natural entity, I am suggesting, is whether we violate our fundamental relationship to that environmental being, be it a non-human animal or a forest or a desert.

On the understanding of environmental rights that I am presenting, this fundamental person–environment relationship should be understood as closely analogous to the person–person relationship. This means that, if there is this relationship, it itself is not created by human beings. Let me elaborate this point by bringing out how this relationship is and must be conceptually different from various created relationships.

Consider first what may be called "utility relationships." We have a utility relationship to an object when our relationship to it is defined by the usefulness of that object for some project or end we have. Often our relationships to our property – our cars, our garden tools and so on – are utility relationships. We may value our property and so recognize in it an instrumental value, but this kind of relationship does not in itself account for the rights of those things that are our property. In fact, if this is the only relationship we see ourselves as having to environmental beings, we in effect deny environmental rights.

However, there are other kinds of created relationships that are not defined by utility. There are, for instance, "relationships of felt significance," as I will call them. A good example of this kind of relationship to an environmental being is provided by Karen Warren in a "first-person narrative about rock-climbing."

> On my second day of climbing, I rapelled down about 200 feet from the top of the Palisades at Lake Superior to just a few feet above the water level... I looked all around me – really looked – and listened... At that moment I was bathed in serenity. I began to talk to the rock in an almost audible, child-like way, as if the rock were my friend. I felt an overwhelming sense of gratitude for what it offered me – a chance to know myself and the rock differently, to appreciate unforeseen miracles like the tiny flowers growing in the even tinier cracks in the rock's surface, and to come to know a sense of *being in relationship* with the natural environment... I felt myself *caring* for this rock and feeling thankful that climbing provided the opportunity for me to know it and myself in this new way.[9]

Warren goes on to say that in this narrative "it is the climber's relationship with the rock she climbs which takes on special significance – which is itself a locus of value"; and, she says, drawing upon Marilyn Frye's category of the "loving eye," "there is no fusion of two into one, but a...*relationship*; they are in relationship if *only* because the loving eye is perceiving it, responding to it, noticing it, attending to it."[10]

We may recognize the kind of experience this narrative describes. Many, perhaps, have felt something similar before a desert vista or a seascape or in some other natural setting. When we have such an experience as this, we do not merely feel that we are in a relationship to the natural object before us – a rock precipice or a desert setting – we *are* in a relationship to that environmental being. It seems to me that Warren is right about this, and, moreover, it seems to me that she is right that the special relationship established and entered when we have this kind of experience is, as she says, a "locus of value." Once we have experienced a natural setting or a natural object, like the rock the narrative's climber rapelled down, in this way, that setting or object takes on a special significance and value for us.

However, our question is whether the kind of entered relationship that Warren describes will do conceptually as the source of environmental rights; and it will not do. It will not do for several reasons. If there are environmental rights analogous to human rights, then they cannot be annulled. But if environmental rights rested on relationships of felt significance, then they could be annulled; for such relationships may end, as they would when one perhaps with the passage of years ceased to feel such significance and, in Warren and Frye's language, turned away the loving eye. Furthermore, if this kind of relationship were the grounding for environmental rights, then environmental beings' having any rights at all would await some human beings creating such a relationship to them by coming to have the requisite experience. If no human beings had such an experience – if we were all rigorously utility-oriented in our approach to the environment – then there would be no environmental rights. And for whom do environmental beings have rights, if the source of environment rights is such a relationship of felt significance? Is it only for those persons who have had the requisite experience and so created a relationship between themselves and the natural objects in question? If environmental rights were understood in accord with these implications, they would end up not being analogous to human rights in the conception embodied in the United Nations Declaration.

There is one other class of created relationships that we should look at – relationships created by entering into an agreement. Such contract relationships are created by a moral agreement, and they carry with them obligations and rights. To use a simple illustration, when I agree to help you fix your fence if you will make my computer program work, thereby entering into this contract relationship with you, I take on the obligation to help fix your fence once you have made my computer program work, and you have the right to expect me to do so. So contract relationships do establish rights. But still they cannot be the foundation of environmental rights any more than they can be the foundation of human rights.

Environmental rights and human rights in the conceptions before us are different from what we may call "contract rights" in that they are not contingent on a moral agreement being made. Also, of course, regarding environmental rights there is the added difficulty that we cannot very well understand environmental beings entering into an agreement with us human beings. Not even non-human animals enter into moral agreements, let alone deserts and mountain ranges, all of which may have environmental rights. If we think of the agreement as an agreement between human persons regarding the environment, there still would be the contingency problem: environmental rights would depend on such agreements being made and would obtain only as long as the agreement was not dissolved.

If there is a relationship that grounds environmental rights that are analogous to human rights in the conception found in the United Nations Declaration, then that relationship must explain rights that environmental beings have irrespective of utility, human attitudes, and agreements. Such a relationship, then, should not itself exist by virtue of utility or human attitudes or an agreement, but by virtue of human persons being who they are and the environment being what it is. As we are related to all persons in the person–person relationship by virtue of being persons, so we are related to the environment by virtue of the environment being what it is; and as we can violate the person–person relationship by not treating persons as persons, so we can violate our relationship to natural entities by not treating them in accord with their worth or integrity. What explains environmental beings' having whatever rights they have is that if we did not act as those rights require us to act, we would violate our fundamental person–environment relationship.

RIGHTS ON RELIGION

In the preceding section I have presented an understanding of human and environmental rights that grounds those rights in relationships. On this understanding there are existing human rights and existing environmental rights, and they exist by virtue of preexisting and uncreated relationships that we human beings are in to one another and to the environment. To what extent is this idea a religious idea or an idea that is compatible with religious traditions?

It has been observed that talk about rights emerges only after 1400.[11] As a blanket claim this is too strong. There are references to rights in the Bible, as in the right of the first-born (Deut. 21:17). But it is true that in Europe and America it was the eighteenth century that saw the first great affirmation of general human rights, and it was then a political affirmation, not a religious one. If human rights are not loudly championed by religious traditions, environmental rights are not even mentioned in the mainstreams of many major traditions. Indeed, for a long time, religion in the West, and Christianity in particular, has been associated with the exploitation of the environment.

Many have thought that the religious view of our relationship to the environment that has prevailed in the West is that of "dominion." In the first book of the Bible, they point out, God gives humankind dominion over the fish of the sea, the birds of the air, and over every creature of the earth. Approved by Aquinas and others, this view is seen as seminal to the Western cultural attitude that nature is to be subdued and made to yield its treasures for the use of human beings. The dominion view, it has been said, is so foreign to the idea of environmental rights that it affirms the right of humans to take animal life when they wish and, by extension, to exploit the environment generally as they wish.[12]

To the extent that Christianity or any religion subscribes to this dominion view, it would be difficult for that religion to allow environmental rights to natural entities. The dominion view, rather, has it that animals and forests have only instrumental value in connection with the projects of human beings. The "good steward" view of our relationship to the environment, as Peter Singer among others appreciates, does not change this equation substantially.[13] It requires us to practice good management of what is in our dominion, so that we are not wasteful of the resources of the world. As stewards of what God has created, we are responsible to God for a proper use of what God has given us dominion over, but the good steward view does not attribute to animals or to any of the beings of nature a moral right to consideration.

However, let us distinguish between these historically held main views of Judaism and Christianity and the views open to Judaism and Christianity, and open to other traditions, on the relationship between human beings and the environment. On the latter score the question for Jews and Christians turns to a great extent on what is scripturally and theologically allowable in these traditions. Thus much could depend on scriptural interpretation and on theological development.

Nevertheless, in regard to Judaism and Christianity, it is fairly clear that the primary tenets that there is a God, that God created all that there is, and that what God created is good do not rule out natural beings having a value in themselves which gives them natural rights. Indeed, these very basic religious beliefs recommend an acceptance of the idea that God has created the world such that the environment and the natural beings of the world have a right to proper and respectful treatment. It is possible to see in the historical development of Judaism and Christianity a growing inclusiveness of moral concern. If at first our concern is with our own, it comes to embrace all the nations (Isa. 9:6), and if at first our notion of neighbor is narrow, we come to understand that it embraces the socially despised (Luke 10:30–37).

One may find a similar expansion of moral concern in the thinking of animal rights and environmental ethicists in our own day. One can see Regan's argument for animal rights as an argument for our extending to non-human animals the category of moral rights that we readily apply to fellow human beings. In fact the seminal environmental ethical thinker Aldo Leopold spoke explicitly of an "extension of ethics." In putting forward his "land ethic," he not only consciously proposed an "extension of ethics" but the affirmation of the "rights" of environmental beings. He proposed an ethic that "enlarges the boundaries of the community," that is, the boundaries of the moral community, to include, beyond the circle of human beings, animals and plants and non-sentient beings of the environment.[14]

Ethical thinkers like Regan and Leopold do not appeal to God's will or place themselves in the prophetic tradition, but they are urging a new and extended understanding of our moral responsibility and concern. While they may prominently speak of rights, as the biblical tradition does not, they, like that tradition, conceive of the ethical extension they urge as one that is required by a proper understanding and recognition of moral realities. Those realities, according to the understanding I have begun to develop in this chapter, are the moral requirements of the relationships we human persons have to one another and to the natural beings of the environment. Furthermore, those moral realities, as the moral requirements of our relationships to one another and to the natural beings of the environment, need not be denied by the religious traditions of Judaism and Christianity, for these accord well with very basic religious beliefs in these traditions about God and God's creation.

NOTES

1. Alasdair MacIntyre, *After Virtue,* 2nd ed. (Notre Dame: University of Notre Dame Press, 1984), p. 70.
2. Iris Marion Young, *Justice and the Politics of Difference* (Princeton: Princeton University Press, 1990), p. 96.
3. For instance, Elizabeth Wolgast, *The Grammar of Justice* (Ithaca and London: Cornell University Press, 1987), pp. 4–5, 6–7, and 25–26; and Jim Cheney, "Eco-Feminism and Deep Ecology," *Environmental Ethics,* 9 (1987), p. 134.
4. For the discussion in this and the preceding paragraph I have drawn upon my *Relationship Morality* (University Park: Pennsylvania State University Press, 1995), pp. 214–220.

5. Jack Donnelly, *Universal Human Rights in Theory and Practice* (Ithaca: Cornell University Press, 1989), p. 65.
6. Ibid., pp. 63–65.
7. Peter Singer, *Animal Liberation*, 2nd ed. (New York: New York Review, 1990), p. 8.
8. Tom Regan, *The Case for Animal Rights* (Berkeley and Los Angeles: University of California Press, 1983), p. 362.
9. Karen Warren, "The Power and the Promise of Ecological Feminism," *Environmental Ethics*, 12 (Summer 1990), pp. 134–135 (Warren's emphasis).
10. Ibid., pp. 135 and 137 (Warren's emphasis); Marilyn Frye, *The Politics of Reality: Essays in Feminist Theory* (Trumansburg, NY: Crossing Press, 1983), pp. 66–72.
11. MacIntyre, *After Virtue*, p. 69.
12. Peter Singer, "Animals and the Value of Life," in *Matters of Life and Death: New Introductory Essays in Moral Philosophy*, ed. Tom Regan (New York: Random House, 1980), p. 230.
13. Ibid., p. 231.
14. Aldo Leopold, *A Sand County Almanac* (New York: Oxford University Press, 1949), p. 204.

Part III

A DECLARATION OF HUMAN RIGHTS BY THE WORLD'S RELIGIONS

Plate 8 Mural proclaiming the importance of understanding human wrongs so that human rights will be instantiated and sustained, found in a residential district of Cape Town, South Africa, during the 1999 Parliament of the World Religions.

Photo: *Nancy M. Martin*

8

TOWARDS *a* DECLARATION *of* HUMAN RIGHTS *by the* WORLD'S RELIGIONS

Arvind Sharma

The relationship between religion and human rights has often been perceived as adversarial, but this is obviously only part of the story.[1] It has been argued, if also contested, that some human rights may actually possess religious roots.[2] The effort to formulate a declaration of human rights from the standpoint of the world's religions constitutes an attempt to further the dialogue between religion and human rights. I shall first deal with the history of the proposed declaration and then with matters that relate to the philosophy underlying it. I shall then proceed to describe the present status of the project. The text of the declaration as it stands today follows.

THE HISTORY OF THE DECLARATION

The genesis of this document can be traced to an initiative called "The Project on Religion and Human Rights," which operated out of New York from July 1993 until June 1995. Its title suffices to explain what it was all about. More specifically it dealt with four themes: (1) religion and the roots of conflict; (2) religious militancy or "fundamentalism"; (3) universality vs. relativism in human rights; and last but not least, (4) positive resources of religion for human rights. The deliberations of the project have since appeared in the form of a book predictably entitled *Religion and Human Rights*.

I was involved in this project as co-chair, with Professor Harvey Cox, of the fourth unit, whose deliberations centered on religion as a positive resource for human rights. As the project drew to a conclusion, before it relocated at Emory University as part of its Religion and Law Program, the suggestion was made that the effort thus initiated to forge a positive link between religion and human rights should be continued. Such continued efforts, it was felt, might lead to two desirable outcomes. They might (1) help overcome the negative image religions in general have in the context of human rights and, even more significantly, (2) enable human rights discourse to be enriched by insights derived from the various religions or, shall we say, by the availability of religious ideas. For instance, it is well known that religions are more prone to talk in terms of duties and responsibilities rather than rights. Might not human rights discourse benefit from a more explicit inclusion of this dimension? The key question, however, remained how this outcome might be brought about.

It was then that the idea of generating declarations of human rights by the world's religions took shape, as a way of mining the religious traditions of the world to serve as a positive resource for human rights. Gradually a two-track approach evolved. One track was to think in terms of each religion producing its own universal declaration or even declarations of human rights individually. The other was to examine the prospect of a universal declaration of human rights by the world's religions jointly.

The approach of the fiftieth anniversary of the United Nations Universal Declaration of Human Rights, which fell on December 10, 1998, provided the catalyst for further developments. Professor John Humphrey, who hailed from Montreal and was a professor in the Faculty of Law at McGill University, had played a key role in the drafting of the Universal Declaration of Human Rights. This fact galvanized human rights organizations and those interested in human rights into organizing a World Conference on the Universal Declaration of Human Rights, which met in Montreal on December 7–9, 1998.

The program committee of this conference accepted the proposal of the Faculty of Religious Studies at McGill University to release a preliminary draft of a universal declaration of human rights by the world's religions on this occasion, as a way of furthering the discourse on human rights. This draft was circulated at this conference in English and French, for comment by the assembled delegates. The tenor of the discussion favored the continuation of the initiative.

Thereafter the draft was circulated amidst a larger audience, and the declaration aroused sufficient interest for it to be made the basic document of discussion at a conference held at Chapman University in California, on April 8–9, 1999, entitled "Human Rights and Responsibilities: The Contribution of the World Religions." At this conference the articles of the declaration were subjected to a detailed analysis from the perspectives of various world religions, and general as well as specific suggestions pertaining to the document were offered. In the fall of the same year (1999), the text of the document discussed at this conference appeared in the *Journal of Religious Ethics* (27: 540–544). Comments from readers were also invited.

This original draft of the declaration was subsequently revised in the light of the comments received. This revised text was then discussed in a special session of the conference on "Ethics and Religion for a Global Twenty-First Century," organized at Chapman and Loyola Marymount Universities on March 23–25, 2000. Parts of the declaration were also discussed in sessions devoted to human rights at the Eighteenth Quinquennial World Congress of the International Association for the History of Religions, when it met in Durban on August 6–12, 2000, and in the inaugural address at the Conference of Religion and Human Rights at the House of World Cultures, Berlin, December 7–9, 2001. In addition, the document was circulated at the Millennium World Peace Summit of Religious and Spiritual Leaders, held at the U. N. and Waldorf-Astoria Hotel in New York on August 28–31, 2000, and was also presented for consideration at the U.N.E.S.C.O. Conference on Mystical Traditions and Interreligious Dialogue at Barcelona, May 23–26, 2002, and at the International Roundtable on the Challenge of Globalization: Towards a Shared Universal, Spiritual, and Moral Ethic, which met at Genting Permai Resort, Genting Highlands, Malaysia, November 25–27, 2002.

This account completes the history of the document. It is now being placed before the world at large through the book you now hold in your hand. Before it is perused, however, the ensuing remarks might be of help. It will be recalled that two possible approaches to preparing a universal declaration of human rights by the world's religions could be taken: (1) the preparation of separate declarations of human rights by the world's religions and (2) the preparation of a single declaration of human rights by the world's religions jointly. Practical considerations led one to prefer the latter course as the more feasible of the two. Such a declaration also seemed more consistent with the Universal Declaration of Human Rights by the United Nations, which was also a single document and which serves as a model for the Universal Declaration of Human Rights by the World Religions. How do we now justify, in terms of thought, what we have just described in terms of action?

UNIVERSALITY WITHOUT IMPERIALISM

Religions can serve as a positive resource for human rights in two ways: (1) by offering something which is unique to them as a religious tradition and

(2) by offering something which they can offer in common to human rights discourse. It is clear that what is unique to a religious tradition is best offered through a declaration of human rights by that tradition, which may enshrine this unique element; and what the religious traditions can offer in common to human rights discourse is best offered through a declaration of human rights by the world's religions as a whole. To illustrate: Hinduism as a religious tradition tends to celebrate not only life but also longevity. An article in a proposed universal declaration of human rights by Hindus might then read not merely that "everyone has the right to life" but that "everyone has the right to life and longevity." Here is something for us to consider and to accept or reject or at least a new point to ponder. I do not plan to unpack this statement here or even to imply that, in the ultimate analysis, we may have something original here. It could be argued that the right to longevity is presupposed in many religious traditions and is contained within the concept of ecological rights as well. I only wish to suggest a point here, not to clinch it.

Similarly, human rights discourse may be enriched by what all the religions of the world are agreed upon, as distinguished from what might be unique to them. For instance, it could well be the case that all of them insist on emphasizing responsibilities and duties. At least one could hypothesize that it might be so. In that case then we may have here something which the religions of the world can offer in common, as distinguished from what they could offer uniquely, to human rights discourse.

What I offered was a hypothetical example. If we now ask "how do we make it real?", we are led to a philosophical point – how do we arrive at a universal and how do we face the problems typically associated with such an enterprise? We have some experience to fall back on here. It is provided by two documents already in existence. The first is the Universal Declaration of Human Rights adopted in 1948 and the second is the statement on the Global Ethic proposed at the Parliament of World Religions in 1993. Both these documents, fairly or unfairly, have attracted the criticism of being Western, and there are no less than twenty-five ways (at the last count) in which this statement could be parsed: as a historical, moral, cultural, or legal statement, and so on. At bottom, however, is the feeling that when such efforts emanate from the West they are merely a further extension of the age of imperialism – an effort on the part of the West to impose its own values on the rest of the world in the guise, or rather disguise, of universalism.

I would at this stage like to share with you a somewhat nightmarish scenario which has been developed by Max L. Stackhouse in another context, as not entirely irrelevant to our own, as something which might also unfold through a perpetuation of this conflation of the universal with the imperial, for then

> Non-Western cultures will gain evidence for the view that human rights *are* merely the artifacts of a phase of modern Western sentiment or merely philosophical intuitions born from peculiar sociological conditions. Fortified by such evidence, they may become more entrenched in their resistance to what then appears to them to be a new colonialism. They will not have to face the question as to whether documents such as the United Nations' *Universal Declaration* represent an ultimately valid insight about and for humanity, an insight about which they will have to marshal careful evidence and make critical decisions. The sentiment will pass, the intuitions will fade, other interests will set the agendas, the international instruments of rights will be revised or ignored, and we will have no basis on which to defend the oppressed, the prisoner, the weak, the dispossessed; to justify civil and political liberties; or to fight for social and economic justice. This, it seems to me, would be a genuine tragic possibility.[3]

What then are we to make of this criticism of the imperial masquerading as the universal, sobered by this scenario, which is looking increasingly less far-fetched as current events unfold? How is the enterprise on hand affected by it?

It seems to me that this criticism could arguably be said to possess two dimensions – one substantive, the other procedural. The substantive part of the criticism would then pertain to the question of whether there are in fact any universals and how they might be arrived at in principle. By contrast, the procedural element would relate to how the various parties to this quest for the universal (and who will be affected by the implications of such a universal once determined) are actually involved in arriving at it, provided it can be determined.

I harbor the suspicion that although these aforesaid universal documents are criticized substantively, as disregarding Asian values for instance,[4] the actual resentment against them is not so much substantive as procedural. In other words, people are really not happy with the way they were drawn up and this dissatisfaction is then expressed in the form of a criticism of the contents of the document, or the document itself – as a form of Freudian transference, if you please. Psychological dissatisfaction at the manner in which they were formulated finds expression as intellectual criticism of the document or its contents.

If one pursues this line of reasoning further, one is naturally led to ask what is wrong with existing procedures, which would explain this psychological discontent of the rest vis-à-vis the West. I now venture to suggest that the source of this discontent may lie in the fact that these documents are perceived as being delivered from on high – like a secular revelation, if you will. It is usually the case that the text of such documents has already been composed – by a committee in the case of the Universal Declaration of Human Rights and mainly by an individual in the case of the Global Ethic.[5] And others are then invited to sign on to it. What is universal is offered as an absolute, as it were.

I am of the view that in formulating such sensitive documents – which claim to enshrine not merely potent current ideas but the cherished long-standing ideals of humanity – the product cannot be severed from the process. How that document has come to be framed is as crucial as, if not even more so than, what it says, so far as its universal acceptance is concerned. If this is so, or may be so, then our previous questions morph into the following one. How could all the parties who will be affected by any universal declaration be brought to the same table, that is to say, be involved in preparing it? There are two ways, it seems to me, of doing this – bottom upwards and top downwards. That is to say, all the religious traditions of the world could be invited independently to generate their own declaration, or even declarations, of human rights from within themselves, and these could then be collected and collated to identify such shared ground as they may possess. This outlines the bottom-up approach. The top-down approach then would represent the approach with which we are familiar, in which a document is prepared and then offered for acceptance.

The fact, however, remains that the document we have in front of us represents the top-down approach, and so let me examine its implications since I have already criticized such an approach and the document as it stands must immediately attract the same criticism that was leveled against the Universal Declaration of Human Rights and the Global Ethic – as essentially apodictic rather than democratic in nature, being handed down from "on high."

THE DECLARATION AS A WORKING DOCUMENT

We are thus led back to the fateful question: can nothing be universal without being imperial? This present project is in the nature of an experiment to see if it might be possible to arrive at a universal without attracting the charge of it being imperial. There seem to be two ways of accomplishing this, already hinted at.

1. It might be accomplished through inviting each religious tradition to prepare its own proposed universal declaration of human rights and then producing a document acceptable to all on the basis of the common ground, however narrow, underlying the documents prepared by each. In such a case the religious traditions will have to be canvassed before any such document is prepared, as well as after.

2. It might be accomplished through preparing a tentative document which might embody this common ground on the basis of our own understanding whetted by the study of comparative religion and comparative ethics. Such a document could be prepared in consultation with various scholars of religion and religious ethics. A document prepared in this manner could then be offered to each religious constituency as something to modify continually until, in its final form, the initial draft is transformed into a text acceptable to all.

These two approaches are not mutually exclusive. In fact, it would be a matter of surpassing interest to compare the outcomes of these two approaches, and the prospect of their hermeneutical interaction is exciting. At the moment, however, we are concerned with the second approach. To be more precise, we are in phase one of the second approach. That is to say, we would like to generate a document in the preparation of which comparativists of all hues have played a role and which could then be offered to various religious constituencies for comment and modification. It is the purpose of the text before you to hopefully initiate this process.

The first few steps were taken in Montreal when comments on this document were invited from various scholars. I would like to share one such response with you. It was proposed, for instance, that in a document such as this the right to food must find a prominent place. It does find a place in existing human rights documents. The right to food can be deduced from article 25, clause 1 of the United Nations Universal Declaration of Human Rights of 1948, which reads: "Everyone has the right to a standard of living adequate for the health and well-being of himself and of his family, including *food*, clothing, housing and medical care." As a result of this proposal, however, the right to food appeared in article 3 of the draft declaration by the world's religions, which read: "Everyone has the right to life, longevity and liveability and the right to food, clothing and shelter to sustain them." Although this right to food was now more explicit and had moved up in the text, as a result of further discussions with concerned scholars and in the light of what is going on in the world, the right to food was then given a more ringing endorsement, being listed as a separate clause by itself under article 3, which reads simply "Everyone has the right to food," period. This discussion is representative of the kind of responses the document has generated and is generating and the evolving nature of the document.

It is here that I would like to distinguish between the concepts of a fixed text and a fluid text. The two documents previously mentioned – the United Nations Universal Declaration of Human Rights and the Global Ethic – were delivered for consideration as prefabricated texts, notwithstanding the chopping and changing which must have been involved at the drafting stage. The text of the Universal Declaration of Human Rights by the World Religions is being offered in a different spirit, in a different manner, and with a different hope. It is being offered as a fluid text, yet to be fixed. What one has now is a draft, to be modified through informed changes as it makes its way through various constituencies, first academic and then subsequently explicitly religious. I need hardly add that the final document which might emerge at the end of the process if the process is successful will not be identical with this document. In fact, in all likelihood, it will be quite different. In fact, it may not resemble the original document any more than a phone number resembles the person to whom it belongs!

The foregoing discussion may now be summarized in terms of its underlying points:

1.   It is desirable to frame a universal declaration of human rights by the world's religions, as a way of tapping into the religious heritage of humanity as a positive resource for human rights discourse.
2.   There are two ways of generating such a document – a top-down approach and a bottom-up approach. According to the former approach, a document could be prepared in advance, to be approved by the various religions. According to the bottom-up approach, various independent declarations by the world's religions would precede the preparation of such a document, which would then capture the common ground among these statements.
3.   Both these approaches possess merit.
4.   The document under discussion is an example of the top-down approach.
5.   Past experience suggests that such an approach is potentially imperialistic, or may be perceived as such – an impression which could fatally compromise its universal acceptance, even if its contents were genuinely universal.

6.   It is therefore proposed that the text of the present document be offered for consideration in the spirit of a rough draft, with its text to be suitably modified as it makes its way through different constituencies. Accordingly, the draft of the Universal Declaration of Human Rights by the World's Religions as it has evolved up to this point is presented here and offered for consideration and modification.

NOTES

1.   See Robert Traer, *Faith in Human Rights* (Washington, DC: Georgetown University Press, 1991).
2.   See Louis Henkin, "Religion, Religions and Human Rights," *Journal of Religious Ethics*, 26, 2 (Fall 1998), p. 229.
3.   Max L. Stackhouse, "The Intellectual Crisis of a Good Idea," *Journal of Religious Ethics*, 26, 2 (Fall 1998), pp. 267–268.
4.   See *The East Asian Challenge for Human Rights*, eds. Joanne R. Bauer and Daniel A. Bell (New York: Cambridge University Press, 1998).
5.   Hans Küng, "Toward a Global Ethic," *The Journal of Religious Pluralism*, 3 (1993), pp. 27–28.

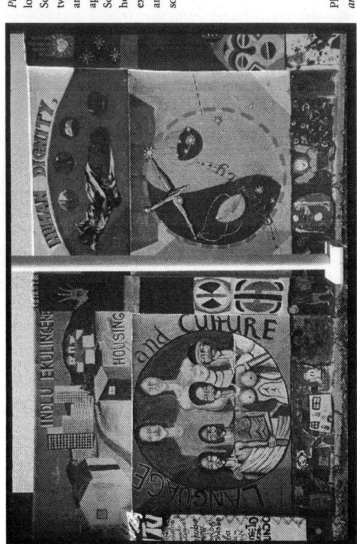

Plate 9 Section of a block-long mural in Durban, South Africa, illustrating two of the human rights articulated in the post-apartheid constitution of South Africa: decent housing and the freedom to express one's own language and culture in a pluralistic society.

Photo: *Nancy M. Martin and Joseph Runzo*

9

A UNIVERSAL DECLARATION *of* HUMAN RIGHTS *by the* WORLD'S RELIGIONS

Whereas human beings are led to affirm that there is more to life than life itself by inspiration both human and divine;

Whereas the Universal Declaration of Human Rights, as adopted by the General Assembly of the United Nations on December 10, 1948 bases itself on the former;

Whereas any exclusion of the world's religions as positive resources for human rights is obnoxious to the evidence of daily life;

Whereas the various communities constituting the peoples of the world must exchange not only ideas but also ideals;

Whereas religions ideally urge human beings to live in a just society and not just in any society;

Whereas one must not idealize the actual but strive to realize the ideal;

Whereas not to compensate victims of imperialism, racism, casteism, and sexism is itself imperialist, racist, casteist, and sexist;

Whereas rights are independent of duties in their protection but integrally related to them in conception and execution;

Whereas human rights are intended to secure peace, freedom, equality, and justice – and to mitigate departures therefrom – when these come in conflict or the rights themselves;

Now, therefore, on the fiftieth anniversary of the Universal Declaration of Human Rights and the fiftieth anniversary of the founding of the Faculty of Religious Studies at McGill University, Montreal, Quebec, Canada.

The signatories to this Universal Declaration of Human Rights by the World's Religions, as legatees of the religious heritage of humanity, do hereby propose the following as the common standard of achievement for the followers of all religions or none, as all people are brothers and sisters on the face of the earth.

ARTICLE 1

All human beings have the right to be treated as human beings and have the duty to treat everyone as a human being.

ARTICLE 2

Everyone has the right to freedom from violence, in any of its forms, individual or collective; whether based on race, religion, gender, caste or class, or arising from any other cause.

ARTICLE 3

1. Everyone has the right to food.
2. Everyone has the right to life, longevity, and liveability and the right to food, clothing, and shelter to sustain them.
3. Everyone has the duty to support and sustain life, longevity, and liveability of all.

ARTICLE 4

1. No one shall be subjected to slavery or servitude, forced labor, bonded labor, or child labor. Slavery and the slave trade shall be prohibited in all its forms.
2. No one shall subject anyone to slavery or servitude in any of its forms.

ARTICLE 5

1. No one shall be subjected to torture or to cruel, inhuman, or degrading treatment or punishment, inflicted either physically or mentally, whether on secular or religious grounds, inside the home or outside it.
2. No one shall subject anybody to such treatment.

ARTICLE 6

1. Everyone has a right to recognition everywhere as a person before law; and by everyone everywhere as a human being deserving humane treatment, even when law and order has broken down.

2.   Everyone has the duty to treat everyone else as a human being both in
      the eyes of law and one's own.

ARTICLE 7

All are equal before law and entitled to equal protection before law without
any discrimination on grounds of race, religion, caste, class, sex, and sexual
orientation. It is the right of everyone to be so treated and the duty of
everyone to so treat others.

ARTICLE 8

1.   Everybody has the right to seek restitution for historical, social,
      economic, cultural, and other wrongs.
2.   Everybody has the duty to prevent the perpetuation of historical,
      social, economic, cultural, and other wrongs.

ARTICLE 9

1.   No one shall be subjected to arbitrary arrest, detention, or exile by the
      state or by anyone else. The attempt to proselytize against the will of
      the person shall amount to arbitrary detention, so also the detention,
      against their will, of teenage children by the parents, and among
      spouses.
2.   It is the duty of everyone to secure everyone's liberty.

ARTICLE 10

Everybody has the right to public trial in the face of criminal charges, and
it is the duty of the state to ensure this. Everyone who cannot afford a
lawyer must be provided one by the state.

ARTICLE 11

Everyone charged with a penal offense has the right to be considered
innocent until proven guilty.

ARTICLE 12

1.   Everyone has the right to privacy. This right includes the right not to
      be subjected to arbitrary interference with one's privacy; of one's own,
      or of one's family, home, or correspondence.
2.   Everyone has the right to one's good name.

3. It is the duty of everyone to protect the privacy and reputation of everyone else.
4. Everyone has the right not to have one's religion denigrated in the media or academia.
5. It is the duty of the follower of every religion to ensure that no religion is denigrated in the media or academia.

ARTICLE 13

1. Everyone has the right to freedom of movement and residence anywhere in the world.
2. Everyone has the duty to abide by the laws and regulations applicable in that part of the world.

ARTICLE 14

Everyone has the right to seek and secure asylum in any country from any form of persecution, religious or otherwise, and the right not to be deported. It is the duty of every country to provide such asylum.

ARTICLE 15

1. Everyone has the right to a nationality.
2. No one shall be arbitrarily deprived of one's nationality or denied the right to change one's nationality.
3. Everyone has the duty to promote the emergence of a constitutional global order.

ARTICLE 16

1. Everyone has the right to marriage.
2. Members of a family have the right to retain and practice their own religion or beliefs within a marriage.
3. Everyone has the right to raise a family.
4. Everybody has the right to renounce the world and join a monastery, provided that one shall do so after making adequate arrangement for one's dependants.
5. Marriage and monasticism are two of the most successful institutional innovations of humanity and are entitled to protection by the society and the state.
6. Motherhood and childhood are entitled to special care and assistance. It is the duty of everyone to extend special consideration to mothers and children.

7. Everyone shall promote the outlook that the entire world constitutes a single extended family.

ARTICLE 17

1. Everybody has the right to own property, alone as well as in association with others. An association also has a similar right to own property.
2. Everyone has a right not to be deprived of property arbitrarily. It is the duty of everyone not to deprive others of their property arbitrarily. Property shall be understood to mean material as well as intellectual, aesthetic, and spiritual property.
3. Everyone has the duty not to deprive anyone of their property or appropriate it in an unauthorized manner.

ARTICLE 18

1. There shall be no compulsion in religion. It is a matter of choice.
2. Everyone has the right to retain one's religion and to change one's religion.
3. Everyone has the duty to promote peace and tolerance among different religions and ideologies.

ARTICLE 19

1. Everyone has the right to freedom of opinion and expression, where the term "expression" includes the language one speaks; the food one eats; the clothes one wears; and the religion one practices and professes, provided that one conforms generally to the accustomed rules of decorum recognized in the neighborhood.
2. It is the duty of everyone to ensure that everyone enjoys such freedom.
3. Children have the right to express themselves freely in all matters affecting the child, to which it is the duty of their caretakers to give due weight in accordance with the age and maturity of the child.

ARTICLE 20

1. Everyone has the right to freedom of assembly and association, and the duty to do so peacefully.
2. No one may be compelled to belong to an association, or to leave one without due process.

ARTICLE 21

1. Everybody over the age of eighteen has the right to vote, to elect or be elected, and thus to take part in the government or governance of the country, directly or indirectly.
2. Everyone has the right of equal access to public service in one's country and the duty to provide such access.
3. It is the duty of everyone to participate in the political process.

ARTICLE 22

Everyone, as a member of society, has a right to social security and a duty to contribute to it.

ARTICLE 23

1. Everyone has the right to same pay for same work and a duty to offer same pay for same work.
2. Everyone has the right for just remuneration for one's work and the duty to justly recompense others for work done.
3. Everyone has the right to form and to join trade unions for the protection of one's interests.
4. Everyone has the right not to join a trade union.

ARTICLE 24

1. Everyone has the right to work and to rest, including the right to support while seeking work and the right to periodic holidays with pay.
2. The right to rest extends to the earth.

ARTICLE 25

1. Everyone has the right to health and to universal medical insurance. It is the duty of the state or society to provide it.
2. Every child has the right to a safe childhood, and it is the duty of the parents to provide it.

ARTICLE 26

Everyone has the right to free education and the right to equality of opportunity for any form of education involving restricted enrollment.

ARTICLE 27

1. Everyone has the right to freely participate in the cultural life of the community and the right to freely contribute to it.
2. Everyone has the right to share scientific advances and their benefits and the duty to disseminate them, and wherever possible to contribute to such advances.
3. Everyone has the right to the protection of their cultural heritage. It is the duty of everyone to protect and enrich everyone's heritage, including one's own.

ARTICLE 28

Everyone has the right to socioeconomic and political order at a global, national, regional, and local level which enables the realization of social, political, economic, racial, and gender justice and the duty to give precedence to universal, national, regional, and local interests in that order.

ARTICLE 29

1. One is duty-bound, when asserting one's rights, to take the rights of other human beings; of past, present, and future generations; the rights of humanity; and the rights of nature and the earth into account.
2. One is duty-bound, when asserting one's rights, to prefer non-violence over violence.

ARTICLE 30

1. Everyone has the right to require the formation of a supervisory committee within one's community, defined religiously or otherwise, to monitor the implementation of the articles of this Declaration; and to serve on it and present one's case before such a committee.
2. It is everyone's duty to ensure that such a committee satisfactorily supervises the implementation of these articles.

Plate 10 Façade of the Sinagoga (Main Synagogue) in Rome, built in 1904 on the site of the former Jewish ghetto. Though Jews had previously lived freely in Rome, the ghetto was established in 1550 with restrictions on Jews in force through 1870. The Torah has a central place on the façade, as it does in Jewish life.

Photo: *Joseph Runzo.*

10

A UNIVERSAL DECLARATION *of* HUMAN RIGHTS *by the* WORLD'S RELIGIONS: A JEWISH PERSPECTIVE

Charlotte Elisheva Fonrobert

Unquestionably, the world's current conflicts with their potential for global destructiveness make it a desperately urgent task to articulate support of human rights wherever and in whichever way we can. This should particularly be the case for leaders in the religious communities, since many of the conflicts are exacerbated by religious perspectives on the world, even when the conflicts themselves may be rooted in economic inequities and political oppressiveness. Therefore, Arvind Sharma and his colleagues' attempt to undertake such an effort is laudable in many respects, in that it seeks to counteract that role of religion in infractions of human rights all over the world.

Curiously, the preamble chooses to emphasize not only the importance of religious traditions as a resource for human rights, but also the negligence of the human rights tradition so far to provide an adequate place for religion: "Whereas any exclusion of the world's religions as positive resources for human rights is obnoxious to the evidence of daily life..." This emphasis is curious, considering that the human rights tradition has served as a critical force against abuse of religious power. One might wish to start a declaration of human rights by the world's religions with a self-critical reflection by any or all religious traditions as to their contribution to the failure of promoting and protecting human rights. Such a step may indeed be the most important contribution of the world's religions to the promotion of human rights. Of course, as in any such project that lays claim to universality, the question of whom such a document might be representative of, whom it may speak for, and therefore its potential authoritativeness has to remain an open one, as Arvind Sharma himself points out.

In what follows I would like to offer some brief remarks on the Declaration from the perspective of a scholar of Judaism that are partially self-critical of Jewish tradition with respect to human rights. Before embarking on the more specific comments on the Universal Declaration of Human Rights by the World's Religions (henceforth H.R.W.R.), and by way of introduction to them, therefore, it is worthwhile to reflect briefly on the question and problem of "universalism" in the context of Jewish culture. Judaism has not particularly been known for its universalism or universal aspirations, for better and for worse. Indeed, for a variety of historical reasons, Judaism has limited its cultural and religious expressions of universalism, or rejected the notion of universal applicability of its rules and rituals. It is not a proselytizing religion. If we overstate the case somewhat, we may say that Judaism has made it its task to mind "its own business" and to stay out of the affairs of the world and humanity at large.

Biblical culture, for sure, may be described as being suspended between the universalism of the prophetic literature and its call for economic justice, on the one hand, and the particularity of the laws that were revealed to one particular people, the people of Israel, on the other. Differently put, the tension is one between the priestly divinity who created the world, who comes into his own in Isaiah 45, and the divinity who revealed himself on Mount Sinai to "his" people. The rabbis of the classical period (the second through sixth centuries CE) expanded most specifically on the particularist legal aspect of biblical literature, and consequently strengthened an ethnocentric notion of Judaism. This was ultimately undergirded by the matrilineal ruling, i.e. that he or she who is born to a Jewish mother is Jewish, a quasi-ethnic notion of identity supplemented by the ritualization of conversion.[1] Rabbinic law (*halakhah*) and its specific commandments were made to circumscribe Jewish identity and as such are applicable only to those regarded as Jewish.

This version of particularism engendered a notion of a fundamental split in humanity, a differentiation into Jews and non-Jews, intersected by the differentiation into men and women. As in other religious traditions, this differentiation has at times produced rather problematic views of non-Jews, sometimes even bordering on what we would today identify as xenophobia. Daniel Boyarin, a prominent scholar of rabbinic Judaism, points out: "The rabbis [i.e. the progenitors of Jewish legal tradition] produced their cultural formation within conditions of Diaspora – that is, in a situation within which Jews did not hold power over others."[2] More often than not, negative views of non-Jews, which led to a disenfranchisement of those deemed to be "idolators," were the product of the historical experience of those who have lived under the oppressive and often murderous conditions of foreign domination, be it by the Romans or by the Christian monarchies in medieval Europe.

At the same time, Jewish (rabbinic) law did develop a concept that provided a "legitimate" place for non-Jews in its view of the world, i.e. the concept of the so-called Noahide laws, or seven commandments incumbent upon the descendants of Noah, by which these people can earn divine acceptance: "The Rabbis taught: Seven commandments were commanded to the descendants of Noah: [to establish] a legal order, and to refrain from blasphemy, idolatry, incest, bloodshed, robbery, and eating (or tearing) the limb off from a living creature" (bSanh. 56a, parallel to Tosefta Av. Zar. 8 (9):4–7). This conceptualization of a binary system of laws – (male) Jews have 613 commandments, non-Jews only 7 – has potential for preserving a sense of particularity and differentiation without automatically objectifying or denigrating the others, even where the individual commandments remain up for interpretation (for how might one define idolatry?),[3] and even where ultimately a sense of spiritual privilege is preserved for those who have the most obligations before God, i.e. male Jews.

Be that as it may, a sense of co-equal existence of Jews and non-Jews before God can be extended into the *eschaton*, as is done by Maimonides, one of the great Jewish philosophers and jurisprudents of the medieval period:

> The Sages and prophets longed for the days of the Messiah, not to rule over the whole world, not to subjugate other nations, not to have other nations exalt them, and not to eat, drink, and rejoice, but rather to be free to study the Torah and its wisdom, and to be free from oppression, so that they can merit the life of the world to come. (*Mishneh Torah, Hilkhot melakhim* 12:2)

The point to be made here is that Judaism is built on a dual heritage of suspicion with respect to non-Jews and the development of a legal system in which non-Jews have a legitimate role as legal subjects. The balance between the two is a delicate one indeed, especially when a religious tradition such as Judaism gains political hegemony, as it did to a certain degree with the establishment of the state of Israel.[4]

In a position of political hegemony each religious tradition has to weigh carefully its treatment of religious minorities in light of human rights. This is certainly true for Jewish tradition, and minds are divided as to how to address this issue. On the one hand, critics of certain forms of Zionist politics may question the possibility of political justice under such circumstances altogether, since the rabbis' "particular discourse of ethnocentricity is appropriate only when the cultural identity is that of a minority, embattled or, at any rate, non-hegemonic."[5] On the other hand, those who deal with the political day-to-day reality of the state of Israel have to be more pragmatic.

Thus, the following excerpt from one of the major Israeli Supreme Court rulings with respect to the status of religious minorities in the state of Israel[6] deserves full citation, to underline the effort of drawing on the resources of Jewish tradition in order to deal with its political hegemony:

> The *Halakhah* has absolutely forbidden the practice – accepted in the ancient world and later – of forcing minority groups to assimilate into the dominant majority of a country, on the basis of the principle of *cuius regio, eius religio*, pursuant to which members of minorities were persecuted until they accepted the religion of the dominant majority. Consequently, when the Jewish people won military victories [quoting Maimonides][7] "the court did not accept proselytes during the entire period of David and Solomon: during the period of David, lest they may have converted because of fear; and during the period of Solomon, lest they may have converted because of the majesty, well-being, and greatness Israel enjoyed." According to the *Halakhah*, a member of a national minority is a "resident alien" (*ger toshav*). The only requisite demanded of him is to abide by the "seven Noahide laws" – the elementary rules viewed by the sages as a type of universal natural law indispensable to a legal order and binding upon all civilized nations. A national minority has all the civil and political rights enjoyed by other residents of the country: "A *ger toshav*, let him live by your side" (Leviticus 25:35). "A *ger toshav* is to be treated with the same respect and kindness accorded a Jew, for we are obligated to sustain them…and since one is obligated to sustain a *ger toshav*, he must be given medical treatment without charge."[8] The Sages also said: "One may not settle a *ger toshav* on the frontier or in an undesirable dwelling, but rather in a desirable dwelling in the center of the Land of Israel, where he may practice his trades, as it is written: 'He shall live with you in any place he may choose among the settlements in your midst, wherever he pleases, you must not ill-treat him' (Deuteronomy 23:17)."[9] The principles governing the relationship of the Jewish state to all of its inhabitants are fundamental principles of the *Halakhah*, as instructively expressed by Maimonides:[10] "For it is stated: 'The Lord is good to all, and His mercy is upon all His works' and it is written:

'Her [referring to the Torah] ways are pleasant ways, and all her paths, peaceful.'"[11]

Jewishly speaking, then, we may propose that the Noahide laws have the potential for a model of a universal declaration of human obligations, as an attempt to define a minimum standard by which others – as others – are to be measured as members of the human community.

Turning now to the Declaration of Human Rights by the World's Religions, we may venture to interrogate first article 7, according to which "all are equal before law and entitled to equal protection before law without any discrimination on grounds of race, *religion*, caste, class, sex, and sexual orientation. It is the right of everyone to be so treated and the duty of everyone to so treat others" (my emphasis). This seems to me where the specific contribution, if any, of the H.R.W.R. to the already existing Universal Declaration of Human Rights of the United Nations would begin, i.e. the commitment to not discriminate against religious minorities where one religious tradition has political hegemony. On that point, the Naiman opinion of the Israeli Supreme Court cited above does entirely concur. At the same time, this may turn out to be the most problematic of the articles of the H.R.W.R.

I will disregard for the time being the inclusion of sex and sexual orientation in this article, with which few religious traditions in the world, sadly, would seem to be able to agree. Rather, let me point out that none of the terms of the article are clear as to their referent, neither "all," nor "equal," nor – most problematically – "before law," nor finally "discrimination." What might "before law" possibly mean here? Before the International Criminal Court in The Hague? Or some diffuse sense of international law? "Equal" in what respect? Who is to say what constitutes discrimination in any particular religious context? To cite but one benevolent example: When the state of Israel declares Saturday the day off from work and hence imposes the Sabbath rest on everybody, including religious minorities, not least by interrupting public transportation services, does this constitute an infringement on the equality of religious minorities "before law"? Similar cautionary questions may of course be raised already on the parallel clause in the Universal Declaration of Human Rights of the United Nations according to which "all are equal before the law and are entitled without any discrimination to equal protection of the law." However, this clause is at least qualified by the statement that "all are entitled to equal protection against any discrimination *in violation of this Declaration* and against any incitement to *such* discrimination" (my emphasis).

Article 7 seems in some sense connected to article 18, paragraph 1, according to which "there shall be no compulsion in religion. It is a matter of choice." Compulsion by whom? By the government of any given state? Such articulation can only emerge from the North American context. What about a context, such as the Jewish context, in which ethnic and religious identity formations are intertwined? This is not to say that I do not sympathize with the sentiment of this article. In fact, Jews in America will whole-heartedly agree with this sentiment and have in the past been at the forefront in support of a political system with a radical separation between religion and state, in the United States and to a more limited degree in the European nation-states.

Similarly, the geopolitical situatedness of the H.R.W.R. in a North American context is true for article 17, which has a rather odd place in a document that seeks to add a religious perspective to the question of human rights. Article 17, paragraphs 1–2, states that "everybody has the right to own property, alone as well as in association with others...Property shall be understood to mean material as well as intellectual, aesthetic, and spiritual property." Perhaps no culture hallows the right to private property as much as the United States. From the perspective of Jewish law one may object to such a promotion of the notion of a *right* to own property.

In biblical law we find the following, much enhanced in the rabbinic corpus:

> When you reap the harvest of your field and overlook a sheaf in the field, do not turn back to get it; it shall go to the stranger, the fatherless, and the widow... When you beat down the fruit of your olive trees, do not go over them again; this shall go to the stranger, the fatherless, and the widow. When you gather the grapes of your vineyard, do not pick it over again; that shall go to the stranger, the fatherless, and the widow. Always remember that you were a slave in the land of Egypt; therefore I do enjoin you to observe his commandment. (Deut. 24:19–20)

These biblical commandments, engendered by the collective Israelite root experience of slavery, actually limit the right to own property, since they prescribe the duty to share property, to whatever limited degree, with those who do not own anything. The ultimate "owner" of the land is considered to be God, and any right to hold property and make use of it is overridden by injunctions such as the Sabbatical or Jubilee year. Owning land and, by extension, owning property, is to be viewed as a privilege rather than a right. The critical perspective that these commandments have to offer to the H.R.W.R. in its present form is that it is not sufficient to declare the right to own property, aside from the problematic effects of celebrating it for notions of economic justice. This right, if it is not to lead to the unjust economic conditions as we currently witness them in this country, needs to be linked to the obligation to share.

Space does not allow me to dwell on every individual article of the H.R.W.R., and I have chosen to discuss only a few. More questions could be raised, such as why only motherhood should be protected but not fatherhood (art. 16, para. 6), or what kind of criterion or authority the "decorum recognized in the neighborhood" (art. 19, para. 1) might be, to attribute to it the power to restrict the freedom of expression.

All these critical questions are not to say that there is not much in the H.R.W.R. that is worthy of support, and could indeed easily find support in an ethic informed by Jewish tradition in its various shades (art. 2: the right to freedom from violence; art. 3: the right to life, etc.). However, in the end, what seems to be of paramount importance for an effort to formulate a declaration of human rights from the perspective of world's religions is that we – and that is not just scholars, but also the communal leaders of religious practitioners – need to theorize the question of religion and its use of power, religion when it is combined with political power. It is not sufficient merely to assume a universal law, before which all are equal, even if we all may wish that "the entire world constitutes a single family" (art. 16).

In order for such a declaration to be effective, we need to integrate into our thinking what it means that religious communities want to, or have their share in, controlling a territory in order to institute their own laws. The best-intentioned declaration that "everyone has the right to freedom of movement and residence anywhere in the world" (why, one might ask?) does not address this question effectively. In fact, under certain circumstances regional local traditions might at times require protection from precisely such "a freedom of movement and residence anywhere in the world," particularly in a world that is increasingly governed by the free movement of capital. Religious traditions must be compelled to address the question of religious minorities in "their" territory in accordance with human rights. After all, some of the world's worst conflicts have been and are exacerbated if not produced by this desire (*cuius regio, eius religio*) rooted in religious beliefs.

NOTES

1. See Shaye Cohen, *The Beginnings of Jewishness: Boundaries, Varieties, Uncertainties* (Berkeley: University of California Press, 1999).
2. Daniel and Jonathan Boyarin, "Diaspora: Generation and the Ground of Jewish Identity," *Critical Inquiry*, 19 (Summer 1993), p. 718.
3. It should be pointed out that the halakhic literature of the medieval people took pains at time to redefine other religious traditions, specifically Christianity and Islam, in such ways as to exclude them from classical definitions of idolatry and therefore the legal disenfranchisement of idolators. Thus, R. Menachen ha-Meiri for instance, a prominent halakhic scholar in fourteenth-century Provence, distinguished between idolatry and non-idolatrous religions by coining a new phrase "nations bound by the ways of religion." See G. Blidstein, "Maimonides and Me'iri on the Legitimation of Non-Judaic Religion," in *Scholars and Scholarship: The Interaction Between Judaism and Other Cultures*, ed. L. Landman (New York: Michael Scharf Publication Trust of the Yeshiva University Press, 1990), pp. 27–35.
4. Albeit not fully. Family laws and personal status laws are relegated to the control of rabbinate. On the complicated role of religious Jewish law in the legal system of the state of Israel, see the monumental work by the former supreme court judge of Israel, Menachem Elon, *Jewish Law: History, Sources, Principles*, 4 vol. (Philadelphia: Jewish Publication Society, 1994).
5. Boyarin and Boyarin, "Diaspora," p. 720.
6. *Naiman v. Chairman, General Elections Committee*, commonly known as the Program List for Peace and Kach Party Case, 1985.
7. Maimonides, *Mishneh Torah, Issurei biah* (forbidden sexual relations), 13:15.
8. Maimonides, *Mishneh Torah, Melakhim* (kings), 10:12.
9. Mishnah *Gerim* (converts) 3:4.
10. Maimonides, *Mishneh Torah, Melakhim*, 10:12.
11. Cited from Elon, *Jewish Law*, vol. 4, pp. 1855–1856.

Plate 11 Stained-glass window from Lincoln Cathedral, England (built between the eleventh and sixteenth centuries), illustrating the parable of the Good Samaritan. In this parable from Jesus, a priest and a Levite (on the right) walk past a man who had been beaten by robbers, while a Samaritan, a despised outsider, stops to help him (Luke 10:29–37).

Photo: *Nancy M. Martin*

11

A CHRISTIAN RESPONSE *to the* UNIVERSAL DECLARATION *of* HUMAN RIGHTS *by* THE WORLD'S RELIGIONS

Jerry Irish

Imagine with me that the pastor of my mainline Protestant church gave the Universal Declaration of Human Rights by the World's Religions to the social action committee of which I am a member. She did so as one of the pastors asked by her bishop to try out the Declaration in their congregations. We were to serve as one of many focus groups reacting to the Declaration as a prelude to its adoption in our denomination.

We were immediately excited to discover that the world's religions are in such agreement on human rights. The Declaration contradicted the false impressions of other religions so often insinuated in the media or overtly proclaimed by some of our own Christian brothers and sisters. We began to imagine actions we might take in concert with Buddhists, Jews, and Muslims in our own city. Working together to extend specific human rights might yield much more in the way of diversity in community – and sooner – than discussing matters of belief.

We were also impressed by the overlap between the Declaration and its United Nations predecessor. Perhaps representatives of the world's religions in the United States could work together more actively in public support of the United Nations and in lobbying Congress and the administration to pay our nation's dues. We decided to ask our pastor to gather a few of her clerical counterparts in other religions that are numerically significant in our district and, if they agree, make a well-publicized visit to our Congressman.

Having exhausted our initial ecumenical euphoria, we turned, somewhat reluctantly, to our own congregation. We began to realize that many of our members, even members of our committee, might not agree with all thirty articles in the Declaration. Furthermore, the logic that dictated the order of the articles and certain of the sub-articles was not clear to us. Knowing that the Declaration would have to become more coherent if it were to play a meaningful role in the life of our congregation, we began to feel a bit overwhelmed. Our committee chair suggested that we each try to prioritize the articles in preparation for our next discussion.

The second meeting was devoted to reaching a consensus on the order and significance of the articles. The process was stimulating, and our frustration with the length of the Declaration gave way to a growing awareness of our own resources. The Decalogue emerged as an important touchstone for our work. With varying degrees of sophistication, committee members exhibited a Max Stackhouse axiom: "Religious ethics might fruitfully focus its attention on how God wants us to live in concrete human relationships."[1] It was not long before a second compass point came into play – Jesus' two Great Commandments recorded in all three of the synoptic gospels and rooted in Deuteronomy and Leviticus. Put simply, what does it take to live together as fully human beings?

By the end of our second meeting we had prioritized the articles and grouped them under seven headings as follows: freedom from want (arts. 1, 3, 25, 26); freedom from fear (arts. 2, 5, 4); freedom to work (arts. 24, 23); freedom before the law (arts. 6–11); freedom of choice (arts. 18–20); freedom in community (arts. 15, 21, 27, 22, 14, 13, 28); and personal freedom (arts. 16, 12, 17, 29, 30). It seemed to us that this arrangement moved from fundamental human rights about which there could be little misunderstanding or argument – at least from a Christian perspective – to more debatable and, perhaps, contentious rights. Grouping the articles also rendered the Declaration more accessible. Admittedly, our organizational logic might differ from others, Christian or non-Christian. But, if we were responsible for presenting the Declaration to our congregation, we would need some such framework, lest disagreement over what seemed to us a secondary right derail the whole process.

Driving home after the meeting, I realized that we had unwittingly employed Sissela Bok's distinction between minimalist and maximalist values. She defines the former as "values that are already known everywhere, whether or not people abide by them." She asserts, "Even the tiniest village or society could not survive if there were no constraints at all on, for example, killing, breaking promises, or lying."[2] So it is that life itself, and food, clothing, shelter, health care, and education constituted our most fundamental grouping of rights. Our second grouping, barely distinguishable from the first in importance and equally minimalist in Bok's sense, included freedom from violence, torture, and slavery. Five of the Ten Commandments and the second of the two Great Commandments illustrate the same logic.

Bok's maximalist values are the necessary working out of minimalist values in particular religious or political settings. Attempts at universal declarations reveal how contested those maximalist values become as one moves from one religion or culture to another. For example, what do we mean by group or communal rights, and under what circumstances, if any, do such rights override individual rights?[3] It is questions such as these that led the social action committee to place articles dealing with property ownership and social security toward the end of the Declaration.

Some members of the committee had started rewriting particular articles in an effort to simplify them. I suspect that was an attempt to make those articles more minimalist and, thus, more convincing or irrefutable. In any case, we decided to resist that temptation lest we get ourselves embroiled in precisely the sort of debilitating debate we were trying to avoid. Such fine-tuning could wait until we decided just how to submit the Declaration to our congregation for discussion. And after all, who were we to second-guess the scholars who had come up with the wording in the first place?

We went home with a good deal of self-satisfaction after that second meeting. We had made the Declaration our own by working through the articles and giving them an integrity that reflected our priorities. "Now," we said to ourselves, "let's sleep on it." At the next meeting we would decide how to report back to the pastor and, with her counsel, determine how best to present the Declaration to the congregation. Well, our "sleep" resulted in a series of rude awakenings. Each of us began to realize what an idealistic document we had on our hands.

In my own case this recognition first came with respect to the articles dealing with the right to life and freedom from violence, torture, and subjection to cruel and inhuman punishment. The governor of my state and the President of the United States – persons for whom I had voted – and the two leading candidates to be the next President were all in favor of capital punishment. Indeed, the Republican contender for the presidency, a self-proclaimed "born-again" Christian, appeared to take some pride in the fact that, while governor of Texas, he had overseen the execution of 120 persons. Furthermore, if national polling results on the death penalty were at all reflective of the views held in my own congregation, many there would not be able to affirm three of the social action committee's "minimalist" articles.

Equally unsettling to me were the articles dealing with food, clothing, and shelter. Many members of my congregation donate food and clothing to the poor of our region. Our church is a major financial contributor to a nearby homeless shelter, and many of our members volunteer at such shelters and food distribution sites. And yet, as a community of faith, we have never dealt critically with the systemic sources of poverty. Perhaps, at some unspoken level, many in my church see food, clothing, and shelter not as human rights but as things people earn or deserve simply by dint of their own efforts. While I honestly do not think I share that view, I cannot deny the fundamental inconsistency between the Christian gospel and global capitalism in its present form. While I may plead helplessness in the face of that economic system's ever-increasing momentum, I am undeniably one of its material beneficiaries. So it is that my volunteer hours at a food-distribution site – where I see the same homeless men and women, the same single mothers, the same mentally ill people return again and again – are a source of profound moral ambivalence, as well as inspiration. Could I myself, in good conscience, affirm the Declaration as anything more than an ideal so distant as to be irrelevant?

Each member of the committee had similar thoughts about one or more of the articles we had so logically rearranged. As you might guess, our third meeting began with considerable anguish as we tried to imagine bringing this human rights agenda to our congregation. How could we, as individuals or as a congregation, champion an ideology so far removed from our actual practice? Most of us on the committee were actively engaged in some form of service or praxis. Ironically, it was that very level of social action that had made some of our individual awakenings so painful. The Declaration had become a mirror, challenging the effectiveness of our best efforts, and, in a way we could not easily articulate, making us deeply uneasy about the motivation for those efforts. We were disheartened and frustrated. Why go to the trouble of endorsing this list of articles that, for the most part, spelled out an obvious set of utopian, even eschatological, ideals, but no more convincingly than the United Nations Declaration that had been around for fifty years? Indeed, why not simply endorse that U.N. Declaration? It was in response to this question that our discussion took a remarkable turn.

The chair of our committee got out a copy of the United Nations Universal Declaration of Human Rights and began reading it aloud. The first "Whereas" recognizes the "inherent dignity" and the "equal and inalienable rights" of all members of the human family as the "foundation of freedom, justice and peace in the world." After sketching the consequences of ignoring or securing those rights, the U.N. Declaration refers to the U.N. Charter wherein the peoples of the U.N. reaffirmed their "faith in fundamental human rights, in the dignity and worth of the human person and in the equal rights of men and women." It was while we were thinking about this U.N. preamble that one of our committee members recited the "preamble" to the Decalogue. "I am the Lord your God, who brought you out of the land of Egypt, out of the house of slavery" (Exod. 20:2). The silence that followed was broken when another committee member recited the first of the two Great Commandments. "You shall love the Lord your God with all your heart, and with all your soul, and with all your mind" (Matt. 22:37).

I cannot remember exactly what was said after that. All I know is we began to rewrite the "preamble" of the Universal Declaration of Human Rights by the World Religions. For us at least, it had to state more simply and boldly the *spiritual* context for human rights. Without that context it was, indeed, little different than its U.N. predecessor. In our case, as Christians, that context is articulated theologically. While we share the respect for human dignity voiced in the U.N. Declaration, that respect is rooted for us in the love of God and in our participation in a common creation story that also includes non-human being. For us, human rights are not objects of faith but fruits of faith. The struggle for their achievement is a response to the grace of an all-loving Creator; the exercise of these rights is a spiritual exercise. It is in loving God with all our heart, soul, and mind that we are empowered to love our neighbors as ourselves, that we not only have respect for their human dignity but experience the connection between their human dignity and our own.

Here, then, is our draft of an alternative preamble to the Declaration. Keep in mind that we are lay members of a Christian social action committee, not religious studies scholars.

Whereas respect for all human beings is affirmed by secular humanism and by the world's religions; and

Whereas the Universal Declaration of Human Rights, as adopted by the Annual Assembly of the United Nations on December 10, 1948, is an expression primarily of the former; and

Whereas this Universal Declaration of Human Rights by the World's Religions complements the United Nations Declaration in spiritual depth and cosmic breadth, to wit:

1. **This Declaration** assumes the dignity of human beings by virtue of their divine origin and destiny and/or their ongoing relation to an all-pervasive spiritual presence; and
2. **This Declaration** acknowledges the universal context of human rights, the web-like interconnectedness of all being, human and nonhuman; and
3. **This Declaration** asserts the necessary connection between human rights and human responsibilities to seek peace with justice and freedom;

Now, therefore, we the signatories to this Universal Declaration of Human Rights by the World Religions, as representatives of those religions, do hereby accept and affirm the following common standard of achievement for the followers of all religions or none, on this the ____ day of _____, 200_.

It is not an exaggeration to say that the recognition on the part of the social action committee that led us to rewrite the preamble was a religious experience, a spiritual awakening. The document that had seemed idealistic, even irrelevant, had become a radical vehicle of empowerment. The mirror that had disheartened us had become a door through which we could embark upon a human rights agenda that was at the same time a spiritual exercise. We realized that the source of our anger at politicians who support the death penalty is not simply their disrespect for human dignity. It is their desecration of the image of God, a desecration made all the more blatant by their self-identification as Christians. We realized that our deep discomfort about our own routinized, band-aid efforts to feed, clothe, and shelter the poor stems not simply from our failure to secure for others an inalienable right but from our misplaced faith in an economic system that pollutes God's creation while it impoverishes an ever-increasing proportion of our sisters and brothers at home and around the world. While these insights were, if anything, more painful still than our failed idealism, they put us in touch with the spiritual power at our disposal.

We decided to bring the Declaration into the very core of our congregational worship so that it could take on the character of prayer or meditation or song. The celebration of human rights is the celebration of the God in whom we live and move and have our being. Intentional, critically conceived congregational efforts to achieve human rights are themselves spiritual exercises, exercises in the interconnectedness of all being. If we encounter God in moments of prayer and meditation, then certainly we encounter her in feeding the hungry, clothing the naked, healing the sick, and visiting those in prison.

Our fourth meeting focused on our report to the pastor and our recommendations for presenting and implementing the Declaration in our congregation. Though it was a strategy session, we found ourselves rehearsing and deepening the spiritual context of our work together. For example, we were able to identify another source of our earlier frustration. We already exercise most, if not all, of the rights listed in the Declaration. In that sense, the document can be read as protective of our power, our material affluence, and the rights and privileges thereof. But read in the spiritual context of God's love, these human rights become responsibilities. The struggle for their full realization for all human beings is at once a response to God and to our neighbors.

One of our members had been reading a book by the British ethicist Jonathan Glover in which the author identifies respect and sympathy for other human beings and a sense of one's own moral identity as the resources we have against atrocity.[4] We concluded that the U.N. Declaration deals with human rights as a matter of respect whereas the Declaration by the World's Religions, at least as we want to understand it, deals with human rights as a matter of spiritual awareness rooted in our connectedness with all being. Thus, in Glover's terms, the sympathy that empowers our action and the sense of moral integrity that accompanies such action are rooted in the love of God for all creation. The struggle to secure human rights is, therefore, a spiritual struggle. Theologically speaking, social praxis consistent with the Declaration is empowered by the presence of God erasing the separation between self and neighbor. Ethically speaking, social praxis consistent with the Declaration hastens the coming of God's kingdom through the transformation of social structures.

In my enthusiasm for the work of the committee, I reported these conclusions in my ecumenical reading group. A regular practitioner of Zen meditation remarked, "That bit about erasing the separation between self and neighbor makes you sound like a Buddhist," at which point a rabbi said he thought social praxis intended to hasten the coming of God's kingdom was *mitzvot* language. My Muslim colleague wondered with a laugh if we were not all talking about Islam. Quite a discussion ensued regarding human rights as a point of convergence among our differing religions. As a result we have scheduled a meeting of social activists from the mosque, the sangha, the temple, and the church to discuss the Declaration and identify joint actions our religious communities might take together locally in collaboration with the impoverished and imprisoned to secure their human rights. We will meet first at the temple where the rabbi will lead us in a brief spiritual exercise characteristic of Judaism as a preamble to and context for our discussion. Subsequent meetings, following a similar format, will be held in each of our places of worship and meditation. We do not want to lose touch with the spiritual reality in which all human rights are grounded and through which our work together will be sustained, enriched, and perhaps even effective.

NOTES

1. Max L. Stackhouse, "Assessing an Assessment," *Journal of Religious Ethics*, 25, 3 (25th Anniversary Supplement), 1998, p. 278.
2. Sissela Bok, panel presentation on "Perspectives on a Global Ethic and Common Values," in *The United Nations and the World's Religions* (Boston: Boston Research Center for the 21st Century, 1995), p. 30.
3. Ibid., pp. 30–32.
4. Jonathan Glover, *Humanity: A Moral History of the Twentieth Century* (London: Jonathan Cape, 1999), pp. 22–30.

Plate 12 Muslims gathering on a rooftop in Osiyan, Rajasthan, to say their midday prayers, visible from the nearby Hindu Devi temple. Daily prayer is an obligation incumbent on Muslims, as is the obligation to give alms to be distributed for those in need. These prayers, shared and recited five times each day, reinforce the central tenet of Islam: that Allah, the Merciful and Compassionate, is all in all.

Photo: *Nancy M. Martin*

12

"THIS TREMOR of WESTERN WISDOM": A MUSLIM RESPONSE to HUMAN RIGHTS and the DECLARATION

Amir Hussain

PROLEGOMENON

One of the most powerful anti-colonial characters created in the last decade is that of Kirpal (Kip) Singh, a Sikh sapper for the British army in Michael Ondaatje's brilliant novel *The English Patient*. In the novel, Kip, who is defusing bombs while stationed in Italy at the end of the Second World War, hears of the atomic bombs dropped by the United States on the civilian populations of Japan. In his outrage, Kip speaks to the English patient:

> I sat at the foot of this bed and listened to you, Uncle. These last months. When I was a kid I did that, the same thing. I believed I could fill myself up with what older people taught me. I believed I could carry that knowledge, slowly altering it, but in any case passing it beyond me to another.
>
> I grew up with traditions from my country, but later, more often, from *your* country. Your fragile white island that with customs and manners and books and prefects and reason somehow converted the rest of the world. You stood for precise behaviour. I knew if I lifted a teacup with the wrong finger, I'd be banished. If I tied the wrong kind of knot in a tie, I was out. Was it just ships that gave you such power? Was it, as my brother said, because you had the histories and printing presses?
>
> You and then the Americans converted us. With your missionary rules. And Indian soldiers wasted their lives as heroes so they could be *pukkah*. You had wars like cricket. How did you fool us into this? Here... listen to what you people have done...

One bomb. Then another. Hiroshima. Nagasaki.

...If he closes his eyes, he sees the streets of Asia full of fire. It rolls across cities like a burst map, the hurricane of heat withering bodies as it meets them, the shadow of humans suddenly in the air. This tremor of Western wisdom.

...My brother told me. Never turn your back on Europe. The deal makers. The contract makers. The map drawers. Never trust Europeans, he said. Never shake hands with them. But we, oh, we were easily impressed – by speeches and medals and your ceremonies. What have I been doing these last few years? Cutting away, defusing, limbs of evil. For what? For *this* to happen?

...All those speeches of civilization from kings and queens and presidents...such voices of abstract order. Smell it. Listen to the radio and smell the celebration in it. In my country, when a father breaks justice in two, you kill the father.[1]

Perhaps not surprisingly, the above scenes were absent from Anthony Minghella's filmed version of the novel. It is Kip's words, particularly "This tremor of Western wisdom," that I use as the main metaphor and guiding principle for my meditations on Muslims and human rights and responsibilities. Note that I do not use the term "Islam," but instead the term "Muslims." Ann Mayer, one of the foremost scholars on Muslims and human rights, has written:

When one discards the abstract rubric "Islam" and moves from a preoccupation with texts and clerical views – which studying "Islam" seems to entail – toward a study of Muslim behavior and manifest attitudes, the doctrinal obstacles to incorporating human rights in the Islamic tradition seem to become surmountable.[2]

There is, of course, a multiplicity of Muslim voices on the issue of human rights and responsibilities. I am privileged to add my own small voice to that discourse.

Kip's words have a deep resonance within me, as I too was born into one culture but educated in another. I am both Canadian and Muslim, and most recently I find myself becoming American. I have been involved for almost fifteen years in issues of peace, justice, and interreligious dialogue. Through this work, I have gained a deep admiration for organizations working for the advancement of rights for all, but as someone who grew up brown, Muslim, and working class, I also understand that sometimes the United States and Canada are guilty of not practicing what they hold to be true in theory. This is particularly true after the events of September 11,

2001. Let me now turn to a discussion of how human rights intersect with Muslims and to the Declaration of Human Rights by the World Religions.

MUSLIMS AND HUMAN RIGHTS

It is important at the outset of any discussion of Muslims and human rights to remember the words of Ann Mayer:

> Muslim views on the relationship of Islam and human rights are so complex that it is extremely difficult to make valid generalizations about this subject. Shaken by a sudden and as yet incomplete modernization process, the Islamic tradition is in a state of ferment. Exposure to diverse intellectual currents, including liberalism and Marxism, has given rise to different interpretations of Islamic scripture and a range of opinions on any given rights issue.[3]

One also needs to keep in mind the complexity of meanings implied by the term for the religious law of Islam, Shari'a. Two general misconceptions are that there is one and only one Shari'a and that all Muslims strive to be governed by it. As explained by another prominent author on Islam and human rights, Bassam Tibi:

> There is no single body of law that constitutes Islamic *shari'a*. Rather, *shari'a* refers to various interpretations of Islamic scripture. That is why *shari'a* can be used to serve modern as well as traditional ends, or to justify the actions of oppressive regimes as well as those of the opposition. There simply is no common understanding of Islamic *shari'a*, particularly with respect to human rights.[4]

Yet within the multi-vocality of Muslim voices with regard to human rights, there are areas of particular perceived conflict between Shari'a and human rights, including corporal punishment, the status of women, and religious liberty.[5] Abdullahi Ahmed An-Na'im, in his chapter in this volume (chapter 2) discusses the latter two areas, and Khaled Abou El Fadl discusses the nature of Shari'a in much greater detail in his chapter which concludes this volume (chapter 21).

One of the early Muslim responses to the U.N. Universal Declaration of Human Rights was by an Iranian Shia writer (and Sufi leader), Sultan Hussein Tabandeh Reza Alishah of Gunabad. He wrote his commentary on the U.D.H.R. in Persian in 1966, and it was translated into English in 1970.[6] His work was "put into the hands of the representatives of every Islamic land who attended the 1968 Tehran International Conference on Human Rights."[7] Tabandeh's work goes through the articles of the U.D.H.R. and compares them to his own understanding of Islam. For most of the articles, Tabandeh points out parallels to Islamic teachings. However, in the case of some articles – such as article 16, which speaks about the equality of men and women in marriage – he writes that "this article contains several points which run directly contrary to Islamic teaching and are therefore wholly unacceptable to Muslims."[8] Specifically, Tabandeh's objections to this article are based on the fact that Muslims are not allowed to marry polytheists, that Muslim women are not allowed to marry non-Muslim men, and that divorce is the prerogative of the male.

Overall, he concludes that:

> In sum, the foregoing notes make it plain that the Universal Declaration of Human Rights has not promulgated anything that was new nor inaugurated innovations. Every clause of it, indeed every valuable regulation needed for the welfare of human society ever enacted by the lawgivers, already existed in a better and more perfect form in Islam. "Islam is the summit and nothing excels it."[9]

Tabandeh exemplifies one Muslim view, namely that anything valuable in the U.D.H.R. can be found within the Islamic tradition. This view is common among apologists for Islam.

On September 19, 1981, the Universal Islamic Declaration of Human Rights (U.I.H.R.) was published in Paris by a London-based organization, the Islamic Council.[10] For those who are fond of the simple dichotomy between "Islam" and the "West," it is instructive to remember that Paris and London are usually categorized as "Western" cities. As explained in the foreword to the U.I.H.R.:

> Islam gave to [hu]mankind an ideal code of human rights fourteen centuries ago. These rights aim at conferring honour and dignity on [hu]mankind and eliminating exploitation, oppression and injustice. Human rights in Islam are firmly rooted in the belief that God, and God alone, is the Law Giver and the Source of all human rights. Due to their Divine origin, no ruler, government, assembly or authority can curtail or violate in any way the human rights conferred by God, nor can they be surrendered.[11]

This opening elicits the conflict that exists for many Muslims, between allegiance to God as the supreme authority, on one hand, and the need for human agency and authority, on the other.

The U.I.H.R. consists of twenty-three articles that are loosely based on the U.D.H.R. In addition, the U.I.H.R. has a reference section that provides

Qur'an verses and *hadith* citations to support each of the twenty-three articles. Like Tabandeh's work, the U.I.H.R. attempts to place statements about human rights within an Islamic framework, thereby subsuming modern human rights discourse under the authority of God. Tibi discusses the U.I.H.R. at some length,[12] and concludes that: "As most students of Islamic history and many Islamists will agree, the claim that the fairly sympathetic interpretation of Islamic texts presented in the twenty-three principles has always been the prevailing interpretation of Islam is historically inaccurate."[13]

A very different Muslim approach to questions of human rights and responsibilities was articulated by Abdullahi Ahmed An-Na'im in his groundbreaking 1990 work, *Toward an Islamic Reformation.*[14] At the time of the book's publication I was beginning my graduate work in the study of Islam and can still recall the excitement of Muslim friends and colleagues who said that I *must* read this work. In his foreword to the book, John Voll wrote of the importance and originality of the work:

> It is neither an attempt to integrate Western and traditional Islamic thought (as is usually the case with modernist positions) nor a fundamentalist effort to return to pristine principles. An-Na'im is attempting to transform the understanding of the very foundations of traditional Islamic law, not to reform them.[15]

In the book's preface, An-Na'im wrote:

> As a Muslim, I am particularly sensitive to the religious implications of attributing inadequacy and injustice to Shari'a, which is perceived by many Muslims to be part of the Islamic faith. Nevertheless, I believe that the questions raised here must be confronted and resolved as a religious as well as a political and legal imperative if the public law of Islam is to be implemented today.[16]

In describing his understanding of the Shari'a, An-Na'im wrote:

> Shari'a is not the whole of Islam but instead is an interpretation of its fundamental sources as understood in a particular historical context. Once it is appreciated that Shari'a was *constructed* by its founding jurists, it should become possible to think about reconstructing certain aspects of Shari'a, provided that such reconstruction is based on the same fundamental sources of Islam and is fully consistent with its essential moral and religious precepts.[17]

An-Na'im's current thoughts are masterfully presented in his chapter in this volume.

Also in 1990, the Cairo Declaration on Human Rights in Islam was published.[18] This document was the product of the Nineteenth Islamic Conference of Foreign Ministers, held in Cairo from July 31 to August 5, 1990. The Cairo Declaration consists of twenty-five articles, written according to the opening: "In contribution to the efforts of mankind to assert human rights, to protect man from exploitation and persecution, and to affirm his freedom and right to a dignified life in accordance with the Islamic Shari'ah." Several of the articles make reference to Shari'a as superordinate in any discussion of human rights, using such phrases as "without a Shari'ah-prescribed reason" (art. 2); "within the framework of the Shari'ah" (art. 12); "provided it is not contrary to the principles of the Shari'ah" (art. 16); or "except as provided for in the Shari'ah" (art. 19). The final two articles explicitly state the importance of Shari'a to the Cairo Declaration: "All the rights and freedoms stipulated in this Declaration are subject to the Islamic Shari'ah" (art. 24); and "The Islamic Shari'ah is the only source of reference for the explanation or clarification of any of the articles of this Declaration" (art. 25). Clearly, the authors of the Cairo Declaration saw Shari'a as being singular and fixed, unlike the understandings of Tibi and An-Na'im that are described above.

Shari'a has a less prominent role in another important document, the Arab Charter on Human Rights.[19] This charter was adopted by the council of the League of Arab States on September 15, 1994. The Arab Charter contains the following clause in its preamble: "Pursuant to the eternal principles of brotherhood and equality among all human beings which were firmly established by the Islamic Shari'a and the other divinely-revealed religions..." Nowhere in the forty-three articles of the Arab Charter is Shari'a mentioned again. Most recently, the Organization of the Islamic Conference held a symposium on March 14 and 15, 2002, at the U.N. headquarters in Geneva on the theme of human rights in Islam.[20]

In addition to the documents described above, a number of Muslim scholars have written about the relationship between Islam and human rights. The work of Bassam Tibi on the Arab world in general and of Abdullahi Ahmed An-Na'im on Sudan in particular have already been mentioned. Abdelwahab El-Affendi also has a recent article on human rights in the Sudan, which includes a discussion on the controversy over slavery.[21] Mohammed Hashim Kamali, a law professor at the International Islamic University of Malaysia, has an excellent book on Islamic understandings of freedom of expression.[22] Farid Esack has written about the issue of human rights in the context of South Africa.[23] Having indicated some of the Muslim literature on Islam and human rights, let me offer an Islamic perspective on the project embodied by the Declaration of Human Rights by the World's Religions.

TOWARD A DECLARATION OF HUMAN RIGHTS BY THE WORLD'S RELIGIONS

Many Muslims are post-colonial people and, in North America, immigrants who have a history with the legacies of colonialism. Mohammed Arkoun, a leading Western scholar of Islam, describes the intersection of colonialism and human rights with respect to Muslims:

> The colonial adventure ended badly. It is difficult to speak to a Muslim audience today about the Western origin of human rights without provoking indignant protests. We must not lose sight of the wars of liberation and the ongoing, postcolonial battle against Western "imperialism" if we want to understand the psychological and ideological climate in which an Islamic discourse on human rights has developed in the past ten or fifteen years.[24]

I began this chapter with Ondaatje's words from *The English Patient,* and it is to those words that I would like to return. I was born in a Christian missionary hospital in Lahore, and so I understand something of the moral ambiguities of the missionary enterprise. Like Kip, I grew up in a world in which my education was largely shaped by white Christian men. Some of these men, like Wilfred Cantwell Smith, himself a former missionary, were extraordinary. They never sought to convert, or to impose, or to colonize, but simply to teach. And having lived in Lahore for six years, decades before the current anthropological trend toward long-term participant observation, Smith and his wife understood much about Indian culture, in its dominant Hindu and Muslim forms. And they saw the horrors that came when one worldview was forced onto people with a different worldview. I think it is for this reason that Smith's work took the direction that it did.

The United Nations Universal Declaration of Human Rights may be perceived as a colonization of sorts, an imposition of one worldview on another. It is, I think, instructive to remember that the U.D.H.R. came after the end of the Second World War, after atomic bombs had been dropped on two Japanese cities. The majority of Muslims in the world are Asian, and perhaps as Asians they think differently about tremors of Western wisdom. This is not to say that there is no merit in the U.D.H.R. In that document there is great merit. But if a document on human rights is to be of any authority, it must come from as many peoples of the world as possible, and not just from one limited group, not even one particular religious group, as is the case with the U.I.H.R. To have any authority with the majority of the world's peoples, it must be more than a "tremor of Western wisdom." Perhaps the Declaration of Human Rights by the World's Religions that is presented and described by Arvind Sharma in this volume is the best possible alternative.

As Muslims join in the project of working toward such a universal declaration of human rights by the world's religions, I am reminded again about the extraordinary contributions of Wilfred Cantwell Smith to discussions of what it means to be Muslim, or how Muslims interact with the world around them. From his deep knowledge, Smith was able to offer critique when it was needed. He was not a Muslim. He was not an apologist for Islam. Yet his critique never did violence to what it meant for other people to be Muslim. Let me quote something from *Islam in Modern History*: "A true Muslim, however, is not a man who believes in Islam – especially Islam in history; but one who believes in God and is committed to the revelation through His Prophet."[25] Those words were published in 1957. In *The Meaning and End of Religion* (1962), he continued: "the essential tragedy of the modern Islamic world is the degree to which Muslims, instead of giving their allegiance to God, have been giving it to something called Islam."[26] Those words could have been written yesterday with equal force and validity. It is a mark of Professor Smith's genius that those words were written forty years ago and yet they continue to inform us today. Perhaps it will be a return to an allegiance to God, rather than to Islam, that will help Muslims in our articulations of what it means to be human.

NOTES

For Ustadh Abdullahi Ahmed An-Na'im who inspired a generation of us with *Toward an Islamic Reformation*. And to the blessed memory of my teacher, Wilfred Cantwell Smith, who I think would disagree with the language that I have used here, but I hope would agree with the sentiment. My thanks also to Pat Nichelson for his diligent reading of various drafts of this chapter.

1. Michael Ondaatje, *The English Patient* (Toronto: McClelland & Stewart, 1992), pp. 283–285.
2. Ann Elizabeth Mayer, "Current Muslim Thinking on Human Rights," in *Human Rights in Africa, Cross-Cultural Perspectives,* eds. Abdullahi Ahmed An-Na'im and Francis M. Deng (Washington: Brookings Institution, 1990), p. 154.

3. Ibid., p. 133.
4. Bassam Tibi, "The European Tradition of Human Rights and the Culture of Islam," in *Human Rights in Africa*, eds. An-Na'im and Deng, p. 124.
5. Heiner Bielefeldt, "Muslim Voices in the Human Rights Debate," *Human Rights Quarterly*, 17, 4 (1995), pp. 587–617.
6. Sultan Hussein Tabandeh, *A Muslim Commentary on the Universal Declaration of Human Rights*, trans. Francis J. Goulding (London: F.T. Goulding, 1970).
7. Ibid., p. x.
8. Ibid., p. 35.
9. Ibid., p. 85.
10. This declaration (along with Tabandeh's earlier work) is discussed in detail by Ann Mayer. Ann Elizabeth Mayer, *Islam and Human Rights: Tradition and Politics* (Boulder: Westview, 1991).
11. The English translation of the U.I.H.R. is available on the web at www.sufism.org/society/islamdecl.html
12. Tibi, "The European Tradition of Human Rights and the Culture of Islam," pp. 117–123.
13. Ibid., p. 119.
14. Abdullahi Ahmed An-Na'im, *Toward an Islamic Reformation: Civil Liberties, Human Rights, and International Law* (Syracuse: Syracuse University Press, 1990).
15. Ibid., p. x.
16. Ibid., p. xiii.
17. Ibid., p. xiv.
18. Available on the website of the Human Rights Library of the University of Minnesota at www1.umn.edu/humanrts/instree/cairodeclaration.htm.
19. Available on the website of the Human Rights Library of the University of Minnesota at www1.umn.edu/humanrts/instree/arabcharter.htm
20. Information on the symposium is available from the website of the O.I.C. at www.oic-oci.org
21. Abdelwahab El-Affendi, "Islam and Human Rights: The Lessons from Sudan," *The Muslim World*, 91 (Fall 2001), pp. 481–506.
22. Mohammed Hashim Kamali, *Freedom of Expression in Islam* (Cambridge: Islamic Texts Society, 1997).
23. Farid Esack, *Qur'an, Liberation and Pluralism: An Islamic Perspective of Interreligious Solidarity Against Oppression* (Oxford: Oneworld, 1997).
24. Mohammed Arkoun, *Rethinking Islam: Common Questions, Uncommon Answers*, trans. Robert D. Lee (Boulder: Westview Press, 1994), p. 109.
25. Wilfred Cantwell Smith, *Islam in Modern History* (Princeton: Princeton University Press, 1957), p. 146.
26. Wilfred Cantwell Smith, *The Meaning and End of Religion* (Minneapolis: Fortress Press, 1991 [1962]), p. 126.

Plate 13 Images of Rama and Sita, enshrined in a Rama temple in Jaipur, India.
Rama, an avatar of the god Vishnu, is the embodiment of the ideal righteous king
and member of the kshatriya or warrior caste. He stands with his wife Sita, who
exemplifies the fulfillment of the duties of a woman (*stridharma*) in her wifely
devotion and obedience to Ram. Their story is told in the *Ramayana*, a tale of
dharma or responsibility and duty and of loving devotion (embodied in the figure
of Hanuman at the lower left). Photo: *Nancy M. Martin*

13

CAN ONE SIZE FIT ALL? INDIC PERSPECTIVES *on the* DECLARATION *of* HUMAN RIGHTS *by the* WORLD'S RELIGIONS

Christopher Key Chapple

Can one size fit all? Is it possible to have a truly universal declaration of human rights by the world's religions? In India today, several important issues have surfaced that touch on some of the core questions raised by the overall human rights philosophy. To rectify past injustices to tribal, low-caste, Muslim, and Anglo-Indian peoples, India has implemented an aggressive affirmative action policy. This has alienated many persons of the upper castes who feel unfairly shut out from some educational and employment opportunities. Another debate has flourished on the issue of personal law, and whether personal matters such as marriage and divorce should be governed by the laws and traditions of one's particular religion or by a uniform civil code that applies to all communities, as with criminal law. However, even beyond these particular concerns and the current debate over the creation of an equitable society through legislation, some underlying philosophical issues within the subcontinent, which apply regardless of whether one is Hindu, Muslim, Sikh, Jaina, Zoroastrian, or Christian, are evident within Indic civilization and merit some attention in regard to human rights. From the perspective of traditional Indic values, I would like to reflect on Indian family structures and cultural expectations in light of the human rights discussion.

The concept of rights by nature focuses on persons as individuals, yet traditional Indic values embrace a relational view of the self. The human person does not arrive in this world alone, but enters immediately into a web of relationships. The child relies utterly on the parents and only after a period of years does the child of whatever culture attain a degree of autonomy. People in India, regardless of caste or creed, celebrate and reinforce the interrelationships among family members in a variety of ways. These include special rituals naming a child and honoring the close bond between brothers and sisters in a ceremony of protection. Additionally, the majority of marriages are arranged by the family, and most families flourish in extended-family communal living arrangements.

A new name is bestowed on babies of about five or six months shortly after they take their first solid food. In this particular ritual, which I observed at Manarassala temple in Kerala, the entire family with assorted friends participate in celebrating the survival and flourishing of the baby who has now reached a position of strength. In another ritual, clearly evident on the wrists of Bengalis and other South Asians worldwide, brothers and sisters pledge protection for one another by tying on a friendship (*rakhi*) bracelet, crafted of loosely braided threads. Both of these rituals confirm the family unit as the central source for one's identity in India.

Another example of India's emphasis on relationality can be found in the wonderfully complex choreography that surrounds marriage even today, in both India proper and the diaspora community. Individuals do not marry individuals based on personal preferences and attractions. Entire families immerse themselves in the process. Today, young people often reserve the right of refusal, but more often than not the parents have a significant say in the choice of their children's life partners. Following marriage, the bride and groom often move to the home of groom's family, where the new wife becomes a working member within the family compound, and where many family businesses might be housed. For instance, during a visit to Madras (now Chennai) a few years ago, I observed a townhouse home with five levels that had been converted into multiple uses. Two grown sons shared quarters with their mother, their wives and children, multiple businesses (in this case, a loan company, an auto repair company, and an insurance brokerage), and a non-profit research facility. One developed the sense that the rhythm of life in this particular home was relaxed, with plenty of hands to help with the necessary work.

These simple examples underscore the centrality of family identity in Indian society. I would like now to explore how this orientation might bring to light interesting insights into Indian attitudes regarding human rights and the draft of the Declaration herein. First and foremost, I want to make the observation that traditional kinship structures of India place emphasis on responsibilities rather than rights. The Universal Declaration of Human Rights by the World Religions, while not abrogating the notion of accountability to one's family and in fact affirming the right to exist within a family, tends to be rooted in a philosophy of individual freedom rather than seeking as its primary purpose to uphold more interconnected complex units.

In the 1970s, South Asian anthropologists developed a series of terms to account for the understanding of the human person in Indian culture. Ronald Inden's study of marriage and rank in Bengal and McKim Marriot's studies of Hindu village life have suggested that the caste system and social relationships in India do not correspond to the idea of class in the West, but rather are grounded in a type of "monism" wherein all persons share in a common, unifying force, regardless of status. Following Dumont's analysis that the concept of the "individual" does not apply to traditional South Asian social structures,[1] Marriot and Inden have offered a theory of the person as "dividual": "Persons are 'dividuals' or unique composites of diverse subtle and gross substances derived ultimately from one source; and they are also divisible into separate particles that may be shared or exchanged with others."[2] Thus, in this interpretation, every person has both a universal and a sub-individual dimension. On the one hand, all persons are derived from "a single, all powerful, perfect, undifferentiated substance or principle"[3] which is referred to elsewhere by Marriot as indicative of an underlying "monism."[4] On the other hand, persons are continually exchanging "pieces" of them-selves with one another, "channeling and transforming heterogeneous ever-flowing, changing substances."[5] The usage of the "monism" indicates the acceptance of a philosophical absolute; the idea of transaction seems to correspond to the mundane or relative level of existence.

In this interpretation, society is maintained by mutual support, each group or unit comprising an integral part of the whole:

> Each caste's inborn code enjoins it to maintain its substance and morality, its particular occupation, and its correct exchanges with other castes. Indian thought does not separate "nature" and "morality" or "law," so that castes are, in Western terms, at once "natural" and "moral" units of society. These units make up a single order, one that is profoundly particularized.[6]

> The act of worship was, then, at both the caste and clan level, the act of *dharma* par excellence, a concise statement or symbol of the ordered unity of the total community. By worshipping a higher more divine genus, by wealth and food in accord with its capacity to give, a genus subordinated its

own gain (*artha*) and enjoyment (*kama*) to the higher goal of nourishing and upholding the embodied Veda, the primary source of community well-being and prosperity, and transformed its own embodied rank into the share of well-being, fame, and respect it rightly deserved.[7]

Through ritual, the underlying unity of Hindu social structure is revealed.

In brief, the interpretation of Marriot and Inden is that indigenous Hindu society is not one of conflict and domination, but rather a system of mutual support through ritual transaction: all castes arise from a monistic source; caste rules are symbolic of that archetypal, monistic structure. Through the interplay of "higher" and "lower," society is maintained in a highly structured fashion, based on the concepts of dharma and *svadharma*. Both personal and societal fulfillment are found in the performance of dharma.

From the perspective of human rights, this could be seen as both inspirational and problematic. On the one hand, this scenario gives dignity to manual labor. The workers hold value as support for the upper echelons of society and provide the nourishment and foundation for all human endeavor. On the other hand, as these roles became prescriptive rather than descriptive with the passing of centuries, this poetic description of specialization of labor became a tool for oppression based on heredity. Hence, the contemporary Indian constitution, composed by B.R. Ambedkar, a member of an untouchable caste who earned a Ph.D. at Columbia University and converted to Buddhism at the end of his life, includes provisions that erode the power of caste and work for a more open, equal-opportunity society.[8] Most recently, Nobel prize winner Amartya Sen has underscored the need for universal education to lift persons from poverty.[9]

The winds of change within India have brought a burgeoning middle class that has begun to claim economic rights and build a lifestyle that benefits from development and progress. However, in traditional rights language, these benefits need to extend also to the lower classes of India, many of whom remain trapped in conditions of bonded labor and have no access to education. Swami Agnivesh, a member of the Arya Samaj, has campaigned tirelessly to draw attention to the nearly 200,000,000 people within India who have little or no hope of gaining an education or sharing in the rapidly developing economy of India.[10] These people, for whom the traditional system of caste and family relationships form no safety net, would be the most important beneficiaries of a Western-style human rights campaign in India.

Today India finds itself caught in a tension between the traditional values and an emerging, uniquely Indian form of modernity. Upper- and middle-caste Hindus continue to celebrate the traditional forms of dharma, which combine personal responsibility with civic awareness expressed through social mores and law. This population continues to fulfill its birth-given duties and does so with a sense of purpose and dignity. At the same time, India continues to define its own version of the modern secularist worldview which, for some, needs to undo all forms of discrimination based on caste or religion. Several persons of low-caste birth have risen to positions in parliament and several have held governorships of India's many states. The vision of Gandhi and Ambedkar of the eradication of all caste distinctions has produced many successes and demonstrated that education and equal opportunity can help empower those whose options have been restricted for generations due to the caste system.

Traditional Hindu values give priority to family and social roles over the individual; modern secular Gandhian values seek to undo the injustices caused by the caste system. A doctrine of universal respect for the human being, like that proposed in the Universal Declaration of Human Rights by the World's Religions, seeks to bridge these two worldviews. In order to be fully successful, the Declaration would need to accommodate some aspects of Indian society that are unique to South Asia. For instance, it tends to emphasize the importance of human wealth and comfort. Traditional Hinduism does not place greatest value on wealth and comfort. It lists wealth (*artha*) as the first of four goals, but considers pleasure (*kama*), social stability (dharma), and spiritual liberation (*moksha*) to be successively superior. Ironically, the highest goal and greatest values are to be achieved by the diminishment of wealth and in some instances the renouncing of food. The greatest saints of Indian culture have been among its poorest citizens. Gandhi's greatest subversion of British colonial rule came through his advocacy that people back away from the economic juggernaut, and renounce consumption of manufactured British goods. His own great campaigns were often punctuated with fasting, and he urged others to follow his example.

As we reflect on the concept of universal human rights from a South Asian religious perspective, we need to acknowledge the specific history of this land steeped in tradition, punctured by two major invasions in the past millennium, and grappling with modernity and post-modernity. Throughout most of its history, India existed as a subcontinent with more than two hundred languages divided into three major language groups

(Dravidian, Indo-European, tribal) and governed by about six hundred different kings at any given time. Occasionally, northern India would be governed by emperors (Buddhist, Hindu, Muslim) who would seek concessions from local kings. The well-being of the people rested in the ruler, who would serve as the model for exemplary behavior and maintain social order. Societal ethics required doing one's birth-given duty and performing one's expected role. The highest modes of religious ethics entailed taking on higher vows that would often remove one from society. In a quest for transcendence, one became a renouncer, giving up name, wealth, status, and family, erasing all of the many connections found in the web of one's relations.

In times of empire or colonial rule, works were not performed solely for one's immediate benefit or for the local king, but for a remote regent. Taxes and goods were sent from one's village to support the wealth of the Mughal ruler or the British king or queen, thus subordinating immediate needs for the sake of a somewhat abstract ruling authority. In the modern period, democracy sought to throw off the allegiance to foreign rulers and establish self-rule or *sva-raj*, which for Gandhi entailed personal discipline and the establishment of both local governance and economies. Resentment remains over the memories of Muslim rule and oppressive British economic policies. Though the loose collection of movements and ideas that now refers to itself as Hindu would in principle support the ideas of the Universal Declaration of Human Rights, it would remain suspicious of any ideology that would seek to undermine the primacy of the family, advocate particular forms of worship, or cede any autonomy to non-local economic entities.

India remains a land of contrasts and multiplicity. Can a single document hope to protect the life-ways of all of its peoples? Can a document that gives priority to food also find a way to protect the right to fast unto death, a religious practice found among the Jainas? The document does support the right to marriage and the right to celibacy. But how would it address issues of polygamy and divorce? Can a document that urges "conformance to the rules of decorum recognized in the neighborhood" allow for full religious diversity? If one's neighborhood includes Muslims, Christians, and Hindus, all of whom follow different codes for personal behavior, what criteria can be used to determine the greatest good for the society? Can the liberal attitudes espoused by the secularists who wish to abolish caste hierarchy prevail in India's complex, multifaceted landscape? As an idealized vision, this document provides the basis for harmonious living, and truly seeks to be universal. To enact the ideals of this document in South Asia will be difficult, given the entrenched differences found in India's many stratified communities.

NOTES

1. Louis Dumont, *Homo Hierarchicus: The Caste System and its Implications*, trans. Mark Sainsbury (Chicago: University of Chicago Press, 1970), pp. 41, 232–233.
2. McKim Marriot and Ronald Inden, "Toward an Ethnosociology of South Asian Caste Systems," in *The New Wind: Changing Identities in South Asia*, ed. Kenneth David (The Hague: Mouton Publishers, 1977), pp. 227–238, at p. 232.
3. Ibid., p. 231.
4. McKim Marriott, "Hindu Transactions: Diversity without Dualism," in *Transaction and Meaning: Directions in the Anthropology of Exchange and Symbolic Behavior*, ed. Bruce Kapferer (Philadelphia: Institute for the Study of Human Issues, 1976).
5. McKim and Inden, "South Asian Caste Systems," p. 233.
6. McKim Marriott and Ronald B. Inden, "Caste Systems," *Encyclopaedia Britannica*, 15th ed. (Chicago, 1981), Macropaedia III, p. 983.
7. Ronald B. Inden, *Marriage and Rank in Bengali Culture: A History of Caste and Clan in Middle Period Bengal* (Berkeley: University of California Press, 1976), pp. 148–149.
8. See Nicholas B. Dirks, *Castes of Mind: Colonialism and the Making of Modern India* (Princeton: Princeton University Press, 2001), pp. 255–275; Eleanor Zelliot, *From Untouchable to Dalit: Essays on the Dalit Movement*, 2nd ed. (New Delhi: Manohar, 1996); Gail Omvedt, *Dalits and the Untouchable Revolution: Dr. Ambedkar and the Dalit Movement in Colonial India* (New Delhi: Sage Publications, 1994).
9. See Amartya Sen, *Development as Freedom* (New York: Knopf, 1999).
10. For articles by Swami Agnivesh, see http://server2042.virtualave.net/swamiagnivesh/articles.htm

Plate 14 Statue of the Laughing Buddha in Beihai Park in Beijing, China, illustrating both compassion toward children and the child-like nature of Zen, which corresponds to Jesus' expression of the Christian ideal, "suffer the little children to come unto me." The Laughing Buddha represents Poe-Tai Hoshang, the Chinese master of Ch'an Buddhism, called Zen Buddhism when it reached Japan in the eleventh century.

Photo: *Joseph Runzo*

14

INTERRELIGIOUS DIALOGUE, GLOBALIZATION, and HUMAN RIGHTS: BUDDHIST REFLECTIONS on INTERDEPENDENCE and the DECLARATION

David W. Chappell

Human rights have an individual and a communal dimension. In the articles of the United Nations Universal Declaration of Human Rights (U.D.H.R.), there are three levels of rights: protection of the individual from the state (arts. 2–21); responsibilities of the state to the individual (arts. 22–27); and a global order (arts. 28–30). Even though not all governments have adopted the U.D.H.R., in the past half century it has become a norm invoked by disadvantaged people around the globe and held up as a standard for humane behavior everywhere. More than any other legislation by the U.N. General Assembly, the U.D.H.R. has become a part of popular discourse in the world community – at least articles 2–21, which protect the individual from the state. But invoking the U.D.H.R. to protect the rights of individuals is different from building a community that meets these standards.

The U.N. addressed the communal dimension of human rights when it dedicated the year 2001 to the theme of a dialogue of civilizations and the creation of cultures of peace. This theme is already expressed in the U.D.H.R. as article 26.2:

> Education shall be directed to the full development of the human person-
> ality and to the strengthening of respect for human rights and fundamental
> freedoms. It shall promote understanding, tolerance and friendship among

all nations, racial or religious groups, and shall further the activities of the
United Nations for the maintenance of peace.

The practice of interfaith dialogue has become an important new tool for
the fulfillment of these goals, and social structures have evolved to present
new challenges, particularly the emergence of transnational corporations.
It is in light of this dialogue and these changes that I will reflect on the
Universal Declaration of Human Rights by the World Religions.

HUMAN RIGHTS AND WORLD RELIGIONS

The motivation behind the 1998 revision of the U.D.H.R. called the Universal
Declaration of Human Rights by the World's Religions (H.R.W.R.) seems, at
least in part, based on the discomfort of religious communities with the
unqualified emphasis on human rights in the U.D.H.R. In contrast, religious
traditions assert that individuals do not have inherent ultimate rights, but
rather that rights are grounded in a larger reality that is foundational to
human life. As the preamble of the H.R.W.R. claims: "There is more to life
than life itself by inspiration human and divine." This "more to life than life
itself" invokes the transcending dimensions of the religious life that seek individual transformation in the name of a larger and truer reality. Another way
in which the religious heritage is present in the H.R.W.R. preamble is its
assertion that ideals are an inherent part of human life. The preamble emphasizes that one must not "idealize the actual but strive to realize the ideal."

The H.R.W.R. also responds to religious communities' discomfort with
the unqualified emphasis on human rights in the U.N. document by
keeping the same number of articles as the U.D.H.R. but coupling duties
with rights as "integrally related to them in conception and execution."
Although the original article 29 of the U.D.H.R. does mention that
"everyone has duties to the community," this single mention of duties is
overshadowed by the long list of individual rights. By including duties next
to rights in the majority of its revised articles, the H.R.W.R. supports individual rights while balancing them with responsibilities. However, this
change breaks down the grouping of the U.D.H.R. articles that distinguished legal minimums for protection for the individual (arts. 2–21) from
the social and political ideals that need to be worked toward locally and
globally (arts. 22–30). An alternative solution might be to keep the
U.D.H.R. as it is, but also to affirm a newly formulated declaration of
human responsibilities as an additional ethical appeal.

HUMAN RIGHTS AND INTERFAITH DIALOGUE

In a strange twist, the H.R.W.R. explicitly drops article 26.2 (quoted in full above). In revising U.D.H.R. article 18 dealing with religious freedom, the H.R.W.R. does add that "everyone has the duty to promote peace and tolerance among different religions and ideologies." But this sentence still omits the goals of education, understanding, and friendship – as well as the full development of the personality – as ideals necessary for achieving religious and social harmony.

Interfaith dialogue has emerged in recent decades as a new tool for building social understanding and harmony,[1] and indeed is assumed by the framers of the initial draft of the H.R.W.R. to be an essential element in the process of moving toward such a declaration. There are two popular sets of guidelines for dialogue, one articulated by Leonard Swidler and the other by Majid Tehranian. Swidler, a Christian theologian and editor of the *Journal of Ecumenical Studies,* formulated ten rules that emphasize sincerity, mutual trust, and empathy between equals in which the partners are minimally self-critical and able to define themselves while engaging in an interchange of mutual learning and growing in their perception and understanding of reality.[2] Swidler's guidelines fully express the methods and goals of "discursive dialogue"[3] and are consistent with the rationalism and individualism of Socratic dialogue and the European Enlightenment that seek intellectual understanding.

Majid Tehranian, a Persian Muslim, professor of communications and director of the Toda Institute for Global Peace and Policy Research in Hawaii, also has a list of ten items that include the roles of silence and deep listening with hearts and minds, honoring diversity while seeking common ground for consensus, and formulating agreements and drawing out their implications for group policy and action.[4] His list emphasizes methods for developing common ground and social integration useful in the arena of conflict resolution and peace work, rather than emphasizing religious or intellectual issues.

A third approach to dialogue is expressed by Asian Buddhists who have worked to build international understanding and global community after the Second World War as a way to prevent future conflict and war. Frequently they sidestep doctrinal differences in order to find and affirm common values and practice.[5] For example, when reflecting on his longtime experience in the Zen–Christian Colloquium begun in Japan in 1967, Nara Yasuaki reported:

> Gradually, I have come to realize... that it is dialogue when we can move each other to the depths. The necessity of exchanging knowledge and of objective discussion is not to be denied; each has its own interest and significance... But, at the same time, thanks to my fellow members, I was able to come in touch with the "world of the spirit", which is sharply distinguishable from knowledge. [6]

The Buddhist members of his dialogue group engaged with other religions "in order to establish a spiritual tie by which all religions can cope with the various problems of the world."[7] In order to develop understanding and solidarity, "controversial issues, which should have been discussed thoroughly, were consciously avoided lest an unpleasant feeling should be left behind among us."[8] Dialogue was a way to develop the social harmony needed to deal more effectively with world problems, but it also facilitated a spiritual understanding that was beyond reason.

Buddhists are diverse and may pursue dialogue in various ways. But in general the tradition gives priority to the reduction of suffering, so a primary goal of dialogue is to be attentive to where there is the most conflict and pain. The Buddhist view of the interdependency of all things tends to relativize doctrines and to emphasize instead the commonality of all people. Diversity is recognized as the distinctiveness of each person based on his or her unique constellation of background influences and present relationships. But these are seen as subject to change. As a result, dialogue begins with the assumption of kinship and works to increase communal friendship and shared responsibility to others and to lessen the suffering of the less fortunate. Since ideas are intellectual constructs that change in different contexts, the goal of Buddhist dialogue is not to reach doctrinal agreement but to increase sensitivity to others in order to be more effective in relieving suffering, which naturally leads to the support of human rights and responsibilities.

The unspoken assumption for all the above views of interreligious dialogue is the separation of religion from state control. When religion is aligned with the state, or seeks to overthrow it, interreligious violence rather than dialogue and understanding may arise. Over a million lives were lost during the partition of India and Pakistan, but the two religious wars that brought the most deaths involved the Taiping Christians and the Muslim Hui in nineteenth-century China, with an estimated twenty million deaths each. The separation of religion from politics is probably the single most important factor in diminishing religious violence in modern times, and facilitating interfaith dialogue and increased social harmony.[9]

Besides the danger of state religion, the other major impediment to dialogue and source of religious violence is the exclusivistic and totalistic religion that is labeled "fundamentalism." Despite extensive study of fundamentalism as a global phenomenon, no clear patterns of causation or evolution have emerged.[10] Nevertheless, increased education, understanding, and sharing across religious lines obviously work to prevent fundamentalism and religious violence.[11]

True dialogue is possible only when the human rights of the participants are already being met. An interview between a prison warden and a prisoner of conscience cannot be dialogue: punishment for expressing one's views and values undermines dialogue. On the other hand, the practice of dialogue raises the level of human relationships beyond merely meeting the standards of human rights. Instead, it works toward the higher goal of creating cultures of peace, personal fulfillment, and social harmony.

DIALOGUE, GLOBALIZATION, AND GUIDING INSTITUTIONS

Whereas the U.D.H.R. focuses mostly on individual rights, the centennial of the Parliament of the World's Religions held in Chicago in 1993 reflected the concern with duties articulated in the H.R.W.R. by emphasizing the need for human transformation and "a readiness to sacrifice" oneself in the cause of global ethical cooperation. Individual transformation, rather than human rights, was made an essential ingredient to social improvement. The parliament affirmed that "Earth cannot be changed for the better unless the consciousness of individuals is changed first."

The 1999 meeting of the parliament went beyond individual transformation to emphasize the communal and institutional dimensions of building a better world. The declaration of the 1999 parliament was entitled "A Call to our Guiding Institutions," where it was asserted that "As new ways are found for religion, government, business and commerce, education, media, and science to cooperate with one another, an unprecedented process of transformation can begin to unfold." As a result, the 1999 parliament sought "a persuasive invitation to these guiding institutions that will encourage new partnerships in building a better world." The major innovation in this document was to broaden responsibility for human well-being beyond the state and to appeal for higher ethical standards from all major institutions.

Half a century ago, nation-states dominated the world. But today it is often not governments that are most powerful but corporations, and their lifeblood is money.[12] Money is not everything, but the global economy is increasingly important in shaping the quality of life on the planet. Moral issues are being framed in economic terms, whether they deal with the environment, health care, or social equity. Even though democracy has lessened violent dictatorships, large corporations are crippling democracy;[13] governments are increasingly being held hostage to global economic institutions.

The rapid growth of the global economy in recent decades is perhaps most clearly shown by the fact that in 1970 the total number of transnational corporations was about 7,000, but grew by 1998 to at least 53,607 transnational corporations who were contracted with at least 448,917 foreign subsidiaries.[14] The six largest corporations in the world (Exxon, General Motors, Ford, Mitsui, Daimler-Chrysler, and Mitsubishi) had combined revenues larger than the combined budgets of 64 nations consisting of 58 percent of the world's population (including India, Indonesia, Brazil, Russia, Pakistan, Bangladesh, Nigeria, and Mexico). Only seven nations have budgets larger than Ford, Exxon, or General Motors – France, the United Kingdom, Italy, China, Japan, Germany, and the United States.

The size of individual corporations in comparison to nations is impressive. However, their growing influence based on their growing number makes them even more powerful. In listing the 200 largest financial budgets in the world, Charles Gray found that only 39 were nations, whereas 161 were corporations. The Fortune 500 companies in 1999 consisted of companies that have budgets over US $9 billion, but only 57 national governments have budgets as large as these 500 corporations.[15]

As corporations increasingly "rule the world"[16] and as corporations function as "fictive persons," it is important to discuss institutional responsibilities as well as individual and state responsibilities. The violence of these institutions is often hidden as it impoverishes and cripples human life through bureaucratic regulations. Johan Galtung has called this "structural violence," since the individuals who work for an institution may be ethical but the procedures and organization may be arranged in such a way that some people are unfairly disadvantaged. The feminist movement has been particularly effective in signaling gender biases in the workplace, for example, but the economic biases in the global economy are even more egregious. Increased communication and regular dialogue are essential methods to learn about the disparity between wages and profits, or between medical budgets and military spending, or between third world and first world consumption, as a way to see structural violence and to seek methods to remove it before it precipitates local war and physical violence. Any declaration of human rights in the twenty-first century must address this structural violence and the changing realities of a world dominated by multinational corporations. Progress on an Earth charter is another initiative to supplement the U.D.H.R. with guidelines to check ecological devastation based on economic exploitation of our natural world.

CONCLUSION

Initiatives to build a global consensus on rights and responsibilities, human and otherwise, offer different views of individual and social responsibilities in building a better world. With corporations, educational institutions, the media, and science playing roles often as decisive as governments, new ways must be established to protect the integrity of the individual and the environment from public and private institutional violence. In response to these changes, the H.R.W.R. created new content for article 30: "Everyone has the right to require the formation of a supervisory committee within one's community...to monitor...and present one's case before such a committee."

Social dialogue is regularly needed to work out fairness for human and natural life. Because of the complexities of technology and institutions, moral developments cannot be easily legislated but need to be constantly improved through regular and inclusive discussion. Without dialogue at all levels of our expanding social organizations, divisions and exclusion will inevitably lead to oppression, fear, hatred, and conflict. Protecting human rights and sponsoring regular dialogue will not solve everything, but they are the best social invention yet for helping government, law, and corporations to evolve a better world.

NOTES

1. For example, the World Conference of Religion and Peace (W.C.R.P.) began its work in 1970 with the major sponsorship of Unitarian Christians and Rissho Koseikai Buddhists. In addition to increasing understanding through dialogue, the W.C.R.P. is very active in areas of social conflict. It was due to W.C.R.P. initiatives at the end of the Kosovo bombing by N.A.T.O. that the leaders of the Greek Orthodox Christians, the Bosnian Muslims, and the Roman Catholics worked together to rebuild social harmony.

2. Leonard Swidler, in "The Dialogue Decalogue," reprinted from *Journal of Ecumenical Studies* 20, 1 (Winter 1983; September 1984 revision), lists ten points:

    1. The primary purpose of dialogue is to learn, that is, to change and grow in the *perception and understanding of reality*, and then to act accordingly.

2. Interreligious, inter-ideological dialogue must be a two-sided project – within each religious or ideological community and between religious or ideological communities.

3. Each participant must come to the dialogue with complete honesty and sincerity. Conversely, each participant must assume a similar complete honesty and sincerity in the other partners.

4. In interreligious, inter-ideological dialogue we must not compare our ideals with our partner's practice.

5. Each participant must *define himself.* Conversely, the one interpreted must be able to recognize herself in the interpretation.

6. Each participant must come to the dialogue with no hard-and-fast assumptions as to where the points of disagreement are.

7. Dialogue can take place only between equals.

8. Dialogue can take place only on the basis of mutual trust.

9. Persons entering into interreligious, inter-ideological dialogue must be at least minimally self-critical of both themselves and their own religious or ideological traditions.

10. Each participant eventually must attempt to experience the partner's religion or ideology "from within."

3.   See Eric Sharpe, "The Goals of Inter-Religious Dialogue," in *Truth and Dialogue in World Religions: Conflicting Truth-Claims,* ed. John Hick, (Philadelphia: Westminster Press, 1975), pp. 77–95; and Eric Sharpe, "Dialogue of Religions," in *The Encyclopedia of Religion,* ed. Mircea Eliade, vol. 4 (New York: Macmillan, 1987), pp. 344–348.

4.   Majid Tehranian's "Ten Commandments of Dialogue" can be found at the home page of Simon Fraser University's Centre for Dialogue Programs (http://buntzen.sfu.ca/continuing-studies/dialogue/commandments.htm) and are engraved on the wall of the Soka Gakkai Peace Memorial in Okinawa. They are:

1. Honor others and listen to them deeply with all your heart and mind.

2. Focus on the agenda while seeking the common ground for consensus, but avoid groupthink by acknowledging and honoring the diversity of views.

3. Refrain from irrelevant or intemperate interventions.

4. Acknowledge others' contributions to the discussion before relating your own remarks to theirs.

5. Remember that silence also speaks; speak only when you have a contribution to make by posing a relevant question, presenting a fact, making or clarifying a point, or advancing the discussion to greater specificity or consensus.

6. Identify the critical points of difference for further deliberation.

7. Never distort other views in order to advance your own; try to restate others' positions to their own satisfaction before presenting your own different views.

8. Formulate the agreements on any agenda item before moving on to the next.

9. Draw out the implications of an agreement for group policy and action.

10. Thank your colleagues for their contribution.

5. See David Chappell, "Buddhist Interreligious Dialogue: To Build a Global Community," in *The Sound of Liberating Truth: Buddhist–Christian Dialogues in Honor of Frederick J. Streng,* ed. Sallie King and Paul Ingram (Richmond: Curzon, 1999), pp. 3–35.

6. Nara Yasuaki, a Soto Zen priest, a scholar of Indian Buddhism, and the former president of the leading intellectual center of the Soto sect, Komazawa University (1994–1998), has been a regular member of the Zen–Christian Colloquium and the Tozai Shukyo Koryu Gakkai. See Nara Yasuaki, "Zen-Colloquium and Me," in *Zen–Christian Pilgrimage: The Fruits of Ten Annual Colloquia in Japan 1967–1976,* ed. Irie Yukio, Isomura Takuro, and Yamanouchi Tayeko (Tokyo: Zen–Christian Colloquium, 1981), p. 88.

7. Ibid.

8. Ibid.

9. The United States often claims that it is the first nation to separate church and state, but a more accurate description might be that it supports religious pluralism, a practice that can be found intermittently in human history from the time of Cyrus the Great of Persia. See Cyrus Masroori, "Cyrus II and the Political Utility of Religious Toleration," in *Religious Toleration: The Variety of Rites from Cyrus to Defoe,* ed. John Christian Laursen (New York: St. Martin's, 1999), pp. 13–36. Asian premodern states who sponsored religious pluralism were Akbar the Great's Mughal India and the Mongol empire. See Richard Fox Young, "*Deus Unus* or *Dei Plures Sunt?* The Function of Inclusivism in the Buddhist Defense of Mongol Folk Religion Against William of Rubruck (1254)," *Journal of Ecumenical Studies* 26, 1 (Winter 1989), pp. 100–137.

10. Rhys Williams, "Movement Dynamics and Social Change: Transforming Fundamentalist Ideology and Organizations," in *Accounting for Fundamentalisms (The Fundamentalism Project, vol. 4),* ed. Martin Marty and R. Scott Appleby (Chicago: University of Chicago Press, 1994), pp. 785–834.

11. I vividly recall Dr. Lynn DeSilva, a Sinhalese Methodist minister, telling how as a young man he sought to convert Buddhist families. However, after visiting them and getting to know them, he was humbled to learn that their depth of spiritual awareness was greater than his own. Similarly, my own students in Hawaii who interviewed Muslim families began in fear of being harassed, but soon were amazed to learn that these Muslims were more humble, trustworthy, and sincere in their life than the students' own families. Education, dialogue, and understanding of others across racial and religious lines are crucial to remove false barriers that can lead to mistrust, fear, and hatred.

12.   It is a chilling experience to see how helpless the members of the United States Congress are when they discuss international economic treaties, such as G.A.T.T. II and N.A.F.T.A., since these political leaders have no power to change any of the regulations, only the choice of accepting the treaty terms. If they reject the treaties, the United States becomes excluded from the international economic partnerships crafted not by representatives elected by the people but by economic leaders.

13.   The decline of democracy because of the global economy is analyzed by Benjamin R. Barber, *Jihad vs. McWorld* (New York: Ballantine, 1996).

14.   Michael Renner, "Corporations Driving Globalization," in Lester Brown, Michael Renner, and Brian Halweil, *Vital Signs 1999* (New York: W.W. Norton, 1999), p. 136.

15.   Charles Gray, "Corporate Goliaths: Sizing Up Corporations and Governments," *Multinational Monitor* (June 1999), pp. 26–27.

16.   See the brilliant and timely work by David C. Korten, *When Corporations Rule the World* (San Francisco: Berrett-Koehler, 1995).

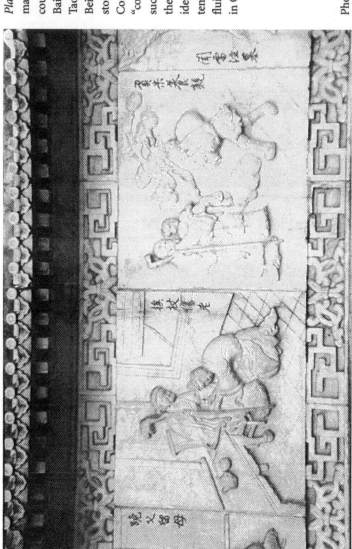

Plate 15 Panels of carved marble on a wall in the courtyard within the Baiyun (White Cloud) Taoist Temple complex in Beijing, China, illustrating stories that exemplify Confucian virtues of "concern consciousness" such as filial piety. To find these clearly Confucian ideals within a Taoist temple vividly shows the fluid boundaries of religion in China.

Photo: *Nancy M. Martin*

15

HUMAN RIGHTS *and* RESPONSIBILITIES: A CONFUCIAN PERSPECTIVE *on the* UNIVERSAL DECLARATION *of* HUMAN RIGHTS

John Berthrong

Recently there has been a heated debate as to whether or not the Confucian Way is compatible with, or even friendly toward, the modern quest for human rights as first defined in the 1948 United Nations Universal Declaration of Human Rights (U.D.H.R.). On the one side are those who hold that, however estimable the Confucian tradition might be in many ways, it was never and is not now capable of articulating anything like the codified rubrics enshrined in the various international human rights protocols promulgated by the U.N. beginning in 1948. On the other side are equally passionate scholars who maintain that the Confucian tradition is fully attuned to a positive appreciation of the modern international human rights project. The debate has become even more complicated by a new chorus of voices who now argue that the U.D.H.R. is a parochial document in the sense that it only incorporates a distinctive modern and Western view of human rights. This group of Asian scholars, public intellectuals, and governmental leaders has made a counter-proposal in terms of what they call "Asian values," as opposed to "Western values."

Attention to the current debate about the definition of human rights is in order to be clear about what exactly is being discussed in the passionate pro and con dispute about Confucian perspectives on human rights and whether or not there is a distinct realm of Asian values that somehow either contravenes or complements the U.D.H.R. and other protocols that represent the modern human rights regime. Some Asian critics make the claim that the language of the documents of the modern human rights regime are entirely derived from the intellectual, social, philosophic, and religious cultures of the Western world and do not represent anything like a global consensus on what a truly universal declaration of human rights would actually be, if indeed it could ever be written.

Nonetheless, many scholars counter that it is still possible to find analogies for human rights language, theory, and practice in other parts of the world, and in this case, specifically in East Asia. For instance, scholars of the Confucian tradition acknowledge that modern human rights language cannot be found in the cumulative Confucian tradition in China, Vietnam, Korea, and Japan. But the same scholars will vehemently go on to point out that if we look beyond the modern English usage and seek the spirit of what the U.D.H.R. seeks to enshrine, then a capacious Confucian affirmation, understanding, and promotion of human dignity has been a major preoccupation of those who took their stand in the *rujiao*, or the teaching of the Confucian Way from the inception of the classical tradition with Master Kong (Confucius) and his great disciple, Master Meng (Mencius).[1]

Nor is it accurate to say Confucian-influenced commissioners played no role in the original formulation of the U.D.H.R. in 1948. The Republic of China dispatched a delegation, including Professor Wu Te-yao, to participate in the process of drafting the original document. The Chinese delegation was both deeply steeped in the theory of Western international law and educated in Confucian history and philosophy. Professor Wu and others made a strong case for including the perspective of Confucian humanism in the language of the U.D.H.R. As Professor Tu Weiming describes the contribution of the Chinese delegation, "[Professor Wu] took part in an unprecedented effort to inscribe, not only on paper but on human conscience, the bold vision of a new world order rooted in respect for human dignity as the central value for political action."[2] From the time of Professor Wu to that of Professor Tu, Confucian-influenced public intellectuals have argued that the Confucian notion of human dignity can be translated effectively, and without significant distortion, into the modern language of the U.D.H.R.

Contemporary Confucian scholars point out that the opening paragraph of the preamble to the Declaration is redolent with Confucian-inspired sensibilities. The paragraph states emphatically, among other things, that there is an inherent dignity for all members of the human family that must undergird the firm foundation of "freedom, justice and peace in the world." The language of dignity for persons as constituent parts of a fiduciary community, from the biological family to the family of nations, resonates with centuries of the best of Confucian political theory. The third paragraph even restates the right of rebellion against tyranny found in the early writings of Mencius, the second of the classical Confucian masters. The right to rebel was no insignificant or overlooked item in the debate between Confucian scholars and the rulers of traditional Asia. Many a Chinese emperor and Japanese shogun sought to either expunge or explain away the clear meaning of Master Meng's defense of human dignity against an unjust tyrant. Generations of Confucian ministers, sometimes at great risk to their own lives and even the lives of their families, resolutely demanded that the passage about the ultimate right of rebellion against intolerable tyranny remain in the text as Mencius intended.

We must then ask, if this is a plausible interpretation of the co-affirmation of core Confucian traditional values *and* the fundamental spirit of the modern human rights regime, why is there such a contentious debate about the conflict between and among Asian and Western disputers concerning the "universal" values of human rights? Again, Tu Weiming summarizes the "core" values of the cumulative Confucian tradition as "the perception of the person as a center of relationships rather than simply as an isolated individual, the idea of society as a community of trust rather than merely a system of adversarial relationships, and the belief that human beings are duty-bound to respect their family, society, and nation."[3] The Confucian analysis of the modern human rights debate is that the problem with most post-Enlightenment Western theory and practice is not that it is wrong but rather that it is simply too narrow in its vision of the role human rights ought to play in human flourishing.

Confucian public intellectuals are often fond of reminding Western audiences of the three cardinal objectives of the French Revolution, namely liberty, equality, and fraternity. From the modern Confucian perspective, Western societies have been quite successful – and this success is a gift to the whole inhabited world from the Confucian perspective – in conceptualizing and sometimes institutionalizing the ideals of liberty and equality. The modern governments of the Euro-American world have enshrined the notions of liberty as positive freedom of the person and equality before the law beginning with the American constitution and bill of rights down to the emerging legal structures of a united Europe. The problem is that, from the Confucian perspective, the Euro-American world has not been equally successful in enculturating fraternity as an ideal for personal and social flourishing.

In regard to expanding the domain of the modern human rights regime, I remember very clearly a conversation with the late Professor Richard McKeon of the University of Chicago at a conference on Chinese philosophy in the early 1980s. Professor McKeon had been a member of the American delegation for the drafting of the U.D.H.R. I asked him – with the power that only hindsight gives after decades of further reflection – what he would have urged the drafting committee to do differently. Professor McKeon did not hesitate in his answer. First, he was proud of the work that was published in 1948. But second, especially based on his further study of Asian philosophies and cultures, he expressed the desire that the Declaration should have included a broader range of rights than what are now called the first generation of political and personal rights described in the 1948 Declaration (often also called civil-political rights).

Professor McKeon went on to explain that he accepted the view of many of his Asian colleagues that the Declaration, including further international conventions on human rights, must include what are called second- and third-generation human rights (often called socioeconomic and collective rights). The second generation should incorporate economic, social, and cultural rights for individuals. The third generation would add more specific rights for social, cultural, or national groups as collectives to the first two iterations of civil-political and socioeconomic rights, seeking a balance between individual and group rights.

Although prepared after Professor McKeon's death, the draft Earth Charter now before the U.N. expands the notion of group rights to include a respect for the natural order. The ecological crisis has caused thoughtful women and men to realize that the planet Earth itself needs a declaration of Earth rights to be articulated and acted upon if the human species is to remain a viable part of the planetary ecology.[4] Professor McKeon noted that Euro-American cultures already had provisions, such as laws for eminent domain for the construction of roads and such, that allowed the rights and needs of groups to trump the specific property rights of individuals.

The points that Professor McKeon made are precisely those articulated by thoughtful Confucian public intellectuals. If human rights are construed solely in terms of individual rights, and if the individual is only considered solely as a social atom without any meaningful connection to other human persons or societies, much less nature itself, then there is a real problem with such protocols from the Confucian perspective. Confucians hold that a person is not just an individual; the person is always a social animal co-constituted by a world far beyond the confines of her or his skin. This is one reason that the early Confucian texts put so much emphasis on the role of the family in the personal and cultural formation of the person and society. Of course Confucians knew that there were bad families; the early Chinese historical records are full of the tales of horribly dysfunctional and even murderous families and societies. The point was rather that, regardless of the actual condition of the natal family, a person grew and flourished within a complicated web of social connections that always began with the family, however empirically flawed the birth family might be.

It is precisely at the focal point of the Confucian emphasis on the root metaphor of the family as the matrix for social ethics that contemporary Confucians seek the fructification of the debate between proponents of personal rights and social duties within the human rights dialogue. From the Confucian perspective, there is simply no way to talk about human rights without also paying equal attention to human duties. As Professor William Theodore de Bary has insightfully written, what we need is a vision of human rights as expressions of rites that promote human flourishing.[5] De Bary's point is that Confucians have always placed human dignity within the broad context of the various rituals of human civility expressing a corporate aspiration for a harmonious and civilized human social world expanding from the family to the nation and now even to the whole natural order.

Confucian public intellectuals refuse to see these three generations of human rights in any kind of fundamental conflict. The debate about universal human rights should be a dialogue between and among the peoples and nations of the earth about what constitutes human flourishing, now including an ecological vision for the whole natural world. From the Confucian viewpoint, it is impossible to conceive of a civilized social order that does not respect human dignity as the foundation of social order. Confucian ritual as respect for human dignity can be transformed into protocols of human rights; ritual can become the basis for a genuine civility between and among persons, families, social groups, societies, nations, and – hopefully – the one natural world all human beings share.

The real task for the Confucian public intellectual is to engage in dialogue with partners from around the world to see what a true expression of human flourishing means for the new millennium. From the Confucian perspective, just as some rituals are particular to a specific family but provide a basis for civilized life together in community, a renewed notion of ritual as comprehensive human civility will encourage genuine dialogue to flourish between and among the nations of the world, articulating what a truly ecumenical vision of human rights must include for the promotion of a new world order of justice and harmony.

TOWARD A DECLARATION OF HUMAN RIGHTS BY THE WORLD'S RELIGIONS

One of the key features of any Confucian approach to the ethics of human rights is embodied in the notion of reciprocity. Confucians believe that reciprocity between and among persons is the pivot that holds rights and obligations together. We have rights because we have obligations, and vice versa. We are persons because we live in community, beginning with our families of origin but expanding in concentric circles out to the widest horizons of the human social order and now to the fragile ecology of the entire planet.

This Confucian sense of the poise between rights and obligations is often thematized as the balance of the sage within and the king without. The world's religions have a special role to play in this balance of sage and king representing the noble ideals of the diverse spiritual dimensions of human insight and the need for effective and humane governance. Religions have, among other things, always been the schools of humanity. It is a prime role of a school to teach, and, according to the Confucian tradition, to teach the cultivation of and respect for the humanity of the other person.

Mou Zongsan (1909–1995), one of the greatest of modern Chinese Confucian thinkers, argued that every religion has two main teaching tasks. The first focus is to direct our mind-hearts toward the ultimate reality, the vision of the *summum bonum* of the tradition. This is the vertical dimension of ultimate concern, what Mou called a concern-consciousness for humanity. The second defining characteristic of the religious dimension of any great wisdom tradition is to provide a set of ethical guidelines and instructions for its members. These axioms and maxims are crucial for the formation of civilized communities even if the specific ethical guidelines and rubrics are the manifestations of human cultures circumscribed by historical conditions. No religion has done its duty until and unless it has explained what it means to be a sage within and a king without.

From a Confucian viewpoint, one of the teaching obligations for each of the world's religions is to reflect on what human rights means for the new global city of the twenty-first century. Moreover, any reflective citizen of the twenty-first century knows that any serious discussion of human rights must be truly ecumenical in scope. There is a reciprocal obligation for the world's religions to help define and refine what the religious dimension of the emerging human rights regimes must include. Confucians must share with other religious persons in seeking to incorporate the most humane religious insights into the framework of international human rights protocols and treaties.

The debates around what should be included in any truly universal declaration of human rights is the kind of conversation Confucians have joined for thousands of years. Confucians do not expect some kind of simplistic harmony or easy agreement, but the discussion must go on. Without such attempts as the draft Declaration of Human Rights by the World's Religions, the conversation cannot be promoted and sustained. Only such conversation can generate the unity of the sage within and the king without, which is as necessary these days as it was in the time of Confucius and his first great disciples.

NOTES

1. For a sample of contemporary scholarship in this and related issues, see Michael C. Davis, *Human Rights and Chinese Values: Legal, Philosophical, and Political Perspectives* (Oxford: Oxford University Press, 1995); and, *The East Asian Challenge for Human Rights*, ed. Joanne R. Bauer and Daniel A. Bell (Cambridge: Cambridge University Press, 1999). For an interpretation of modern Japan, see T.R. Reid, *Confucius Lives Next Door: What Living in the East Teaches us Living in the West* (New York: Random House, 1999).

2. *Confucianism and Human Rights*, ed. W. Theodore de Bary and Tu Weiming (New York: Columbia University Press, 1998), p. 298.

3. Ibid., p. 299.

4. For Confucian perspectives on ecology, see *Confucianism and Ecology: The Interrelationship of Heaven, Earth, and Humans*, ed. Mary Evelyn Tucker and John Berthrong (Cambridge, MA: Harvard University Press, 1998).

5. See especially W. Theodore de Bary, *The Liberal Tradition in China* (New York: Columbia University Press, 1983).

Part IV

RIGHTS AND RELIGIOUS TRADITIONS

Plate 16 Stained-glass window in Lincoln Cathedral, England (built between the eleventh and sixteenth centuries), illustrating the giving of the Ten Commandments through Moses to the Hebrews. This tradition of divine commands is central to the Jewish, Christian, and Islamic understanding of the basis of morality. Photo: *Joseph Runzo*

16

A JEWISH PERSPECTIVE *on* HUMAN RIGHTS

Elliot N. Dorff

The expression "human rights" involves a double assumption: first, that we can speak intelligibly of a universal humanity, without regard to subcategories such as race, creed, nationality, sex, or social rank; and, second, that specific entitlements accrue to anyone who belongs to the community of humanity. Where membership in any of the subcategories I just listed entails lesser rights, we must either conclude that the person in some sense is less than human, or that the full rights spoken of may not be characterized as rights qua human. It is this stark logic that makes the call for human rights in the face of discrimination so powerful, for we are not willing to accept either conclusion. Denying human rights to any group calls into question the claim to human rights of any other group and, ultimately, of humanity as a whole. Nothing less than the status and dignity of human beings as a species is thus at stake.

At the same time, what people do does affect their claim on human rights. So, for example, the "self-evident" rights that Jefferson listed in the Declaration of Independence include both life and liberty, and yet we routinely take away liberty and sometimes even life from those convicted of crimes. We also intentionally kill people in war. In doing so, we are not saying that criminals and soldiers are less than human, for we insist that prisoners of war and criminals retain some rights. We are rather acknowledging that these "human rights" of life and liberty are "human" in that they apply to all human beings, regardless of subcategories of status, but not regardless of the actions they commit. Thus, as much as we may honor those who go to war to defend our country or even the rights of others, such as the ethnic Albanians in Kosovo, we must simultaneously recognize that both in fact and in theory they put their lives in jeopardy by doing so, that neither American nor Serb soldiers can claim that a universal human right to life has been violated if they die in the conflict.[1]

Human rights can be, and have been, defended by humanists, secularists, utilitarians, and pragmatists without any appeal to theological or metaphysical presuppositions. And yet, as the Universal Declaration of Human Rights by the World's Religions maintains, religious reasons for asserting human rights can and should be invoked as well. Since so much is at stake in establishing the authority of human rights, and since large numbers of the world's peoples derive meaning from their religious convictions, grounding human rights in religion makes great sense on practical grounds alone.

There is also, though, a theoretical reason to establish the moral mooring of human rights in religion. The word "religion" comes from the same Latin root from which we get the word "ligament." That root means ties, links, or bonds. Religions, by their very nature, describe the linkages we have to each other as members of a family, a community, and a species, and they also describe our ties to the environment and to the transcendent. The various religions of the world present different pictures of the way the world is and ought to be, and each religion's moral code is rooted in its vision of how we are and how we ought to be. Secular philosophies also present such visions, but the world's major religions have the advantages of the rootedness of long traditions and the availability of rituals, myths, and sacred texts to remind people constantly of their vision and of their commitment to make it real. Thus in looking at how religions can ground human rights, we are asking both how their theoretical convictions justify human rights and how their specific moral demands help to make human rights a reality in people's lives.

THEORETICAL GROUNDS FOR HUMAN RIGHTS IN JUDAISM

One of Judaism's fundamental theoretical convictions is that God both created the world and owns it.[2] This immediately establishes a ground for moral claims completely different from secular alternatives. The whole drama of life, from the point of view of Judaism, is not played out on the stage of individuals with inherent, inalienable rights; it is rather played on the stage of both positive and negative duties to God. So, for example, the right to life is not phrased as such in the Torah; rather, as God told Noah in the early chapters of Genesis, God forbids both suicide and murder and will punish those who engage in either: "For your own life-blood I will require a reckoning: ...of man, too, will I require a reckoning for human life, of every man for that of his fellow man! Whoever sheds the blood of man, by man shall his blood be shed; for in His image did God make man" (Gen. 9:5–6).

This last doctrine, that God created humanity in the divine image, is a second foundation for the Jewish view of human rights. The most obvious ramification of that tenet, the one just quoted, is that murder is to be banned, for it diminishes the instances of God's image in the world. Even murderers, though, are created in the divine image, as are others guilty of a capital offense. The Torah therefore prescribes that after we execute such people for their crimes, we must honor the divinity of their bodies (and the holiness of the land of Israel) by burying them quickly:

> If a man is guilty of a capital offense and is put to death, and you impale him on a stake, you must not let his corpse remain on the stake overnight, but must bury him the same day. For an impaled body is an affront to God; you shall not defile the land that the Lord your God is giving you to possess. (Deut. 21:22–23)

Exactly which feature of the human being reflects this divine image is a matter of debate within the tradition. The Torah itself seems to tie it to humanity's ability to make moral judgments – that is, to distinguish good from bad and right from wrong, to behave accordingly, and to judge one's own actions and those of others on the basis of this moral knowledge.[3] Another human faculty connected by the Torah and by the later tradition to divinity is the ability to speak.[4] Maimonides claims that the divine image resides in our capacity to think, especially discursively.[5] Locating the divine image within us may also be the Torah's way of acknowledging that we can love, just as God does,[6] or that we are at least partially spiritual and thus share God's spiritual nature.[7]

In the biblical account, humanity was not only created in the divine image; humanity was created, initially, in the form of one human being, Adam. In an oft-quoted passage in the Mishnah, the Rabbis, in describing how the judges in a capital case are to be warned, spell out several implications of God's creating first a single human being. Two of those ramifications add further to the worth of each individual.

First, killing one person is also killing all of his or her potential descendants – indeed, "an entire world." Conversely, someone who saves an individual "saves an entire world." That makes the murder of any one individual all the more serious – and, conversely, saving a human life all the more praiseworthy. It also ascribes value to each of us as the possible pro-genitor of future generations.

Second, when people use a mold to create coins, the image on each coin is exactly the same. God, however, used the first form of Adam to create every other human being as a unique individual. In accordance with the laws of supply and demand, a one-of-a-kind thing demands a far higher price than something that is plentiful on the market. Think, for example, of the comparative value of a Picasso original, each of a few hundred prints of that work, and, finally, a photograph of that work; the more unique the product, the greater its value. Thus the fact that each of us is unique imparts to each of us immense value.

> How were witnesses [in capital cases] inspired with awe?...[The judges told them this:] Know that capital cases are not like monetary cases. In civil suits, one can make restitution [for false testimony] and thereby effect atonement, but in capital cases the false witness is held responsible for the accused's blood and the blood of his [potential] descendants until the end of time. For thus we find in the case of Cain, who killed his brother, that it is written, "The bloods of your brother cry out to Me" [Genesis 6:10] – not [just] the blood of your brother, but the bloods of your brother, i.e., his blood and the blood of his [potential] descendants...For this reason was man created alone: to teach you that with regard to anyone who destroys a single soul [of Israel], Scripture imputes guilt to him as though he had destroyed a complete world; and with regard to anyone who preserves a single soul [of Israel], Scripture ascribes merit to him as though he had pre-served a complete world. Furthermore, [man was created alone] for the sake of peace among men, that one might not say to his fellow, "My father was greater than yours." And [man was created alone] so that the sectarians might not say, "There are many powers in heaven." Additionally, [man was created alone] to proclaim the greatness of the Holy One, blessed be He: for if a man strikes many coins from one mold, they all resemble one another, but the Supreme King of kings, the Holy One, blessed be He, fashioned every person in the stamp of the first person, and yet not one of them looks the same as anyone else. Therefore every single person is obligated to say: "The world was created for my sake." (Sanh. 4:5)

Thinking that the world was created for your sake can, of course, produce more than a little arrogance. The following, lovely Hasidic saying intro-duces an appropriate balance: "A person should always carry two pieces of paper in his/her pockets. On one should be written, 'For me the world was created,' and on the other, 'I am but dust and ashes'" (quoting Genesis 18: 27).[8] Still, the Mishnah, like the other sources we have reviewed, expresses the immense worth that each individual has due to the specific way in which the Torah describes God's creation of human beings.

The Rabbis, like the Torah before them, invoke the doctrines that God created human beings in the divine image and uniquely not only to describe aspects of our nature, but also to prescribe behavior. Specifically, the Rabbis maintain that because human beings are created in God's image, we affront God when we insult another person.[9] Conversely, "one who welcomes his friend is as if he welcomes the face of the Divine Presence" (jEruv. 5:1).[10] Moreover, when we see someone with a disability, we are to utter this blessing: "Praised are you, Lord our God, *meshaneh ha-briyyot*, who makes different creatures," or "who created us different." Precisely when we might recoil from a deformed or incapacitated person, or thank God for not making us like that, the tradition instead bids us to embrace the divine image in such people – indeed, to bless God for creating some of us so.[11] Those who suffer from a disability have a right to be angry with God and even to argue with God, as Jews have done from the time that Abraham questioned God's justice in his plans for Sodom and Gomorrah,[12] but the rest of us must look beyond the disability and see the person for the image of God embedded in him or her. Finally, the non-utilitarian basis of the Rabbis' assertion of human worth is graphically illustrated in their ruling that no one person can be sacrificed to save even an entire city unless that person is named by the enemy or guilty of a capital crime:

> Caravans of men are walking down a road, and they are accosted by non-Jews who say to them: "Give us one from among you that we may kill him; otherwise we shall kill you all." Though all may be killed, they may not hand over a single soul of Israel. However, if the demand is for a specified individual like Sheva, son of Bikhri [who, according to the biblical story in II Samuel 20, was also subject to the death penalty], they should surrender him rather than all be killed. (jTer. 7:20; Genesis Rabbah 94:9)[13]

Thus the doctrine that each person is created in the divine image, with its corollaries that each person is unique and that each person can legitimately say, "For me the world was created," constitute firm foundations for claims of human rights.

One other aspect of the Jewish conception of the individual is important for our understanding of the Jewish approach to human rights. Our duties to one another are rooted not only in God's creation of us in the divine image and as unique individuals, but also in God's covenant with us. God made a covenant with the Jewish people at Mount Sinai consisting of 613 commandments, and many of the Torah's laws guaranteeing specific human rights are included in that list and their expansion at the hands of the Rabbis. We are to cherish human rights, then, as part of our duties to God under our covenant with him and as one way to worship him.

For three reasons, though, the covenant between God and Israel does not mean that Judaism restricts human rights to fellow Jews. First, the Jewish covenant was to be a model for all other nations, as God makes clear in the first mention of it to Abraham: "Abraham is to become a great and populous nation and all the nations of the earth are to bless themselves by him. For I have singled him out, that he may instruct his children and his posterity to keep the way of the Lord by doing what is right and good" (Gen. 18:18–19). Similarly, Isaiah later was to depict Israel as "a light unto the nations" (Isa. 49:6).[14] Thus the Jewish covenant was to serve as model of how all peoples, Jews certainly included, were to treat each other.[15]

Second, the Rabbis maintain that God made another covenant with all children of Noah, consisting of six prohibitions and one positive command – to wit, the interdictions of murder, incest/adultery, idolatry, tearing a limb from a living animal, blasphemy, and theft, and the positive command to establish a system of justice.[16] Thus Jews have never been missionary, for according to Jewish theology non-Jews do all that God expects of them by abiding by the Noahide covenant. This non-missionary stance, rooted in the doctrine of the Noahide covenant, is an important foundation for respecting the convictions and rights of others.

Finally, while Jews could only reasonably be expected to fulfill all the 613 commandments toward those fellow Jews who took upon themselves a reciprocal burden, Jewish law specifies that Jews were to bear some of the responsibilities of the Jewish covenant, beyond those of the Noahide covenant, toward non-Jews. Thus according to talmudic law, Jews were to visit the sick among non-Jews, take care of their poor, and see to their burial if nobody else was available.[17] This was for the "sake of peace" and also, one would presume, as part of the modeling that Jews were to do.

Note, though, that both God's covenant of Mount Sinai with the children of Israel and God's covenant with all children of Noah speak of obligations, not rights. In many cases, my duty to you establishes a reciprocal right that you have toward me, but the mapping of duties onto rights is not completely congruent. I may have duties to God vis-à-vis you even though you do not have a legal right to expect something of me. So, as Jewish commentators note, Leviticus 19 specifies a number of duties to other people with mention of "I am the Lord" following the duty, thus indicating that we have these duties to others because God commands them even though they cannot be enforced by human courts. Such duties include our obligations to leave crops for the poor and to refrain from cursing the deaf, putting a stumbling block before the blind, or spreading gossip about someone else. Moreover, even if there were a complete one-to-one mapping of duties onto rights, my frame of mind is completely different if I begin by assuming that I have duties toward others rather than rights that I can demand from others; in the former, Jewish mode, I owe the world, while in the latter, American mode, the world owes me. Thus the Jewish framework for this discussion in terms of duties rather than rights must be translated into the Enlightenment paradigm of rights, and, like all translations, some important assumptions and nuances get lost in the process.

SPECIFIC DEMANDS TO UPHOLD HUMAN RIGHTS

We have already seen how the theoretical foundation for human rights within Judaism has immediate implications for action in such matters as protecting the lives of others, respecting others, including the indigent and disabled, and caring for others, including the poor and the sick. The Jewish tradition, though, does not rest with general pronouncements of theology or morality; it transforms those theoretical commitments into very specific demands through the instrument of Jewish law. As Mortimer Adler put it:

> The Pharisees took up the religion of the prophets and brought it to bear upon the lives of the people in a way and to an extent which the prophets had never been able to accomplish...Religion is not a matter of living on the "peaks" of experience. That is for the saint and the mystic. More fundamentally, religion must mean transposing to a higher level of spiritual awareness and ethical sensitivity the entire plateau of daily living by the generality of men...[18]

Therefore, when we are asked to describe Judaism's approach to human rights, it is critical to look at the ways in which Jewish law spelled out those rights in concrete, legal detail. Haim Cohn, formerly a justice of the Supreme Court of Israel, wrote a book entitled *Human Rights in Jewish Law*[19] in which he did just that. In a series of 26 chapters spanning 231 pages, he describes how Jewish law provides for a variety of human rights. I will not repeat his work here, but I will list the subjects of the chapters in order to provide an idea of just how extensive Jewish law is on these matters, and then I will investigate one of them at some length and in a different way than he did, namely, the right to privacy.

Cohn divides his book into three sections. Under the first, entitled "Rights of Life, Liberty, and the Pursuit of Happiness," he includes chapters on the rights to life, to liberty and security of person, to privacy, to reputation, to freedom of movement and residence, to asylum, to marriage and procreation, to property, to work and remuneration, to leisure, to freedom of thought, speech, and conscience, to freedom of information, and to education and participation in culture. He also discusses slaves and slavery under that heading. In the second section, entitled "Rights of Equality," the first chapter is entitled "All Men are Born Equal," and the remaining chapters discuss Jewish law's aversion to discrimination on account of race, religion, national origin, sex, and social and economic status – all the while providing for special duties and rights among the People Israel toward each other. In the third section, entitled "Rights of Justice," he includes chapters describing Jewish law's insistence on equality before the law, on judicial standards, and on procedural and legislative safeguards, as well as a chapter on Jewish law's prohibition of torture and cruel punishments.

As you can see simply from this list, the Jewish tradition took concrete steps to assure human rights in a wide variety of areas. In some cases – as, for example, in its treatment of women – classical Jewish law did not go as far in establishing egalitarianism as we moderns might like, but it went considerably farther than most other cultures of its time, and the modern Conservative and Reform movements in Judaism have gone much further toward becoming fully egalitarian.[20] In other areas, the Jewish tradition's demand for human rights antedated modern sensitivities by thousands of years. So, for example, the Torah states no less than thirty-six times in social, ritual, and judicial settings that the alien is to be treated as the citizen is, a standard that few societies achieve even today.[21] The Torah also prohibits holding parents responsible for their children or the reverse.[22] In England, it was not until 1830 that the possibility of attaint, under which descendants would suffer for their ancestors' treason, was abolished. Corruption of attaint and attaints or forfeitures that extend beyond the life of the criminal were banned by article 3, section 3 of the United States Constitution in 1789.

ONE EXAMPLE: THE RIGHT TO PRIVACY

To illustrate the interaction of how these theological and methodological underpinnings work in applying the Jewish tradition to modern contexts of human rights, we shall look at the issue of privacy. Contemporary computer technology and other communications techniques have seriously compromised our abilities to keep anything confidential in both our personal and professional lives. Businesses are increasingly called upon to see what they can do to restore at least some measure of privacy.

The Values and Concepts Inherent in Privacy

Why is privacy a concern at all? It is, putting it bluntly, because the right to privacy is at the core of human dignity. As one loses privacy, one loses individuality and respect – and one, in turn, trusts others less. Privacy also enables creativity to flourish, for it protects nonconformist people from interference by others.[23] In addition, privacy is a prerequisite for friendship, for the bond of friendship includes sharing feelings and vulnerabilities which one often does not want to reveal to others.[24] Moreover, privacy is a prerequisite for a free and tolerant society, for each person has secrets which "concern weaknesses that we dare not reveal to a competitive world, dreams that others may ridicule, past deeds that bear no relevance to present conduct or desires that a judgmental and hypocritical public may condemn."[25]

If these are moral concerns in a secular society, they are even more urgent in a religious tradition like Judaism, for it is not only the individual's welfare that must be protected, but God's. Since human beings, according to the Torah, are created in God's image, honoring them is a way to honor God, and, conversely, degrading them is tantamount to dishonoring God.[26] Moreover, God intends that the Israelites be "a kingdom of priests and a holy people,"[27] not just a nation which observes the minimal necessities of maintaining order and providing for basic needs. As the Torah specifies, to be a holy people requires, among other things, that a lender not intrude on a borrower's home to collect on a loan, and that nobody be a talebearer among the people.[28] Thus both intrusion and disclosure were forbidden so that a person's home, reputation, and communication were all protected as part of the effort to create a holy people.

In addition to this religious mission which mandates privacy, Jewish theology does as well. "You shall be holy, for I, the Lord your God, am holy"; "Walk in all His ways"; and "Follow the Lord your God."[29] The Rabbis understood these biblical verses as establishing the principle of *imitatio dei*, of modeling ourselves after God: "as God is gracious and compassionate, you too must be gracious and compassionate...; as the Holy One is righteous, you too must be righteous; as the Holy One is loving, you too must be loving."[30] But God, as understood in the Jewish tradition, is in part known and in part hidden; God is related to human beings through revelation and through divine acts in history, but no human being, not even Moses, can know God's essence.[31] Furthermore, the Mishnah declares that one who probes God's essence beyond what God has chosen to reveal to us should not have been born, for, as the Jerusalem Talmud explains, to know more about God than the Holy One chooses to reveal to us is an affront to his dignity.[32] If God is to be a model for us in this, then we too must preserve both our own privacy and that of others to enable us to be like God.[33]

Intrusion

In interpreting the biblical laws prohibiting intrusion, the Rabbis maintain that these laws bar not only physical trespass, but also visual penetration of a person's domain (*hezek re'iyah*). Thus they insist that two joint landowners contribute equally to erect a wall between their respective halves of the property to serve as a deterrent to visual intrusion, and they prohibit making a hole in the wall opposite the neighbor's window. They interpret Balaam's praise of the tents of the Israelites – "How fair are your tents, O Jacob, your dwelling places, O Israel" – as arising from his observation that the Israelite tents were so situated that the tent openings did not face each other.[34]

In the Middle Ages, when the mail system expanded, Rabbenu Gershom (Germany, c. 960–1028) issued a decree prohibiting mail carriers and others from reading other people's mail lest they learn trade secrets or spread gossip. According to the decree, violators would be subject to excommunication even if they did not publicize the improperly read letter. Privacy was thus recognized as an important value in its own right apart from its importance in protecting people from harm.[35]

Rabbi Norman Lamm, currently president of Yeshiva University in New York, has argued that, in modern circumstances, this can and should be applied not only to visual incursions, but to aural ones as well. He notes that Rabbi Menahem Meiri (France, 1249–1316) ruled that the biblical laws interdict visual surveillance alone, not because eavesdropping is any less heinous than spying as an invasion of privacy, but because people normally speak softly when they think they can be overheard and therefore the wall which Jewish law demands between neighbors needs to be high but not thick. That reasoning, though, clearly does not apply to wiretapping and other forms of electronic bugging, and so, for Rabbi Lamm, "all forms of surveillance – natural, mechanical, and electronic, visual and aural – are included in the Halakhah's [Jewish law's] strictures on *hezek re'iyah*."[36]

There are, though, several ways in which Jewish practices specifically promote intrusion.[37] So, for example, Jewish law demands that as many friends and family as possible attend a funeral, comfort the mourners in their home, and join them there in prayer for a full seven days after the burial. Similarly, friends and family are expected to celebrate the *brit milah* (ritual circumcision) of a newborn boy with his parents, even though that is surgery on his most private parts. Here social needs to express appropriate emotions and to articulate traditional Jewish understandings of a life cycle event, as well as the needs of the people themselves for communal support on such occasions, outweigh the needs for privacy.[38] These are exceptions, though, to the general rule that people were not allowed to spy on others and, in turn, people must value their own privacy enough to erect walls to protect it.

The practice common in some businesses today in which employers "spy" on their employees presents an interesting case for applying these Jewish principles. When an airline, for example, announces to callers that their call "may be monitored to assure better service," is that an illegitimate intrusion on either the employee or the caller? Is it legitimate for employers to download their employees' computer data or check an employee's telephone record in the office to see how much time the employee is spending on business and how much on personal matters or to evaluate the employee's efficiency and effectiveness for purposes of determining his or her future job status?

What must be balanced in these cases is the right of the employer to ensure that employees are doing their job well, as against the right of employees to privacy. It is clear that, according to Jewish sources, employees do not give up their rights to privacy just because they have entered the workplace. The sources do not even contemplate that possibility, in part because the sophisticated ways in which that can be done with contemporary technology did not exist until very recently. At the same time, employers historically certainly did have the right to supervise their employees and to determine their job status on the basis of performance.

In our own time, then, I personally would balance these conflicting principles by establishing clear guidelines to make the ground rules clear to everyone concerned. Specifically, if the employer intends to monitor employee performance through examining computer files and telephone communications, that policy must be announced to employees when they first apply for a job so that they know that that is part of the conditions of employment and can choose to accept or reject employment on those terms. Similarly, if the employer's policy is that no personal use may be made of the telephones or computers belonging to the business, that policy too must be disclosed at the time of employment. These policies must then be reiterated in periodic training sessions or bulletins. With that amount of fair warning, it seems to me that employers would have the right to supervise their employees electronically. Doing that may not be a wise way to build employee morale, but employers have the right to make that business judgment.

On the other hand, without such warning, employees have the right to assume that their computer and telephone records will remain private, even those within the employer's office. The right to privacy, in other words, is the default assumption in employment as well as in other arenas of life, an assumption which is rebuttable only when clear and complete warning is given ahead of time as to the conditions of using the machines belonging to the business. Without such prior specifications, repeated often so that there is no chance of misunderstanding, Jewish strictures prohibiting opening someone else's mail would apply to electronic communications as well, even within a business environment owned and operated by the employer.

Disclosure

The Rabbis also took steps to ensure privacy of communication. A judge was forbidden to reveal his vote lest the privacy of the other judges on the panel be compromised, and the Talmud records that a student was ejected from the house of study when he revealed that information a full twenty-two years after the trial![39] Private individuals were also enjoined to maintain confidentiality: according to the Talmud, a person may not reveal a private conversation, even if there is no harm intended or anticipated, unless the original speaker gives explicit permission to do so.[40]

The limits to the protections of privacy are, in part, what one would anticipate. Specifically, the claim to privacy was set aside when that was necessary to protect an individual, family, or group. So, for example, the Torah imposes a duty to testify in court when one knows of relevant facts, even though they may be incriminating.[41]

What is probably less expected is that Jewish law also insisted on breaking confidentiality when it would harm someone in non-judicial settings, based on the Torah's command, "Do not stand idly by the blood of your neighbor" (Lev. 19:16).[42] So, for example, Rabbi Israel Meir Ha-Kohen (Poland, 1838–1933), the "Hafetz Hayyim," asserts, based on that verse, that

A must warn B of potential problems in a business deal that B is contemplating with C if five conditions apply: (1) A must thoroughly examine the extent to which B will be harmed by the business deal; (2) A must not exaggerate the extent of the potential harm; (3) A must be motivated solely by the desire to protect B and not by dislike of C, let alone by A's own financial gain; (4) A can enable B to avoid the partnership without defaming C to B; and (5) A must only harm C to the extent of thwarting the partnership and must not tell B anything that will cause C to be publicly embarrassed.[43]

Individualistic and Communitarian Approaches to Privacy

Even with such exceptions, the Jewish tradition clearly understands and values privacy. How do stringent protections of an individual's privacy square with the tradition's focus on our communitarian ties? In what way, in other words, is this any different from what an Enlightenment ideology would produce?

The answers to both questions, I think, lie not so much in the content of the rules – which are, in the case of privacy, quite similar to those of Enlightenment societies – but in the motivation for creating the rules and for obeying them. Enlightenment ideology requires protections of privacy as part of society's duty to preserve individuals' rights; a Jewish approach requires protections of privacy because it is demanded by God as part of creating a holy community. God demands such protections, as stated above, to preserve the dignity of God's creatures created in the divine image and to enable people to be like God in being partially unknown. Each individual, in turn, should respect another person's privacy on the basis of Enlightenment ideology because each wants the same right, while, in Jewish terms, privacy must be respected because that is what God wants of us, as indicated by the laws to that effect in the Torah and in rabbinic interpretations throughout the ages.

I deliberately chose the example of privacy precisely to highlight the important role of these different motivations even when the content of the moral rules is similar. Even in the case of privacy, however, the content of the rules is affected by these differing ideological convictions. So, for example, the Torah's requirement that we not stand idly by the blood of our neighbor entails that, when writing a letter of recommendation for a job applicant, the writer has the duty to the potential employer to reveal the applicant's weaknesses as well as his/her strengths for the position, even though that compromises vulnerabilities which the applicant may prefer to keep hidden. In Enlightenment ideology, the duty to tell the whole truth to the potential employer does not clearly outweigh the applicant's right to privacy; indeed, after the Buckley Amendment and other legislation established the right of an applicant to read such letters of evaluation, people are wary of writing anything negative about a person lest they be sued.

Although I have not seen any specific rabbinic rulings on this, I would imagine, to take a second example, that Jewish law would be much more supportive of employers having the right to monitor the computers and telephones of their employees while at work because employers have the right to be assured that their employees are doing their job. The good of the business, which is a community of its own, would, I think, take precedence over individual rights to privacy when the invasion of privacy is clearly connected to job performance; it would not extend to surveillance cameras in rest rooms or the like.

Contemporary Implications

Still, for the reasons cited above, privacy is an important Jewish value, one which can only be superseded if a substantial burden of proof is sustained. In line with this, Rabbi Elie Spitz (Conservative) suggests that the Jewish tradition should impel Jews to lobby for the following four changes in American society and law:

1. Confidentiality as a value. Like Rabbenu Gershom's insistence that a letter's confidentiality must not be breached even if the mail carrier only reads it and does not publicize its contents, so too American law should not demand a showing of damages to enforce confidentiality. Instead, businesses should be permitted to gather from potential clients only that information which is directly relevant to the product or service they are providing and then only with the person's explicit consent, and the law should ban the sharing of information among businesses without the individual's explicit permission.

2. Duty to prevent temptation. Jewish law requires that owners of a divided common courtyard erect a wall so that they are not even tempted to invade each other's privacy. Similarly, argues Rabbi Spitz, American law should seek to limit the temptation to take data stored in computers. Some measures that he suggests are laws that permit data to be held no longer than is necessary for the purpose collected, allow data subjects to examine personal data files at a nominal fee, require businesses and government agencies promptly to correct any inaccuracies and permit the party to dispute any piece of the computer file and note

that disagreement within the file itself, and demand that the data be maintained in a reasonably secure manner so as to prevent access to the data by any unauthorized person using any device, such as a remote terminal or another computer system.[44]

3.   Considered restraint. The five preconditions of the Hafetz Hayyim on revealing confidential information – need, accuracy of the information, proper intent, lack of alternatives, and no unnecessary harm – are, according to Rabbi Spitz, appropriate measures to be built into American law. Thus "considered restraint in regard to personal data would allow transfer only if the data subject consented or public need overrode the privacy concern." Public need would include, for Rabbi Spitz, not only those occasions when the law compelled disclosure but also when the person had acted adversely to a business interest and it was necessary for the business to protect itself or, to give another instance, when the disclosure was limited, customary, and usual among businesses, was for the sole purpose of providing business or employment references, and when it avoided any unnecessary embarrassment of the data subject. Before turning information over to a third party, the business should notify the data subject, unless prohibited by law, release only the information legally requested, and, if possible, respond to a subpoena or legal process in a time frame which allows the person on whom the information is being sought legally to challenge the request.[45]

4.   Sanctions. Finally, just as Jewish law backed up its demands for preserving confidentiality with threats as severe as social ostracism, so too American law should provide for fines and/or damages when information was improperly gathered or shared or when businesses refused to correct information in a timely manner. These remedies should, suggests Rabbi Spitz, include attorney and court expenses and "restitutionary relief from the violator for the collection of any gain which resulted from the invasion of privacy."[46]

To Rabbi Spitz's suggestions concerning the law, I would add one comment. American practice is not only a matter of law and sanctions, as important as they are; it is also a function of what people learn to expect of each other and of themselves. Consequently, educators and religious and political leaders have an important role to play in restoring privacy to American life. This should be done, first, by teaching people to expect and respect reasonable bounds of privacy even within their own families, let alone in the public arena. The tie between privacy and dignity must be clearly explained so that citizens understand that this is not just a matter of freedom, but of the quality of life in our society. These lessons must be reiterated in churches and synagogues, where the specific religious significance which privacy entails within a given denomination's theology should be spelled out, repeated often, and employed in the religious institution's dealings with its members and with others. At the same time, as the Jewish materials indicate, privacy is not an absolute right; there are some limits to it which must be carefully delineated and justified in these non-legal settings as well as in legal ones. These are only some of the small, but important, steps, then, in which privacy can be retained and protected within our lives while still preserving the needs of the community to invade it for specified purposes and while still enjoying the immense gains in communication which modern technology affords us.

HUMAN RIGHTS AS DIVINE RIGHTS

The secular, Western approach to human rights arose specifically in opposition to the divine right of kings. Now everyone, regardless of social position, would inherit rights "from their Creator" that would be inalienable by any government. This, then, transforms the American Declaration of Independence from a selfish writ of rebellion by subjects who no longer want to pay taxes to a charter asserting the divinely bestowed rights of equality, life, liberty, and the pursuit of happiness for everyone.

The Jewish approach to human rights preserves these moral claims but roots them more firmly in God. God created each one of us in the divine image and uniquely, and so our very being demands to be respected. Moreover, God entered into a covenant with us, and so our rights and duties to each other are grounded in our promises to God. These aspects of the greater vision that a religion like Judaism provides links our claims to human rights to the fundamental nature of human beings and of God. As Joseph Hertz, in commenting on the Torah's verse, "Justice, justice shall you pursue" (Deut. 16:20), has said:

> These passionate words may be taken as the keynote of the humane legislation of the Torah, and of the demand for social righteousness by Israel's Prophets, Psalmists, and Sages. "Let justice roll down as the waters, and righteousness as a mighty stream," is the cry of Amos. Justice is not the only ethical quality in God or man, nor is it the highest quality; but it is the basis for all the others. "Righteousness and justice are the foundations of Thy throne," says the Psalmist: the whole idea of the Divine rests on them.[47]

NOTES

1.   I am not here taking account of pacifism, which may be offered variously as a principled objection to killing anyone or a strategy to minimize killing; in the former case, pacifists give up their own right to life for the sake of not violating the right to life of others, and in the latter, strategic, version of the doctrine, pacifists maintain that aggregate loss of life will be least if they, at least, refuse to go to war. The latter claim has yet to be proven empirically, and the former claim involves the questionable theoretical position that my own life should be sacrificed rather than kill an aggressor. In any case, my analysis here assumes the more commonly held position that we have a right to imprison criminals and to defend ourselves against aggressors.

2.   See, for example, Exodus 19:5; Deuteronomy 10:14; Psalms 24:1. See also Genesis 14:19, 22 (where the Hebrew word for "Creator" [*koneh*] also means "Possessor," and where "heaven and earth" is a merism for those and everything in between) and Psalms 104:24, where the same word is used with the same meaning. The following verses have the same theme, although not quite as explicitly or as expansively: Exodus 20:11; Leviticus 25:23, 42, 55; Deuteronomy 4:35, 39; 32:6.

3.   See Genesis 1:26–27; 3:1–7, 22–24.

4.   See Genesis 2:18–24; Numbers 12:1–16; Deuteronomy 22:13–19. Note also that *ha-middaber*, "the speaker," is a synonym for the human being (in comparison to animals) in medieval Jewish philosophy.

5.   Maimonides, *Guide for the Perplexed*, part I, chapter 1.

6.   See Deuteronomy 6:5; Leviticus 19:18, 33–34, and note that the traditional prayer book juxtaposes the paragraph just before the Shema, which speaks of God's love for us, with the first paragraph of the Shema, which commands us to love God. (The Shema is the fundamental Jewish statement of faith and commitment found in Deuteronomy 6:4–9, which begins "Hear O Israel: The Lord our God is one Lord: and you shall love the Lord your God with all your heart, and with all your soul, and with all your might" [verses 4–5, RSV].)

7.   Consider the prayer in the traditional, early morning weekday service, "*Elohai neshamah she-natata bi*," "My God, the soul (or life-breath) which you have imparted to me is pure. You created it, You formed it, You breathed it into me; You guard it within me...": Jules Harlow, *Siddur Sim Shalom* (New York: Rabbinical Assembly and United Synagogue of America, 1985), pp. 8–11. Similarly, the Rabbis describe the human being as part divine and part animal, the latter consisting of the material aspects of the human being and the former consisting of that which we share with God; see Sifre Deuteronomy, para. 306, 132a. Or consider this rabbinic statement in Genesis Rabbah 8:11: "In four respects man resembles the creatures above, and in four respects the creatures below. Like the

animals he eats and drinks, propagates his species, relieves himself, and dies. Like the ministering angels he stands erect, speaks, possesses intellect, and sees [in front of him and not on the side like an animal]."

8. Rabbi Bunam, cited in Martin Buber, *Tales of the Hasidim* (New York: Schocken, 1948), vol. 2, pp. 249–250.

9. Genesis Rabbah 24:7.

10. Barukh Halevi Epstein suggests that this is a scribal error, that because the previous aphorisms in this section of the Talmud refer to welcoming scholars, here too the Talmud meant to say that one who welcomes a scholar is like one who welcomes the Divine Presence: Barukh Halevi Epstein, *Torah Temimah* (Tel Aviv: Am Olam, 1969), p. 182 (on Exod. 18:12, note 19). He may well be right contextually, but the version that we have states an important, broader lesson that expresses the divine image in every person, regardless of their level of scholarship. Along the same lines, Shammai, who was not known for his friendliness and who in the immediately previous phrase warns us to "say little and do much," nevertheless admonishes, "Greet every person with a cheerful face" (Pirkei Avot [Ethics of the Fathers] 1:15), undoubtedly in recognition of the divine image in each of us.

11. For a thorough discussion of this blessing and concept in the Jewish tradition, see Carl Astor, "...*Who Makes People Different:" Jewish Perspectives on the Disabled* (New York: United Synagogue of America, 1985).

12. Genesis 18:25. For many other examples and a discussion of the implications of this approach, see Anson Laytner, *Arguing with God: A Jewish Tradition* (Northvale, NJ: Jason Aronson, 1990). This is, of course, the approach taken in the popular book by Harold Kushner, *When Bad Things Happen to Good People* (New York: Schocken, 1981).

13. Even when a person is named by the enemy and condemned to capital punishment, the Rabbis were not convinced that the people within the city should hand him or her over to the enemy (jTer. 47a):

> Ulla, son of Qoseb, was wanted by the [non-Jewish] government. He arose and fled to Rabbi Joshua ben Levi at Lydda. They [troops] came, surrounded the city, and said: "If you do not hand him over to us, we will destroy the city." Rabbi Joshua ben Levi went up to him, persuaded him to submit and gave him up [to them]. Now Elijah [the prophet], of blessed memory, had been in the habit of visiting him [Rabbi Joshua], but he [now] ceased visiting him. He [Rabbi Joshua] fasted several fasts and Elijah appeared and said to him: "Shall I reveal myself to informers [betrayers]?" He [Rabbi Joshua] said: "Have I not carried out a mishnah [a rabbinic ruling]?" Said he [Elijah]: "Is this a ruling for the pious (*mishnat hasidim*)?" [Another version: "This should have been done through others and not by yourself."]

For more on this, see Elliot N. Dorff, *Matters of Life and Death: A Jewish Approach to Modern Medical Ethics* (Philadelphia: Jewish Publication

Society, 1998), pp. 291–299. See also Elijah J. Schochet, *A Responsum of Surrender* (Los Angeles: University of Judaism, 1973).

14.   Cf. Isaiah 42:1–4; 51:4–5.

15.   While that was certainly the ideal, many of the commandments' demands were restricted to fellow Israelites, "your neighbor" (*ra'ekha*) or "your brother" (*a'hikha*), for only they took upon themselves in a reciprocal way the demands of all 613 commandments. Herbert Chanan Brichto provides an interesting analogy to this: "For a relevant analogy, consider how misleading it would be to censure as discriminatory a life-insurance company on the grounds that it does not extend death benefits to non-policyholders, or denies them to those in default of premium payments": Herbert Chanan Brichto, "The Hebrew Bible on Human Rights," in *Essays on Human Rights: Contemporary Issues and Jewish Perspectives*, ed. David Sidorsky (Philadelphia: Jewish Publication Society, 1979), p. 219.

16.   The doctrine of the Noahide covenant is first recorded in the Tosefta, a work commonly believed to have been edited late in the second century CE: see T. Av. Zar. 8:4. It is later recorded and discussed in the Talmud, at bSanh. 56b. For an extended discussion on this, see David Novak, *The Image of the Non-Jew in Judaism* (New York and Toronto: Edwin Mellen Press, 1983).

17.   BGit. 61a; M.T. Laws of Gifts to the Poor 7:7. According to bGit. 59b, obligations that are for the sake of peace, as this one is, have pentateuchal, and not just rabbinic, authority.

18.   Mortimer Adler, *The World of the Talmud* (New York: Schocken, 1958), pp. 61–65.

19.   Haim Cohn, *Human Rights in Jewish Law* (New York: Ktav, 1984).

20.   The Torah already recognizes the rights of women to food, clothing, and sex (Ex. 21:11), and it provides that in divorce the man must give the woman a writ so that she can have proof that she is eligible for remarriage (Deut. 24:1). The Rabbis went much further in this direction in using the wedding contract as the vehicle for guaranteeing the woman rights to health care, to ransom from captivity, to visit her parents, and to a number of other financial provisions. See Mishnah, Ket. 4:7–12. Moreover, the Rabbis applied all the tort laws of the Bible to both men and women equally, both as tortfeasors and as victims, on the basis of the fact that Numbers 5:6 speaks specifically of "a man or a woman": see Mekhilta on Exodus 21:18.

Modern women often see the early morning blessings in the daily liturgy as a stark reminder that women are unequal in Judaism, for the man says "Blessed are you, Lord, Sovereign of the universe, who has not made me a woman." While that blessing certainly does differentiate between men and women, it does so not on the basis that women are inferior to men, but that they have fewer obligations under Jewish law than men do. That becomes clear when one considers the context of that blessing. First the man blesses God for not making him a non-Jew, for non-Jews are only responsible for the seven commandments of the Noahide covenant; then he thanks God for not making him a slave, for slaves can only be held accountable for the 365 negative commandments, given that their master determines whether or not they can fulfill the 248 positive commandments; and finally he thanks God for not making him a woman, for women are exempt from approximately twenty of the 613 commandments. The series of blessings, then, expresses the man's joy at being obligated by the full complement of the Torah's laws, given that the Torah is seen not so much as a burden as a gift of love on God's part. To avoid misunderstandings, though, the Conservative movement in 1945 changed all three blessings to the positive: "Blessed are You, Lord our God, who has made me a Jew, ... who has made me free, ... who has made me in His image." See Morris Silverman, *Sabbath and Festival Prayerbook* (New York: Rabbinical Assembly of America and United Synagogue of America, 1945), p. 45; Harlow, *Siddur Sim Shalom* p. 11. More than 80 percent of Conservative synagogues, and 100 percent of Reform synagogues, are now fully egalitarian in their ritual practices, a development in part influenced by modern feminism but in part the product of the internal development within Judaism to equalize the position of women.

21. The count of thirty-six appears in bBM 59b. Some examples: Exodus 22:20; 23:9, 12; Leviticus 17:12, 13, 15; 19:33–34; Deuteronomy 24:17–18; etc.

22. Deuteronomy 24:16.

23. Ruth Gavison, "Privacy and the Limits of the Law," *Yale Law Journal,* 89 (1980), pp. 421, 447.

24. Charles Fried, "Privacy," *Yale Law Journal,* 77 (1983), p. 475.

25. David L. Bazelon, "Probing Privacy," *Gonzaga Law Review,* 12 (1977), pp. 587, 589. See also E. Shils, *The Torment of Secrecy* (Carbondale: Southern Illinois University Press, 1956), pp. 22–24; Martin Bulmer, *Censuses, Surveys and Privacy* (London: Macmillan, 1979); and P. Westin and F. Allan, *Privacy and Freedom* (New York: Atheneum, 1967).

     These sources and those cited in the previous two notes are suggested in Elie Spitz, *Jewish and American Law on the Cutting Edge of Privacy: Computers in the Business Sector* (Los Angeles: University of Judaism, 1986), p. 1. Moreover, much of the material included in my exposition of the Jewish sources was collected by Rabbi Spitz in that article, and I am indebted to him for his thorough and insightful work. I shall cite some of his own conclusions based on this material anon.

26. Mekhilta, "Yitro," on Exodus 20:23 (*Mekhilta'* de Rabi Yishma'el, 2nd edn, eds. Saul Horovitz and I. A. Rabin [Jerusalem: Bamberger & Wahrman, 1960], p. 245); Sifra, "Kedoshim," on Leviticus 19:18 (also in jNed. 9:4 and Genesis Rabbah 24:7); Deuteronomy Rabbah 4:4.

27. Exodus 19:6.

28. Deuteronomy 24:10–13; Leviticus 19:16.

29. Leviticus 19:2; Deuteronomy 11:22, 13:5; Sifre Deuteronomy, "Ekev"; see also Mekhilta, "Beshalah" 3; bShab. 133b; bSot. 14a.

30. Sifre Deuteronomy, "Ekev"; see also Mekhilta, "Beshalah" 3; bShab. 133b; bSot. 14a.

31. Exodus 3:6; 33:20–23. See also Deuteronomy 29:28, according to which "secret matters belong to the Lord our God, while revealed matters are for us and for our children forever to carry out the words of this Torah." Similarly, in the visions of the heavenly chariot in Isaiah (chap. 6) and Ezekiel (chap. 1), both prophets can only see God's attendants and not God himself. M. Hag. 2:1; jHag. 2:1 (8b).

32. M. Hag. 2:1; jHag. 2:1 (8b).

33. Norman Lamm makes this point; see, "The Fourth Amendment and its Equivalent in the Halacha," *Judaism* 16, 4 (Fall 1967), pp. 300–312; reprinted as "Privacy in Law and Theology," in his *Faith and Doubt: Studies in Traditional Jewish Thought* (New York: Ktav, 1971), pp. 290–309, esp. pp. 302–303.

34. Numbers 24:5; bBB 60a; see also 2b, 3a. M.T. Laws of Neighbors 2:14. The legal requirements mentioned were enforced through monetary fines and, if necessary, excommunication; see Nahum Rakover, *The Protection of Individual Modesty* (Jerusalem: Attorney General's Office), pp. 7, 8 (Hebrew). See also "Hezek Re'iya," Encyclopedia Talmudit 8:559–602 (Hebrew); and Lamm, "Privacy in Law and Theology," pp. 294–295.

35. Louis Finkelstein, *Jewish Self-Government in the Middle Ages* (New York: Jewish Theological Seminary of America, 1924), pp. 31, 171ff., 178, 189. "Herem d'Rabbenu Gershom," *Encyclopedia Talmudit*, 7:153, footnotes 877–904 (Hebrew), cites Ashkenazic and Sephardic codes and responses which adopted and extended Rabbenu Gershom's mail decree.

    Jewish communities also sought to ensure confidentiality in the collection of taxes. Some demanded that the collectors be sequestered while working. The Frankfurt Jewish tax collectors refused to reveal entries in their books even to their superiors, the city treasurers, and the Hamburg community imposed severe fines for breaches of confidence. See Salo W. Baron, *The Jewish Community* (Philadelphia: Jewish Publication Society, 1942), vol. 2, p. 281.

36. Lamm, "Privacy in Law and Theology," p. 295. The comment of Rabbi Menahem Meiri is in his *Bet Ha-behirah* (Bava Batra), ed. Avraham Sofer (Jerusalem: Kedem, 1972), p. 6.

37. Gladys Sturman has written a humorous spoof of these invasions of privacy mandated by Jewish practice; see her "Privacy, Clearly a Goyish Invention," *Sh'ma* (Purim ed.) 22/430 (March 20, 1992), p. 73. There are, of course, many truths revealed in humor.

38. Sturman (see ibid.) points out another common Jewish practice which is, frankly, harder to justify. When a woman goes to the *mikveh* (ritual pool)

to become ritually cleansed after her menstrual flow so that she and her husband can resume conjugal relations, she is often witnessed by other such women and greeted with good wishes of fertility. With regard to a wedding, though, the Rabbis specifically point out that everyone knows that the bride and groom are getting married, at least in part, in order to be allowed to engage in sexual relations, but the wedding guests are forbidden to mention that out of respect for their privacy and dignity. See bShab. 33a; M. Sanh. 3:7; bSanh. 31a.

39. M. Sanh. 3:7; bSanh. 31a.

40. BYoma 4b. According to Magen Avraham (S.A. Orah Hayyim 156:2), even if the party revealed the matter publicly, the listener is still bound by an implied confidence until expressly released. Likewise Hafetz Hayyim 10:6; Leviticus 5:1. See also bBK 56a; Gordon Tucker, "The Confidentiality Rule: A Philosophical Perspective with Reference to Jewish Law and Ethics," *Fordham University Law Journal*, 13 (1984), pp. 99, 105; and A. Cohen, *Everyman's Talmud* (New York: Schocken, 1949), p. 307.

41. Leviticus 5:1. See also bBK 56a; Tucker, "The Confidentiality Rule"; and Cohen, *Everyman's Talmud*, p. 307.

42. The Rabbis' interpretation (in the Sifra on that verse and in Targum Pseudo-Jonathan there) was: "Do not stand idly by when your neighbor's blood is shed. If you see someone in danger of drowning or being attacked by robbers or by a wild beast, you are obligated to rescue that person."

43. Zelig Pliskin, *Guard your Tongue* (based on the Hafetz Hayyim) (Jerusalem: Aish Ha-Torah, 1975), p. 164; see also Alfred S. Cohen, "Privacy and Jewish Perspective," *The Journal of Halacha and Contemporary Society* 1 (1981), pp. 74–78.

44. Spitz, *Jewish and American Law*, p. 12.

45. Ibid., pp. 12–13.

46. Ibid., p. 13.

47. Joseph H. Hertz, *Pentateuch and Haftorahs*, 2nd ed. (London: Soncino Press, 1936, 1960), pp. 820–821. The verse from Amos that he quotes is Amos 5:24. The verse from Psalms that he quotes is Psalms 89:15.

Plate 17 A human rights display, located in one of the bays of Wells Cathedral, England, where Christians have worshiped since the twelfth century. The burning candle encircled by barbed wire – a trademark of Amnesty International – invokes hope for a future of freedom, and the poster behind enjoins first world countries – in this case Britain – to rescind the crushing foreign debt of the world's poorest countries, invoking the biblical precedent of the Jubilee year. Photo: *Joseph Runzo*

17

CHRISTIAN ETHICS *and* HUMAN RIGHTS

Philip Quinn

City of God is a book about religion, among other things, in a time of social strife and threatened cultural chaos. It concerns a quest for authentic spirituality in a troubled century. In this fine new novel by E.L. Doctorow, set at the end of the twentieth century, one of the characters, Sarah Blumenthal, who is a rabbi, addresses the Conference of American Studies in Religion. In her talk, Sarah says:

> Constitutional scholars are accustomed to speak of the American civil religion. But perhaps two hundred or so years ago something happened, in terms not of national history but of human history, that has yet to be realized. To understand what that is may be the task of the moment for our theologians. But it involves the expansion of ethical obligation democratically to be directed all three hundred and sixty degrees around, not just upon one's co-religionists, a daily indiscriminate and matter-of-fact reverence of human rights unself-conscious as a handshake. Dare we hope the theologians might emancipate themselves, so as to articulate or perceive another possibility for us in our quest for the sacred? Not just a new chapter but a new story.[1]

I think it is not wholly fanciful to suppose that the new occurrence in human history of some two hundred years ago was the dawning of an era of universal human rights. They have, of course, not yet been fully realized everywhere. Reverence for them has not yet become a daily indiscriminate and matter-of-fact affair, unselfconscious as a handshake. And it may well be that religious communities, and not merely the theologians of those that have them, have a special responsibility to weave human rights deeply into the fabric of their narratives of quests for the sacred, even if doing so does not require telling an entirely new story. But why should this enterprise be problematic for any of the world religions?

In a special issue of the *Journal of Religious Ethics* commemorating the fiftieth anniversary of the Universal Declaration of Human Rights, Louis Henkin proposes an answer to this question. Henkin has been concerned with human rights in the course of a distinguished career in the academy and government service, and so he speaks on this topic with a voice that deserves our attention. In the first part of this chapter, I summarize his rather negative assessment of the relations between religions and the human rights movement. I then narrow my focus to Christianity. In the second part, I present what I take to be the strongest objection to endeavoring to weave human rights into the fabric of Christian ethical theory, and I go on to argue that it yields no insurmountable obstacle to supporting human rights, in most cases, from within a Christian ethical perspective.

HENKIN'S INDICTMENT AND CHALLENGE

According Henkin, religious apologists sometimes make their task too easy when they speak in an essentialist way of religion and then write off the practices of actual religions as aberrations. So he insists that we keep firmly in mind the plurality of religions and of smaller religious groups. When we do, he thinks we will see that "every religion at some time, in some respect, has had to answer to the human rights idea for human rights violations, many of them unspeakable."[2] From the point of view of the human rights movement, in other words, religions have a bad historical track record. Nor is this a mere coincidence; it springs from differences in worldview between the human rights movement and the religions. Religions typically try to ground their moralities in a vision of cosmic order while the human rights movement appeals at the most fundamental level only to a freestanding secular conception of human dignity, a conception perhaps derived from Kant's idea of the humanity in each of us that the categorical imperative requires us to treat always as an end in itself and never as a mere means. As Henkin sees it, "human rights discourse has rooted itself entirely in human dignity and finds its complete justification in that idea."[3] The result is that, to the extent that religions incorporate into their ethical thought an idea of human dignity, their conception of it is not fully congruent with the conception endorsed by the human rights movement.

Henkin gives four examples to illustrate the lack of congruence. First, the human rights movement considers freedom of conscience and religious choice to be a human right. Religions have in the past condemned idolatry and killed idolaters, and even today many of them condemn apostasy and resist the proselytizing of their adherents by others. Second, for the human rights movement, human dignity requires equality and non-discrimination, including non-discrimination on religious grounds. In contrast, religions have accepted discrimination on religious grounds, and even mandated it when it was feasible to do so, distinguishing invidiously between the faithful and the infidel. Third, the human rights movement insists that many gender distinctions are unacceptable because they are inconsistent with human dignity today. Yet some religions continue to hold that men and, even more so, women must find their human dignity within a system of such distinctions. And fourth, the human rights movement aims at the abolition of capital punishment, seeing it as derogation from the human dignity of both its victims and the other members of a society in which it is practiced. But some religions continue to endorse retributive accounts of criminal justice that underwrite the practice of capital punishment.

Henkin thinks of religions as in competition with the human rights movement and as a source of resistance to the idea of human rights. He claims that religions "have not always welcomed the human rights idea, or recognized its kinship, or sought its cooperation."[4] As an example, he cites the biblical injunction to love one's neighbor. The Bible, he tells us, "mandates a duty upon me to love my neighbor; but it does not present my neighbor as having a right to be loved by me; he/she, one might say, is only a third-party beneficiary of my duty to God."[5] What is more, the human rights movement's insistence on secular foundations makes many religious people uncomfortable. In a religiously pluralistic world, this is the only feasible strategy for a movement whose aspiration is to gain universal acceptance for human rights and get them entrenched in a common morality for all humankind. But it is a strategy that worries those who yearn to anchor morality in a cosmic order. And so, as Henkin notes, "spokesmen for religion have declared secular foundations for human rights to be weak, unstable, and doomed to fail and pass away. Some religions resist what they see as the concentration on, indeed the apotheosis of, the individual and the exaltation of individual autonomy and freedom."[6]

Henkin's argument up to this point has been a severe indictment of religions. He concludes it with an expression of modest hope and a ringing challenge. Religions today, he observes, are aware of the degree to which their own interests would be served if a right to religious freedom were generally acknowledged. They "have begun to welcome, and claim, human dignity as a religious principle implicit in teachings concerning the *imago dei*, the fatherhood of God, the responsibility for the neighbor."[7] Some of them are in the process of trying "to assure that religions, polities, societies, communities, all respect and ensure our common morality."[8]

But the record remains decidedly mixed. After the Cold War ended, churches became more powerful in some formerly repressive countries. However, they "rarely cooperate with human rights organizations in support of the human rights of their own country's population, not even in support of the specifically religious rights of other religious bodies and their adherents."[9] In various parts of the world, fundamentalist religious movements that view human rights with contempt abound and grow alarmingly. In the United States, there continues to be no sustained cooperation between the world of religion and the human rights movement. Understandably, the "human rights bodies still tend to see religions as sensitive and alert only to threats to their own denomination, their own believers and institutional arrangements – or, at most, to threats to the religious rights of others, but not to other rights, to freedom of expression, or to political dissidence."[10]

Yet there is, Henkin believes, cause for hope. It is that religions and the human rights movement share some common ground, a commitment to a core of common morality, that could provide the basis for a common agenda for action. He claims that "there is now a working consensus that every man and woman, between birth and death, counts, and has a claim to an irreducible core of integrity and dignity."[11] So we may, in effect, hope for what John Rawls describes as an overlapping consensus of various religions (each from the perspective of its own comprehensive doctrine) and of the human rights movement (from the perspective of its secular comprehensive doctrine) on a morality that includes a robust array of human rights.[12]

To be sure, as Henkin realizes, human rights will not exhaust morality for the religions; they will not comprise what he describes as a total ideology. But we may nevertheless hope that the religions will come to see this much about human rights: "If they do not bring kindness to the familiar, they bring – as religions have often failed to do – respect for the stranger. Human rights are not a complete, alternative ideology, but rights are a *floor*, necessary to allow other values – including religions – to flourish."[13] And so, in order to promote the realization of this hope, Henkin ends with a challenge to the religions. He calls on the religions themselves to acknowledge that "in the world we have and are shaping, the idea of human rights is an essential idea, and religions should support it fully, in every way, everywhere."[14] Presumably this support should go beyond lip-service and unite the religions and the human rights movement on a common agenda for action to foster and defend human rights.

How should Christians react to Henkin's indictment? Should they endorse his hope? How should they respond to his challenge? I next try to answer these questions.

A CHRISTIAN RESPONSE

Christians may find it tempting to dismiss or downplay the indictment, arguing that the historical track record of Christianity is not as bad as Henkin's sketch suggests. Consider, as Nicholas Wolterstorff does, the abolitionist movement in nineteenth-century America; the civil rights movement in twentieth-century America; the resistance movements in Nazi Germany, in communist Eastern Europe, in apartheid South Africa. All these movements were on the side of human dignity, and all of them were supported by Christians for religious reasons. Wolterstorff thinks secular academics have a blind spot about the role of religion in these movements that conceals reality and distorts scholarship. They assume without argument that religion is epiphenomenal.

Wolterstorff attempts to drive this point home in the following rather scathing remarks:

> The people in Leipzig [in the later 1980s] assembled in a meeting space that just happened to be a church to listen to inspiring speeches that just happened to resemble sermons; they were led out into the streets in protest marches by leaders who just happened to be pastors. Black people in Capetown were led on protest marches from the black shanty-towns into the center of the city by men named Tutu and Boesak – who just happened to be bishop and pastor, respectively, and who just happened to use religious talk in their fiery speeches.[15]

But such protests did not just happen to be religiously based; the leadership role Christian clergy played in them was no mere accident. Or consider the social teaching of the Roman Catholic Church. In 1891, Pope Leo XIII argued for social and economic rights in his encyclical, *Rerum Novarum* ("new things"). His views have been reaffirmed, refined, and expanded by Pius XI's *Quadragesimo Anno* ("after forty years"), Paul VI's *Octogesima Adveniens* ("on the eightieth anniversary"), and John Paul II's *Centesimas*

Annus ("on the hundredth anniversary"). And a declaration endorsing religious freedom was promulgated by the Second Vatican Council. So the track record of Christianity on human rights can be read in a way that emphasizes its positive features and makes it appear less bleak than it does in Henkin's portrait.

Though I have some sympathy with this defensive line of argument, I think what it can accomplish is quite limited. Even if those who, like Wolterstorff, advance it are correct, the historical track record of Christianity on human rights is mixed. And it remains an open question whether Christians have good reasons to be suspicious of Henkin's hope and ambivalent about his challenge to strive for rapprochement with the human rights movement.

Indeed, it might be thought that there are general ethical reasons for reservations about human rights morality. In discussions in biomedical ethics of the norms that ought to govern physician–patient relationships, some theorists have proposed a social-contract model according to which the norms can be represented in terms of a purely hypothetical contract that specifies rights and correlative duties for both parties. A forceful objection to this model is that it encourages minimalist moral thinking, allowing physicians to consider themselves in the clear, morally speaking, provided they have not violated any of their patients' contractual rights.[16] As Howard Brody puts the point, "So long as one's view of oneself as a free, self-interested negotiator is the *primary* moral conception that one brings into a relationship, one is unlikely to 'go the extra mile' for the other party in ways likely to make the relationship grow and flourish over time."[17] It is easy to see how to generalize the objection. A moral framework in which human rights are given pride of place will encourage minimalism and thereby work to the detriment of flourishing human relationships with one's loved ones, friends, and colleagues. In short, human rights morality is fit only to govern relations among strangers.

I do not think this is an impressive objection. Human rights are, as Henkin notes, a moral floor; they are not also a moral ceiling. Of course morality asks much more of us in our relationships with loved ones, friends, and colleagues than that we respect their rights. But it requires that we do at least that. As medicine is currently practiced, it is also worth emphasizing, patients can expect to have different kinds of relationships with different sorts of physicians. It may well be that we want relationships with our primary-care physicians that approximate to friendship and so demand more of both parties than a minimalist honoring of rights.

However, most of us will inevitably also have relationships with various medical specialists on occasion, and we cannot reasonably expect that specialists with whom we interact only infrequently will ever be much more than strangers to us. Yet we surely want to insist that they too, at a minimum, respect our rights and do not, for example, violate our autonomy out of misguided benevolent motives. And we want something similar from the many strangers we encounter casually in our daily lives or deal with formally in large bureaucratic institutions as well as from the billions of living humans who, because we will never encounter them at all, will forever remain utter strangers to us. And, needless to say, all these strangers want parallel conduct from us. In our relations with strangers, though we may sometimes be morally required to do more than merely honor their rights, we are never morally permitted to do less. So we should not fault human rights morality for being minimalist once we are clear that it specifies only the moral floor and is not meant to do anything more.

If we are to find some reason for Christians in particular to have reservations about rising to meet Henkin's challenge, therefore, we would do best to look for its ground in features that are distinctive of Christian ethics. Christian morality is, above all, a love ethics in some sense. About this, different Christian denominations, though they disagree about much else in the moral realm, are of one mind. Recall Henkin's clever remark that, though the biblical text imposes a duty to love one's neighbor, it nowhere speaks of the neighbor's right to be loved. Is this to be explained solely on historical grounds? Or is there something in a Christian ethics of love that is repugnant to a human rights morality? I will probe the latter question by reflecting briefly on two discussions of Christian love I find especially attractive.

One is contemporary. It is to be found in the theistic Platonism espoused by Robert M. Adams in his recent book, *Finite and Infinite Goods*. According to Adams, God is the Good itself, the paradigm or standard of goodness, and finite things are good by virtue of being images of God. A principle of his ethical theory is that it is good to love good things, and so love of God and of God's finite images is also good. Such love is gracious and in central cases is a type of love for persons. In these cases, Adams identifies gracious love with the Hebrew Bible's *hesed*. The Hebrew word has no exact English translation, being commonly rendered in the King James Version by "loving kindness" or "mercy" and in the Revised Standard Version by "steadfast love."

As Adams understands it, *hesed* has two aspects. One is that it is a loyal and dependable devotion. *Hesed* "issues in particular acts of kindness, but they are done out of a *commitment* to a person whom one loves, or with whom one has, at least, a valued relationship."[18] The other is that it goes beyond obligation to encompass kindnesses such as forgiveness to which the agent is not strictly bound. If one only does one's duty, one may well have fallen short of showing *hesed*, for it "goes beyond anything that should be demanded as a duty."[19] Nevertheless, it is an important virtue because community cannot long endure if we do no more than we are obligated to do.

Adams concludes that *hesed*'s "pattern of dependable commitment that is open-ended in its giving, and forgiving but not always undemanding, represents a virtue that is needed in any society, even if ours has not seen fit to give it a name."[20] When Christian love is construed as involving *hesed*, as I think it should be, it is clear that Christian ethics asks of those who try to live up to its vision of the good that they do much that is above and beyond the call of duty. It therefore calls on them to do more for their fellow humans than merely to respect and honor their rights.

Indeed, the second discussion I wish to consider, the classical view of Christian ethics presented in Sören Kierkegaard's *Works of Love*, insists that Christian love speaks with the voice of stern duty. Infuriated by the complacency of the Christendom he found around him in Golden Age Denmark, Kierkegaard was fond of stressing, both in his pseudonymous authorship and in works published in his own name, the terrible difficulty of becoming a Christian. In ethics, his campaign against the laxity of his contemporaries takes the form of an argument emphasizing that love, in the Christian New Testament, is the subject of a commandment. Christian love is a divinely commanded love, and so Kierkegaard, unlike Adams, contends that it is an obligatory love. And the duty to love one's neighbor can be extremely demanding, since love of one's neighbor includes love of one's enemy.

Kierkegaard makes the connection in the following way:

> Therefore he who in truth loves his neighbor loves also his enemy. The distinction *friend* and *enemy* is a distinction in the object of love, but the object of love to one's neighbor is without distinction. One's neighbor is the absolutely unrecognizable distinction between man and man; it is eternal equality before God – enemies, too, have this equality. Men think that it is impossible for a human being to love his enemies, for enemies are hardly able to endure the sight of one another. Well, then, shut your eyes – and your enemy looks just like your neighbor. Shut your eyes and remember the command that *you* shall love; then you are to love – your enemy? No. Then love your neighbor, for you cannot see that he is your enemy.[21]

If you can shut your eyes, there is no distinction among your neighbors, and your enemy is your neighbor too. But shutting your eyes is by no means easy to do. Obeying the divine command to love one's neighbor is a very stringent duty.

Kierkegaard is well aware that it is. He acknowledges that the divine command to love one's neighbor will repel many people; it is, he says, a command, "which to flesh and blood is offence, and to wisdom foolishness."[22] Yet obedience is not impossible. The following story provides an actual example of it:

> The Armenian Christians are a people who have experienced centuries of suffering and know that their worship is surrounded by a cloud of martyred witnesses. A Turkish officer has raided and looted an Armenian home. He killed the aged parents and gave the daughters to the soldiers, keeping the eldest daughter for himself. Sometime later she escaped and trained as a nurse. As time passed, she found herself nursing in a ward of Turkish officers. One night, by the light of a lantern, she saw the face of this officer. He was so gravely ill that without exceptional nursing he would die. The days passed, and he recovered. One day, the doctor stood by the bed with her and said to him, "But for her devotion to you, you would be dead." He looked at her and said, "We have met before, haven't we?" "Yes," she said, "we have met before." "Why didn't you kill me?" he asked. She replied, "I am a follower of him who said 'Love your enemies.'"[23]

Perhaps the Turkish officer in the story had a right to medical care despite his past barbaric mistreatment of Armenian civilians. If Kierkegaard's view is correct, the Armenian nurse had a Christian duty of love to care for him.

But did he have a right to receive medical care, in particular heroic, live-saving care, from her? I think not. By virtue of his mistreatment of her he forfeited any such right against her. If she had a Christian duty to provide loving care to him, it was not because he had a correlative right to receive loving care from her. Nor was he, as Henkin suggests, merely a third-party beneficiary of her duty to God. Rather, she had a duty to him, a duty not only not to kill him but also to care for him; but it was a duty grounded in a divine command and not in some right he possessed against her. So on the stringent Kierkegaardian interpretation of the Christian ethics of love, Christian duties of love go far beyond our duties to honor and respect the universal human rights of others.[24]

I take it, then, that Adams and Kierkegaard would agree that the Christian ethics of love asks far more of those who would live by its standards than that they respect human rights. I concur with this view. Yet it does not follow that, as a general rule, Christian ethics asks for less. Christian love of neighbor can, to return to Henkin's metaphor, regard respect for the neighbor's rights as a moral floor in many instances. Christians can, therefore, share the moral agenda of the human rights movement, at least most of the time, provided they do not consider it exhaustive of ethics and so fall into the error of minimalism by confusing the floor with the ceiling.

But maybe this happy means of reconciliation will not be available in all cases. In order to see why, consider the story recounted in Genesis 22 of the *akedah*, the binding of Isaac. In the story, God is said to command Abraham to sacrifice Isaac, his beloved son; and Abraham agrees to do so. Did Abraham, by agreeing to kill his innocent son, consent to violate Isaac's right to life? Kant, whom Henkin mentions as a possible historical source for the principle of human dignity, would have thought so; he holds that there could have been no such divine command. In *The Conflict of the Faculties*, Kant tells us that Abraham should have responded to the supposedly divine voice as follows: "That I ought not to kill my good son is quite certain. But that you, this apparition, are God – of that I am not certain, and never can be, not even if this voice rings down to me from (visible) heaven."[25]

No doubt other moral theorists, including some Christians, will find Kant's response to the *akedah* compelling. But Kierkegaard suggests a different and more disturbing possibility for a Christian appropriation of the story of Genesis 22. It is that there was such a divine command and that it brought about for Abraham a teleological suspension of the ethical. In *Fear and Trembling*, Johannes de Silentio, Kierkegaard's pseudonym, says of Abraham that "by his act he overstepped the ethical entirely and possessed a higher teleos outside of it, in relation to which he suspended the former."[26] According to de Silentio, God's command imposed on Abraham an absolute duty of obedience, and the ethical duty to respect the right to life of innocent Isaac was overridden or suspended by that duty. "If such is not the position of Abraham," de Silentio goes on to say, "then he is not even a tragic hero but a murderer."[27] Absent a teleological suspension of the ethical, Abraham would not be, as de Silentio thinks he is, a knight of faith. In my opinion, Christian ethics should not lightly dismiss the possibility of a teleological suspension of the ethical.[28]

Of course some ethical theorists who are committed to both human rights and monotheism do reject this Kierkegaardian possibility. Work on Jewish ethics by Lenn E. Goodman provides a particularly clear and instructive example. In his recent *Judaism, Human Rights, and Human Values*, Goodman argues that foundations for human rights can be discerned in Jewish traditions of moral thinking as far back as the Torah. He sums up what he hopes to show in the book's chapter on Judaism and human rights as follows: "The idea of rights, as I will argue, is not a modern conception in any but a question-begging sense. Indeed, we almost stumble over the impressive metaphysical roots given to that idea in two of the great Jewish rationalists of the Middle Ages, Saadia Gaon (882–942) and Moses Maimonides (1138–1204)."[29] And he dissents from and severely criticizes the Kierkegaardian reading of the *akedah*.

In an earlier book, *God of Abraham*, which reproduces Rembrandt's *The Angel Prevents the Sacrifice of Isaac* (1655) on its dust jacket, Goodman discusses the binding of Isaac at some length. He argues that the angel's command to Abraham to stay his hand indicates that "God never intended Isaac to be slain."[30] Abraham is not punished for obeying the angel's command and sacrificing a ram instead of Isaac. According to Goodman, this shows that "the binding had been sufficient, the slaying was not required."[31] Abraham has been tested, and he has passed the test. All along, the test was meant to reinforce Abraham's belief that God is good "by refining, strengthening, giving substance to his nascent conviction of God's goodness."[32]

Goodman thinks Kierkegaard has radically misunderstood the lesson of Genesis 22. In order to drive this point home, he scathingly remarks: "Blinded by his own inner struggle, Kierkegaard reads an academic Kantian morality into Abraham's mind and projects his own (rather pagan) notion of faith's conflict with that morality, at the very moment where the Torah seeks to awake our consciousness to the indissoluble linkage of goodness to the idea of God."[33] Though I do not agree with this sharply negative assessment of Kierkegaard, I do think that many monotheists and, in particular, some Christians will find it very plausible. So I must acknowledge that my view of the *akedah*, according to which Christian ethics should not lightly dismiss the Kierkegaardian possibility of a religious suspension of the ethical, is highly controversial.

Not dismissing this possibility out of hand does not, of course, commit one to agreeing with every claim one encounters to the effect that human rights violations are to be condoned or even approved in the name of some higher religious imperative. If I were to discover my next-door neighbor building an altar in his backyard, and he told me he planned to sacrifice his son on it and invited me to take part in the ceremony, my first thought would surely be that he had gone mad. And though I have great sympathy for the Branch Davidians in Waco and the Heaven's Gate community in San Diego, I do not approve of their actions. However, I do think that a Christian who takes seriously the possibility of a teleological suspension of the ethical should not be an absolutist about honoring human rights and should not concede that respecting them must always be given priority over pursuing religious goals of other kinds in cases of conflict. Hence, while I believe Christian ethics can comfortably ally itself with what Henkin describes as the human rights ideology, at least most of the time, I suspect that secular members of the human rights movement would rightly see its convergence with Christian ethics as fragile and their relationship, if cooperative, as a rather uneasy alliance.

NOTES

I presented an earlier version of this chapter at a session of the Conference on Ethics and Religion for a Global Twenty-First Century that was held at Chapman University and Loyola Marymount University in March 2000. I am grateful to the conference participants for stimulating discussion.

1.   E.L. Doctorow, *City of God* (New York: Random House, 2000), p. 256.
2.   Louis Henkin, "Religion, Religions and Human Rights," *Journal of Religious Ethics*, 26 (1998), pp. 229–230.
3.   Ibid., p. 231.
4.   Ibid., p. 232.
5.   Ibid., p. 233.
6.   Ibid.
7.   Ibid., p. 236.
8.   Ibid., p. 237.
9.   Ibid.
10. Ibid.
11. Ibid., p. 239.
12. John Rawls, *Political Liberalism* (New York: Columbia University Press, 1993), pp. 133–172.
13. Henkin, "Religion, Religions and Human Rights," p. 239.
14. Ibid.
15. Robert Audi and Nicholas Wolterstorff, *Religion in the Public Square: The Place of Religious Convictions in Political Debate* (Lanham, MD: Rowman & Littlefield, 1997), p. 80.
16. See Daniel Callahan, "Minimalist Ethics," *Hastings Center Report*, 11, 2 (1981), pp. 19–25.
17. Howard Brody, "The Physician/Patient Relationship," in *Medical Ethics*, ed. Robert M. Veatch (Boston and Portola Valley: Jones & Bartlett Publishers, 1989), p. 72.

18. Robert Merrihew Adams, *Finite and Infinite Goods: A Framework for Ethics* (New York and Oxford: Oxford University Press, 1999), p. 171.

19. Ibid., p. 172.

20. Ibid., p. 173.

21. Sören Kierkegaard, *Works of Love*, trans. Howard Hong and Edna Hong (New York: Harper Torchbooks, 1962), p. 79.

22. Ibid., p. 71.

23. Stephen E. Fowl and L. Gregory Jones, *Reading in Communion: Scripture and Ethics in Christian Life* (Grand Rapids, MI: Eerdmans, 1999), pp. 79–80. Fowl and Jones report in a note that this story is taken from Geoffrey Wainwright, *Doxology* (New York: Oxford University Press, 1980), p. 434.

24. For more on Kierkegaard's ethics, see Philip L. Quinn, "The Divine Command Ethics in Kierkegaard's *Works of Love*," in *Faith, Freedom, and Rationality*, ed. Jeff Jordan and Daniel Howard-Snyder (Lanham, MD: Rowman & Littlefield, 1996), pp. 29–44.

25. Immanuel Kant, *The Conflict of the Faculties*, trans. Mary J. Gregor (Lincoln and London: University of Nebraska Press, 1992), p. 115.

26. Sören Kierkegaard, *Fear and Trembling*, trans. Walter Lowrie (Princeton: Princeton University Press, 1968), p. 69.

27. Ibid., p. 77.

28. For an argument that the *akedah* confronts Abraham with a tragic dilemma rather than a teleological suspension of the ethical, see Philip L. Quinn, "Agamemnon and Abraham: The Tragic Dilemma of Kierkegaard's Knight of Faith," *Journal of Literature and Theology*, 4 (1990), pp. 181–193.

29. Lenn E. Goodman, *Judaism, Human Rights, and Human Values* (New York and Oxford: Oxford University Press, 1998), p. 49.

30. L.E. Goodman, *God of Abraham* (New York and Oxford: Oxford University Press, 1996), p. 21.

31. Ibid., p. 22.

32. Ibid., p. 23.

33. Ibid., p. 27.

Plate 18 Small porcelain image of Kuanyin, the Chinese form of the Bodhisattva of Compassion, on the altar of the Lum Sai Ho Tong Society Taoist temple in Honolulu, Hawaii. The compassion represented by this female figure transcends the distinctions between religions. Mahayana Buddhism affirms the interconnectedness of all beings, and an outpouring of compassion marks the enlightened mind. Thus the followers of this Buddhist path make the "bodhisattva vow" to work for the liberation of all beings. The challenge facing Buddhism today is whether that vow obligates one to work for physical and social liberation as well as spiritual liberation. Photo: *Nancy M. Martin*

18

BUDDHISM *and* HUMAN RIGHTS: THE RECENT BUDDHIST DISCUSSION *and its* IMPLICATIONS *for* CHRISTIANITY

James Fredericks

"The question of human rights is so fundamentally important," according to the Dalai Lama, "that there should be no difference of views on this."[1] This statement, made at the Non-Governmental Organizations United Nations World Conference on Human Rights, on June 15, 1993, in Vienna, was greeted with broad approval. On the issue of human rights, however, there are in fact many differences in views. Some Asian governments, as is well known, criticize the rhetoric of human rights as yet another form of neo-colonialism. Later, in his speech to the N.G.Os. in Vienna, the Dalai Lama observed that opposition to the concept of human rights comes mainly from "the authoritarian and totalitarian regimes."[2] Although this is largely the case, a lively discussion concerning human rights is going on within the Dalai Lama's own religious tradition, Buddhism.

As a Christian theologian, I find this continuing conversation among Buddhists particularly rich. In this chapter, I want to review some of the current Buddhist discussion about human rights and then reflect (much more briefly) on the import this discussion might have for Christians.

BUDDHISM AND HUMAN RIGHTS

B.R. Ambedkar, India's first minister of law and one of the chief architects of the Indian constitution, converted to Buddhism in 1956. Ambedkar was born a member of the Mahar caste, a community which had been considered "untouchable." After years of struggle against caste-based oppression, his hopes for a "Protestant" Hinduism (i.e. a Hinduism that would renounce hierarchical caste distinctions) had failed to materialize in an independent India. Buddhism, with its ancient renunciation of the caste system, offered the best hope for low-caste Indians to secure their human rights in his view.[3]

Ambedkar was not alone in finding support for human rights within Buddhism. Dr. Tilokasundari Kariyawasam, president of the World Fellowship of Buddhist Women, claims that "Buddhism is an all pervading philosophy and a religion, strongly motivated by human rights or rights of everything that exists, man, woman, animal and the environment they are living in."[4]

Not all Buddhists, however, are confident about the suitability of the concept of human rights for their religion. Their concerns may be organized into the following points of contention.

1.   Is there an implicit doctrine of human rights within the pre-modern Buddhist tradition?
2.   As a moral framework, does the notion of human rights measure up to the demands of Buddhist ethics?
3.   Is the concept of human rights compatible with Buddhist teachings?
4.   Is the defense of human rights mounted by Buddhists the same as the defense of rights made by Western secular Liberals?

The current Buddhist discussion of human rights is quite convoluted, and imposing this framework on it will of necessity lead to some distortion. Nevertheless, I believe that organizing the major themes of the discussion under these headings will be helpful in summarizing a great deal of material.

AN IMPLICIT DOCTRINE OF HUMAN RIGHTS IN BUDDHISM?

Ananda Guruge, Sri Lankan diplomat and Buddhist scholar, in writing about the United Nations Declaration on Human Rights, states that "every single Article of the Universal Declaration of Human Rights – even the labour rights to fair wages, leisure and welfare – has been adumbrated, cogently upheld and meaningfully incorporated in an overall view of life and society by the Buddha."[5] Guruge's convictions regarding the pre-existence of a concept of human rights within the classical Buddhist tradition is shared by Sulak Sivaraksa, an internationally respected Buddhist social activist based in Bangkok. Sulak claims that a notion of human rights can be found in the Buddhist values and customs of traditional Thai society. Prior to the influx of Western cultural influences, Thai society took as its ideal the first community of Buddhist monks (the historical Buddha and his disciples), a community free of all egoistic attachment. According to Sulak, human rights flow naturally from such non-attachment to ego. Thus, in order to realize human rights today, the people of Thailand should not turn to the modern West, which is often designated as the birthplace of the concept of human rights. On the contrary, respecting human rights means that Thais should reject modern Western influences (such as consumerism) and return to the time-honored values of their own Buddhist tradition with its implicit doctrine of human rights.[6]

Damien Keown, a Western Buddhist, acknowledges that there is no specific word in either Pali or Sanskrit for a "human right" understood as an individual entitlement or immunity. Nevertheless, he joins Guruge, Sulak, and others in his belief that there exists in Buddhist tradition an implicit or "embryonic" concept of rights.[7] Therefore, in order to appreciate classical Buddhism's contribution to the human rights movement today, we will need to distinguish between having a value (rights) and having a clear concept of it. According to Keown, Buddhism's implicit notion of human rights can be seen in the Buddhist precepts. Not only do the precepts spell out what the Buddhist is to do, they also bring with them implications regarding what is due to others. Therefore, my duty, as adumbrated by the precepts, constitutes someone else's right. Keown also acknowledges that Buddhist ethics has traditionally preferred to speak about duties, not rights. For example, the precepts establish the duty of a husband to support his wife, without stating explicitly that the wife has a right to be supported. However, according to Keown, the husband's duty implicitly establishes the wife's right.[8]

Sallie King, a prominent figure in the "Engaged Buddhism" movement, also recognizes an implicit doctrine of human rights in the Buddhist precepts. Like Keown, she argues that an explicit assertion of responsibilities in the precepts contains within it an implicit assertion that others have rights. In fact, for Buddhists, "rights and responsibilities are interdependent to the point almost of fusion."[9] This is so much the case that King believes it is perhaps better for Buddhists to drop the language of "rights" and "responsibilities" and speak instead of "mutual obligation."[10]

Keown asks why the embryonic notion of human rights has been so long gestating in the womb. He answers his own question by noting that, although Buddhism holds within itself many resources for criticizing social hierarchy, the conditions necessary for the emergence of an explicit doctrine of rights may be an egalitarian ethos and democratic institutions, "neither of which have been notable features of Asian polity before the modern era."[11] Keown and Sulak would seem to be in agreement about an implicit doctrine in the tradition, but in disagreement about the role of Western influence in making what is implicit explicit.

Robert Thurman, a scholar of Tibetan Buddhism and translator for the Dalai Lama, is in agreement with Guruge when he observes confidently that "the principles of human rights were all there in the Buddha's earliest teachings."[12] His voice harmonizes with Sulak's when he goes on to add that these principles of human rights were given concrete form in the historical Buddha's original monastic community. Thurman is in agreement with Keown, however, when he notes that Buddhist human rights principles "never led to any sort of institutional democracy until modern times, which only happened with outside help."[13] Nevertheless, Thurman holds up pre-1959 Tibet as a model society based on Buddhism's notion of human rights. "As a Buddhist effort in furthering human social and cultural rights [Tibet] is an example of what one long-term Buddhist experiment actually did produce."[14]

Is there an implicit doctrine of human rights to be found within the pre-modern Buddhist tradition? Soraj Hongladarom, an observer of Thai Buddhism, seems to be in disagreement with Sulak. According to Soraj, the Thai word for human rights, *sitthi manussayachon*, carries with it a distinctly foreign ring. For most Thais, this phrase brings to mind the image of one who has cast aside "the traditional pattern of compromise and harmonization of social relations, someone, that is, who is quite out of touch with the traditional Thai mores."[15]

In a response to Keown, Craig Ihara states flatly that "there is no concept of rights in classical Buddhism" and that introducing such a notion "would significantly transform the nature of Buddhist ethics."[16] Rights may imply duties, but the reverse is not the case: the fact that the Buddhist precepts impose duties on Buddhist practitioners does not imply that other people have a right to an entitlement or immunity. Let me offer a concrete example. Dr. Haing Ngor, the Cambodian doctor who played the journalist Dith Pran in the film *The Killing Fields*, was himself a survivor of the Khmer Rouge cultural revolution. During four years as a slave laborer in the countryside, Haing was tortured horribly on three separate occasions. On each occasion, he had been denounced to his tormentors by Pen Tip, a former medical technician who had known Haing in Phnom Penh prior to the "liberation." Pen accused Haing of stealing food and, more dangerous still, of being a doctor before "year zero" (1975, the fall of Phnom Penh). By betraying

Haing, Pen significantly enhanced his own position in the labor camps. In the tumult that followed the North Vietnamese invasion of Cambodia, Haing succeeded in making it to a refugee center in Thailand. There he began once again to practice as a doctor, attending to the considerable medical needs of refugees. In the camp, Haing wondered what had happened to his betrayer. What if Pen should have turned up as a patient in need of treatment at the refugee center? According to the Buddhist precepts, Haing would have the duty to respond to his betrayer's medical needs with compassion. As a Buddhist, Haing's responsibility is clear. Does the doctor's religious responsibility imply that the betrayer also has a right to treatment? Secular understandings of human rights would affirm that the betrayer has a right to medical treatment, but would not insist that Dr. Haing be the physician to administer the treatment. Buddhist ethics requires Dr. Haing to treat his betrayer, but says nothing about the betrayer's "right" to be treated. Indeed, to insist on the betrayer's right to treatment tends to obscure the religious meaning of Haing Ngor's responsibility.[17]

ADEQUATE TO THE DEMANDS OF BUDDHIST ETHICS?

As a moral framework, the concept of human rights may be described as a "minimalist ethics" or "moral floor." Here, a considerable contrast has to be drawn between approaches to social problems based on the notion of human rights and Buddhist social ethics. Is the human rights approach adequate to the demands of Buddhist ethics?

On this issue, Keown acknowledges that the various lists of specific human rights do not form a complete account of the good. Rather, they constitute a bare minimum guide for social behavior. For a complete account of the good and the moral requirements to be derived therefrom, Keown directs us to religious traditions.[18] Ihara expands on this theme, arguing that although human rights affirmations may be of some limited good in dealing with social problems, the human rights perspective does little to alleviate the problem of suffering at its roots, which is the goal of Buddhist ethics. In fact, by promoting an adversarial mentality, the human rights approach can actually begin to compete with the Buddhist practice of compassion.[19] Thus, in falling short of the demands of Buddhist ethics, human rights can become a stumbling block for Buddhist practitioners. Given these reservations, Ihara concludes that "it probably would be a mistake to introduce the notion of rights into Buddhist ethics."[20]

Jay Garfield, writing in defense of the Dalai Lama's use of human rights language, also underscores the limitations of the human rights approach for Buddhism. The roots of the moral minimalism that characterizes the asserting of human rights are to be found in the presuppositions of Liberal political theory, which gave birth to the concept of human rights in the first place. Buddhism, according to Garfield, is more ethically demanding than Western Liberalism. Buddhist ethics is based on the demand for infinite compassion, not the assertion of rights. When human rights replace compassion as the moral starting point, too much evil and indifference to suffering is permitted. According to Western Liberalism, society is a contractual construct made up of autonomous and competing individuals. Within such a society, social relations must be regulated by rights. In this understanding of society, compassion is relegated to the realm of private choice, that is, as one of a number of purely optional ways of responding to people within the social contract. Liberalism, therefore, is much at odds with the Buddhist understanding of society and social solidarity. The promotion of human rights may not be inimical to Buddhism, but it does not measure up to the demands of Buddhist ethics.[21]

Phra Dhammapidok, a Thai monk much respected for his scriptural erudition and his writings on the social implications of Buddhism, has received multiple honorific names from the King of Thailand.[22] Unlike Sulak Sivaraksa, Phra Dhammapidok is generally skeptical about what he calls the "human rights mentality," although he concedes that asserting rights may have some benefits for contemporary Thai society.[23] The human rights approach, however, is by no means adequate to the needs of modern human beings or equal to the demands of Buddhist ethics.

> While human rights are useful within the environment of dissension, they are not very far reaching. They are only a compromise. Compromise is not capable of leading human beings to true unity and harmony. Compromise is a situation in which each side agrees to give in a little to the other in order to attain some mutual benefit. A quality of force or mental resignation is involved.[24]

In effect, Phra Dhammapidok looks suspiciously on human rights because they present themselves as lasting remedies when in fact they merely treat symptoms, leaving the real malady – suffering (*dukkha*) – untouched. Worse, by treating symptoms, human rights can distract us from the need to attack the disease at its root cause – craving (*tanha*). Asserting rights entails a compromise that may establish an uneasy peace. True peace, however, requires human beings to outgrow old ways of thinking, including the human rights mentality.[25]

COMPATIBLE WITH BUDDHIST TEACHINGS?

Of the several voices in this Buddhist conversation, one stands out from the rest as particularly opposed to Buddhists adopting the language of human rights. Peter Junger, a practicing Buddhist and a specialist in Anglo-American common law, is by no means in favor of torture or slavery, economic exploitation, or political oppression of any sort. He is, however, convinced that the very idea of human rights is antithetical to Buddhism and should not be adopted by Buddhists.[26]

Junger argues that human rights is a Western idea, alien to Buddhist ethics and incompatible with Buddhist doctrine. In this he places himself in opposition to Buddhists such as Sulak, Thurman, Guruge, Keown, and King. And more so than Ihara and even Phra Dhammapidok, Junger is opposed to Buddhists adopting a human rights approach to social problems. Many of the rights enumerated in the 1948 United Nations Universal Declaration of Human Rights assert immunities from interference. Rights such as these presume a "negative notion of freedom," that is, freedom understood in a characteristically modern Western sense as an immunity from interference based on the innate autonomy of the individual. Buddhism knows nothing of such an individual. Some of the rights listed in the U.N. Declaration assert entitlements, a point of view that is silent about social responsibilities, moral duties, or Buddhist virtues such as compassion. Both as immunities and as entitlements, the assertion of human rights raises severe difficulties for Buddhism.

The human rights mentality, according to Junger, is incompatible with the Four Noble Truths. "Rights" are merely an impermanent mental construction. As is the case with all mental constructions, human rights are dependently arisen *(pratitya-samutpada)* and therefore contingent, not absolute. Since rights have no inherent existence, to claim that rights are inalienable is unintelligible for a Buddhist. Therefore clinging to human rights, insisting on the universality of rights, and most of all asserting our own rights is yet another form of thirst which leads to the creation of more suffering, in accordance with the Second Noble Truth's teaching that suffering arises through craving. The pursuit of rights, according to Junger, also entails a denial of the First Noble Truth, which teaches the universality of suffering. Buddhism does not teach that human beings have a *right* to be secure from suffering or immune from the fact of impermanence *(anicca)*. Suffering and impermanence are universal facts, what Buddhism calls a "mark of existence," and are unavoidable regardless of what "rights" might be attributed to human beings as "inalienable."[27]

As a law theorist, Junger notes that the concept of human rights is a recent historical development, the result of the interplay of two Western legal traditions: the Continental civil law and the Anglo-American common law.[28] As such, fairness and justice are important concerns of human rights activists. Fairness and justice, however, are not the concerns of Buddhists, even though they may be desirable in social and political life.[29] Unfairness and injustice are unavoidable facts in accordance with the First Noble Truth. To believe otherwise is to cling to ignorance which only breeds more suffering. The human rights mentality can also trace its roots back to Christian natural law theory, according to Junger. Roman Catholics, such as Jacques Maritain who made a significant contribution to the 1948 U.N. Declaration, argued that natural law requires all human beings to recognize that human rights are rooted in human nature, which is endowed by God with an innate dignity.[30] Argumentation such as this, in Junger's view, is unintelligible to Buddhists.[31]

As mentioned above, Junger does not reject the concept of human rights as legitimate secular policies and ideals. Problems present themselves, however, when the human rights mentality is adopted by Buddhists as an expression of the Buddha's dharma.

> There is little that is wrong, and much that is right, with the Western European concept of "human rights" when that concept is viewed from within that tradition; but problems arise when efforts are made to impose that concept with all its Western trimmings upon traditions – like those of Buddhism – that have quite different concepts, if only because they have quite different histories.[32]

Good Buddhists will not cling to their rights. This non-clinging to rights constitutes "right action" as understood within the Buddha's Eightfold Path. For this reason, human rights language is not particularly useful for Buddhists and very well may be harmful to Buddhists who try to work skillfully with people who do not come from societies shaped by the worldview of Western Liberalism.[33]

ARE BUDDHIST RIGHTS THE SAME AS WESTERN RIGHTS?

When Buddhists affirm human rights, do they mean the same thing that secular Western Liberals mean when they talk about human rights? A final theme which runs through the current conversation among Buddhists about human rights has to do with the need to distinguish between Buddhist human rights and secular human rights.

King, who embraces the language of human rights and, as discussed above, sees within Buddhist tradition an implicit doctrine of human rights, also recognizes the need to distinguish between Buddhist rights and the Western Liberal notion of rights. This is made necessary because "the conceptual world which Buddhist 'human rights' language inhabits... differs from Western concepts in important ways."[34]

In King's view, differences between Buddhist rights and Liberal rights are fundamental. The differences that separate Buddhists from Western Liberals have to do with the nature of society and the individual. Buddhism rejects the notion that society consists in a contractual relationship of contending individuals. Instead, it begins with the view that social existence arises in the fundamental connectedness of all sentient beings. Properly grasped, social existence is non-adversarial and non-contentious.

Given the difference King sees in their fundamental presuppositions, the differences between Buddhist and Western rights must be manifold.

1. For Buddhism, human rights have to do with whole communities. They do not presume or promote the illusion of the autonomous individual. In practice, Buddhist human rights are not about protecting individual autonomy; rather, they are about securing the well-being of all.

2. For this reason, Buddhist human rights language conscientiously avoids the rhetoric of self-assertion in favor of a rhetoric of selfless compassion. Rights are realized when self-assertion is renounced.

3. Therefore, Buddhist human rights, in contrast to rights as understood by Western Liberalism, are non-adversarial.

4. Moreover, Buddhist rights do in fact recognize value in the individual, but not in the same way that Western Liberalism does. Instead of asserting the immunities and entitlements of autonomous individuals, Buddhism roots the value of each and every individual in the potential, enjoyed by every sentient being, for Buddhahood.

5. Additionally, human rights, in the Buddhist perspective, are not fundamentally suspicious of governmental and political structures. Rather, Buddhist human rights reflect the true interconnectedness of all sentient beings by recognizing the potential of all social institutions to contribute to the enlightenment of all.

6. And finally, Buddhist understanding of rights never pits the human good against the good of other sentient beings, in contrast to the anthropocentrism of Western Liberal notions of *human* rights.

The need to distinguish between Buddhist affirmations of human rights and their secular Western counterparts is the motive force behind Garfield's defense of the Dalai Lama's use of human rights language. In fact, Garfield argues that Buddhist use of the language of human rights is coherent only if a clear distinction is made between the Buddhist defense of rights and those made by Western Liberals. For Garfield, the distinction between Western and Buddhist rights begins in their respective starting points. Liberalism's plea for human rights is based, as King also argues, on a social contract theory which assumes that autonomous individuals are fundamentally competitive and thus need to be self-assertive about their "rights." In contrast, Buddhism bases its defense of human rights on the virtue of compassion. In this respect, Buddhist affirmations of rights are qualitatively different from the affirmations made by Western Liberals. The concept of human rights in the Western Liberal tradition, given its starting presupposition, constitutes a minimalist ethics of constraint imposed on competitive individuals. In this scheme, a virtue ethics, such as Buddhism, is relegated to the private sphere of individual choice. Thus the virtue of compassion can in no way serve as an adequate basis for affirming human rights. In this respect, the affirmations of human rights made by Buddhist figures such as the Dalai Lama are qualitatively different than those made by Western Liberals.[35] Of course Garfield believes strongly that Buddhists such as the Dalai Lama should continue to speak out in defense of human rights, but not on the basis of the worldview of Western Liberalism.

The call to distinguish a properly Buddhist notion of human rights from the Western notion can be heard not only among Buddhists who want to justify Buddhist championing of human rights like Garfield, but also among Buddhists who are fundamentally skeptical about human rights as well. For example, Phra Dhammapidok, after arguing that human rights are historically contingent human inventions, which reflect a mentality based on division and competition, and which do not really address the mental motivations that lie at the core of social problems, then argues that there is a specifically Buddhist way to look on human rights. Buddhism makes a distinction between two types of law. On the one hand, there is the *dhamma*, or "true reality," the way things really work. On the other hand, there is *vinaya*, the law governing Buddhist society. Unlike *dhamma*, *vinaya* is merely a human convention which is more or less useful in helping human being to find release from suffering. According to Phra Dhammapidok, human rights can be affirmed as an aspect of the *vinaya*. In this respect, the affirmation of human rights is of value only to the extent that it is useful for the realization of the *dhamma.* Therefore, Buddhists can affirm human rights, but in a way that is rather different than the affirmations made by Western Liberals. For Buddhists, human rights are not absolute. They are dependently arisen human conventions and will not last. Therefore, although rights are not "natural" or absolute, they may have some usefulness in achieving a Buddhist goal in certain circumstances.

Like Phra Dhammapidok, Ihara is generally skeptical about Buddhist affirmations of human rights. The language of human rights is foreign to classical Buddhism, and the introduction of such language brings with it the potential to distort Buddhist tradition. For this reason, he approaches the question of human rights with an "intellectual presumption" against them. Nevertheless, Ihara acknowledges that there are "some conditions" in which Buddhists should use such language.[36] "It may be that... rights-talk is the best way of coping with a world without common customs and traditions." But this would not be the only consideration to which Buddhists would have to attend. Even if the language of human rights provides human beings today with a kind of universal discourse, Ihara argues that Buddhists will have to discern whether human rights language can be used skillfully, i.e. in a way that, on the one hand, does not distort the dharma and, on the other hand, is helpful in leading human beings to find release from suffering. Significantly, Ihara notes that there exist within the tradition materials to do precisely this.[37]

CHRISTIANITY AND HUMAN RIGHTS

Christians who support human rights tend to be in agreement on two important issues. First, they believe that the roots of human rights can be traced back, at least in part, to Christianity itself. Second, they believe that Christianity's support for human rights should not only be unwavering, but also unambiguous. Calling these two assumptions into question can only enrich Christian thinking about human rights. The debate among Buddhists regarding the role of human rights in their own tradition will be helpful to Christians in this respect.

Can the concept of human rights be traced back to Christianity? Many Christians assume this to be the case. For example, Thomas Hoppe admits that "the idea of legally defensible individual human and basic rights was unknown" in the European medieval feudal order. However, he also claims that the origins of human rights can be found in what he calls "the Judeo-Christian religion." Heinrich Rommen claims that "all through the Middle

Ages...the struggle for securing the rights of life, liberty and property was going on" and that these rights were based on a person's particular dignity as a Christian called to a "higher citizenship in the true City of God." T. Payzs argues that "It was...the classic interpretation of St. Thomas that served for centuries as the philosophical foundation of human rights."³⁸

Is there an implicit doctrine of human rights to be found within Christian tradition? This question recapitulates one of the major themes in the Buddhist discussion of human rights. Political scientists such as Louis Henkin and Jack Donnelly are surprised to hear of religious believers (Christian, Buddhist, or otherwise) claiming that the origin of the concept of human rights can be located in a religious worldview of any sort.³⁹ Henkin, in an influential essay, criticizes religious believers for their tendency to speak about their faith in ideal terms, heedless of the decidedly mixed track record of religions in regard to human rights. Violations of human rights have been and continue to be perpetrated by religious believers, in the name of religious institutions, justified by religious beliefs.⁴⁰ In light of Christianity's mixed record in regard to human rights, the claim that there is an "embryonic" doctrine of rights in Christianity deserves to be debated as vigorously among Christians as it is among Buddhists.

The issue raised by Keown and others may be an especially useful way for Christians to begin their discussion: does Christianity's imposition of an ethical duty on its believers imply that others have rights? The example offered above, regarding Dr. Haing Ngor and his betrayer in Cambodia's "killing fields," serves as a test case not only for the Buddhist understanding of compassion in relation to rights, but also for the Christian understanding of love. As a Buddhist, Haing's duty would be to respond to his betrayer with compassion (*karuna*). A Christian's duty would be to respond with love (*agape*). In either case, does the religious duty establish the betrayer's implicit right? The betrayer may indeed have a right to treatment, but the question currently being discussed by Buddhists has to do with whether or not this right is established by Haing's religious duty to show compassion. Does insisting that the religious duty establishes a human right obscure the radical religious meaning of compassion for Buddhists and love for Christians? This question leads us to the second assumption often made by Christian supporters of human rights.

Christianity's support for human rights should be not only unwavering, but unambiguous as well. This is a second assumption often found among Christians who champion human rights. Here again, the Buddhist discussion of human rights raises fruitful questions for Christians. Is the human rights approach adequate to the demands of Buddhist ethics? Is the assertion of human rights compatible with basic Buddhist teachings? Do we need to distinguish human rights in a properly Buddhist sense from the human rights affirmed by Western Liberalism? These difficult questions, the answers to which are by no means obvious, can be asked of Christianity as well. As is the case with the Buddhist discussion, the issue here is not whether Christians should be unconcerned with social problems. Rather, it has to do with the religious character of Christianity's concern and the propriety of the contemporary human rights approach for Christian believers.

In Thailand, Phra Dhammapidok criticizes human rights as mere political compromises ("band-aids") which do not address mental motivation, the actual root of social problems. The demanding religious vision of Buddhist ethics exceeds by far the limitations of the human rights "mentality." Can something similar be said of human rights in relation to Christian ethics? Instead of "mental motivations," Christians see social problems rooted in personal and structural sin. All creation will be saved from sin only in the eschatological coming of the Kingdom of God. Short of the Kingdom of God, Christians must be critical of all social structures and political systems. What role should the defense of human rights play in relation to Christianity's eschatological hope in the Kingdom of God? The justice of this world (human rights) does not fulfill the mercy of God (the Kingdom). Does worldly justice anticipate the Kingdom of God? Questions such as these suggest that Christians should reflect on Phra Dhammapidok's reservations about human rights as temporary measures which may be necessary, but are not ultimate solutions to social problems.

Ihara believes that Buddhists who embrace human rights do violence to their religion. The assertion of rights as subjective entitlements (e.g. to employment) promotes an adversarial mentality inimical to Buddhist ethics and begins to compete with the practice of compassion. Let me offer my own example here. Article 13.1 of the Universal Declaration of Human Rights by the World's Religions states that "everyone has the right to freedom of movement and residence anywhere in the world." Asserting that everyone has a right to residency "anywhere in the world" has different effects in different parts of the world. Do Han Chinese people have a right to residence in Tibet? Tibetan Buddhists, who are not shy about asserting human rights, have vehemently objected to this "right." Chinese nationals should be treated with compassion in Tibet, but they do not have a "right" to residence in the Land of Snows. Tibet as a land of contending and adversarial rights would seem to compete with Tibet as a land of compassion. Ihara's concerns about human rights should be taken seriously by Christians, even though Christians may very well come to different conclusions about the role of human rights within their own religion. Are there circumstances in which the assertion of rights can begin to compete with the healing practice of Christian love? If Christians can answer yes to this question, then are not certain kinds of human rights assertions incompatible with the Gospel's message of reconciliation?

Junger is particularly concerned about the distorting effect the notion of human rights has on Buddhism. The historical Buddha did not teach that human beings have a *right* to be secure from suffering or immune from the fact of impermanence (*anicca*). Suffering and impermanence are universal facts, and are unavoidable regardless of what "rights" might be attributed to human beings as "inalienable." Suffering, of course, plays a central role in Christian spirituality. Did Jesus of Nazareth teach that his disciples have a "right" to be free of suffering and death? On the contrary, redemptive suffering and the necessity of the cross are central themes in the preaching of Jesus. Taking Junger as a guide, Christians might well ask how the theology of the cross requires them to qualify their affirmation of human rights.[41]

Today, Buddhists like Craig Ihara, Sallie King, Jay Garfield, and Phra Dhammapidok claim that the Buddhist understanding of human rights should not be equated with that of secular Western Liberals. Must not the same be said of Christian support for human rights? Christianity is by no means fully compatible with the individualism and secularity that motivates Western Liberals in their assertion of rights. Many Christians are aware that what motivates their support of human rights must be distinguished, at times sharply, from the motivations of secular Liberals or other religious believers.[42] This suggests the possibility for creative cooperation among Buddhists and Christians who recognize a distinctly religious foundation to their support for human rights. How are Buddhist and Christian affirmations of rights similar and how are they different? What might Buddhists and Christians learn from one another in this respect? What might they learn from secular Liberals?

I am particularly interested in Buddhist–Christian discussions of what Charles Taylor calls an "overlapping consensus" on human rights.[43] Taylor argues that we may distinguish between a human right as a norm of conduct and the justification of that norm. There can be agreement on norms even if there is significant disagreement on how that norm is to be justified. In this respect, Taylor sees more hope in the possibility of wide (if not universal) agreement on norms of conduct even though there may be no agreement on the justification for the norms. As norms, human rights would not be Western or Buddhist or Christian particularly. Justifications for the norm, however, would be rooted in the specific cultural, political, or religious traditions. Taylor believes that such an "overlapping consensus" on human rights might provide a basis for a fruitful discussion of differing justifications of human rights. This may prove to be a particularly practical way to bring Buddhists, Christians, and secular Liberals together for fruitful dialogue.

Today, Buddhist and Christian voices can often be heard in defense of human rights. In promoting rights, I believe that both communities have a genuine intuition into the correspondences that exist between what is best in their religious traditions and the ideals of the modern human rights movement. However, there are good reasons for both Christians and Buddhists to be ambiguous about human rights. By sharing their own deliberations and doubts, Buddhists can be helpful to Christians as Christians discern how ambiguous the Christian affirmation of human rights must be.

NOTES

1. Dalai Lama, *A Policy of Kindness: An Anthology of Writings by and about the Dalai Lama* (Ithaca, NY: Snow Lion Publications, 1990), p. xviii.
2. Ibid., p. xix.
3. Sangharakshita, *Ambedkar and Buddhism* (Glasgow: Windhorse Publications, 1986), pp. 162–163.
4. Robert Traer, *Faith in Human Rights: Support in Religious Traditions for a Global Struggle* (Washington, DC: Georgetown University Press, 1991), p. 139.
5. "Introduction" to L.P.N. Perera, *Buddhism and Human Rights: A Buddhist Commentary on the Universal Declaration of Human Rights* (Colombo: Karunaratne & Sons, 1991), p. xi.
6. Sulak Sivaraksa, *A Socially Engaged Buddhism* (Bangkok: Khana Radom Tham, 1982), pp. 42–47. See also "Buddhism and Development – A Thai Perspective," *Ching Feng*, 26 (1983), pp. 123–133.
7. Damien Keown, "Are There Human Rights in Buddhism?" in *Buddhism and Human Rights*, ed. Damien Keown, Charles Prebish, and Wayne Husted (Richmond: Curzon, 1998), p. 20.
8. Ibid., pp. 20–23.
9. Sallie King, "Human Rights in Contemporary Engaged Buddhism," in *Buddhist Theology: Critical Reflections by Contemporary Buddhist Scholars*, ed. Roger R. Jackson and John J. Makransky (Richmond: Curzon, 2000), p. 300.
10. Ibid.
11. Keown, "Are There Human Rights in Buddhism?", p. 22.

12. Robert Thurman, "Social and Cultural Rights in Buddhism," in *Human Rights and the World's Religions*, ed. Leroy S. Rouner (Notre Dame: University of Notre Dame Press, 1988), p. 148.

13. Ibid. Compare Thurman's idealized Tibet (pp. 160–161) with the views of David Lopez, *Prisoners of Shangri-La: Tibetan Buddhism and the West* (Chicago: University of Chicago Press, 1998).

14. Thurman, "Social and Cultural Rights in Buddhism," p. 161.

15. Soraj Hongladarom, "Buddhism and Human Rights in the Thoughts of Sulak Sivaraksa and Phra Dhammapidok (Prayudh Prayutto)," in *Buddhism and Human Rights*, ed. Keown, Prebish, and Husted, p. 97. Similar statements could be made in regard to other Asian societies. For example, the term for "human rights" in Japan, *jinken*, has a distinctly modern and foreign connotation. The word was non-existent before the Meiji Period (1867–1912) and came into common use only after the end of the Second World War. A word with a more domestic and traditional character is "harmony," *wa*, the preservation of which can be juxtaposed to the idea of defending human rights in Japan.

16. Craig Ihara, "Why There are no Rights in Buddhism," in ibid., p. 44.

17. Haing Ngor and Roger Warner, *Haing Ngor: A Cambodian Odyssey* (New York: Macmillan, 1987).

18. Keown, "Are There Human Rights in Buddhism?" p. 31.

19. The adversarial character of human rights is an important issue for Sallie King. In contrast to Ihara, King argues that Buddhists can affirm human rights and work to promote them in a way that is non-adversarial. See King, "Human Rights in Contemporary Engaged Buddhism," pp. 298–300.

20. Ihara, "Why There are no Rights in Buddhism," p. 51.

21. Jay L. Garfield, "Human Rights and Compassion: Towards a Unified Moral Framework," in *Buddhism and Human Rights*, ed. Keown, Prebish, and Husted, pp. 111–140.

22. This sometimes makes identifying his work difficult. Prayudh Prayutto is the monk's original name. The titles Phra Rajavaramuni, Phra Depvedi, and most recently Phra Dhammapidok have been bestowed honorifically by the king. He is also the author of the widely respected exposition of basic Buddhist teachings, *Buddhadhamma* (Bangkok: Kledthai Press, 1974).

23. For a comparison of Sulak Sivaraksa and Phra Dammapidok on the question of human rights, see Hongladarom, "Buddhism and Human Rights in the Thoughts of Sulak Sivaraksa and Phra Dhammapidok (Prayudh Prayutto)," pp. 97–109.

24. As translated by Soraj Hongladarom, in ibid., p. 104.

25. Somewhat analogously to Phra Dhammapidok, Thurman speaks of human rights as the West's "desperate, perhaps ultimately ineffective, band-aid" used to "plaster over the mortal wound to human dignity inflicted by modernity's metaphysical materialism, psychological

reductionism, and nihilistic ethical relativism." See Thurman, "Social and Cultural Rights in Buddhism," p. 149.

26. Peter Junger, "Why the Buddha has no Rights," in *Buddhism and Human Rights*, ed. Keown, Prebish, and Husted, pp. 53–96.

27. Ibid., pp. 60–61.

28. Ibid., p. 67.

29. Ibid., pp. 81–82.

30. On Roman Catholic natural law theory, Junger quotes at length from Jacques Maritain, *The Rights of Man and Natural Law*, trans. Doris Anson (New York: Charles Schribner & Sons, 1943).

31. Junger, "Why the Buddha has no Rights," pp. 74–75.

32. Ibid., p. 56.

33. Ibid., pp. 55–56.

34. King, "Human Rights in Contemporary Engaged Buddhism," p. 293.

35. Garfield, "Human Rights and Compassion," pp. 122–123.

36. Ihara, "Why There are no Rights in Buddhism," p. 49.

37. Ibid., p. 50.

38. For Hoppe, see "Human Rights," in *The New Dictionary of Catholic Social Teaching*, ed. Judith Dwyer (Collegeville, MN: Liturgical Press, 1994), pp. 454–470, esp. pp. 455, 461. For Rommen, see "The Church and Human Rights," in *Modern Catholic Thinkers*, ed. R. Caponigri (New York: Harper Torchbooks, 1960), vol. 2, p. 398. For Payzs see his article on "Human Rights" in *The New Catholic Encyclopedia*, vol. 7, p. 212.

39. Louis Henkin, "Religion, Religions and Human Rights," *Journal of Religious Ethics* 26, 2 (1998), pp. 229–230; Jack Donnelly, "Human Rights and Asian Values: A Defense of 'Western' Universalism," in *The East Asian Challenge for Human Rights*, ed. Joanne Bauer and Daniel Bell (Cambridge: Cambridge University Press, 1999), pp. 60–87.

40. Roman Catholic Christianity provides one obvious example. Claiming that there is an implicit doctrine of human rights within the Roman Catholic tradition does much to obscure the fact that popes have generally been opposed to human rights, at least in the generally accepted understanding of the notion, until the last hundred years. Discussions of official Roman Catholic teaching on human rights often begin in 1891 with the promulgation of *Rerum Novarum* by Leo XIII, the first of a series of "social encyclicals" affirming human rights which continue to this day. In fact, explicit papal teaching on human rights can be traced at least to 1791 when Pius VI, in *Quod Aliquantum*, rejected the Declaration of the Rights of Man for its support of freedom of opinion and expression. In 1864, Pius IX condemned the freedom of religion in his *Syllabus of Errors*. In fact, the first official statement by the Roman Catholic Church in support of freedom of religion was issued only in 1965, the Document on Religious Liberty of the Second Vatican Council. Since the popes continue to teach that human dignity plays out in gender-specific roles,

many have argued that the Roman Catholic Church has yet to recognize the human rights of women.

41.   On this issue, see James V. Schall, "Human Rights: the 'So-Called' Judaeo-Christian Tradition," *Communio*, 8 (1981), p. 56.

42.   Nor is this awareness particularly recent. Jacques Maritain, a Roman Catholic thinker who made a seminal contribution to the 1948 Universal Declaration of Human Rights of the United Nations, was well aware that his way of justifying human rights was at times "entirely different" or "opposed" to the justifications offered by others who signed the Declaration. See his "Introduction" to UNESCO, *Human Rights: Comments and Interpretations* (London: Allan Wingate, 1949), pp. 10–11.

43.   The phrase originates with John Rawls. See the Fourth Lecture of his *Political Liberalism* (New York: Columbia University Press, 1993). For an application of this idea to the problem of the criticism of the human rights movement by certain East Asian governments, see Charles Taylor, "Conditions of an Unforced Consensus on Human Rights," in *The East Asian Challenge for Human Rights*, ed. Bauer and Bell, pp. 124–144.

Plate 19 Bhil tribal singers, Gauribai and her husband, in Rajasthan, India, singing the songs of the devotional Hindu saints, as do other Hindu and Muslim devotees from very low castes and tribal groups. Through songs attributed to the saints, Hindu devotees express the dignity and equality of all before God and resist the value system that privileges material wealth and high-caste status.

Photo: Nancy M. Martin

19

RIGHTS, ROLES, *and* RECIPROCITY *in* HINDU DHARMA

Nancy M. Martin

Bhimrao Ramji Ambedkar, a leading figure in the drafting of India's constitution, famously declared, "I will not die a Hindu," and after careful study of other religious traditions, he converted to Buddhism in 1956 along with nearly 500,000 members of his low-caste community, the Mahars. What might have driven Ambedkar to say such a thing and take such a radical step? The immediate cause was his realization that, after twelve years of working successfully to open all of India's temples to members of every caste, thereby ending the practice of excluding those people who belong to the castes considered most impure (formerly called "untouchables"), the status of these low-caste people remained unchanged in the eyes of their fellow Hindus. The degrading treatment and the abuse of members of the "untouchable" castes continued.

Out of his own experience, Ambedkar felt that he had come to recognize an unrelenting hierarchy in Hindu tradition which necessarily led to oppression, and so he chose to abandon his natal tradition in a very public manner. He began by exhorting a gathering of 10,000 low-caste leaders in 1935, saying,

> If you want to gain self-respect, change your religion.
> If you want to create a cooperating society, change your religion.
> If you want power, change your religion.
> If you want equality, change your religion.
> If you want independence, change your religion.[1]

Interestingly, Ambedkar did not choose to abandon religion altogether but chose to embrace a different religion and to continue to work for the protection of the rights of low-caste people by helping to instantiate the protection of human rights legally in the Indian constitution.[2]

Was Ambedkar correct in his assessment? Is Hinduism irrevocably hierarchical in a way that makes it unable to protect human rights and uphold the dignity of all? It is true, and important to recognize, that Hindu dharma *can* be construed to endorse a view of society as functioning under a type of social organization which I will designate "hierarchical complementarity," such that people have different but complementary roles within the society based on caste, gender, and life stage, and such that relations between people of different castes, genders, and ages are hierarchically defined. But is such a model of hierarchical complementarity necessarily and irrevocably oppressive? Another world tradition that functions under a similar model is Confucianism. This same question must be directed toward Confucianism and any other tradition that, along with Hinduism, embraces a hierarchical complementarity at its base.

Undoubtedly Ambedkar was correct that in India, in the early twentieth century, people within the "lower" castes too often suffered verbal and physical abuse, conscripted labor, and severe restrictions on such things as how and where they were allowed to live, what they were allowed to wear, and how they were allowed to practice religious ritual, and were systematically blocked from educational and economic advancement. The situation was exacerbated by British colonial rule, for the British seemingly found it easier to understand and to rule India through a hierarchy and instantiated dharmic texts like the *Laws of Manu* as the law of the land, as if they were universally accepted as definitive of Hindu practices and universally followed.[3] But the *Laws of Manu* is a law book composed by upper-caste Brahmin men for Brahmin men, with a number of very negative things to say about people of low caste and about women. For example, with respect to members of the lowest of the four major divisions of caste – the Shudras – the text reads: "But a Shudra, whether bought or unbought, he [the Brahmin] may compel to do servile work: for he was created by the Self – existent to be the slave of the Brahmin."[4] And of the requirements for a wife: "Though destitute of virtue, or seeking pleasure (elsewhere), or devoid of good qualities, (yet) a husband must be constantly worshipped as a god by a faithful wife."[5] This text neither was nor is today definitive of Hinduism nor was it or is it universally followed. Yet the British, whose dealings were primarily with Brahmins, seemingly preferred the simplicity of an ancient text to the complexities of custom and precedent and narrative that carry equal weight along with law books such as the *Laws of Manu* in solving disputes around matters of caste and gender relations.

Mahatma Gandhi agreed with Ambedkar's assessment that caste oppression must be fought. Both men worked tirelessly to better the conditions of the people whom Gandhi called Harijans or "children of God" and who call themselves Dalits, the "oppressed" or "broken." After independence, caste prejudice was outlawed in the emerging nation of India, the protection of human rights was written into the constitution, and "reservations" were made for people from oppressed groups so that they might have opportunities for educational and economic advancement and develop a political voice. Yet, unlike Ambedkar, Gandhi did not choose to abandon Hinduism. He did not share Ambedkar's assessment that Hinduism was irrevocably oppressive.

What Gandhi saw instead was the potential within Hinduism for a vision of a social order marked by what we might call "egalitarian complementarity," with a reciprocity of roles and an organic vision of society in which all members are vital participants and where personal and direct relationships of reciprocity are key. Gandhi's vision was fundamentally grounded in a Hindu worldview in which the ultimate oneness of all beings in the one reality, Brahman, generated a strong doctrine of non-violence and respect for the dignity and potential of all humans. And he drew inspiration from the devotional traditions of India and from such texts as the *Bhagavad Gita* as well as from the words of Jesus in the Sermon on the Mount. His understanding of dharma moved beyond notions of structure and duty to stress truth, a truth that called each person to act with non-violence, dignity, and compassion and thus to call forth the dignity and compassion of others.

Hinduism offers both views of social relations – that of hierarchical complementarity and that of egalitarian complementarity. In what follows I will begin with a closer examination of the Hindu notion of dharma and the basis for these two views – hierarchical and egalitarian complementarity – within Hinduism, and then, disagreeing with Ambedkar, I will argue that Hinduism has a valuable contribution to make to global discourse on human rights, both (1) through the teachings of Hinduism which advocate non-violence and compassion and thus relativize the meaning of hierarchies of difference and (2) through the Hindu vision of human community as marked by an egalitarian complementarity which incorporates both responsibilities and difference in a rich manner that a call for individualistic egalitarianism does not and indeed cannot attain.

HIERARCHY AND COMPLEMENTARITY IN HINDU DHARMA

Any viable discussion of human rights and responsibilities is grounded in both the fabric of social relations and ethical reasoning. Within the purview of the wide-ranging beliefs and practices arising in South Asia that are collectively called "Hinduism," there is a perceived order inherent in the world which is at once natural, social, and moral.[6] This structuring principle is dharma. And as Julius Lipner has suggested with respect to Hinduism's view of how human beings should live, "dharma has both a prescriptive and a descriptive connotation. Traditionally one's dharma is what one has to do to live an upright life, because one *ought* to do it (the moral aspect) and because that is the way one *is* (the natural aspect)."[7] With respect to its prescriptive aspect and the question of rights and responsibilities, dharma encompasses two levels of "privileges, duties and obligations" – those that are common or universal (*sadharana dharma*), i.e. incumbent on all people; and those that are specific, depending on one's gender, caste, and life-stage.[8]

The first sort of dharmic privileges, duties, and obligations which are shared by all people come closest to what we would call "universal human rights and responsibilities," though, in the Hindu view, one begins with duties and obligations, the fulfillment of which then confers privileges (rather than "rights" per se).[9] According to Gautama's *Dharma* (one of the earliest texts on dharma), elements of this common or universal dharma include the virtues of "compassion for all creatures, patience, lack of envy, purification, tranquility, having an auspicious disposition, generosity and lack of greed," and other texts offer additional listings.[10] Most important among these is the principle of *ahimsa* or non-injury, from which many of the other virtues flow.[11]

Implied in the type of virtues Gautama lists are basic responsibilities toward others – namely, to cause no injury and to treat them with compassion, patience, and generosity, without greed or envy. Therefore, these virtues, if practiced, would clearly offer motivational support for the protection of the basic rights of others – even, one might add, at the expense of one's own "rights."[12] Madhu Kishwar, the social activist and editor of the women's journal *Manushi*, recalls a story her mother told her repeatedly as a child when she would want to retaliate for some perceived wrong. The story tells of a saintly man who was bathing in a river. A scorpion had fallen into the water and the man reached in to rescue it from drowning. The scorpion immediately stung him, causing him to drop it again into the water. The man reached out again and again to rescue the scorpion and each time it stung him, causing him to drop it. A curious onlooker asked why he persisted. His response was "The scorpion's dharm is to sting, my dharm as a human is compassion. How can I forgo my dharm and return injury for injury, when even the scorpion is not willing to leave his own?"[13] Hinduism is replete with similar stories which explore the application of dharmic virtues and obligations and take account of the complexity of real-life situations as only narrative can do. Significantly, those Hindu texts that serve as resources for ethical decision making and judgment include not only the *dharmashastra* law books but also this vast body of narrative including the epic traditions of the *Ramayana* and the *Mahabharata*.[14]

It is noteworthy that the emphasis in the story Madhu Kishwar relates is on inalienable responsibilities rather than inalienable rights. In addition, human beings may share a common dharmic nature, but there is a distinction between human beings and other beings, for each class has its own dharma, and thus non-hierarchical complementarity also arises here in the difference between humans and other beings. The dharmic nature shared by humans and defined by the dharmic virtues is precisely that nature which Gandhi, in his non-violent campaign against the British, called upon people to mobilize within themselves and live up to, and it is this aspect of dharma that offers a strong foundation within Hinduism for upholding human rights through upholding human responsibilities.

In addition to this universal feature of dharma, human dharma also includes duties, privileges, and obligations which are not universally applicable to all humans but rather particular and related to a person's caste, gender, and age. Underlying these differing duties and privileges is an organic view of society and a relational understanding of the human person. A person is defined as a member of both a family and a community with particular responsibilities at different stages in his or her life. Roles and responsibilities are further understood to be a function of one's nature as defined by gender, by the kinship group into which one is born – i.e. one's caste – and by one's individual abilities.

Ideally such an organic understanding of society facilitates the well-being of all through the division of labor and mutual responsibility and reciprocity. The image of society as divided in this manner in terms of roles appears in earliest Hindu text, the *Rig Veda*. In the hymn to Purusha (*Rig Veda* 10:90) the world is said to be created through the sacrifice of the Cosmic Person. From the mouth the Brahmin priests are made, the Kshatriya rulers and warriors from the arms, the Vaishya merchants and artisans from the thighs, and the Shudras or servants from the feet. This hymn suggests social stratification and role division quite apart from any consideration of heredity.

Yet hierarchy seems inherent in such an image of the mutual division of labor, and indeed these divisions appear to be ossified in a hereditary and hierarchically related manner based on an understanding of purity. The underlying conception is that those at the highest level of society are to remain pure in order that they might carry out the necessary ritual interaction with the divine on behalf of the society as a whole and preserve and teach the wisdom of the sages. With each descending level, impurity increases. The lowest of the Shudras traditionally carried out the most impure functions needed within the society, such as sweeping up excrement and dealing with the bodies of dead animals in the making of leather goods.

Such distinctions do not necessarily imply prejudice, and they need not result in oppression and the violation of human rights. Gandhi argued forcefully that they should not do either. As a clear example, he required all members of his community to undertake the cleaning of latrines. That one's role should be defined simply by kinship without concern for individual proclivities and capabilities was, for Gandhi, an unreasonable limitation. Thus Gandhi argued that one's responsibilities within such an organic social structure ought to be based on one's individual nature and abilities.

All that being said, it is true that when heredity and hierarchy enter this system, those at the bottom have sometimes suffered terribly. This led some to agree with Ambedkar that this system of hierarchical complementarity is hopelessly flawed and should just be scrapped for what we might call an individual egalitarianism, such as is often affirmed in the West. But is it really necessary that to be "equal" must mean "interchangeable," as it has tended to mean in the West? And does complementarity necessarily have to be hierarchical? This has long been an issue in international feminist discourse, where feminists in India, for example, rankled under the critiques of Western feminists who saw complementarity as inherently oppressive.

To get rid of caste is not such an easy matter in any case. Castes are extended kin groups within which one marries and which form a fundamental element of social identity and belonging. The actual closed endogamous groups to which people belong, called *jatis*, number in the thousands, all hierarchically related to one another within the four larger categories of Brahmin, Kshatriya, Vaishya, and Shudra, called *varna*. Within the dharmic structure, caste relations are complex and not simply hierarchical. Castes interrelate in multiple ways – not only in hierarchical terms of purity, but also in terms of centrality and mutuality.[15] Relationships of centrality refer to the responsibility of the economically and socially dominant caste (which may fall anywhere on the purity scale) ritually to remove inauspiciousness or misfortune from the community as a whole through a series of gifts given to members of other specified castes (from high to low) within a given community. These ritual gifts are understood to diffuse misfortune or bad luck away from the community to individuals, but this is also a way to distribute wealth so that basic needs of community members are addressed. Thus it is also a facet of the caste system that those with economic and political power are responsible to care for those within their realm of influence.

THE RELIGIOUS JUSTIFICATION OF OPPRESSION

In addition to relationships marked by hierarchy and centrality, castes relate in terms of mutuality. Each caste provides goods and services to others in established relationships of reciprocity maintained across generations between specific families. There is a certain equality in relationships of mutuality, an egalitarian complementarity arising from the reciprocal exchange of services and the fulfillment of responsibilities. Yet this balance of reciprocity works only when relationships are maintained. If there is a surplus of workers, those more socially advantaged might choose to hire the person who will provide the service at the lowest cost rather than honoring these multigenerational relationships of exchange. Then the reciprocity of mutual obligation breaks down.

When hierarchy becomes the dominant mode of interaction between people of different castes, the system can become oppressive, particularly so when acceptance of one's low status (and the deprivation that may come with it) is religiously justified in terms of dharma and when a reward for endurance is promised in future lives by way of compensation. For instance, the *Bhagavad Gita* states unequivocally that it is better to do one's own dharma, even if poorly, than to try to do another's dharma.[16] Emphasis is also sometimes put on one's karma as a justification for the social position of one's caste or gender in any given birth, so that low status and a difficult life becomes a kind of penance for past wrongs, with a promise of improved future lives through the proper fulfillment of one's caste and/or gender duties in this life.

Practitioners of Hinduism are not alone in offering religious justifications for oppression and human rights violations. We can find a multitude of examples from nearly every religious tradition where religiously based language is used to keep the "poor" (broadly defined) and women in their "place," whether or not they espouse a view of hierarchical complementarity like that embodied in some Hindu understandings of dharma. A similar use of religious language to justify human rights violations can be gleaned from the history of Christianity which ostensibly advocates equality.

In the antebellum south of the United States, sermons delivered to enslaved people of African descent consisted of biblical passages emphasizing that a slave should obey his or her master and that one should turn the other cheek, coupled with the assurance that one's reward would come in heaven and that justice belonged to God alone. While these are indeed important teachings within Christianity, the masters and mistresses of the slaves did not have the same message preached in their own churches. (Nor, it should be noted, did the enslaved people simply accept this language and reproduce it among themselves, any more than low-caste Hindus like Ambedkar accepted everything in the *dharmashastra* texts – a point Ambedkar made by publicly burning them.) The language of rights dominated the sermons the masters and mistresses heard, upholding their economic and social position as divinely ordained – God's blessing upon the righteous and the "chosen" – even as the language of privilege dominated references to Brahmin men within the *Laws of Manu*.[17]

To continue this comparison, alternative religiously based voices have arisen out of both Hinduism and Christianity as well as other religious traditions, articulating equality and challenging the use of religion to justify the mistreatment and dehumanization of others. Without reciprocity, Christian teachings such as "turn the other cheek" quite readily become teachings designed to perpetuate slavery or the subordination of women, in contradistinction to the biblical insistence that before God there is "neither Jew nor Greek... neither slave nor free... neither male nor female" (Gal. 3:28, RSV). However, it is also significant that Christians were prime movers in the abolitionist and civil rights movements in the United States. So just as we should not dismiss Christianity as having no resources to support human rights because of the use of Christian texts to reinforce slavery or because there are racists who identify themselves as Christians, so we should not dismiss Hinduism because of caste-based or gender-based oppression, though certainly these actions and prejudices must be challenged in both traditions. Turning our attention to Hinduism, there are other voices coming from within the

Hindu tradition which do radically challenge such oppression and uphold the dignity of all.

RELIGIOUS CHALLENGES TO THE VIOLATION OF HUMAN RIGHTS

One principal mode of challenge to the danger of oppression embedded in the hierarchical complementarity of the dharmic system is to deemphasize the importance of this structure on religious grounds and emphasize the universal and egalitarian aspects of dharma and of human beings. For example, the Upanishads radically relativized existing notions of caste, suggesting that the true self of all individuals is one with the true self of all that is – Atman – and that this unity, rather than caste, is what ultimately matters. One implication of belief in the oneness of all is a sense of responsibility for all that happens in the world, including human rights abuses, because as the *Chandogya Upanishad* says, "all that is you."[18]

Irawati Karve has written eloquently about this realization, suggesting that it is easy for us to feel a oneness with nature during a beautiful sunset or with those we love, but much more sobering to come to the realization of our oneness with the victims and with the perpetrators of horrific violence, which is equally implied in this Upanishadic idea.[19] In response to such a realization, it becomes one's duty to work against such violence, for as the *Bhagavad Gita* makes clear, human beings in the world must act. Not to act is also to act. The only question is how we will act. The *Gita* advocates acting according to dharma and not for self, a call to which Gandhi responded in affirming virtuous action, marked by non-violence and compassion for both the British colonizers and the colonized Indians. Such a realization of oneness indeed makes it very difficult to establish the sense of separation required to assume a superior position and to see another as less than oneself, the precursor to rights violations and violence, as Gerrie ter Harr has indicated.[20]

The later devotional or *bhakti* traditions that began to appear in India in the sixth century in the south make even more radical statements suggesting that all are equal in the presence of the one divine reality of which we are all a part, conceived of in personalistic terms as God. The particulars of one's current incarnation – including gender and caste – have no relevance before God. Religious authority lies not in heredity but in religious experience and the ability to draw others into relationship with the one divine reality who is loved by and loves the devotee. The ninth-century saint and devotee of Vishnu, Nammalvar (whose songs are still popular today), sings thus of caste:

> The four castes
> Uphold all clans;
> Go down, far down
> To the lowliest outcastes
> Of outcastes...

If they are the servants of God, he says:

> Then even the slaves of their slaves
> Are our masters.[21]

In so saying, Nammalvar does not deny the existence of castes or the complementarity of their roles and responsibilities, but he does deny the ideal of hierarchy that would value and privilege the Brahmin over the outcaste.

The twelfth-century Virashaiva poet–saint Dasimayya offers a similar perspective which relativizes gender distinctions, suggesting that people often focus inappropriately on mere physical features – seeing facial hair, they call that person a man; seeing breasts and long hair, they call that one a woman:

> But, look, the self that hovers
> In between
> Is neither man nor woman.[22]

For Dasimayya, a fundamental equality underlies and relativizes gender distinctions although it does not erase them.

Nammalvar and Dasimayya are not isolated cases. The *bhakti* movements had spread rapidly across India by the sixteenth century. The songs of these and other devotional or *bhakti* saints are sung now regularly in evening village gatherings in homes or local temples and played across the airwaves of *akashwani*, all-India radio. They are sung by Muslims as well as Hindus, and popular devotional singers like Anup Jalota and Lata Mangeshkar have the same kind of following that secular rock stars might in the West. These songs and the life stories of the saints, many of whom belonged to formerly "untouchable" castes or were women, permeate people's awareness, and devotion is by far the most widely practiced form of Hinduism. Indeed, Ambedkar's family was deeply devoted to Kabir, the iconoclastic saint who condemned caste hierarchy and undermined the notion of purity that is the basis of Brahmin claims to superiority well as condemning the religious exclusivism that focuses on the external practices of both Hindus and Muslims rather than on relationship to God.

As a premier example of one who practiced non-violent resistance, Gandhi also turned to the devotional saints, choosing the upper-caste saint Mirabai, who renounced her life of privilege and endured great persecution for, among other things, her perceived violations of a woman's dharmic duties to her husband and because she associated with people of all castes and with men outside her family (albeit with holy men or *sadhus*) in the practice of her devotion. Songs attributed to Mirabai and Kabir and other devotional saints are typically sung by those of low caste, providing a language to articulate resistance and assert human dignity as well as to express theological understanding and religious experience.[23] The *bhakti* saints were not social revolutionaries, but the traditions that surround them present an alternate value system which honors the dignity of all and challenges the valuation of individuals on the basis of material possessions or social position.

Sometimes these religious statements of equality are interpreted in strictly spiritual terms that do not extend outside the realm of religious practice, particularly as movements become institutionalized, but some interpret them as also calling for radical social change. In the history of religious traditions, we find real world attempts to establish societies where hierarchical distinctions are not made and where the needs of all are provided by the whole. An example would be the Jesuit work during the time of the conquistadors in the highlands of South America. In Hinduism, the Virashaivas of South India (the Kannada-speaking region) established the "Mansion of Experience" in Kalyana in the twelfth century under the leadership of the saints Basavanna and Allama Prabhu (fellow devotees with Dasimayya, quoted earlier) – a community 190,000 strong, where authority was based solely on religious experience and where caste distinctions were left behind.[24] Unfortunately the wider society, in both this Indian case and that of the Jesuits mentioned above, would not tolerate such experiments for long. The Jesuit mission was brutally destroyed, and the Mansion of Experience collapsed after a formerly low-caste man and a formerly Brahmin woman married and the king had their fathers dragged to death through the streets. Some less spiritually advanced members of the Virashaiva community responded with violence, assassinating the king, in spite of Basavanna's entreaty not to react in kind, and unleashed massive riots that scattered the community.

These relatively small experiments within larger cultural systems that opposed them perhaps could not succeed at the time, but they offer us inspiration and testify to the deep roots of challenge within these traditions to human rights violations. Envisioning a new future of equality is vastly strengthened when it can be rooted in a past marked by courageous action which provides an identity for a people as part of a lineage that opposes dehumanization and seeks equality. Similar experiments today may still meet with similar resistance and violence, as the assassinations of Gandhi and Martin Luther King, Jr. attest, but we can see the important role that religious motivation has played in change around the world when we consider the civil rights movement in the U.S., the Indian independence movement, and the South African rejection of apartheid.

A HINDU CALL TO HUMAN RIGHTS AND RESPONSIBILITIES

Although India today has a good legal system supporting individual rights, hierarchies remain, as Ambedkar predicted, as does poverty and caste and gender oppression. Ambedkar's and India's embrace of rights language and laws, while extremely helpful, has by itself proved insufficient to the task without a fuller integration with the existing religiously based social structure of dharma. The solution, it seems, lies in between the hierarchical complementarity of roles and the individualist egalitarianism of rights in a language and action that will honor both equality and individual rights *and* mutual responsibilities and complementarity.

To advocate, as Gandhi did, a possible vision of community structured by an egalitarian complementarity (rather than a hierarchical complementarity or an individualistic egalitarianism) is not to advocate the "separate but equal" understanding of the segregationist southern United States. It is to challenge any hierarchical valuing of human differences radically and to call for the full recognition of the humanity and dignity of all, and in so doing to erase the degradation and oppression of those deemed "lower" that might result from hierarchical valuing. But to advocate egalitarian complementarity is also to advocate a deep recognition of interrelationship and interdependence in a way that values and cherishes difference as a vital part of the world community. This is the model that Hinduism challenges us to consider, as we seek to uphold human rights worldwide – an egalitarian complementarity, where roles and differences both find a place without hierarchy and where reciprocity ensures that the rights and dignity of all can be upheld.

NOTES

1. Ambedkar, quoted by Christopher S. Queen in "Dr. Ambedkar and the Hermeneutics of Buddhist Liberation," in *Engaged Buddhism: Buddhist Liberation Movements in Asia*, ed. Christopher S. Queen and Sallie B. King (Albany: State University of New York Press, 1996), p. 51.

2. See John Carmen, "Duties and Rights in Hindu Society," in *Human Rights and the World's Religions*, ed. Leroy S. Rouner (Notre Dame: University of Notre Dame Press, 1988), esp. pp. 117–118.

3. Nicholas B. Dirks offers a history of the development of understandings of caste in his *Castes of Mind: Colonialism and the Making of Modern India* (Princeton: Princeton University Press, 2001).

4. *Laws of Manu* 8.413, in *A Sourcebook in Indian Philosophy*, ed. Sarvepalli Radhakrishnan and Charles A. Moore (Princeton: Princeton University Press, 1957), p. 189.

5. *Laws of Manu* 5. 154, ibid., p. 191.

6. See Julius Lipner, "A Hindu View of Life," in *The Meaning of Life in the World Religions*, ed. Joseph Runzo and Nancy M. Martin (Oxford: Oneworld Publications, 2000), pp. 111–135.

7. Ibid., p. 121.

8. Vasudha Narayanan, "Hindu Ethics and Dharma," in *Ethics in the World Religions*, ed. Joseph Runzo and Nancy M. Martin (Oxford: Oneworld Publications, 2001), pp. 178, 181–182.

9. Carmen, "Duties and Rights in Hindu Society," p. 124.

10. Narayanan, "Hindu Ethics and Dharma," p. 182.

11. See Arindam Chakrabarti's discussion of the virtues delineated in Patanjali's *Yogasutras* in chapter 3 of this volume, pp. 57–58 above.

12. See Vrinda Dalmiya, "Dogged Loyalities: A Classical Indian Intervention in Care Ethics," in *Ethics in the World Religions*, ed. Runzo and Martin, pp. 293–306.

13. Madhu Kishwar, "In Defense of our Dharma," *Manushi* 79 (Nov.–Dec. 1990), reprinted in Madhu Kishwar, *Religion in the Service of Nationalism and Other Essays* (New Delhi: Oxford University Press, 1998), p. 122.

14. See, for example, Dalmiya, "Dogged Loyalities."

15. Gloria Raheja, *The Poison in the Gift: Ritual, Prestation, and the Dominant Caste in a North Indian Village* (Chicago: University of Chicago Press, 1988), pp. 239–254.

16. *Bhagavad Gita* III: 35.

17. See Albert J. Raboteau, *Slave Religion: The "Invisible Institution" in the Antebellum South* (Oxford: Oxford University Press, 1978); and James C. Scott, *Domination and the Arts of Resistance* (New Haven and London: Yale University Press, 1990), esp. pp. 115–117.

18. *Chandogya Upanishad*, sixth prapathaka.

19. Irawati Karve, "All that is you," in *The Experience of Hinduism: Essays on*

Religion in Maharashtra, ed. Eleanor Zelliot and Maxine Berntsen (Albany: State University of New York Press, 1988), pp. 213–222.

20.   See chapter 5 of this volume.

21.   A.K. Ramanujan, trans., *Hymns for the Drowning: Poems for Visnu by Nammalvar* (Delhi: Penguin Books, 1993 [1981]), p. 60.

22.   A.K. Ramanujan, *Speaking of Siva* (Delhi: Penguin Books, 1973), p.110.

23.   See Nancy M. Martin, "Kabir and Mirabai in Folk Traditions of Western Rajasthan: Meghwal and Mauganiyar Repertoires," in *The Banyon Tree: Essays in Early Literature in New Indo-Aryan Languages*, vol. 2, ed. Mariola Offredi (Delhi: Manohar, 2000), pp. 391–418; and "Homespun Threads of Dignity and Protest: Songs of Kabir in Rural Rajasthan," in *Image of Kabir*, ed. Monika Horstmann (Delhi: Manohar, 2002), pp. 199–214.

24.   Ramanujan, *Speaking of Siva*, pp. 62–64.

Plate 20 Statue of Confucius, standing at the stairway into the Confucian Temple and Imperial Academy in Beijing, China. In the Confucian tradition, the web of responsibilities between persons defines social order, which, in turn, is a reflection of the divine order. This Beijing temple is one of the largest Confucian temples outside Qufu, the birthplace of Confucius. Photo: *Joseph Runzo*

20

CONFUCIAN VALUES *and* HUMAN RIGHTS

Sumner B. Twiss

A common perception of the Confucian tradition is that it is authoritarian, meritocratic, and intrinsically resistant to human rights of any sort. Indeed, it is claimed by some scholars of the tradition that at its deepest moral and conceptual level Confucianism is simply incompatible with human rights as understood by the international community.[1] I believe that such perceptions are shortsighted and need to be countered, especially if it is possible that the Confucian tradition may reemerge as a stronger social and political force in the People's Republic of China. Contrary to these views, I wish to propose that all three "generations" (or types) of human rights – civil-political, socio-economic, and collective-developmental – are compatible with the Confucian tradition and that fundamental Confucian values can support universal human rights in a surprisingly robust manner. The case that I present has three parts: (1) overview hypotheses relating the three generations of human rights to the Confucian tradition (here mentioning broad moral–political themes of the tradition); (2) explicit attention to the political thought of the seventeenth-century Neo-Confucian Huang Tsung-hsi (whose essentials of humane governance provide functional analogues of human rights); and (3) brief discussion of the Confucian contributions of P.C. Chang, the Chinese delegate to and vice-chair of the commission that drafted the United Nations Universal Declaration of Human Rights in 1947–1948.

OVERVIEW HYPOTHESIS

Let me begin by offering a brief characterization of the Confucian tradition that I believe many scholars and adherents would accept.[2] The Confucian tradition is communitarian in outlook. That is to say, it holds that persons are essentially socially interrelated beings, and it emphasizes duties that people must pursue toward the common good as well as virtues needed for the fulfillment of these duties. Furthermore, Confucianism holds that certain reciprocal role relationships (e.g. parent–child, elder–younger siblings, ruler–subject) are crucial in achieving a flourishing community of basic trust among persons all working together in a mutually supportive way to achieve a good life for all.[3]

At the same time, the tradition also emphasizes for all its adherents, from ruler to commoner, the importance of personal moral self-cultivation in relationship with others – "a benevolent man helps others to take their stand in so far as he himself wishes to take his stand, and gets others there in so far as he himself wishes to get there."[4] This notion of self-cultivation incorporates the view that all people have the moral potential to develop the interrelated virtues of humaneness (benevolence), righteousness (justice), propriety (civility), and wisdom (moral discernment), particularly when they are guided by moral exemplars (sages) who are themselves guided by their own discerning interpretations of the tradition's basic texts and history.

This strong emphasis on persons interrelated in community is further grounded in a cosmological vision of the interdependence of all beings in the universe, which in turn sustains and develops a basic human sympathy for the whole and its constituent parts. This ideal of sympathy (humane caring) is cast in the image of extending care from within family relationships into ever-larger concentric circles of care for others. As a consequence of this vision, the Confucian tradition is greatly concerned about all those conditions – e.g. social, economic, educational – that bear on people's ability to cultivate their moral potential to flourish as responsible members of an organically flourishing community in a harmoniously functioning universe.

The tradition has historically emphasized, in both its classical and subsequent phases, the responsibility of the ruler or state to ensure the material welfare of the people – providing, for example, subsistence, livelihood, education, famine relief. Such benefits are conceived as conditions necessary for people's self-cultivation of their moral potential, and to deny them these benefits would mean denying them the opportunity to fulfill their human and cosmological destiny. This is a primary theme in both Confucius (fifth century BCE) and Mencius (third century BCE), whose works contain much advice to and remonstration with kings along these lines. The theme is even taken so far as to impose limits on political legitimacy, thus bordering on a claim of social guarantee of such benefits. Mencius, for example, arguably advances the notion of righteous revolt against an emperor who, in materially oppressing the people, loses the "Mandate of Heaven" (the ultimate source of political legitimacy).[5] Now it seems to me a short step from this kind of position to the contention that the tradition has the resources to appreciate and support socio-economic human rights. In fact, we may arguably discern this compatibility and support in the background to the openness of twentieth-century Chinese regimes to the idea of socio-economic rights.[6]

There is also reason to suggest that the Confucian tradition may be more open to civil–political human rights than is usually perceived. Here I would begin by citing Mencius' ideas of human moral potential that is shared equally by all human beings and of the "natural nobility" (or "nobility of Heaven") that is attainable by all who self-consciously develop this potential.[7] These ideas clearly strike themes of equality, human dignity, and voluntarism similar to those associated with civil–political human rights. Even more to the point are those later Neo-Confucian thinkers (eleventh–seventeenth centuries) who, in building on the ideas of Mencius, advanced strong claims about the moral nature of humankind, individual perfectibility, and the autonomy of the moral mind and individual conscience.[8] These thinkers also advanced provocative proposals regarding the self-governance of local communities, a reformed conception of the law as a necessary check on political abuse of the people, and a conception of public education as a means of enhancing people's political participation in their communities. I believe that notions such as these move in the direction of recognizing civil–political human rights as positive empowerments for people's mutual involvement in social and political processes aimed at communal flourishing. I will return to these notions in more detail shortly in connection with the thought of Huang Tsung-hsi.

I would also suggest that the Confucian worldview is open to collective–developmental human rights. This suggestion is supported in part by the aforementioned notion of righteous rebellion by the people collectively against material oppression as well as the Neo-Confucian recognition of the importance of communal self-governance, both of which tend in the direction of collective rights to political self-determination and community development. This tendency may also be supported by that highest of Confucian ideals – "the unity of Man and Heaven" or "one body with heaven, earth, and the myriad things" – which defines humankind in cosmological moral terms.[9] This ideal extends Confucian humanism and its sense of moral responsibility to a planetary or even universal scale, recognizing collective claims to peace, harmony, and the well-being of the entire holistic community of interdependent beings.

There are, then, reasons for thinking that the Confucian tradition has the resources to recognize, appreciate, and accept the priority of those values represented by international human rights. This recognition remains true even if the tradition itself prefers not to employ internally the language of human rights.[10] The point is that the tradition nonetheless recognizes and supports the content of human rights even to the degree of social guarantee in some cases.

HUANG TSUNG-HSI

Thus far I have been speaking in generalities about the Confucian tradition and its values, offering what I regard as reasonable hypotheses about their compatibility with human rights. In order to make my case more convincing, it might be useful to focus briefly on the forward-looking political thought of the seventeenth-century Neo-Confucian thinker Huang Tsung-hsi whose views appear to provide functional analogues to human rights. Huang's thought was particularly influential in the late nineteenth and early twentieth centuries when he came to be acclaimed by reformers and revolutionaries alike as a champion of indigenous Chinese "democratic" ideas.[11] I focus particular attention here on Huang's views concerning the essentials of governance, legal reform, the role of prince and ministers, the role of education and schools, and the importance of land and tax reform. Unfortunately, space constraints prevent me from quoting extensively from Huang's work *Waiting for the Dawn: A Plan for the Prince*, so I will confine myself to characterizing his thinking on these topics.

Let me begin with a brief orientation to Huang's manuscript. He prefaces his work by stating that he intends to itemize "the essentials of a grand system of governance," which I interpret to mean those functional requisites and priorities for ensuring a stable, peaceful, and just society.[12] Huang himself subsequently uses terms and phrases such as these (followed by my identification of basic themes): "peace or disorder in the world depends upon the happiness or distress of the people" (foundation of peace and justice); "safeguarding the world for the sake of all-under-Heaven, providing means of subsistence, education, social institutions" (freedom from want); "esteem for those at court and for those in the countryside...imbuing all with the broad and magnanimous spirit of the classics" (equal human dignity and worth);

"only if there is governance by law can there be governance by men" (protection by the rule of law); "outspoken discussion of important issues without fear of those in power" (freedom of speech and freedom from fear).[13]

I want to suggest that Huang's essentials of governance have an aim and aspiration approximating that of international human rights, by quoting these remarkable parallels from the United Nations Universal Declaration of Human Rights.[14] (1) "providing the foundation of freedom, justice and peace in the world"; (2) "freedom of speech and belief and freedom from fear and want are the highest aspiration of the common people"; (3) "if man is not to have recourse to rebellion against tyranny and oppression... human rights should be protected by the rule of law"; (4) "affirmation of the dignity and worth of the human person." These similarities suggest to me that Huang's essentials of governance may well be functional analogues of human rights.

Huang's essentials of governance crucially involve the notion of the rule of law understood as functioning to safeguard the world for the sake of the people. According to Huang, there will be proper governance by humans only if there is governance by laws designed to serve the people so that they are assured of adequate subsistence, education, physical security, regulative rules and social institutions, and peace.[15] That is to say, true law or just law, as contrasted with what Huang calls "un-lawful laws," is needed as a check on political abuse by the ruler so that (1) the people are safeguarded and treated fairly; and (2) governance by humans is possible, with the latter involving the notion of shared decision making between the prince and his ministers and open to public input (more on this below). Huang's view of the importance of law for the people's welfare and proper governance is certainly compatible with and functionally analogous to the regulative role of human rights and their explicitly stated concern to mitigate "tyranny and oppression" and to protect people by "the rule of law."[16]

After introducing the idea that the ancient "Law of the Three Dynasties [symbolizing true law] safeguarded the world for the sake of all-under-Heaven," Huang further claims that "high esteem was not reserved to those at court; nor were those in the countryside... held in low esteem." [17] Taken contextually, this claim suggests the notion that, while accepting social hierarchical distinctions among people, Huang nevertheless regards the people as equal before the law. This interpretation is strengthened when, in subsequently discussing reforms for subofficials, Huang explicitly cites as the first evil of the then current system: "When [the riff-raff subofficials] are put in [a] position where it is possible to profit themselves, there is no limit to what they may do. In order to serve their own ends they devise all sorts of legal snares. The legal code in effect today is entirely their creation."[18] In order to counter this evil, among others he identifies, Huang recommends restoring a draft service system at the local level, assigning posts of lower responsibility (e.g. policing) on a yearly rotational basis to the households of a local district, and assigning higher positions of responsibility (e.g. courts) to scholar-officials for fixed terms of office. One effect of such reform would be to eliminate legal abuses from the system, and it seems plausible to suggest that this reform heads in the direction of "equal protection of the law."[19]

Erected upon his ideas of governance by law is Huang's notion of shared governance between the prince and his ministers, which involves the idea that their proper role is to work together for the sake of all-under-Heaven according to the Way (sagacious determination of right and wrong courses of action). Huang images this notion of shared governance in the analogy of the "hauling of great logs," where "the men in front call out, 'Heave!', those behind, 'Ho!'" so that "the prince and his ministers should be log-haulers working together" in cooperative harmony. Huang subsequently speaks of ministers sharing the function of the prince, and he argues vigorously for the reestablishment of the office of prime minister, who sets up meetings involving the prince, himself, and other ministers of state for the discussion and deliberation of public affairs. Says Huang, these deliberations are to be specifically informed by memorials from people "all over the land...so that no matter fails to come to the government's attention."[20] I believe that Theodore de Bary is substantially correct in regarding this notion of shared governance based on governance by law as analogous to constitutional limitation of the ruler's power and as heading in the direction of a constitutional order resembling the British system of government.[21] These resemblances become even more striking when considering Huang's views on the political roles of schools (see below).

The important thing to note at this point is that even in the highest corridors of political power, Huang mandates a cooperative decision-making process, controlled by the rule of law, dedicated to the priority interests of the people, and open to considering information, views, and ideas from people outside the government. These features tend in the direction of opening the door (albeit just a crack) to a functional analogue to the human right of political participation and the notion of "the will of the people" serving as "the basis of the authority of government."[22] It also opens the door (again just a crack) to a functional analogue to "freedom of opinion and expression," including the freedom to "impart information and ideas."[23] These doors open even wider when we consider Huang's discussion of the function of schools, the importance of education for all the people, and the selection of scholar-officials for government service.

In Huang's treatment of these topics, we encounter a veritable mother lode of concepts and ideas functionally analogous to a number of important human rights. According to Huang, the schools function not only to train scholar-officials but also to produce "all the instrumentalities for governing all-under-Heaven." A particularly important instrumentality is the "outspoken discussion of important issues without fear of those in power." The protection of such discussion is to be accomplished by granting local autonomy to school districts so that participants in public discussions (i.e. scholars and students) can speak out without reserve.[24] This is not far from the notion of the free exchange of information and ideas, and, as de Bary suggests, the schools appear to function as parliaments encouraging ever broader discussion of administrative, political, social, and economic issues.[25] Protected public discussion and collective deliberation and decision making are the watchwords here, connoting processes which clearly enhance political participation and consensual government (though these are admittedly restricted to the educated).

The prime function of schools, of course, is to educate people, and the above can be construed broadly as an educational process plugging into the system of governance. But Huang has much more to say about education and who ought to be educated and how. He explicitly says that schools are "meant to imbue all men, from the highest at court to the humblest in country villages, with the broad and magnanimous spirit of the Classics." He also says that "the height of inhumanity" is to allow people to lose all education and that "the youngsters of each district should proceed to school," including here both elementary and more advanced schools. He would also use the property of temples for "the support of poor students."[26] My point here is that Huang appears to hold that education is such a high priority interest that it ought to be universal so that all, including the humblest and the poorest, have access to it. Huang also holds that education primarily serves the purpose of moral and humanistic education in the classics, which I interpret to mean the advancement of self-cultivation in the central Confucian virtues as well as knowledge of the world needed to equip people to be sagacious deliberators about the common good. In his discussion of the training and examination of scholar-officials, Huang displays considerable commitment to education in history, creative thinking, various practical sciences, and the arts.[27]

Furthermore, students are to advance through the education system only on the basis of meritorious achievement.

I contend that this picture of the priority of education is not far removed from the human right to education. Quoting from the U.D.H.R.

> Everyone has the right to education. Education shall be free, at least in the elementary and fundamental stages. Elementary education shall be compulsory. Technical and professional education shall be made generally available and higher education shall be equally accessible to all on the basis of merit. Education shall be directed to the full development of the human personality and to the strengthening of respect for human rights.[28]

Here we have a strong functional analogue to a human right.

Now what is interesting about this right is the fact that it is internally complex and involves many conceptual features ordinarily associated with different types or generations of human rights.[29] For example, it is often argued that a minimal level of education is necessary for political participation and for socio-economic advancement through work. Education also develops one's personality and character and equips one to participate in cultural development. Education requires the investment of social resources so as to maintain schools effectively and to provide access to them. To do their job properly, educational institutions must have a degree of autonomy in order to protect open discussion without fear of reprisal. And so the list could go on. The point is that a full understanding of the right to education involves aspects analogous to or presupposing civil–political liberties and protections, socio-economic rights, and collective–developmental rights. A further point is that Huang, without the use of rights language, is clearly aware of this sort of internal complexity, seeing education as a set of priority interests in a similar interdependent web of requirements.

A final element of Huang's views on education that I want to consider briefly is the selection of scholar-officials.[30] Here Huang argues that in order to advance the quality of governance and meet the needs of the people, it is absolutely essential to have a liberal selection system at the points of initial access – so as to identify and encourage as much talent as possible – and a strict employment system as the process proceeds – so as to weed out those unsuitable for governing with moral commitment, judicious deliberation, and creative thinking. It bears remarking that Huang is advocating a system that broadens access to the education system from all social and economic classes, while weeding out those who do not live up to expectations. This system is aimed at ensuring scholar-officials of the highest caliber who will be more likely to contribute to advancing the welfare of the people, with the side benefit of bringing ever more people into the system of governance. This latter feature, when combined with universal education, has the effect of further enhancing the extent and quality of political participation as well as the tendency toward consensual government.

Huang expends considerable effort on designing and recommending reforms for land and tax policies because he believes them to be unjust as they have developed over the years – indeed, centuries.[31] At the outset of his discussion of these topics, Huang is clearly attracted to the egalitarian fairness of the ancient system of land shared in common with its use distributed by the ruler on the basis of people's needs, soil fertility, population changes, and alterations in the general conditions of life. After this system was ended and private ownership of land introduced, the people became subject to taxes initially calculated on the basis of the poorest land serving as the standard for taxation, which is already somewhat of an unfair bargain from Huang's viewpoint, since "the people had to take care of themselves" and "in addition…became subject to taxes." Worse still, subsequently the tax rates were increased in such a way that "the best land served as the standard," resulting in even higher taxes and considerable and inescapable suffering of the people. Huang comments, "if a true king should arise, I believe he should revise the taxes of the empire, and…take the poorest land as the standard."

The system that Huang eventually recommends involves a concession to private land ownership – "today people own their own land and to deprive them of it by decree would be 'doing even one act that is not right' [Mencius]" – combined with the redistribution of land sufficient for subsistence from imperial private estates and official lands to people in need – all with a differential tax rate, lower for land already privately owned, higher for new plots gained from the redistribution.[32] He is essentially advocating an egalitarian reassignment of what he regards as common lands to the people in need and supporting the subsistence of each household, combined with the acceptance of extant private ownership. In connection with land distribution, Huang further advocates that the land be classified according to its agricultural capacity and assigned accordingly – more land if of low capacity, less land if of better capacity.

The first thing to be remarked is that Huang apparently regards the individual or household as an active subject of its socio-economic welfare and development, expected to meet subsistence needs individually or in intimate association (family household). Thus the person or household needs to have or to be given resources to use for subsistence. Not having or being provided with these subsistence resources is, for Huang, a basic social injustice. Providing resources for subsistence is a priority interest, and it tends in the direction of the human right to "a standard of living adequate for the health and well-being" of self and family, which includes "equitable distribution" of essential goods "in relation to need."[33]

Second, it should be observed that while Huang prefers a broader understanding of property as contributing to what amounts to a decent standard of living that does not conflict with the common good (i.e. emphasizing the use of property in accordance with the common good), he also appears to accept the narrower conception of private property which is to be protected from arbitrary deprivation. The U.D.H.R. states: "Everyone has the right to own property alone as well as in association with others. No one shall be arbitrarily deprived of his property."[34] Huang's views are quite consistent with this understanding, and with respect to the notion of "no arbitrary deprivation," his attempts to eliminate oppressive and inequitable taxes fit within this notion as well.

P.C. CHANG

Although I believe that Huang's political proposals make it reasonably clear that Confucianism can support functional analogues to human rights from its own resources, it may further strengthen my case if I were to show that Confucian ideas were historically used to influence the drafting of the U.D.H.R. and the debates surrounding it in 1947–1948. The official U.N. records of this period, as well as the recently published private diaries of John Humphrey, principal coordinator of the drafting process, clearly show that the Chinese delegate P.C. Chang introduced a number of Confucian ideas, strategies, and arguments into the deliberative process leading up to the final formulation of the U.D.H.R., adopted on December 10, 1948, by the U.N. General Assembly.[35]

Prior to his official assignment to the U.N., where he served as vice-chair of the Commission on Human Rights, Chang had a distinguished career as professor of philosophy at Nankai University, followed by a briefer diplomatic career during the war years, first as ambassador to Turkey and then as ambassador to Chile.[36] Although his higher education was in the United States – B.A., Clark University; M.A. and Ph.D., Columbia University (studying with John Dewey, among others) – Chang was also significantly shaped by classical Chinese thought (especially Confucianism), as indicated by his two books on Chinese culture as well as his public lectures on Chinese history and culture delivered in Baghdad while ambassador to Turkey. In these books and lectures (as well as other writings), Chang consistently displays erudition in the thought of, for example, Confucius, Mencius, and Huang Tsung-hsi, and a propensity to utilize Confucian texts, such as the *Analects*, *Mencius*, *The Great Learning*, and *Li Chi*, in his argumentation about the importance of achieving a balance in cultural change between the processes of modernization and the retention of classical humane values.

It is noteworthy that particularly important to Chang are Confucius' ideas on *jen* (humaneness, benevolence) and its extension to others, the inclusiveness of human responsibility for improving life, the cultivation of the completely humanized person, and a humanistic attitude of tolerance regarding spiritual matters, as well as Mencius' notions of the essential goodness of human nature, fundamental respect for what is human in all persons, and the priority of the people in humane governance, empha-sizing the rights of the people as well as the obligations of the ruler to provide for the people's good, not to mention Huang's criticism of later ruling dynasties for their oppression of the people. In addition, Chang is eloquent about the fact that the general Confucian contributions to political thought in world history include the democratizing effects of the competitive civil service examination system, the right of the people to rebellion against unworthy rulers, and the emphasis given to education by the state.

This background well positioned Chang to make distinctive Confucian-inspired contributions to the U.D.H.R. in 1947–1948. I divide these contributions into three kinds: (1) substantive contribution to the drafting of article 1 of the Declaration; (2) strategic contributions to the conception and role of the Declaration; and (3) specific interventions in the debates over specific articles of the Declaration. The final wording of article 1 of the U.D.H.R. is as follows: "All human beings are born free and equal in dignity and rights. They are endowed with reason and conscience and should act towards one another in a spirit of brotherhood."[37] In the case of Chang's substantive contribution to this article, it is reported in some secondary literature that Chang argued for the inclusion of *jen* ("two-men-mind-edness" – Chang's English translation – or humaneness) in addition to the mention of reason in the early version of this article.[38] At the forefront of Chang's mind apparently was the idea of a fundamental sympathy or compassion (represented in the thought of Mencius) as constitutive of human beings generally and at the basis of human dignity and human rights. The wording finally adopted included "conscience" in addition to "reason," with the understanding by the drafting committee that conscience was not the voice of an internal moral court but rather the emotional or sympathetic basis of morality, "a germ objectively present" in all persons, which reason must cultivate.[39]

With respect to Chang's strategic contributions to the Declaration as a whole, three are particularly noteworthy: (1) that the U.D.H.R. be conceived as the basis and program for the humanization of humankind, here appealing to the Confucian idea of humankind's innate capacity to become truly human in the sense of moral growth and achievement; (2) that the Declaration incorporate a pragmatic agreement on norms of conduct despite persisting differences of philosophy and ideology among peoples of the world, here appealing to the Confucian emphasis on the art of living as contrasted with metaphysics; and (3) that the Declaration be written in a manner readily comprehensible to all people, here using the Confucian emphasis on the priority of the people to support the role of the U.D.H.R. as a people's document, not a scholars' or lawyers' document.

Space constraints prevent me from discussing each of these contributions in detail, but perhaps I can give a flavor of Chang's contributions by indicating how he went about supporting the notion of pragmatic agreement on norms without ideology. In stoutly resisting the incorporation of any language that would raise "metaphysical problems" in "a declaration designed to be universally applicable," Chang argued that "in the field of human rights popular majority should not be forgotten," adumbrating as follows: "The Chinese representative recalled that the population of his country comprised a large segment of humanity…with ideals and traditions different from those of the Christian West…[e.g.] good manners, decorum, propriety, and consideration for others." Yet, despite the importance of all these to the Chinese, he "would refrain from proposing that mention of them should be made in the declaration," with the hope "that his colleagues would show equal consideration and withdraw some of the amendments…raising metaphysical problems."[40] A subsequent intervention against those wishing to import a theological foundation to the U.D.H.R. put the point eloquently and subtly: "without these words [e.g. God, natural law]…those who believed in God could still find the idea of God [if they wished to so interpret], and at the same time others with different concepts would be able to accept the text [since theology was not its basis]".[41] Chang's point was clearly that pragmatic agreement was possible despite persisting differences of philosophy, theology, and metaphysics. His point and argument carried through the remainder of the deliberations.

With respect to Chang's interventions in the debates about specific articles of the draft declaration, again for reasons of time, I note the following briefly:

1. He appealed to Confucian concepts of human moral capacity and *jen* to support and interpret the claims of article 1 about the dignity of human beings and the importance of acting in the spirit of brotherhood.

2. He used the Confucian orientation to moral pragmatism to support what he called "pluralistic tolerance" of thought, conscience, and religious belief protected by article 18.

3. He used the Confucian emphasis on the priority of the people and appealed to the tradition's experience with a competitive civil service system to support, respectively, governance based on the will of the people and equal access to public service forwarded by article 21.

4. He appealed to the Confucian emphasis on duties to the community to support the balancing of rights with duties in article 29. Chang's contribution to the debate over article 18 must suffice to provide a flavor of how he went about his task with respect to specific articles.

Amid the heated debate over protecting freedom of religious belief, most pointedly the freedom to change one's religious adherence – a problematic point for the Saudi delegate representing a conservative Islamic view on the question – Chang introduced his understanding of Confucian tolerance.[42] First, he affirmed that this article dealt with "one of the most important principles in the declaration," stemming "from the eighteenth century, when the idea of human rights was born in Western Europe." Second, in the interest of "studying the problem of religious expression in its true perspective," he wished to explain "how the Chinese approached the religious problem."

What followed was a Confucian-informed argument in five steps based on Chang's interpretation of *Analects* 6:22 regarding Confucius' humanistic respect for religious matters.

1. "Chinese philosophy was based essentially on a firm belief in a unitarian cause" (a reference to intraworldly, organic cosmology).

2. "That philosophy considered man's actions [also called by Chang 'the art of living'] to be more important than metaphysics" (also called by him "knowledge of the causes of life").

3.   "The best way to testify to the greatness of the Divinity [used by Chang in an all-encompassing way to refer to both theistic and non-theistic beliefs] was to give proof of an exemplary attitude in this world."

4.   "In the eyes of Chinese philosophers, it was pluralistic tolerance in every sphere of thought, conscience, and religion, which should inspire men if they wished to base their relations on benevolence and justice" (the exemplary attitude or art of living).

5.   Q.E.D.: against "the objection of the representative from Saudi Arabia," freedom of religion was to be protected, to which Chang added the pragmatically compelling point: not "to ensure the inviolability of that profound part of thought and conscience...was apt to lead mankind into unreasoned conflict."

Shortly after this intervention, article 18 was adopted by the committee deliberating on the draft declaration.

I conclude by suggesting that Chang's Confucian-inspired contributions to the U.D.H.R. drafting and debate appear quite consistent with my previous discussions of the tradition's fundamental values and openness to human rights. In examining the tradition's ethos and philosophical sources, we find considerable evidence for compatibility with and support of human rights, even though the language of rights is not employed.

NOTES

A version of this chapter was presented at the panel on Moral Universals, Human Rights, and World Religions, Eighteenth Congress of the International Association for the History of Religions, Durban, South Africa, in August 2000.

1.   See, for example, Henry Rosemont, Jr., "Why Take Rights Seriously? A Confucian Critique," in *Human Rights and the World's Religions*, ed. Leroy Rouner (Notre Dame: University of Notre Dame Press, 1988), pp. 167–182, and his more recent "Human Rights: A Bill of Worries," in *Confucianism and Human Rights*, ed. W. Theodore de Bary and Tu Weiming (New York: Columbia University Press, 1998), pp. 54–66.

2.   This section of the present chapter is drawn from my earlier simultaneously published essays, "Religion and Human Rights: A Comparative Perspective," in *Explorations in Global Ethics: Comparative Religious Ethics and Interreligious Dialogue*, ed. Sumner B. Twiss and Bruce Grelle (Boulder and Oxford: Westview Press, 1998; repr. 2000), pp. 155–175; and "A Constructive Framework for Discussing Confucianism and Human Rights," in *Confucianism and Human Rights*, ed. de Bary and Tu, pp. 27–53.

3. The theme of a community of basic trust is developed extensively in Tu Weiming, *Centrality and Commonality: An Essay on Confucian Religiousness* (Albany: State University of New York Press, 1989), pp. 39–66.

4. Confucius, *The Analects*, trans. D.C. Lau (London: Penguin Books, 1979), VI: 30.

5. *Mencius*, trans. D.C. Lau (London: Penguin Books, 1970), 1B: 8, 1B: 12, 1A: 7, 7B: 14. Whether this notion of righteous rebellion amounts to a "right to rebellion" is contested; see, for example, de Bary's "Introduction," in *Confucianism and Human Rights*, ed. de Bary and Tu, pp. 7–9.

6. This position is explicitly argued by Ann Kent in her *Between Freedom and Subsistence: China and Human Rights* (Hong Kong and New York: Oxford University Press, 1993), chap. 2.

7. For an extensive discussion of this point, see Irene Bloom, "Fundamental Intuitions and Consensus Statements, in *Confucianism and Human Rights*, ed. de Bary and Tu, pp. 94–116.

8. For development of this and the following points, see especially W. Theodore de Bary, *The Liberal Tradition in China* (Hong Kong: Chinese University Press, 1983) and his "Neo-Confucianism and Human Rights," in *Human Rights and the World's Religions*, ed. Rouner, pp. 183–198. On communal self-governance specifically, see his *Asian Values and Human Rights: A Confucian Communitarian Perspective* (Cambridge, MA: Harvard University Press, 1998), chapter 5.

9. See Tu Weiming, *Confucian Thought: Selfhood as Creative Transformation* (Albany: State University of New York Press, 1985), pp. 180–181, where he reflects on this ideal as found in the classic Doctrine of the Mean (Chung-yung).

10. This point is developed more extensively in my "A Constructive Framework for Discussing Confucianism and Human Rights," in *Confucianism and Human Rights*, ed. de Bary and Tu, pp. 35–37, 43–46.

11. This characterization is drawn from W. Theodore de Bary, *Waiting for the Dawn: A Plan for the Prince – Huang Tsung-hsi's Ming-I-tai-fang lu* (New York: Columbia University Press, 1993), pp. xi–xii, a work which includes a translation of Huang's text as well as de Bary's extensive commentary and notes on it. For subsequent clarity of reference to this work, I adopt the convention of using Huang's name when referring to the translated text of his manuscript, and de Bary's name when referring to the commentary on that text. This section of the present chapter was first articulated in my unpublished paper, "Confucianism, Humane Governance, and Human Rights," presented at the Conference on Confucianism and Humanism, East–West Center, University of Hawaii, May 1996.

12. Huang, *Waiting for the Dawn*, p. 89.

13. Quotations are from ibid., pp. 95, 97–98, 104–105.

14. I use the edition of the Universal Declaration of Human Rights (U.D.H.R.) found in *The International Bill of Human Rights* (New York: United Nations, 1993); quotations will be cited by section or article. Quotations in this paragraph are from U.D.H.R., Preamble.
15. Huang, *Waiting for the Dawn*, p. 96.
16. U.D.H.R., preamble.
17. Huang, *Waiting for the Dawn*, p. 98.
18. Ibid., pp. 162–163; see also de Bary's helpful discussion on pp. 41–42.
19. U.D.H.R., article 7.
20. Huang, *Waiting for the Dawn*, pp. 94–95, 100–101, 103.
21. De Bary, *Waiting for the Dawn*, p. 56.
22. U.D.H.R., article 21.
23. Ibid., article 19.
24. Huang, *Waiting for the Dawn*, pp. 103–107.
25. De Bary, *Waiting for the Dawn*, p. 56.
26. Huang, *Waiting for the Dawn*, pp. 104–106.
27. Ibid., pp. 111–121.
28. U.D.H.R., article 26.
29. See, for example, Manfred Nowak, "The Right to Education," in *Economic, Social, and Cultural Rights*, ed. Asbjorn Eide, Catarina Krause, and Allan Rosas (Dordrecht: Martinus Nijhoff, 1995), pp. 189–211.
30. Huang, *Waiting for the Dawn*, pp. 115–117.
31. Ibid., pp. 128–134, 136, 138.
32. See de Bary's clarifying discussion in *Waiting for the Dawn*, pp. 42–50.
33. U.D.H.R., article 25.
34. Ibid., article 17.
35. This section of the present chapter draws from and briefly summarizes my more extensive discussion of Chang's background and contribution to the U.D.H.R. in an as yet unpublished paper, "Confucian Contributions to the Universal Declaration of Human Rights: A Historical and Philosophical Perspective," shorter versions of which were delivered at the Academic Seminar on Perceptions of Being Human in Confucian Thought, International Confucian Association, Beijing, June 1998, and the Fairbank Center for East Asian Research, Harvard University, April 1999. The final version is slated for eventual publication in a volume on "Confucianism and Human Values," edited by W. Theodore de Bary and Tu Weiming. This material as briefly summarized also comprises part of another paper to be published later this year by the journal *China Forum*. The Humphrey diaries have been published by McGill University: *On the Edge of Greatness: The Diaries of John Humphrey, the First Director of the United Nations Division of Human Rights*, ed. A.J. Hobbins, vol. 1 (1948–1949) and vol. 2 (1950–1951) (Montreal: McGill University Libraries, 1994 and 1996, respectively); a third volume has recently appeared but is not germane to the U.D.H.R. See especially vol. 1, pp. 55–56, 58, and 88.

36. This information on the biography and career of Chang is drawn from
     the following sources: "Peng Chun Chang, Diplomat, 65, Dies"
     (obituary), *New York Times*, Sunday, July 21, 1957; *Yearbook of the United
     Nations, 1947–48* (Lake Success, NY: United Nations Department of
     Public Information, 1948), p. 1055; "Dr. Peng-chun Chang," on-line biog-
     raphy produced by the National Coordinating Committee for UDHR50,
     Franklin and Eleanor Roosevelt Institute, revised April 12, 1998
     (http://w.w.w.udhr50.org/history/biographies/biopcc.htm); and *Peng
     Chun Chang 1892–1957: Biography and Collected Works*, ed. Ruth H.C.
     Cheng and Sze-Chuh Cheng (privately published by Chang's family),
     p. 8 (Chang's own resume) and 20–36 ("A Chronological Biography" by
     the editors, Chang's daughter and her husband). The latter source is the
     most comprehensive and useful. Chang's books include: *Education for
     Modernization in China* (New York: Columbia University Teachers'
     College, 1923) and *China at the Crossroads: The Chinese Situation in
     Perspective* (London: Evans Brothers Ltd., 1936). The texts of his Baghdad
     lectures and U.N. presentations can be found in *Peng Chun Chang*, ed.
     Cheng and Cheng, pp. 143–153.

37. U.D.H.R., article 1.

38. Pier Cesare Bori, *From Hermeneutics to Ethical Consensus Among Cultures*
     (Atlanta: Scholars Press, 1994), chapter 7. I have previously reported
     Bori's findings in my "A Constructive Framework for Discussing Confu-
     cianism and Human Rights," in *Confucianism and Human Rights*, ed. de
     Bary and Tu, endnote 35 (pp. 50–51).

39. The phrase is Bori's.

40. *Official Records of the Third Session of the General Assembly, Part I, Social,
     Humanitarian and Cultural Questions, THIRD COMMITTEE, Summary
     Records of Meetings 21 September–8 December, 1948*, with annexes,
     printed in both English and French (Lake Success, NY: United Nations,
     1948), p. 98. It should be noted that these records represent a historical
     summary of proceedings, not necessarily a precise word-for-word tran-
     scription of quotations from speakers.

41. Ibid., p. 114.

42. Ibid., p. 397.

Plate 21 Muslim worshipers purify themselves through ablutions before entering the Mosque of Suleiman for midday prayers. The largest mosque in Istanbul, Turkey, this mosque, like other imperial mosques in the city, was traditionally surrounded by a hospital, soup kitchen, schools, accommodations for travelers, and a bath house, which served the city's poor, regardless of whether they were Muslims, Christians, or Jews.

Photo: *Nancy M. Martin*

21

THE HUMAN RIGHTS COMMITMENT *in* MODERN ISLAM

Khaled Abou El Fadl

O f all the moral challenges confronting Islam in the modern age, the problem of human rights is the most formidable. This is not because Islam, as compared to other religious traditions, is more prone to causing or inducing behavior that disregards or violates the rights of human beings. In fact, the Islamic tradition has generated concepts and institutions that could be utilized in a systematic effort to develop social and moral commitments to human rights. But the cause of the formidable challenge to the Islamic tradition pertains to the particular historical dynamics that Muslims have had to confront in the modern age. Here, I am referring to the political realities that have plagued Muslims, especially since the rise of the hegemonic power of the West, and the destruction of the traditional institutions of authority and learning in most Muslim polities. As discussed below, political realities – such as colonialism, the persistence of highly invasive and domineering despotic governments, the widespread perception, and reality, of Western hypocrisy in the human rights field, and the emergence and spread of supremacist movements of moral exceptionalism in modern Islam – have contributed to modes of interpretation and practice that are not consistent with a commitment to human rights.[1]

These political developments, among others, have led to an aggravated process of moral disengagement, and even callousness, toward human suffering, even when such suffering is inflicted in God's name. Put simply, there has in the contemporary era been a systematic undermining and devaluing of the humanistic tradition in Islam, and a process of what could be described as a vulgarization of Islamic normative doctrines and systems of belief. Therefore, exploring the relationship of Islam to the concept of human rights implicates the crucial issue of Islam's self-definition: What will Islam stand for and represent in the contemporary age? What are the symbolic associations that Muslims and non-Muslims will draw when it comes to thinking about the Islamic tradition? A corollary issue will be the relationship between modern Islam and its own humanistic tradition: To what extent will modern Islam associate with and develop the historical experience of Islamic humanism?[2]

In recent times, and well before the tragedy of 9/11, Muslim societies have been plagued by many events that have struck the world as offensive and even shocking. Morally offensive events, such as the *Satanic Verses* and the death sentence against Salman Rushdie; the stoning and imprisoning of rape victims in Pakistan and Nigeria; the public flogging, stoning, and decapitation of criminal offenders in Sudan, Iran, and Saudi Arabia; the degradation of women by the Taliban; the destruction of the Buddha statues in Afghanistan; the sexual violation of domestic workers in Saudi Arabia; the excommunication of writers in Egypt; the killing of civilians in suicide attacks; the shooting in 1987 of over four hundred pilgrims in Mecca by Saudi police; the taking of hostages in Iran and Lebanon; the burning to death in 2002 of at least fourteen schoolgirls in Mecca because they were not allowed to escape their burning school while not properly veiled; and the demeaning treatment that women receive in Saudi Arabia, including the ban against women driving cars, as well as many other events, seem to constitute a long Muslim saga of ugliness in the modern world.

For many non-Muslims around the world, Islam has become the symbol for a draconian tradition that exhibits little compassion or mercy toward human beings. When one interacts with people from different parts of the world, one consistently finds that the image of Islam is not that of a humanistic or humane religion. This has reached the extent that, from Europe and the United States to Japan, China, and Russia, one finds that Islamic culture has become associated with harshness and cruelty in the popular cultural imagination of non-Muslims. This saga of ugliness has forced Muslims, who are embarrassed and offended by this legacy, to adopt apologetic rhetorical arguments that do not necessarily carry much persuasive weight.

My purpose in this chapter is not necessarily to explain the sociopolitical reasons for the pervasiveness of acts of ugliness in the modern Islamic context. In addition, although, admittedly, I discuss the Islamic tradition as an insider, I do not aim, so to speak, to vindicate or defend Islam by proving that Islamic beliefs and convictions are consistent with human rights. For reasons explained below, I think that adopting such an approach would be intellectually dishonest and ultimately not convincing or effective. Rather, the purpose of this chapter is to discuss the major points of tension between the Islamic tradition and the human rights system of belief and to explore the possibilities for achieving a normative reconciliation between the two moral traditions.

There is an initial difficulty with the discourse on human rights that warrants some cautionary comments. In the West, the issue of human rights has become the subject of an extensive philosophical, theological, legal, political, and anthropological discourse that defies citation.[3] The origins, nature, and meaning of human rights as well as the relationship between human rights and religion have been widely debated in the West, to the point that human rights has become a fairly developed and sophisticated field of inquiry. This poses something of a challenge because, considering the broadness of the subject in the West, it is necessary to specify the particular concept of human rights to which we refer.

For instance, in speaking about Islam and human rights, it is important to specify whether we are addressing a scheme of individual rights or of collective or communitarian rights.[4] Furthermore, there is a material difference between schemes of human rights based on natural law conceptions and notions of human rights derived from positivist and contractual premises. In addition, human rights as identified and defined by international law instruments, and contractual obligations applicable to nation-states, pose their own particular sets of issues and challenges. Finally, another fairly complex issue is whether conceptions of universal human rights can accommodate any degree of cultural or indigenous variation without undermining the very rationale for universal rights.[5] It will not be possible to address, let alone resolve, these various multi-faceted issues in this chapter, but in order for a coherent discourse to emerge on Islam and human rights, these issues do, in fact, need to be engaged in a rigorous and systematic fashion. Otherwise, Islamic discourses on the subject will remain very partial, and largely unconvincing.

What I can hope to achieve in this chapter is to identify some of the main obstacles that hamper a serious Islamic engagement with the field, and analyze potentialities within Islamic doctrine for realizing a vision of human rights. In essence, this chapter will focus on potentialities – i.e. the doctrinal aspects in Muslim thought that could legitimize, promote, or subvert the emergence of a human rights practice in Muslim cultures. In principle, doctrinal potentialities exist in a dormant state until they are co-opted and directed by systematic thought, supported by cumulative social practices, toward constructing a culture that honors and promotes human rights. This chapter will focus on the doctrinal potentialities or concepts constructed by the interpretive activities of Muslim scholars (primarily jurists), but not on the actual sociopolitical practices in Islamic history.

One of the powerful attributes of doctrine – especially theological and religious doctrine – is that it does not necessarily have to remain locked within a particular sociopolitical-historical practice. Religious doctrine can be distilled from the aggregations and accumulations of past historical practices, and reconstructed and reinvented in order to achieve entirely new social and political ends. I do admit that I suffer from a certain amount of optimism about the possibilities of reinterpreting religious doctrine in order to invent new sociopolitical traditions, without necessarily having to sacrifice either the appearance or substance of authenticity. Put differently, I do believe that even if Islam has not known a human rights tradition similar to that developed in the West, it is possible, with the requisite amount of intellectual determination, analytical rigor, and social commitment, to demand and eventually construct such a tradition.[6] This is to say that the past influences – but does not completely determine – the future and if one did not at all believe in the transferability of ideas, and in the possibility of cultural transplants, there would be little point to speaking about a possible relationship between Islam and human rights.

COLONIALISM, APOLOGETICS, AND THE MUSLIM HUMAN RIGHTS DISCOURSE

The construct of human rights has achieved notable symbolic significance in the modern world. Politically, whether in fact a nation regularly violates the rights of its citizens or not, most nations go through the pretense of claiming to honor some version of human rights. In the past half-century, human rights has become a significant part of international relations, as there has been a globalization of human rights concerns and discourses.[7] At least since the widespread adoption of what has been referred to as the International Bill of Rights,[8] the idea of human rights has become established as a powerful symbolic construct often used to shame or embarrass governments into exhibiting a higher degree of restraint in dealing with their citizens.[9]

Importantly, in the case of the Muslim world, the human rights movement has, so to speak, won indigenous converts, and as a result, it is not unusual to observe the language of human rights being used as a medium for expressing dissent, and making demands on local governments. This is the case particularly for women's rights activists in the Muslim world who frequently cite international standards and obligations as a means of exerting pressure upon their domestic governments.[10] But aside from localized support and co-optation of the language and paradigms of international human rights by some activists in the process of articulating social and political demands, there has been quite a different dynamic taking place in Muslim countries.

Despite the active involvement of countries such as Egypt, Lebanon, and Tunisia in drafting the aspirational language of several international human rights documents, there remained a considerable tension between traditional Islamic law and the normative demands of human rights. This was particularly so in matters relating to personal status laws, equal rights for women, freedom of religion, and harsh Islamic criminal penalties for offenses such as theft, adultery, and apostasy.[11] However, the primary intellectual and theological response to the challenge of international human rights followed a pattern that had become well ingrained since the onslaught of colonialism and the taunting criticisms of Orientalists against the Islamic tradition and systems of belief.

Colonialism, and its accompanying institution of Orientalism, had not only played a pivotal role in undermining the traditional institutions of Muslim learning and jurisprudence, but it had also posed a serious challenge to traditional Muslim epistemologies of knowledge and sense of moral values.[12] Although international human rights law was enshrined in various treaties during a period in which most Muslim countries had gained political independence, the experiences of colonialism and post-colonialism influenced the Muslim intellectual response in several important respects. Muslims did not first encounter Western conceptions of human rights in the form of the Universal Declaration of Human Rights (U.D.H.R.) of 1948, or in the form of negotiated international conventions.[13] Rather, they encountered such conceptions as part of the "White Man's Burden" or the "civilizing mission" of the colonial era, and as a part of the European natural law tradition, which was frequently exploited to justify imperialistic policies in the Muslim world.[14]

This experience has had a significant impact on the understanding of human rights in the Muslim social imagination, and on the construction of Islamic discourses on the subject.[15] The most important, among Muslim intellectuals, was the perception that the human rights field is thoroughly political, and that it is plagued by widespread Western hypocrisy.[16] The aggravated politicization of the issue of human rights meant that, quite frequently, the field became a battleground for competing cultural orientations within Muslim societies. In the writings of some dogmatists such as Sayyid Qutb, Abu A'la al-Mawdudi, and Jalal Kishk, the human rights discourse was portrayed as a part of the Western cultural invasion of Muslim lands, and as a tool for instilling Muslims with a sense of cultural inferiority. Although in the late nineteenth and early twentieth centuries there were several systematic efforts to come to terms with the Western natural law tradition in general[17] and human rights more specifically, increasingly the Muslim intellectual response could be summed up within two predominate orientations, the first apologetic and the second defiant or exceptionalist.

The apologetic orientation consisted of an effort by a large number of Islamists to defend and salvage the Islamic system of belief and tradition from the onslaught of Westernization and modernity by simultaneously emphasizing both the compatibility and the supremacy of Islam. Apologists responded to the intellectual challenges of modernity and to universalist Western paradigms by adopting pietistic fictions about the presumed perfection of Islam, and eschewed any critical evaluation of Islamic doctrines. A common heuristic device of apologetics was to argue that any meritorious or worthwhile modern institutions were first invented and realized by Muslims. Therefore, according to the apologists, Islam liberated women, created a democracy, endorsed pluralism, and protected human rights, long before these institutions ever existed in the West.[18]

Muslim apologists generated a large body of texts that claimed Islam's inherent compatibility with international human rights, or even claimed that Islam constituted a fuller and more coherent expression of human rights. These texts followed the same basic pattern and methodology – they produced a list of rights purportedly guaranteed by Islam, and the rights listed coincided, or were correlated, most typically with the major human rights articulated in the U.D.H.R. Most often, in order to demonstrate the point, these texts would selectively cite a Qur'anic verse, or some anecdotal report attributed to the Prophet, for each of the purported rights.[19]

Nonetheless, these rights were not asserted out of critical engagement with Islamic texts, or the historical experience that generated these texts, or even out of a genuine ideological commitment or a rigorous understanding of the implications of the rights asserted. Rather, they were asserted primarily as a means of resisting the deconstructive effects of Westernization, affirming self-worth, and attaining a measure of emotional empowerment. The apologetic orientation raised the issue of Islamic authenticity in relation to international human rights, but did not seriously engage it. By simply assuming that Islam presented a genuine and authentic expression of international human rights, the apologetic orientation made those international rights redundant.

According to the apologetic orientation, all society needed to do in order to attain fully the benefits of human rights was to give full expression to real and genuine Islam. But what naturally flowed from this position was an artificial sense of confidence, and an intellectual lethargy that neither took the Islamic tradition nor the human rights tradition very seriously. One of the serious consequences of this orientation was that to date, a serious analytical Islamic discourse on human rights has not emerged. By pietistically affirming the place of human rights in Islam instead of investigating it, the apologetic movement simply avoided confronting the points of tension between the two convictional systems.[20]

An incidental effect of the apologetic movement was that it contributed to the secularization, and therefore to the marginalization, of human rights movements in the Muslim world. It is notable, for instance, that human rights activists in Muslim countries most often belonged to a Western-educated secular elite, who typically possessed no more than a superficial familiarity with the Shari'a tradition. I am not arguing that all human rights activists in Muslim countries were committed to a secular paradigm, or that they entirely ignored the Islamic tradition. The point is that activists who articulated human rights demands in society did so while armed with Western categories and paradigms, but their demands did not arise from a dynamic engagement with Islamic Shari'a imperatives. Shari'a, if cited by most human rights activists, was as an afterthought, or as a formalistic stamp applied for the purposes of bolstering the perception of Islamic authenticity.

Significantly, many of the more serious scholarly, and less apologetic, works written on the subject of human rights were authored by lawyers who had the benefit of a secular education in the civil law legal system, whether obtained in Muslim countries or in Europe. Although they attempted to present a more rigorous treatment of the relationship between human rights and Islam, these jurists clearly possessed a greater mastery of the international legal system than of the classical legal tradition. Epistemologically, these lawyers were far more anchored in the Western intellectual tradition than in its Islamic counterpart, and as a result, their claim to authenticity was tentative at best. In effect, the intellectual product of this relatively small number of legal theorists was *de facto* secularist, and because of its superficial engagement of the Islamic tradition, and result-oriented approach, *de facto* apologetic.[21]

Demonstratively, in this regard, one notices a near-complete absence of any systematic philosophical and theological treatment of the issue of human rights in Islam.[22] As discussed later, in contrast to speculative theological works of classical Islam, and the often complex rights conceptions of premodern Islam, contemporary Islamist approaches remained superficial. For instance, during the heyday of socialist ideologies in the third world, a large number of Islamists insisted that the essential character of the Islamic approach to rights is collectivist, and not individualistic. But in the 1980s, with the increasing influence of the United States on the world scene, a large number of Islamists claimed that Islam emphasized individualistic conceptions of rights and guaranteed the right to private property.

PURITANISM, ANTI-WESTERNISM, AND EXCEPTIONALISM IN MUSLIM DISCOURSES

In the 1970s, much of the Muslim world witnessed an Islamic resurgence, which took the form of a powerful puritan movement demanding a return to an authentic Islamic identity through the re-implementation of Shari'a law. The return to an authentic Islamic identity as well as the call for the reassertion of Shari'a law were recurrent themes during the colonial era. Both the Wahhabi[23] and Salafi[24] theological movements – the main proponents of puritan Islam – had emerged during the colonial era and remained active throughout the twentieth century. But for a variety of reasons, including aggressive proselytizing and the generous financial support of Saudi Arabia, these two movements became practically indistinguishable from each other, and they also became a dominant theological force in contemporary Islam.

Puritanism resisted the indeterminacy of the modern age by escaping to a strict literalism in which the text became the sole source of legitimacy. It sought to return to the presumed golden age of Islam, when the Prophet created a perfect, just polity in Medina. According to the puritans, it was imperative to return to a presumed pristine, simple, and straightforward Islam, which was believed to be entirely reclaimable by a literal implementation of the commands and precedents of the Prophet and by a strict adherence to correct ritual practice. The puritan orientation also considered any form of moral thought that was not entirely dependent on the text to be a form of self-idolatry and treated humanistic fields of knowledge, especially philosophy, as "the sciences of the devil." It also rejected any attempt to interpret the divine law from a historical or contextual perspective and, in fact, treated the vast majority of Islamic history as a corruption or aberration of the true and authentic Islam. The dialectical and indeterminate hermeneutics of the classical jurisprudential tradition were considered corruptions of the purity of the faith and law, and the puritan movement became very intolerant of the long-established Islamic practice of considering a variety of schools of thought to be equally orthodox and attempted to narrow considerably the range of issues upon which Muslims may legitimately disagree.

In many respects, the puritan movement reproduced the mental sets adopted by the apologetic movement. It eschewed any analytical or historical approaches to the understanding of the Islamic message and claimed that all the challenges posed by modernity are eminently resolvable by a return to the original sources of the Qur'an and Sunna. Unlike the apologetic orientation, however, the puritans insisted on an Islamic particularity and uniqueness and rejected all universalisms, except the universals of Islam. The puritans reacted to the eagerness of the apologists to articulate Islam in a way that caters to the latest ideological fashion by opting out of the process. In the puritan paradigm, Islam is perfect, but such perfection meant that ultimately Islam does not need to reconcile itself or prove itself compatible with any other system of thought. According to this paradigm, Islam is a self-contained and self-sufficient system of beliefs and laws that ought to shape the world in its image, rather than accommodate human experience in any way.

This attitude, in good part, emerged from what is known as the *hakimiyya* debates in Islamic history (dominion or sovereignty). According to the puritans, in Islam dominion properly belongs to God alone, who is the sole legislator and lawmaker. Therefore, any normative position that is derived from human reason or sociohistorical experience is fundamentally illegitimate. The only permissible normative positions are those derived from the comprehension of the divine commands, as found in divinely inspired texts. Not surprisingly, the puritan orientation considered all moral approaches that defer to intuition, reason, contractual obligations, or social and political consensus to be inherently whimsical and illegitimate. All moral norms and laws ought to be derived from a sole source, the intent or will of the Divine.

In some of its more extreme forms, the puritans explicitly demanded that Muslims must show enmity and hostility toward the unbelievers (*mushrikun*), insisting that a Muslim should not adopt the customs of unbelievers and should not befriend them. According to these puritans, Muslim displays of enmity and hostility toward the unbelievers must be visible and unequivocal. In this particular puritan orientation it was argued that it is entirely immaterial what a non-Muslim might think about Muslim practices, and in fact, it was a sign of spiritual weakness to care about whether non-Muslims were impressed by Muslim behavior or not.[25] In general, the puritans espoused a self-sufficient and closed system of belief that had no reason to engage or interact with the other, except from a position of dominance.[26]

As to the issue of universal human rights, it is not entirely accurate to describe the puritan orientation as exceptionalist because the puritans did not seek a relativist or cultural exception to the universalism of human rights. Rather, the puritan claim was that whatever rights human beings are entitled to enjoy, they are entirely within the purview of Shari'a law. It is important to realize that the puritans did not deny, in principle, that human beings have rights; they contended that rights could not exist unless granted by God. Therefore, one finds that in puritan literature there is no effort to justify international rights on Islamic terms but simply an effort to set out the divine law, on the assumption that such a law, by definition, provides human beings with a just and moral order.

Nevertheless, despite the practice of waving the banner of Islamic authenticity and legitimacy, the puritan orientation was far more anti-Western than it was pro-Islamic. The puritans' primary concern was not to explore or investigate the parameters of Islamic values or the historical experience of the Islamic civilization but to oppose the West. As such, Islam was simply the symbolic universe in which they functioned and not the normative imperative that created their value system. Although the puritans pretended that the Shari'a comprised a set of objectively determinable divine commands, the fact is that the divine law was the byproduct of a thoroughly human and fallible interpretive process. Whatever qualified as a part of the Shari'a law, even if inspired by exhortations found in religious texts, was the product of human efforts and determinations that reflected subjective sociohistorical circumstances. As such, the determinations of the puritans were as subjective and contextual as any of the earlier juristic interpretations in Islam.

However, the most noticeable aspect regarding the puritan determinations was their reactive nature. The puritan orientation was as alienated and superficially anchored in the Islamic tradition as the apologetic orientation.

Puritanism understood and constructed Islam only through the prism of seeking to be culturally independent from the West. As such, its primary operative mode was to react to Western supremacy in the modern world by, effectively, constructing Islam into the antithesis of the West, or at least the antithesis of an essentialized view of the West.[27] This reactive stance was significant because it shaped much of the puritan discourse on the idea of universal human rights.[28] Since international human rights were seen as distinctly Western in origin, they were opposed on these grounds alone, and in fact, Islamic scholars who espoused some form of doctrinal reconciliation were thought of as suffering from Westoxification and, consequently, treated as betrayers of the Islamic tradition.[29]

THE HUMAN RIGHTS COMMITMENT AND AMBIGUITY IN ISLAM

Between the two dominant responses of apologetics and puritanism, Islamic discourse on the subject of human rights has remained vastly underdeveloped.[30] Consequently, there has been much ambiguity surrounding what may be called the human rights commitment in modern Islam. In essence, a human rights commitment emerges from a convictional paradigm – human rights is a moral and normative belief about the basic worth and standard of existence that ought to be guaranteed for any human being.[31] Whether this belief is founded on a vision of human dignity, rational capacity, or freedom from harm and suffering, in its essence it expresses a commitment to the well-being of the human being. Even collectivist or communitarian visions of rights are often forced to justify their commitments by claiming to provide for the well-being of most of the members of the imagined community or collectivity.[32]

Importantly, visions of human rights do not necessarily seek to exclude subjective or contextual perceptions of rights or entitlements. Such visions are not necessarily premised on the idea that there is a fixed set of human rights that is immutable and unevolving from the dawn of history until today. However, human rights visions do tend to objectify and generalize the subjective experiences of human beings.[33] By evaluating the socio-historical experience of human beings – the demands made for protection and the resistance offered to these demands – and by evaluating the impact of practices that cause suffering, degradation, or deny people the ability to develop, it becomes possible to articulate objectified visions of a universal set of rights that ought to be enjoyed by all human beings.[34]

At the legalistic level, arguably the so-called Bill of International Human Rights has already recognized what ought to be objective standards for human conduct, and such standards are binding on all nations of the world, even as to states that have not become signatories to the two human rights covenants.[35] But whether the legal argument is valid or not, the universal human rights schemes have the unmistakable characteristic of an ideology that, very much like a religious faith, believes that human beings ought to be treated in a certain way because, quite simply, as a matter of conviction it is what is right and good.[36] Once a claim of right is objectified, unless it goes through a process of deconstruction and de-objectification, as a matter of commitment and belief, it becomes binding to all, and it also becomes a measure by which to judge the behavior of violators.[37]

One of the major aspects that human rights schemes share with religious systems is the objectification of subjective experience. The tension between religion and human rights, as systems of convictional reference, is not in the subjective experience. Genuine regard for human rights may be subjectively experienced in a fashion that is entirely consistent with one's religious convictions.[38] Put differently, a religious person's unique set of experiences may resolve all possible tensions between his/her own personal religious convictions and human rights. At the subjective level, individuals may feel that they have not experienced any irreconcilable conflicts between their commitment to human rights and their religious convictions.

Rather, the tension between the convictional systems of religion and human rights exist in the objectified standards and realities that each system claims.[39] Put rather bluntly, which of the two generalized and objectified systems warrants deference and which constitutes the ultimate frame of reference? Unless one argues, as was claimed in the classical natural law tradition, that God willed that human beings have a particular set of rights, the tension between the two systems becomes inevitable.[40] If the generalized and objectified set of human rights asserted by people just happens to be exactly the same as the divinely ordained set of rights, then, in effect, the tension is resolved, or such a tension never really existed in the first place. The tension is most pronounced, however, when the objectified religious experience is inconsistent with the objectified claims to human rights. This is especially the case when, as is the situation today, such claims arise from a fundamentally secular paradigm.[41]

The ambiguity one finds in modern Muslim discourses regarding a commitment to human rights is due to the failure to confront the two objectified experiences of Islam and human rights. The apologetic discourse avoided the issue by assuming that the two experiences must be one and the same, and that God has granted human beings the same set of rights found in the international human rights discourse. But such a claim was not made out of a process of re-objectifying or reconstructing Islam so as to engineer such a consistency. In light of the colonial experience and the perception of the vast hypocrisy in human rights practices, many Muslims did not take the human rights discourses seriously enough to effectuate such an engineering of the objectified experience of Islam.[42]

The puritan orientation, on the other hand, opted out of the process altogether and, asserting the supremacy of Islam as a convictional system, rejected as a matter of principle the process of reengineering or re-objectifying Islam in order to resolve such a tension. This is what accounts for the puritan orientation's defiant stance toward contemporary international human rights claims and its assumption that Islamic imperatives must necessarily be very different from the imperatives set by human rights commitments. The irony, however, is that by taking such a stance, the puritan orientation ended up negating the integrity of the Islamic experience and, in the name of being different, voided what could be genuinely Islamic and, at the same time, consistent with the international human rights tradition.

Acknowledging the primacy of the apologetic and puritan approaches in modern Islam does not mean that the problematic relationship between the two convictional systems of Islam and human rights is fundamentally irre-solvable. In fact, such an acknowledgment is a necessary precondition for developing a critical mass of analytically rigorous Islamic treatments of the issue. There have been some serious efforts, especially in Iran, to deal with the tension between the two systems, but to date such efforts have not reached a critical mass where they may constitute a serious intellectual movement.[43]

Methodologically, many of these efforts have tried to locate a primary Islamic value, such as tolerance, dignity, or self-determination, and utilize this value as a proverbial door by which the human rights tradition may be integrated into Islam. Other efforts, however, have relied on a sort of original-intent argument, namely, that God's original intent was consistent with a scheme of greater rights for human beings but that the socio-historical experience was unable to achieve a fulfillment of such an intent.[44] My point here is not to critique these methodological approaches, and I do not necessarily even disagree with them. I do think, however, that Islamic discourses need to go further than either identifying core values or constructing arguments about a historically frustrated divine will.

It is not an exaggeration to say that what is needed is a serious rethinking of the inherited categories of Islamic theology. Nonetheless, in my view, what is needed is not a human-centered theology, but a rethinking of the meaning and implications of divinity, and a reimagining of the nature of the relationship between God and creation. It is certainly true that in Qur'anic discourses God is beyond benefit or harm, and therefore all divine commands are designed to benefit human beings alone and not God. One of the basic precepts of Shari'a is that all laws are supposed to accrue to the benefit of human beings, who are ultimately charged with fulfilling the divine covenant.[45] But in and of itself, this avowed goal of Islamic law is not sufficient to justify a commitment to human rights. Rather, the challenge is to reimagine the nature of the divine covenant, which defines the obligations and entitlements of human beings, in order to centralize the imperative of human rights, and to do so from an internally coherent perspective in Islam.

From an internal perspective, the question is: Is the subjective belief of human beings about their entitlements and rights relevant to identifying or defining those entitlements and rights? May human beings make demands upon each other, and God, for rights and, upon making such demands, become entitled to such rights? As Islamic theology stands right now, the answer would clearly be that, in the eyes of God, the demands of human beings are irrelevant to their entitlements. God is not influenced one way or the other by human demands, and it is heretical to think otherwise. This response given by traditional Islamic theology does not necessarily preclude a recognition of human rights, but I do believe that such a response creates the potential for foreclosing the possibility of giving due regard to the evolving field of universal human rights.

As I noted earlier in this chapter, I am dealing with potentialities, and not absolute determinations. Therefore, as argued below, giving a different response to these questions could contribute to, or could create, a potential for resolving what I described as the problematic tension between human rights schemes and Islam. I will argue that in order to create an adequate potential for the realization of a human rights commitment in Islam, it is important to visualize God as beauty and goodness, and that engaging in a collective enterprise of beauty and goodness, with humanity at large, is part of realizing the divine in human life.

GOD'S SOVEREIGNTY AND THE SOVEREIGNTY OF HUMAN WELL-BEING

The well-known Muslim historian and sociologist Ibn Khaldun (d. 784/1382) separated all political systems into three broad types. The first he described as a natural system, which approximates a primitive state of nature. This is a lawless system in which the most powerful dominates and tyrannizes the rest. The second system, which Ibn Khaldun described as dynastic, is tyrannical as well but is based on laws issued by a king or prince. However, due to their origin, these laws are baseless and capricious, and so people obey them out of necessity or compulsion, but the laws themselves are illegitimate and tyrannical. The third system, and the most superior, is the caliphate, which is based on Shari'a law. Shari'a law fulfills the criteria of justice and legitimacy, and binds the governed and governor alike. Because the government is bound by a higher law that it may not alter or change, and because the government may not act whimsically or outside the pale of law, the caliphate system is, according to Ibn Khaldun, superior to any other.[46]

Ibn Khaldun's categorization is not unusual in premodern Islamic literature. The notion that the quintessential characteristic of a legitimate Islamic government is that it is a government subject to and limited by Shari'a law is repeated often by premodern jurists.[47] Muslim jurists insisted that a just caliph must apply and himself be bound by Shari'a law – and in fact, some such as the jurist Abu al-Faraj al-Baghdadi Ibn al-Jawzi (d. 597/1200) asserted that a caliph who tries to alter God's laws for politically expedient reasons is implicitly accusing the Shari'a of imperfection.[48] Ibn al-Jawzi elaborated upon this point by contending that under the guise of political expediency or interests, innocent Muslims could be murdered, imprisoned, or tortured. In reality, he argued, no political interest could ever justify the killing or imprisonment of a Muslim without legitimate legal cause.[49]

In the imaginary constructs of Muslim jurists, Shari'a was seen as the bulwark against whimsical government, and as the precondition for a just society. Although this point is often ignored in modern discourses, Shari'a was, at least at the symbolic level, presented as a constraint on the power of the government. The very notion that informed the concept of Shari'a law was that Shari'a is not the law of the state but the law that limits the state.[50] The premodern jurists insisted that the state or the ruler cannot make or formulate Shari'a law. Particularly after the third/ninth century, it had become fairly well established that it was the jurists ('ulama') who were the legitimate spokespersons for the divine law – an idea that was expressed in the oft-repeated phrase that the 'ulama' are the inheritors of the Shari'a.

The state could pass and adopt rules and regulations, as might be necessary in order to serve the public interest, but only as long as such rules and regulations did not violate Shari'a law. Any rules or regulations enacted by the state did not constitute a part of Shari'a law, but were treated as merely administrative in nature. Administrative laws, or what might be called executive laws, were, unlike Shari'a law, considered temporal and mundane; they were a legitimate means for achieving specific contextual ends, but such laws had no claim to divinity and had no precedential value beyond their specific context and time.

In order to ensure compliance with Shari'a law, however, the classical jurists argued that the caliph should consult with the jurists before undertaking to implement any law or before passing any executive regulations. So, for instance, emphasizing this point, the influential Hanbali jurist Ibn al-Qayyim (d. 751/1350) wrote the following:

> Properly speaking, the rulers (al-umara') are obeyed [only to the extent] that their commands are consistent with the [articulations] of the religious sciences (al-'ilm). Hence, the duty to obey them [the rulers] derives from the duty to obey the jurists (fa ta'atuhum taba'a li al-'ulama'). [This is because] obedience is due only in what is good (ma'ruf), and what is required by the religious sciences (wa ma awjabahu al-'ilm). Since the duty to obey the jurists is derived from the duty to obey the Prophet, then the duty to obey the rulers is derived from the duty to obey the jurists [who are the experts on the religious sciences]. Furthermore, since Islam is protected and upheld by the rulers and the jurists alike, this means that the laity must follow [and obey] these two [i.e. the rulers and jurists].[51]

Although the jurists often argued that the caliph ideally should himself be trained in law and qualify for the rank of a *mujtahid* (jurist of the highest rank capable of generating *de novo* law), this did not mean that he was empowered to implement laws without regard to the opinions of the jurists. Even a caliph who is a *mujtahid* is bound by the well-established principles and rules of law.[52]

The notion of a government constrained by laws, and the denial to the executive power of unfettered discretion in dealing with the ruled, does tend to support conditions that are conducive for the protection of human rights. Arguably, Shari'a law, as articulated by jurists, could support a conception of rights that, in most situations, are immune from government interference or manipulation. The fact that the interpretations of jurists are endowed with a certain measure of sanctity, as long as such interpretations tend to respect the honor and dignity of human beings, could empower these juristic interpretations against the vagaries and indiscretions of political powers and contribute to the protection of human dignities.

In fact, in Islamic historical practice, Muslim jurists did form a class that exercised considerable moral power against the government and helped to play a mediating role between the rulers and ruled. Historically, Muslim jurists often represented the ruler to the ruled, and the ruled to the ruler, and acted to stem and balance against political absolutism. They did so by negotiating power, and yielding their moral authority in favor of the ruler or ruled, depending on the sociohistorical context and the competing normative demands confronting them. Throughout Islamic history, the *'ulama'* performed a wide range of economic, political, and administrative functions, but most importantly, they acted as negotiative mediators between the ruling class and the laity. As Afaf Marsot states: "[The *'ulama'*] were the purveyors of Islam, the guardians of its tradition, the depository of ancestral wisdom, and the moral tutors of the population."[53]

While they legitimized and often explained the rulers to the ruled, they also used their moral weight to thwart tyrannous measures, and, at times, led or legitimized rebellions against the ruling classes.[54] As Marsot correctly points out, "to both rulers and ruled they were an objective haven which contending factions could turn to in times of stress."[55] Importantly, until the modern age Muslim jurists, as a class of legal technocrats, never assumed power directly and did not demand that they be allowed to assume direct political power.[56] Therefore, theocratic rule, until the contemporary age, was virtually unknown in Islam.[57]

The problem, however, is that Shari'a is a general term for a multitude of legal methodologies and a remarkably diverse set of interpretive determinations.[58] In fact, the negotiative role played by Muslim jurists points to the subjective element in Shari'a interpretations. Despite the dogmatic assumptions of many Muslim activists, Shari'a law constitutes the sum total of the subjective engagements of legal specialists with texts that purport to represent the divine will. The extent to which Shari'a law will provide for certain rights, to be retained by individuals or even communities, which are held as immunities against possible transgressions by others, to a large extent depends on the subjective determinations of Muslim jurists.

I am not arguing that Islamic texts do not provide for objectivities whatsoever, or that they do not constrain, and even limit, the interpretive activities of jurists. My argument is that the idea of limited government in Islam is as effective as the constraints and limitations that the subjective interpreter is willing to place upon such a government. In other words, the reliance on Shari'a, or on Islamic texts, is not in and of itself a sufficient guarantee of human rights. What is needed is a normative commitment by the subjective interpreters of the law in favor of such rights.

It is quite possible for a government to implement faithfully the technical rules of Shari'a, but otherwise violate the rights of human beings. A government could implement Shari'a's criminal penalties, prohibit usury, dictate rules of modesty, and so on, and yet remain a government of unrestrained powers against its citizens. This is because unless the conception of government is founded around core moral values about the normative purpose of Shari'a and unless there is a process that limits the ability of the government to violate those core moral values, the idea of a government bound by Shari'a remains vague.

Much of the debate on the subjective moral commitments that underlie the implementation of Shari'a harks back, however, to the issue of God's legislative sovereignty. This is known in Islamic discourses as the *hakimiyya* debate. Arguably, it is meaningless to speak of normative moral commitments to human rights in the context of Islamic law. Put simply, since only God is sovereign and since God is the sole legislator, God is also the giver and taker of rights. Therefore, it is often argued, human beings only have such rights as God has chosen to give to them, and they are also denied the rights that God has denied them, and one may not add or subtract anything to this basic and fundamental principle. As a result, it is often maintained that the sole focus ought to be on compliance with the technical rules of Islamic law, without paying particular attention to whether the implementation of such laws grant or deny rights to human beings. Interestingly, a very similar issue was debated in the context of a famous political controversy in early Islam. It will be helpful to review briefly this historical debate.

The issue of God's dominion or sovereignty (*hakimiyyat Allah*) was raised by a group known as the Haruriyya (later known as the Khawarij) when they rebelled against the fourth Rightly Guided Caliph, 'Ali ibn Abi Talib (d. 40/661). Initially, the Haruriyya were firm supporters of 'Ali, but they rebelled against him when he agreed to arbitration in his political dispute with a competing political faction led by a man named Mu'awiya. Ultimately, the effort at reaching a peaceful resolution to the political conflict was a failure, and, after 'Ali's assassination, Mu'awiya was able to establish himself as the first caliph of the Umayyad dynasty. At the time of the arbitration, however, the Khawarij, a puritan and pietistic group of zealots, believed that God's law clearly supported 'Ali and, therefore, an arbitration or any negotiated settlement was inherently unlawful. The Khawarij maintained that the Shari'a clearly and unequivocally supported 'Ali's claim to power, and that any attempt at a negotiated settlement in effect challenged the rule of God and thus God's sovereignty or dominion, and therefore, by definition, was illegitimate.

Ironically, 'Ali himself had agreed to the arbitration on the condition that the arbitrators be bound by the Qur'an, and that they would give full consideration to the supremacy of the Shari'a, but, in 'Ali's mind, this did not necessarily preclude the possibility of a negotiated settlement, let alone the lawfulness of resorting to arbitration as a way of resolving the dispute. In the view of the Khawarij, by accepting the principle of arbitration and by accepting the notion that legality could be negotiated, 'Ali himself had lost his claim to legitimacy because he had transferred God's dominion to human beings. 'Ali's behavior, according to the Khawarij, had shown that he was willing to compromise God's supremacy by transferring decision making to human actors instead of faithfully applying the law of God. Not surprisingly, the Khawarij declared 'Ali a traitor to God, rebelled against him, and eventually succeeded in assassinating him.

Typically, the story of the Khawarij is recounted as an example of early religious fanaticism in Islamic history, and I have no doubt that this view is substantially correct. However, one ought not to overlook the fact that the Khawarij's rallying cry of "dominion belongs to God" or "the Qur'an is the judge" (*al-hukm li-Allah* or *al-hukm li al-Qur'an*) was a call for the symbolism of legality and the supremacy of law.[59] This search for legality quickly descended into an unequivocal radicalized call for clear lines of demarcation between what is lawful and unlawful. The anecdotal reports about the debates between 'Ali and the Khawarij regarding this matter reflect an unmistakable tension about the meaning of legality, and the implications of the rule of law.

In one such report, members of the Khawarij accused 'Ali of accepting the judgment and dominion (*hakimiyya*) of human beings instead of abiding by the dominion of God's law. Upon hearing of this accusation, 'Ali called upon the people to gather and brought a large copy of the Qur'an. 'Ali touched the Qur'an, commanding it to speak to the people and to inform them about God's law. The people gathered around 'Ali and one of them exclaimed, "What are you doing! The Qur'an cannot speak, for it is not a human being." Upon hearing this, 'Ali exclaimed that this is exactly the point he was trying to make! The Qur'an, 'Ali stated, is but ink and paper, and it is human beings who give effect to it according to their limited personal judgments.[60]

Arguably, anecdotal stories such as this do not relate only to the role of human agency in interpreting the divine word, but they also symbolize a search for the fundamental moral values in society. These moral values might differentiate between issues that are subject to political negotiation and expedience and those that constitute unwavering matters of principle and are strictly governed by law. Furthermore, one can discern in such reports a search for the proper legal limits that may be placed upon a ruler's range of discretion. But they also point to the dogmatic superficiality of proclamations in support of God's dominion or sovereignty.

For a believer, God is thought of as all-powerful, and as the ultimate owner of the heavens and earth, but what are the implications of this claim for human agency in understanding and implementing the law? As I argue below, arguments claiming that God is the sole legislator and only source of law engage in a fatal fiction that is not defensible from the point of view of Islamic theology. Such arguments pretend that human agents could possibly have perfect and unfettered access to the mind of God and could possibly become the mere executors of the divine will, without inserting their own human subjectivities in the process. Furthermore, and more importantly, claims about God's sovereignty assume that there is a divine legislative will that seeks to regulate all human interactions. This is always stated as an assumption, instead of a proposition that needs to be argued and proven.

It is possible that God does not seek to regulate all human affairs, a point to which I will return. It is also as possible that God leaves it to human beings to regulate their own affairs as long as they observe certain minimal standards of moral conduct, and that such standards include the preservation and promotion of human dignity and honor because, after all, according to the Qur'an, humans are the vicegerents of God and the inheritors of the earth and are the most valued invention among God's creation. In the Qur'anic discourse, God commanded creation to honor human beings because of the miracle of the human intellect, which is the microcosm of the abilities of the divine itself. Arguably, the fact that God honored the miracle of the human intellect and also honored the human being as a symbol of divinity is sufficient, in and of itself, to justify a moral commitment to whatever might be needed to protect and preserve the integrity and dignity of that symbol of divinity.[61]

SHARI'A AND THE HUMAN RIGHTS COMMITMENT

At this point, it will be useful to deal more systematically with the very concept and epistemology of Shari'a, and the possibility of moral commitments within such an epistemology. This is important because of the centrality of Shari'a to the whole conception of government in Islam, and because the epistemological basis of Shari'a itself is poorly understood by contemporary Muslims, let alone by non-Muslims. As noted earlier, the primacy of the apologetic and puritan trends in contemporary Islam has made Shari'a discourses more like an arena for political slogans than a serious intellectual discipline. But the issue of God's sovereignty and the possibility of moral commitments within a Shari'a paradigm needs to be analyzed through a more informed understanding of the epistemology of Shari'a. Only then can one hope to get beyond the prevalent contemporary dogma in the process of justifying a human rights commitment in Islamic jurisprudence.

As discussed earlier, the difficulty with the concept of Shari'a is that it is potentially a construct of limitless reach and power, and any institution that can attach itself to that construct becomes similarly empowered. Shari'a is God's Way, and it is represented by a set of normative principles, methodologies for the production of legal injunctions, and a set of positive legal rules. Shari'a encompasses a variety of schools of thought and approaches, all of which are equally valid and equally orthodox.[62] Nevertheless, Shari'a as a whole, with all its schools and variant points of view, is considered the Way of God. It is true that the Shari'a is capable of imposing limits on government and of generating individual rights, both of which would be considered limits and rights dictated by the divine will. Yet, whatever limits are imposed or whatever rights are granted may be withdrawn in the same way they are created – through the agency of human interpretation.

In other words, the Shari'a for the most part, is not explicitly dictated by God. Rather, it relies on the interpretive act of the human agent for its production and execution. This creates a double-edged conceptual framework – on the one hand, Shari'a could be the source of unwavering and stolid limitations on government and an uncompromising grant of rights; but on the other hand, whatever is granted by God can also be taken away by God. In both cases, one cannot escape the fact that it is human agents who determine the existence, or non-existence, of the limits on government and the grant of individual rights. This is a formidable power that could be yielded, in one way or another, by the human agent who attaches himself or herself to the Shari'a.

To propose secularism as a solution in order to avoid the hegemony of Shari'a and the possibility of an abuse of power is, in my view, unacceptable. There are several reasons for this. First, given the rhetorical choice between allegiance to the Shari'a and allegiance to international human rights, quite understandably most Muslims will make the equally rhetorical decision to ally themselves to the Shari'a. Second, secularism has become an unworkable and unhelpful symbolic construct. In the Muslim world, secularism is normally associated with what is described as the Western intellectual invasion, both in the period of colonialism and of post-colonialism. Furthermore, secularism has come to symbolize a misguided belief in the probity of rationalism and a sense of hostility to religion as a source of guidance in the public sphere. Third, beyond the issue of symbolism, as noted earlier, there is a considerable variation in the practice of secularism. It is entirely unclear to what extent the practice of secularism requires a separation of church and state, especially in light of the fact that there is no institutional church in Islam. Put differently, to what extent does the practice of secularism mandate the exclusion of religion from the public domain, including the exclusion of religion as a source of law?[63]

Finally, to the extent that the secular paradigm relies on a belief in the guidance-value of reason as a means for achieving utilitarian fulfillment or justice, it is founded on a conviction that is not empirically or morally veri-fiable. One could plausibly believe that religion is an equally valid means of knowing or discovering the means to happiness or justice.[64] But the fact that secularism is a word laden with unhelpful connotations in the Islamic context should not blind us to the fact that the discourse of Shari'a enables human beings to speak in God's name, and effectively empowers human agency with the voice of God. This is a formidable power that is easily abused.

However, I wish to focus on one aspect of Islamic theology that might contribute to the development of a meaningful discourse on human rights in the Islamic context. As noted above, Muslims developed several legal schools of thought, all of which are equally orthodox. But paradoxically, Shari'a is the core value that society must serve. The paradox here is exem-plified in the fact that there is a pronounced tension between the obligation to live by God's law and the fact that this law is manifested only through subjective interpretive determinations. Even if there is a unified realization that a particular positive command does express the divine law, there is still a vast array of possible subjective executions and applications. This dilemma was resolved somewhat in Islamic discourses by distinguishing between Shari'a and *fiqh*. Shari'a, it was argued, is the divine ideal, standing as if suspended in mid-air, unaffected and uncorrupted by the vagaries of life. The *fiqh* is the human attempt to understand and apply the ideal. Therefore, Shari'a is immutable, immaculate, and flawless – *fiqh* is not. [65]

As part of the doctrinal foundations for this discourse, Muslim jurists focused on the tradition attributed to the Prophet stating: "Every *mujtahid* [jurist who strives to find the correct answer] is correct," or "Every *mujtahid* will be [justly] rewarded."[66] This implied that there could be more than a single correct answer to the same question. For Muslim jurists, this raised the issue of the purpose or the motivation behind the search for the divine will. What is the divine purpose behind setting out indicators to the divine law and then requiring that human beings engage in a search? If the Divine wants human beings to reach *the* correct understanding, then how could every interpreter or jurist be correct?

The juristic discourse focused on whether or not the Shari'a had a determinable result or demand in all cases; and if there is such a deter-minable result or demand, are Muslims obligated to find it? Put differently, is there a correct legal response to all legal problems, and are Muslims charged with the legal obligation of finding that response? The over-whelming majority of Muslim jurists agreed that good faith diligence in searching for the divine will is sufficient to protect a researcher from liability before God. As long as the researcher exercises due diligence in the search, he or she will not be held liable nor incur a sin, regardless of the result.

Beyond this, the jurists were divided into two main camps. The first school, known as the *mukhatti'ah*, argued that ultimately there is a correct answer to every legal problem. However, only God knows what the correct response is, and the truth will not be revealed until the Final Day. Human beings, for the most part, cannot conclusively know whether they have found that correct response. In this sense, every *mujtahid* is correct in trying to find the answer; however, one seeker might reach the truth while the others might be mistaken. On the Final Day, God will inform all seekers who was right and who was wrong. Correctness here means that the *mujtahid* is to be commended for putting in the effort, but it does not mean that all responses are equally valid.

The second school, known as the *musawwibah*, included prominent jurists such as Imam al-Haramayn al-Juwayni (d. 478/1085), Jalal al-Din al-Suyuti (d. 911/1505), al-Ghazali (d. 505/1111), and Fakhr al-Din al-Razi (d. 606/1210), and it is reported that the Mu'tazilah were followers of this school as well.[67] The *musawwibah* argued that there is no specific and correct answer (*hukm mu'ayyan*) that God wants human beings to discover, in part because if there were a correct answer, God would have made the evidence indicating a divine rule conclusive and clear. God cannot charge human beings with the duty to find the correct answer when there is no objective means of discovering the correctness of a textual or legal problem. If there were an objective truth to everything, God would have made such a truth ascertainable in this life. Legal truth, or correctness, in most circumstances, depends on belief and evidence, and the validity of a legal rule or act is often contingent on the rules of recognition that provide for its existence.

Human beings are not charged with the obligation of finding some abstract or inaccessible legally correct result. Rather, they are charged with the duty to investigate a problem diligently and then follow the results of their own *ijtihad*. Al-Juwayni explains this point by asserting:

> The most a *mujtahid* would claim is a preponderance of belief (*ghalabat al-zann*) and the balancing of the evidence. However, certainty was never claimed by any of them [the early jurists]…If we were charged with finding [the truth] we would not have been forgiven for failing to find it.[68]

According to al-Juwayni, what God wants or intends is for human beings to search – to live a life fully and thoroughly engaged with the Divine.

Al-Juwayni explains: it is as if God has said to human beings, "My command to My servants is in accordance with the preponderance of their beliefs. So whoever preponderantly believes that they are obligated to do something, acting upon it becomes My command."[69] God's command to human beings is to search diligently, and God's law is suspended until a human being forms a preponderance of belief about the law. At the point that a preponderance of belief is formed, God's law becomes in accordance with the preponderance of belief formed by that particular individual. In summary, if a person honestly and sincerely believes that such and such is the law of God, then, for that person "that" is in fact God's law.[70]

The position of the *musawwibah*, in particular, raises difficult questions about the application of the Shari'a in society.[71] This position implies that God's law is to search for God's law, otherwise the legal charge (*taklif*) is entirely dependent on the subjectivity and sincerity of belief. The *mukhatti'ah* teach that whatever law is applied is potentially God's law, but not necessarily so.[72] In my view, this raises the question: Is it possible for any state-enforced law to be God's law? Under the first (*mukhatti'ah*) school of thought, whatever law the state applies, that law is only potentially the law of God, but we will not find out until the Final Day. Under the second (*musawwibah*) school of thought, any law applied by the state is not the law of God unless the person to whom the law applies believes the law to be God's will and command. The first school suspends knowledge until we are done living, and the second school hinges knowledge on the validity of the process and ultimate sincerity of belief.

Building upon this intellectual heritage, I would suggest that Shari'a ought to stand in an Islamic polity as a symbolic construct for the divine perfection that is unreachable by human effort. It is the epitome of justice, goodness, and beauty as conceived and retained by God. Its perfection is preserved, so to speak, in the mind of God, but anything that is channeled through human agency is necessarily marred by human imperfection. Put differently, Shari'a as conceived by God is flawless, but as understood by human beings, it is imperfect and contingent. Jurists ought to continue exploring the ideal of Shari'a and expounding their imperfect attempts at understanding God's perfection. As long as the argument constructed is normative, it is an unfulfilled potential for reaching the divine will. Significantly, any law applied is necessarily a potential unrealized. Shari'a is not simply a bunch of *ahkam* (a set of positive rules) but also a set of principles, methodology, and a discoursive process that searches for the divine ideals. As such, it is a work in progress that is never complete.

To put it more concretely, a juristic argument about what God commands is only potentially God's law, either because on the Final Day we will discover its correctness (the first school) or because its correctness is contingent on the sincerity of belief of the person who decides to follow it (the second school). If a legal opinion is adopted and enforced by the state, it cannot be said to be God's law. By passing through the determinative and enforcement processes of the state, the legal opinion is no longer simply a potential – it has become an actual law, applied and enforced. But what has been applied and enforced is not God's law – it is the state's law. Effectively, a religious state law is a contradiction in terms. Either the law belongs to the state or it belongs to God, and as long as the law relies on the subjective agency of the state for its articulation and enforcement, any law enforced by the state is necessarily not God's law. Otherwise, we must be willing to admit that the failure of the law of the state is, in fact, the failure of God's law and, ultimately, God himself. In Islamic theology, this possibility cannot be entertained.[73]

Institutionally, it is consistent with the Islamic experience that the *'ulama'* can and do play the role of the interpreters of the divine word, the custodians of the moral conscience of the community, and the curators reminding and pointing the nation towards the Ideal that is God.[74] But the law of the state, regardless of its origins or basis, belongs to the state. It bears emphasis that under this conception, there are no religious laws that can or may be enforced by the state. The state may enforce the prevailing subjective commitments of the community (the second school), or it may enforce what the majority believes to be closer to the divine ideal (the first school). But in either case, what is being enforced is not God's law.

This means that all laws articulated and applied in a state are thoroughly human, and should be treated as such. This also means that any codification of Shari'a law produces a set of rules that are human, and not divine. These laws are a part of Shari'a law only to the extent that any set of human legal opinions can be said to be a part of Shari'a. A code, even if inspired by Shari'a, is not Shari'a – a code is simply a set of positive commandments that were informed by an ideal, but do not represent the ideal. As to the fundamental rights that often act as the foundation of a just society, a Muslim society would have to explore the basic values that are at the very core of the divine ideal.

It is important to note that the paradigm proposed above does not exclude the possibility of objectified and even universalistic moral standards. It simply shifts the responsibility for moral commitments, and the outcome of such commitments, to human beings. Morality could originate with God or could be learned by reflecting upon the state of nature that God has created, but the attempts to fulfill such a morality and give it actual effect are human. In fact, the paradigm proposed here would require certain moral commitments from human beings that ought to be adopted as part of their discharge of their agency on God's behalf.[75] For instance, arguably, the fulfillment of this paradigm is not possible unless it is recognized that people must enjoy certain immunities that are necessarily implied by the very purpose of creation in Islam.

Neither the first nor second view of Shari'a epistemology is possible unless people are guaranteed the right to rational development. Furthermore, the right to rational development means that people ought to be entitled to minimum standards of well-being, in both the physical and intellectual senses. It is impossible to pursue rational development if one is not fed, housed, educated, and, above all, safe from physical harm or persecution. In addition, people cannot pursue a reflective life unless they are guaranteed freedom of conscience, expression, and assembly with like-minded people. Premodern Muslim jurists approached the same type of concerns expressed here by arguing that human needs should be divided into necessities, needs, and luxuries, and that the necessities should be conceptualized in terms of the five core values of protecting religion, life, intellect, honor, and property.[76] I have more to say about the juristic divisions, and five core values, but my point is that even these juristic divisions, for example, are fundamentally human, and thus fallible attempts at fulfilling a divine ideal or moral commitment. As such, they can be re-thought, deconstructed, and re-developed if need be. I think that once Muslims are able to assert that morality is divine, but law and legal divisions and rules are mundane, this will represent a major advancement in the attempt to justify a paradigm of human rights in Islam.

More concretely, reflecting upon divinity, I, as a Muslim, might be able to assert that justice and mercy are objective and universal moral values. I might even try to convince others that justice and mercy are part of the divine charge to humanity – God wants humans to be merciful and just. This represents a moral commitment that I am inviting other human beings to adopt as well. But, under the paradigm proposed here, while I can claim that moral rules emanate or originate from God – a claim which people are free to accept or dispute – I cannot claim that any set of laws that attempt to implement or give effect to this moral commitment is divine as well. Under the first and second views discussed above, this would simply be a conceptual impossibility. Giving effect to this paradigm, I will argue below that justice is a core divine and moral value and further attempt to justify a human rights commitment in Islam.

JUSTICE AS A CORE VALUE AND HUMAN RIGHTS

One of the basic issues commonly dealt with in Islamic political thought was the purpose of government (or the caliphate). The statement of al-Juwayni is fairly representative of the argument of premodern jurists. He states:

> The *imama* (government) is a total governorship and general leadership that relates to the special and common in the affairs of religion and this earthly life. It includes guarding the land and protecting the subjects, and the spread of the message [of Islam] by the word and sword. It includes correcting deviation, redressing injustice, aiding the wronged against the wrongdoer, and taking the right from the obstinate and giving it to those who are entitled to it.[77]

The essential idea conveyed here is that government is a functional necessity in order to resolve conflict, protect religion, and uphold justice.

In some formulations, justice is the core value that justifies the existence of government. Ibn al-Qayyim, for example, makes this point explicit when he asserts the following:

> God sent His message and His Books to lead people with justice... Therefore, if a just leadership is established, through any means, then therein is the Way of God... In fact, the purpose of God's Way is the establishment of righteousness and justice... so any road that establishes what is right and just is the road [Muslims] should follow.[78]

In the Qur'anic discourse, justice is asserted as an obligation owed to God and also owed by human beings to one another. In addition, the imperative of justice is tied to the obligations of enjoining the good and forbidding the evil and the necessity of bearing witness on God's behalf.

Although the Qur'an does not define the constituent elements of justice and in fact seems to treat it as intuitively recognizable, it emphasizes the ability to achieve justice as a unique human charge and necessity.[79] In essence, the Qur'an requires a commitment to a moral imperative that is vague, but recognizable through intuition, reason, or human experience.[80] Importantly, a large number of Muslim jurists argued that God created human beings weak and in need of cooperating with others in order to limit their ability to commit injustice. Furthermore, God created human beings diverse and different from each other so that they will need each other, and this need will cause them further to augment their natural tendency to assemble and cooperate in order to establish justice.

The relative weakness of human beings and their remarkably diverse abilities and habits will further induce people to draw closer and cooperate with each other. If human beings exploit the divine gift of intellect and the guidance of the law of God, through cooperation, they are bound to reach a greater level of strength and justice. The ruler, the jurists argued, ascends to power through a contract with the people pursuant to which he undertakes to further the cooperation of the people, with the ultimate goal of achieving a just society or at least maximizing the potential for justice.[81]

This juristic discourse is partly based on the Qur'anic statement that God created people different, and made them into nations and tribes so that they will come to know one another. Muslim jurists reasoned that the expression "come to know one another" indicates the need for social cooperation and mutual assistance in order to achieve justice.[82] Although the premodern jurists did not emphasize this point, the Qur'an also notes that God made people different, and that they will remain different until the end of human existence. Further, the Qur'an states that the reality of human diversity is part of the divine wisdom, and an intentional purpose of creation.[83]

The Qur'anic celebration and sanctification of human diversity, in addition to the juristic incorporation of the notion of human diversity into a purposeful pursuit of justice, creates various possibilities for a human rights commitment in Islam. This discourse could be appropriated into a normative stance that considers justice to be a core value that a constitutional order is bound to protect. Furthermore, this discourse could be appropriated into a notion of delegated powers in which the ruler is entrusted to serve the core value of justice in light of systematic principles that promote the right of assembly and cooperation in order to enhance the fulfillment of this core value. In addition, a notion of limits could be developed that would restrain the government from derailing the quest for justice, or from hampering the right of the people to cooperate in this quest. Importantly, if the government fails to discharge the obligations of its covenant, then it loses its legitimate claim to power.

However, there are two considerations that militate against the fulfillment of these possibilities in modern Islam. First, modern Muslims themselves are hardly aware of the Islamic interpretive tradition on justice. Both the apologetic and puritan orientations, which are the two predominant trends in modern Islam, have largely ignored the paradigm of human diversity and difference as a necessary means to the fulfillment of the imperative of justice. The second consideration, and the more important one, is that even if modern Muslims reclaim the interpretive traditions of the past on justice, the fact is that, at the conceptual level, the constituent elements of justice were not explored in Islamic doctrine.

There is a tension between the general obligation of implementing the divine law and the demand for justice. Put simply, does the divine law define justice, or does justice define the divine law? If it is the former, then whatever one concludes to be the divine law, therein is justice. If it is the latter, then whatever justice demands is, in fact, the demand of the Divine. For instance, many premodern and modern jurists asserted that the primary purpose of a Muslim polity is to guard and apply the divine law, and the primary charge of a Muslim ruler is to ensure that the people cooperate in giving effect to God's law. In effect, this paradigm makes the organizing principle of society the divine law, and the divine law becomes the embodiment of justice.

Under this paradigm, there is no point in investigating the constituent elements of justice. There is no point in investigating whether justice means equality of opportunities or results, or whether it means maximizing the potential for personal autonomy, or whether it means, perhaps, the maximization of individual and collective utility, or the guarding of basic human dignity, or even the simple resolution of conflict and the maintenance of stability, or any other conception that might provide substance to a general conception of justice. There is no point in engaging in this investigation because the divine law preempts any such inquiry. The divine law provides particularized positive enactments that exemplify but do not analytically explore the notion of justice. Conceptually, according to this paradigm, organized society is no longer about the right to assembly, about cooperation, or about the right to explore the means to justice, but simply about the implementation of the divine law. This brings us full circle to the problem noted above, which is that the implementation of the divine law does not necessarily amount to the existence of limited government, or the protection of basic human rights.

It is important to note, however, that considering the primacy of justice in the Qur'anic discourse, coupled with the notions of human vicegerency, and the notion that the divine charge of justice has been delegated to humanity at large, it is plausible to maintain that justice is what ought to control and guide all human interpretive efforts at understanding the law. This requires a serious paradigm shift in Islamic thinking. In my view, justice and whatever is necessary to achieve justice is the divine law and is what represents the supremacy and sovereignty of the Divine.[84]

God describes God's-self as inherently just, and the Qur'an asserts that God has decreed mercy upon Godself.[85] Furthermore, the very purpose of entrusting the divine message to the Prophet Muhammad is as a gift of mercy to human beings.[86] In the Qur'anic discourse, mercy is not simply forgiveness or the willingness to ignore the faults and sins of people.[87] Mercy is a state in which the individual is able to be just with himself or herself and with others by giving each their due. Fundamentally, mercy is tied to a state of true and genuine perception – that is why, in the Qur'an, mercy is coupled with the need for human beings to be patient and tolerant with each other.[88] Most significantly, diversity and differences among human beings are claimed in the Qur'anic discourse as a merciful divine gift to humankind.[89]

Genuine perception that enables persons to understand and appreciate – and become enriched by – the difference and diversity of humanity is one of the constituent elements for the founding of a just society, and for the achievement of justice. The divine charge to human beings at large, and Muslims in particular, is, as the Qur'an puts it, "to know one another," and utilize this genuine knowledge in an effort to pursue justice. Beyond mere tolerance, this requires that Muslims, and human beings in general, engage in a collective enterprise of goodness, in which they pursue the fulfillment of justice through mercy.[90] The challenge is not simply for people to coexist, but to take part in an enterprise of goodness by engaging in a purposeful moral discourse.[91] Although coexistence is a basic necessity for mercy, in order to pursue a state of real knowledge of the other and aspire for a state of justice, it is imperative that human beings cooperate in seeking the good and beautiful. The more the good and beautiful is approached, the closer humanity comes to a state of divinity.

However, implementing legalistic rules, even if such rules are the product of the interpretation of divine texts, is not sufficient for the achievement of genuine perception of the other, of mercy, or ultimately of justice. The paradigm shift of which I speak requires that the principles of mercy and justice become the primary divine charge. In this paradigm, God's sovereignty lies in the fact that God is the source and authority that delegated to human beings the charge to achieve justice on earth by fulfilling the virtues that are approximations of divinity.[92] Far from negating human subjectivities through the mechanical enforcement of rules, such subjectivities are accommodated and even promoted to the extent that they contribute to the fulfillment of justice.

Significantly, according to the juristic discourses, it is not possible to achieve justice unless every possessor of right (*haqq*) is granted his or her right. [93] As discussed below, God has certain rights, humans have rights, and both God and humans share some rights. The challenge of vicegerency is to first recognize that a right exists, then to understand who is the possessor of such a right, and ultimately to allow the possessor of a given right the enjoyment of the warranted right. A society that fails to do so, regardless of the deluge of rules it might apply, is not a merciful or just society. This puts us in a position to explore the possibility of individual rights in Islam.

THE RIGHTS OF GOD AND THE RIGHTS OF PEOPLE

This is the most challenging topic, and I cannot possibly do it justice in the space of this chapter. The very notion of individual rights is elusive, in terms of both the sources and the nature of those rights. Furthermore, whether there are inherent and absolute individual rights or simply presumptive individual entitlements that could be outweighed by countervailing considerations is debatable.[94] In addition, while all constitutional democracies afford protections to a particular set of individual interests, such as freedom of speech and assembly, equality before the law, right to property, and due process of law, exactly which rights ought to be protected, and to what extent, is subject to a large measure of variation in theory and practice. In this context, I am using a minimalist – and, hopefully, non-controversial – notion of individual rights.

By individual rights, I do not mean entitlements but qualified immunities – the idea that particular interests related to the well-being of an individual ought to be protected from infringements, whether perpetuated by the state or other members of the social order, and that such interests should not be sacrificed unless for an overwhelming necessity. This, as noted, is a minimalist description of rights and, in my view, a largely inadequate one. I doubt very much that there is an objective means of quantifying an overwhelming necessity, and thus, some individual interests ought to be unassailable under any circumstances. These unassailable interests are the ones that, if violated, are bound to communicate to the individual in question a sense of worthlessness, and that, if violated, tend to destroy the faculty of a human being to comprehend the necessary elements for a dignified existence.[95] Therefore, for instance, under this conception, the use of torture, the denial of food or shelter, or the means for sustenance, such as employment would, under any circumstances, be a violation of an individual's rights. For the purposes of this chapter, however, I will assume the minimalist description of rights.

It is fair to say, however, that the premodern juristic tradition did not articulate a notion of individual rights as privileges, entitlements, or immunities. Nonetheless, the juristic tradition did articulate a conception of protected interests that accrue to the benefit of the individual. However, as demonstrated below, this subject remains replete with considerable ambiguity in Islamic thought. As noted earlier, the purpose of Shari'a in jurisprudential theory is to fulfill the welfare of the people. The interests or the welfare of the people is divided into three categories: the necessities (*daruriyyat*), the needs (*hajiyyat*), and the luxuries (*kamaliyyat* or *tahsiniyyat*). The law and political policies of the government must fulfill these interests in descending order of importance – first, the necessities, then the needs, and then the luxuries. The necessities are further divided into five basic values – *al-daruriyyat al-khamsah*: religion, life, intellect, lineage or honor, and property.[96] But Muslim jurists did not develop the five basic values as conceptual categories and then explore the theoretical implications of each value. Rather, they pursued what can be described as an extreme positivistic approach to these rights.

Muslim jurists examined the existing positive legal injunctions that arguably can be said to serve these values, and concluded that by giving effect to these specific legal injunctions, the five values have been sufficiently fulfilled. So, for example, Muslim jurists contended that the prohibition of murder served the basic value of life, the law of apostasy protected religion, the prohibition of intoxicants protected the intellect, the prohibition of fornication and adultery protected lineage, and the right of compensation protected the right to property.[97] Limiting the protection of the intellect to the prohibition against the consumption of alcohol or the protection of life to the prohibition of murder is hardly a very thorough protection of either intellect or life. At most, these laws are partial protections to a limited conception of values, and in any case, cannot be asserted as the equivalent of individual rights because they are not asserted as immunities to be retained by the individual against the world. It is reasonable to conclude that these five values were emptied of any theoretical social and political content and were reduced to technical legalistic objectives. This, of course, does not preclude the possibility that the basic five values could act as a foundation for a systematic theory of individual rights.[98]

To argue that the juristic tradition did not develop the idea of fundamental or basic individual rights does not mean that that tradition was oblivious to the notion. In fact, the juristic tradition tended to sympathize with individuals who were unjustly executed for their beliefs or those who died fighting against injustice. Jurists typically described such acts as a death of *musabara*, a description that carried positive or commendable connotations. Muslim jurists produced a formidable discourse condemning the imposition of unjust taxes and the usurpation of private property by the government.[99] Furthermore, the majority of Muslim jurists refused to condemn or criminalize the behavior of rebels who revolted because of the imposition of oppressive taxes or who resisted a tyrannical government.[100]

In addition, the juristic tradition articulated a wealth of positions that exhibit a humanitarian or compassionate orientation. I will mention only some of these positions, leaving the rest to a more extensive study. Muslim jurists developed the idea of presumption of innocence in all criminal and civil proceedings and argued that the accuser always carries the burden of proof (*al-bayyina 'ala man idda'a*).[101] In matters related to heresy, Muslim jurists repeatedly argued that it is better to let a thousand heretics go free than to punish a single sincere Muslim wrongfully. The same principle was applied to criminal cases; the jurists argued that it is always better to release a guilty person than to run the risk of punishing an innocent person.[102] Moreover, many jurists condemned the practice of detaining or incarcerating heterodox groups that advocate their heterodoxy (such as the Khawarij) and argued that such groups may not be harassed or molested until they carry arms and form a clear intent to rebel against the government.[103]

Muslim jurists also condemned the use of torture, arguing that the Prophet forbade the use of *muthla* (the use of mutilations) in all situations[104] and opposed the use of coerced confessions in all legal and political matters.[105] A large number of jurists articulated a doctrine similar to the American exculpatory doctrine – confessions or evidence obtained under coercion are inadmissible at trial. Interestingly, some jurists asserted that a judge who relies on a coerced confession in a criminal conviction is, in turn, to be held liable for the wrongful conviction. Most argued that the defendant or his family may bring an action for compensation against the judge, individually, and against the caliph and his representatives, generally, because the government is deemed to be vicariously liable for the unlawful behavior of its judges.[106]

But perhaps the most intriguing discourse in the juristic tradition is that which relates to the rights of God and the rights of people. The rights of God (*huquq Allah*) are rights retained by God, as God's own through an explicit designation to that effect. These rights belong to God in the sense that only God can say how the violation of these rights may be punished and only God has the right to forgive such violations.[107] These rights are, so to speak, subject to the exclusive jurisdiction and dominion of God, and human beings have no choice but to follow the explicit and detailed rules that God set out for the handling of acts that fall in God's jurisdiction. In addition, in the juristic theory, all rights not explicitly retained by God accrue to the benefit of human beings.

In other words, any right (*haqq*) that is not specifically and clearly retained by God becomes a right retained by people. These are called *huquq al-'ibad, huquq al-nas,* or *huquq al-adamiyyin.*[108] Importantly, while violations of God's rights are only forgiven by God through adequate acts of repentance, the rights of people may be forgiven only by the people. For instance, a right to compensation is retained individually by a human being and may only be forgiven by the aggrieved individual. The government, or even God, does not have the right to forgive or compromise such a right of compensation if it is designated as part of the rights of human beings. Therefore, the Maliki jurist Ibn al-'Arabi (d. 543/1148) states:

> The rights of human beings are not forgiven by God unless the human being concerned forgives them first, and the claims for such rights are not dismissed [by God] unless they are dismissed by the person concerned...The rights of a Muslim cannot be abandoned except by the possessor of the right. Even the *imam* [ruler] does not have the right to demand [or abandon] such rights. This is because the *imam* is not empowered to act as the agent for a specific set of individuals over their specific rights. Rather, the *imam* only represents people, generally, over their general and unspecified rights.[109]

In a similar context, the Hanafi jurist al-'Ayini (d. 855/1451) argues that the usurper of property, even if a government official (*al-zalim*), will not be forgiven for his sin, even if he repents a thousand times, unless he returns the stolen property.[110]

Most of these discourses occur in the context of addressing personal monetary and property rights, but they have not been extended to other civil rights, such as the right to due process or the right to listen, to reflect, and to study, which may not be abandoned or violated by the government under any circumstances. This is not because the range of the rights of people was narrow – quite to the contrary, it is because the range of these rights was too broad. It should be recalled that people retain any rights not explicitly reserved by God. Effectively, since the rights retained by God are quite narrow, the rights accruing to the benefit of the people are numerous. Juristic practice has tended to focus on narrow legal claims that may be addressed through the processes of law rather than on broad theoretical categories that were perceived as non-justiciable before a court.

As such, the jurists tended to focus on tangible property rights or rights for compensation instead of on moral claims. So, for instance, if someone burns another person's books, that person may seek compensation for destruction of property, but he could not bring an action for injunctive relief preventing the burning of the books in the first place. Despite this limitation, the juristic tradition did, in fact, develop a notion of individual claims that are immune from governmental or social limitation or alienation.

There is one other important aspect that needs to be explored in this context. Muslim jurists asserted the rather surprising position that if the rights of God and those of people (mixed rights) overlap, the rights of people should, in most cases, prevail. The justification for this was that humans need their rights, and need to vindicate those rights on earth. God, on the other hand, asserts God's rights only for the benefit of human beings, and in all cases God can vindicate God's rights in the Hereafter if need be. As to the rights of people, Muslim jurists did not imagine a set of unwavering and generalizable rights that are to be held by each individual at all times. Rather, they thought of individual rights as arising from a legal cause brought about by the suffering of a legal wrong. A person does not possess a right until he or she has been wronged and, as a result, obtains a claim for retribution or compensation.

Shifting paradigms, it is necessary to transform the traditional conceptions of rights to a notion of immunities and entitlements. As such, these rights become the property of individual holders, before a specific grievance arises and regardless of whether there is a legal cause of action. The set of rights that are recognized as immutable and invariable are those that are necessary to achieve a just society while promoting the element of mercy. It is quite possible that the relevant individual rights are those five values mentioned above, but this issue needs to be re-thought and re-analyzed in light of the current diversity and particularity of human existence.

The fact that the rights of people take priority over the rights of God, on this earth, necessarily means that a claimed right of God may not be used to violate the rights of human beings. God is capable of vindicating whichever rights God wishes to vindicate in the Hereafter. On this earth, we concern ourselves only with discovering and establishing the rights that are needed to enable human beings to achieve a just life, while – to the extent possible – honoring the asserted rights of God.[111] In this context, the commitment to human rights does not signify a lack of commitment to God, or a lack of willingness to obey God. Rather, human rights become a necessary part of celebrating human diversity, honoring the vicegerents of God, achieving mercy, and pursuing the ultimate goal of justice.

ISLAM AND THE PROMISE OF HUMAN RIGHTS

I have argued that God's sovereignty is honored in the pursuit of a just society and that a just society must, in pursuit of mercy, respect human diversity and richness and must recognize the immunities that are due to human beings. I have justified this position on Islamic grounds, and, while acknowledging that this approach is informed by the interpretive traditions of the past, it is not the dominant approach to the subject or even a well-established approach among Muslims in the modern era. Unfortunately, the only well-established approaches to the subject today are the apologetic and puritan approaches. As far as contemporary discourses are concerned, they are replete with unjustified assumptions and intellectual shortcuts that have seriously undermined the ability of Muslims to confront such an important topic as human rights.

In addition, partly affected by Muslim apologists, many Western scholars repeat generalizations about Islamic law that, to say the least, are not based on historical texts generated by Muslim jurists. Among those unfounded generalizations are the claims that Islamic law is concerned primarily with duties, and not rights, and that the Islamic conception of rights is collectivist, and not individualistic.[112] Both claims, although they are often repeated, are somewhat inconsistent, but more importantly, they are not based on anything other than cultural assumptions about the non-Western "other." It is as if the various interpreters, having decided on what they believe is the Judeo-Christian or perhaps Western conception of rights, assume that Islam must necessarily be different.[113] The reality, however, is that both claims are largely anachronistic.

Premodern Muslim jurists did not assert a collectivist vision of rights, just as they did not assert an individualistic vision of rights. They did speak of *al-haqq al-'amm* (public rights) and often asserted that public rights ought to be given preference over private entitlements. But as a matter of juristic determination, this amounted to no more than an assertion that the many should not be made to suffer for the entitlements of the few. For instance, as a legal maxim, this was utilized to justify the notion of public takings or the right to public easements over private property. This principle was also utilized in prohibiting unqualified doctors from practicing medicine.[114] But, as noted above, Muslim jurists did not, for instance, justify the killing or the torture of individuals in order to promote the welfare of the state or the public interest. Even with regard to public takings or easements, the vast majority of Muslim jurists maintained that the individuals affected are entitled by the state to compensation equal to the fair market value of the property taken.

Pursuant to a justice perspective, one can argue that a commitment to individual rights, taken as a whole, will accrue to the benefit of the many (the private citizens) over the few (the members of ruling government). I do believe that the common good is greatly enhanced, and not hampered, by the assertion of individual rights, but this point needs to be developed in a more systematic way in a separate study.[115] My point here, however, is that the juristic notion of public rights does not necessarily support what is often described as a collectivist view of rights.[116]

Likewise, the idea of duties (*wajibat*) is as well established in the Islamic tradition as the notion of rights (*huquq*) – the Islamic juristic tradition does not show a preference for one over the other. In fact, some pre-modern jurists have asserted that to every duty there is a reciprocal right, and vice versa.[117] It is true that many jurists claimed that the ruler is owed a duty of obedience, but they also, ideally, expected the ruler to safeguard the well-being and interests of the ruled. The fact that the jurists did not hinge the duty to obey on the obligation to respect the individual rights of citizens does not mean that they were, as a matter of principle, opposed to affording the ruled certain immunities against the state. In some situations, Muslim jurists even asserted that if the state fails to protect the well-being of the ruled, and is unjust toward them, the ruled no longer owe the state either obedience or support.[118]

The widespread rhetoric regarding the primacy of collectivist and duty-based perspectives in Islam points to the reactive nature of much of the discourse on Islamic law in the contemporary age. In the 1950s and 1960s, most Muslim countries, as underdeveloped nations, were heavily influenced by socialist and national development ideologies which tended to emphasize collectivist and duty-oriented conceptions of rights. Therefore, many Muslim commentators claimed that the Islamic tradition necessarily supports the aspirations and hopes of what is called the third world. But such claims are as negotiative, re-constructive, and inventive of the Islamic tradition as is any particular contemporaneous vision of rights. In my view, however, from a theological perspective, the notion of individual rights is easier to justify in Islam than a collectivist orientation.

God created human beings as individuals, and their liability in the Hereafter is individually determined as well. To commit oneself to safeguarding and protecting the well-being of the individual is to take God's creation seriously. Each individual embodies a virtual universe of divine miracles – in body, soul, and mind. Why should a Muslim commit himself/herself to the rights and well-being of a fellow human being? The answer is because God has already made such a commitment when God invested so much of the God-self in each and every person. This is why the Qur'an asserts that whoever kills a fellow human being unjustly, it is as if he/she has murdered all of humanity – it is as if the killer has murdered the divine sanctity and defiled the very meaning of divinity.[119]

The Qur'an does not differentiate between the sanctity of a Muslim and that of a non-Muslim.[120] It repeatedly asserts that no human being can limit the divine mercy in any way or even regulate who is entitled to it.[121]

I take this to mean that non-Muslims, as well as Muslims, could be the recipients and the givers of divine mercy. The measure of moral virtue on this earth is who is able to come closer to divinity through justice, and not who carries the correct religious or irreligious label. The measure in the Hereafter is a different matter, but it is a matter that is in the purview of God's exclusive jurisdiction.

Does it matter what the general world community has come to believe are the minimal standards of conduct that ought to be observed when dealing with human beings? Concretely, does it matter if the world community has come to see the cutting of the hands of the thief, the stoning of an adulterer or adulteress, or the male privilege enjoyed in matters of divorce or inheritance to be violative of the basic standards that should be observed in dealing with human beings? It is relevant if the concept of mercy and human diversity is going to be taken seriously. The real issue is that as Muslims we have been charged with safeguarding the well-being and dignity of human beings, and we have also been charged with achieving justice.

If my argument is sound, dignity and justice need compassion and mercy. Muslims are charged with the obligation to teach mercy, but in the same way that one cannot learn to speak before learning to listen, one cannot teach unless one is also willing to learn. To take the ethic of mercy seriously, we must first learn to care, and this is why it does matter what humanity at large thinks of our interpretations and applications of the divine mandate. If other humans cannot understand our version of mercy, then claiming cultural exceptionalism or relativism, from a theological point of view, avails us nothing. This is especially so if we, as Muslims, are engaging the rest of humanity in a collective enterprise to establish goodness and well-being on this earth. Considering the enormous diversity of human beings, we have no choice but to take each contribution to a vision of goodness seriously, and to ask which of the proffered visions comes closer to attempting to fulfill the divine charge.

Yet we cannot lose sight of the fact that, as human beings, the charge, and ultimate responsibility, is ours. This means that, acting upon the duties of vicegerency on this earth, we must take the imperative of engaging in a collective enterprise of goodness seriously, and in doing so we must be willing to persuade and be persuaded as to what is necessary for a moral and virtuous existence on this earth. God will most certainly vindicate God's rights in the Hereafter in the fashion that God deems most fitting, but, on this earth, our primary moral responsibility is the vindication of the rights of human beings. Put this way, perhaps it becomes all too obvious that a commitment in favor of human rights is a commitment in favor of God's creation, and ultimately, it is a commitment in favor of God.

NOTES

1. See Ann E. Mayer, "Rhetorical Strategies and Official Policies on Women's Rights: The Merits and Drawbacks of the New World Hypocrisy," in *Faith and Freedom: Women's Human Rights in the Muslim World*, ed. Mahnaz Afkhami (Syracuse: Syracuse University Press, 1995), pp. 104–132.

2. On the humanistic tradition in Islam, see George Makdisi, *The Rise of Humanism in Classical Islam and the Christian West* (Edinburgh: Edinburgh University Press, 1990); Joel L. Kraemer, *Humanism in the Renaissance of Islam: The Cultural Revival During the Buyid Age* (Leiden: E.J. Brill, 1992); Lenn Evan Goodman, *Islamic Humanism* (Oxford: Oxford University Press, 2003); Marcel Boisard, *Humanism in Islam* (Indianapolis: American Trust Publications, 1987).

3. On the development of natural rights theory in the West, see Knud Haakonssen, *Natural Law and Moral Philosophy: From Grotius to the Scottish Enlightenment* (Cambridge: Cambridge University Press, 1996); Brian Tierney, *The Idea of Natural Rights* (Atlanta: Scholars Press, 1997). For a useful review of the broad range of theories in the field, see Carlos Santiago Nino, *The Ethics of Human Rights* (Oxford: Clarendon Press, 1993); Tibor Machan, *Individuals and their Rights* (La Salle, IL: Open Court, 1989).

4. There has been a considerable amount of literature about what has been described as the East Asian challenge to liberal Western human rights conceptions. The debate centers on the legitimacy, effectiveness, and morality of individualistic as opposed to communitarian or collectivist human rights schemes. This debate is relevant to the Islamic context because a number of commentators have claimed that communitarian or collectivist human rights schemes are more consistent with Islamic morality and ethics. On the debate, see *The East Asian Challenge for Human Rights*, eds. Joanne R. Bauer and Daniel A. Bell (Cambridge: Cambridge University Press, 1999) (two of the articles in this collection deal with predominantly Muslim nations); W.M. Theodore de Bary, *Asian Values and Human Rights: A Confucian Communitarian Perspective* (Cambridge, MA: Harvard University Press, 1998); *Confucianism and Human Rights* ed. W.M. Theodore De Bary and Tu Weiming (New York: Columbia University Press, 1998); Daniel A. Bell, *East Meets West: Human Rights and Democracy in East Asia* (Princeton: Princeton University Press, 2000), esp. pp. 3–172; Andrew J. Nathan, "Sources of Chinese Rights Thinking," in *Human Rights in Contemporary China*, eds. R. Randle Edwards, Louis Henkin, and Andrew J. Nathan (New York: Columbia

University Press, 1986), pp. 123–164; Henry J. Steiner and Philip Alston, *International Human Rights in Context: Law, Politics, Morals* (Oxford: Clarendon Press, 1996), pp. 166–255; and *Debating Human Rights: Critical Essays from the United States and Asia,* ed. Peter Van Ness (London: Routledge, 1999) (several of the articles in this collection deal with debates in predominantly Muslim countries). On the African critique of individual human rights, and what the author believes is the "Muslim approach" to human rights, see Rhoda E. Howard, *Human Rights and the Search for Community* (Boulder: Westview Press, 1995), pp. 79–104.

5.   On the natural law origins of the human rights discourse, and the emancipatory role natural law paradigms played against the state, see Costas Douzinas, *The End of Human Rights* (Oxford: Hart Publishing, 2000), pp. 1–145. Douzinas argues that claims of rights played a powerful role in critiques of legal conservatism. However, the endless expansion of potential rights led to the co-optation of the natural rights discourses by state actors, and to false polarization between universalists and cultural relativists. For a critical overview of the development of the human rights discourse in modern times, see Upendra Baxi, *The Future of Human Rights* (New Delhi: Oxford University Press, 2002).

6.   For the argument that some of what are believed to be ancient traditions are in reality recently crafted constructs, see the introduction and concluding chapter written by Hobsbawm in *The Invention of Tradition,* ed. Eric Hobsbawm and Terence Ranger (Cambridge: Cambridge University Press, 1983), pp. 1–14, 263–307.

7.   Jack Donnelly, "The Social Construction of International Human Rights," in *Human Rights in Global Politics,* eds. Tim Dunne and Nicholas J. Wheeler (Cambridge: Cambridge University Press, 1999), pp. 71–102; Jack Donnelly, *International Human Rights: Dilemmas in World Politics,* 2nd ed. (Boulder: Westview Press, 1998), pp. 3–17, 86–114; David P. Forsythe, *Human Rights in International Relations* (Cambridge: Cambridge University Press, 2000), pp. 139–60, 217–36; Peter Schwab and Adamantia Pollis, "Globalization's Impact on Human Rights," in *Human Rights: New Perspectives, New Realities,* eds. Adamantia Pollis and Peter Schwab (Boulder: Lynne Rienner, 2000), pp. 209–223; Paul Gordon Lauren, *The Evolution of International Human Rights: Visions Seen* (Philadelphia: University of Pennsylvania Press, 1998), pp. 241–280; A.H. Robertson and J.G. Merrills, *Human Rights in the World: An Introduction to the Study of the International Protection of Human Rights,* 3rd ed. (Manchester: Manchester University Press, 1992), pp. 286–304. For a useful collection of articles on the topic, see *The Power of Human Rights: International Norms and Domestic Change,* eds. Thomas Risse, Stephen Ropp, and Kathryn Sikkink (Cambridge: Cambridge University Press, 1999); see also the collection of articles in *The Politics of Human Rights,* ed. Obrad Savic (London: Verso, 1999). For useful anthropological

studies on the "globalization of human rights," see *Human Rights, Culture and Context*, ed. Richard A. Wilson (Chicago: Pluto, 1997). For a study that analyzes this phenomenon, but is critical of the American contribution, see Diana G. Zoelle, *Globalizing Concern For Human Rights: The Failure of the American Model* (New York: St. Martin's, 2000).

8. The so-called International Bill of Rights comprises the Universal Declaration of Human Rights, the International Covenant on Economic, Social, and Cultural Rights, and the International Covenant on Civil and Political Rights. See Jimmy Carter, Adolfo Perez Esquivel, and Tom J. Farer, *The International Bill of Rights* (Glen Ellen, CA: Entwhistle Books, 1981). See also Johannes Morsink, *The Universal Declaration of Human Rights: Origins, Drafting, and Intent* (Philadelphia: University of Pennsylvania Press, 1999).

9. See Michael Ignatieff, *The Rights Revolution* (Toronto: House of Anansi, 2000); Carl Wellman, *The Proliferation of Rights: Moral Progress or Empty Rhetoric?* (Boulder: Westview, 1999); Kirsten Sellars, *The Rise and Rise of Human Rights* (Stroud: Sutton, 2002); Norberto Bobbio, *The Age of Rights* (Cambridge: Polity, 1996); Louis Henkin, *The Age of Rights* (New York: Columbia University Press, 1990).

10. For instance, see Susan E. Waltz, *Human Rights and Reform: Changing the Face of North African Politics* (Berkeley and Los Angeles: University of California Press, 1995), esp. pp. 14–34, 216–230; Kevin Dwyer, *Arab Voices: The Human Rights Debate in the Middle East* (Berkeley and Los Angeles: University of California Press, 1991); George Black, ed., *Islam and Justice: Debating the Future of Human Rights in the Middle East and North Africa* (New York: Lawyers' Committee for Human Rights, 1997); Joe Stork, *Debating Human Rights in the Middle East* (Cambridge: Cambridge University Press, forthcoming); Eugene Cotran and Mai Yamani, eds., *The Rule of Law in the Middle East and the Islamic World, Human Rights and the Judicial Process* (London: I.B. Tauris, 2000). On the impact of the international human rights discourse on Egypt, see Kevin Boyle, "Human Rights in Egypt: International Commitments," in *Human Rights and Democracy: The Role of the Supreme Constitutional Court in Egypt*, eds. Kevin Boyle and Adel Omar Sherif (The Hague: Kluwer Law International, 1996), pp. 87–114. For a more general assessment, but which also focuses on Algeria, see Mahmood Monshipouri, *Democratization, Liberalization, and Human Rights in the Third World* (Boulder: Lynne Rienner, 1995). A particularly insightful analysis is offered by Katerina Dalacoura in *Islam, Liberalism and Human Rights* (London: I.B. Tauris, 1998).

11. On the issue of the general tension between Islamic law and human rights law, see Bassam Tibi, "Islamic Law/Shari'a and Human Rights: International Law and International Relations," in *Islamic Law Reform and Human Rights: Challenges and Rejoinders*, eds. Tore Lindholm and Kari Vogt (Oslo: Nordic Human Rights Publications, 1993), pp. 75–96. On the

response of several Muslim countries to international human rights obligations, see Ann Mayer, *Islam and Human Rights: Tradition and Politics,* 3rd ed. (Boulder: Westview, 1999). Mayer critiques the practice of several Muslim countries of entering reservations to human rights treaties providing that they are bound by human rights law only to the extent that such international obligations are consistent with Shari'a law. See also Ann Mayer, "Cultural Particularism as a Bar to Women's Rights: Reflections on the Middle Eastern Experience," in *Women's Rights, Human Rights: International Feminist Perspectives,* eds. Julie Peters and Andrea Wolper (London: Routledge, 1995), pp. 176–188. On the treatment of religious minorities in traditional Islamic law, and the tension with international human rights law, see Mohammad Tal'at Al Ghunaimi, *The Muslim Conception of International Law and the Western Approach* (The Hague: Martinus Nijhoff, 1968), pp. 212–216. See also John Kelsay, "Saudi Arabia, Pakistan, and the Universal Declaration of Human Rights," in *Human Rights and the Conflicts of Culture: Western and Islamic Perspectives on Religious Liberty,* eds. David Little, John Kelsay, and Abdulaziz Sachedina (Columbia: University of South Carolina Press, 1988), pp. 33–52. For two very critical perspectives on the status of women under traditional Shari'a law, see Mahnaz Afkhami, "Gender Apartheid and the Discourse of Relativity of Rights in Muslim Societies," pp. 67–77, and Asma M. Abdel Halim, "Reconciling the Opposites: Equal but Subordinate," pp. 203–213, both in *Religious Fundamentalisms and the Human Rights of Women,* ed. Courtney W. Howland (New York: St. Martin's, 1999). See also Miriam Cooke and Bruce B. Lawrence, "Muslim Women Between Human Rights and Islamic Norms," in *Religious Diversity and Human Rights,* eds. Irene Bloom, J. Paul Martin, and Wayne L. Proudfoot (New York: Columbia University Press, 1996), pp. 313–328. On Islamic criminal punishments and human rights, see Abdullahi An-Na'im, "Toward a Cross-Cultural Approach to Defining International Standards of Human Rights: The Meaning of Cruel, Inhuman, and Degrading Treatment or Punishment," in *Human Rights in Cross-Cultural Perspectives: A Quest for Consensus,* ed. Abdullahi An-Na'im (Philadelphia: University of Pennsylvania Press, 1992), pp. 19–43. See also Ann Mayer, "A Critique of An-Na'im's Assessment of Islamic Criminal Justice," in *Islamic Law Reform,* eds. Lindholm and Vogt, pp. 37–60. On freedom of religion in Islam, see Nathan Lerner, *Religion, Beliefs, and International Human Rights* (Maryknoll, NY: Orbis, 2000), pp. 47–48.

12.   See J.N.D. Anderson, *Islamic Law in the Modern World* (New York: New York University Press, 1959); J.N.D. Anderson, *Law Reform in the Muslim World* (London: Athlone, 1976); Wael Hallaq, *A History of Islamic Legal Theories* (Cambridge: Cambridge University Press, 2001), pp. 207–211. On the adoption of secularized law, and the emergence of Western legal professionals in Egypt, see Farhat J. Ziadeh, *Lawyers, the Rule of Law, and*

Liberalism in Modern Egypt (Stanford: Hoover Institution Publications, 1968), pp. 3–61.

13. See Lynn Hunt, "The Paradoxical Origins of Human Rights," in *Human Rights and Revolutions*, ed. Jeffrey Wasserstrom, Lynn Hunt, and Marilyn Young (Lanham, MD: Rowman & Littlefield, 2000), pp. 3–17.

14. The classic studies on Orientalism and its effects remain those of Edward Said, *Orientalism* (New York: Random House, 1979) and *Culture and Imperialism* (New York: Vintage Books, 1994). For a probing survey of Orientalism and its practices, see Bryan S. Turner, *Orientalism, Postmodernism and Globalism* (London: Routledge, 1994), pp. 3–114. See also *Orientalism, Islam, and Islamists*, eds. Asaf Hussain, Robert Olson, and Jamil Qureshi (Brattleboro, VT: Amana Books, 1984). For an informative survey of Orientalism and its practices, see A.L. Macfie, *Orientalism* (London: Pearson Education, 2002). Roxanne L. Euben in *Enemy in the Mirror: Islamic Fundamentalism and the Limits of Modern Rationalism* (Princeton: Princeton University Press, 1999) argues somewhat persuasively that Islamic fundamentalism is a form of critique or protest against rationalist modernism. On the emergence of the feminist discourse and the "White Woman's Burden", see Leila Ahmed, *Women and Gender in Islam* (New Haven: Yale University Press, 1992); Mounira Charrad, *States and Women's Rights: The Making of Postcolonial Tunisia, Algeria, and Morocco* (Los Angeles: University of California Press, 2001); Kumari Jayawardena, *The White Woman's Other Burden: Western Women and South Asia During British Rule* (London: Routledge, 1995); Azra Asghar Ali, *The Emergence of Feminism Among Indian Muslim Women 1920–1947* (New Delhi: Oxford University Press, 2000);*Western Women and Imperialism: Complicity and Resistance*, eds. Nupur Chaudhuri and Margaret Strobel (Bloomington: Indiana University Press, 1992); Shaheen Sardar Ali, *Gender and Human Rights in Islam and International Law: Equal Before Allah, Unequal Before Man?* (The Hague: Kluwer Law International, 2000).

15. See David Rieff, "A New Age of Liberal Imperialism," in *Human Rights and Revolutions*, eds. Wasserstrom, Hunt, and Young, pp. 177–190.

16. See also Richard Falk, "A Half Century of Human Rights: Geopolitics and Values," in *The Future of International Human Rights*, eds. Burns H. Weston and Stephen P. Marks (Ardsley, NY: Transnational, 1999), pp. 1–24.

17. This period has been described by some scholars as the liberal age of modern Islam. See Albert Hourani, *Arabic Thought in the Liberal Age: 1798–1939* (Cambridge: Cambridge University Press, 1983); Leonard Binder, *Islamic Liberalism: A Critique of Development Ideologies* (Chicago: Chicago University Press, 1988); Daniel Brown, *Rethinking Tradition in Modern Islamic Thought* (Cambridge: Cambridge University Press, 1996); Robert D. Lee, *Overcoming Tradition and Modernity: The Search for Islamic Authenticity* (Boulder: Westview, 1997). Lee focuses on the reformative

thought of four modern influential Islamic thinkers. For excerpts from the works of Muslim liberals, see *Liberal Islam: A Sourcebook*, ed. Charles Kurzman (Oxford: Oxford University Press, 1998). See also Huseyn Hilmi Isik, *The Religion Reformers in Islam*, 3rd ed. (Istanbul: Wakf Ikhlas, 1978).

18.   For a critical, and similarly grim, assessment by a Muslim intellectual of the impact of apologetics upon Muslim culture, see Tariq Ramadan, *Islam, the West and the Challenges of Modernity*, trans. Said Amghar (Markefield: Islamic Foundation, 2001), pp. 286–290. For an insightful analysis of the role of apologetics in modern Islam, see Wilfred Cantwell Smith, *Islam in Modern History* (Princeton: Princeton University Press, 1977).

19.   Examples of such works in Arabic, Persian, Urdu, and English are too numerous to cite. I will restrict my citations here to representative works from the genre published in different parts of the Muslim world: Mohammad Khoder, *Human Rights in Islam*, trans. Zaid Al-Husain (Beirut: Dar Khoder, 1988); *Human Rights in Islamic Law*, ed. Tahir Mahmood (Delhi: Khowaja Press, 1993); Abul A'la Mawdudi, *Human Rights in Islam* (London: Islamic Foundation, 1976); Abdur Rahman Shad, *The Rights of Allah and Human Rights* (Delhi: Adam, 1987); International Commission of Jurists, *Human Rights in Islam* (Kuwait: Kuwait University Press, 1982); Sulieman Abdul Rahman al-Hageel, *Human Rights in Islam and Refutation of the Misconceived Allegations Associated with these Rights* (Riyadh: Muhammad Ibn Saud Islamic University, 1999); *Human Rights in Islam: Papers Presented at the 5th Islamic Thought Conference* (Tehran: Islamic Propagation Organization, 1987); Ibrahim Abdulla al-Marzouqi, *Human Rights in Islamic Law* (Abu Dhabi: n.p., 2000); N.K. Singh, *Social Justice and Human Rights in Islam* (Delhi: Gyan Publishing House, 1998); Muhammad Zafrullah Khan, *Islam and Human Rights* (Islamabad: Islam International Publications, 1967); Shaikh Shaukat Hussain, *Human Rights in Islam* (New Delhi: Kitab Bhavan, 1990); Hilmi Zawati, *Is Jihad a Just War? War, Peace, and Human Rights under Islamic and Public International Law* (New York: Edwin Mellen, 2002). Some Western scholars have noticed the superficiality of the treatment offered by many Muslim writers, but they reach the unsupported and careless conclusion that this superficiality of treatment is due to the fact that there are no individual rights in Islam. See Jack Donnelly (Rhoda Howard is listed as a co-author in the section on non-Western conceptions of rights), *Universal Human Rights in Theory and Practice* (Cornell: Cornell University Press, 1989), pp. 50–52.

20.   See on this subject the collection of articles in *Human Rights and Religious Values: An Uneasy Relationship?*, ed. Abdullahi An-Na'im, Jerald Gort, Henry Jansen, and Hendrik Vroom (Grand Rapids: Eerdmans, 1995).

21.   For examples of this genre, see Mohammad Tal'at Al Ghunaimi, "Justice and Human Rights in Islam," in *Justice and Human Rights in Islamic Law*, ed. Gerald E. Lampe (Washington D.C.: International Law Institute,

1997), pp. 1–22; Noor ul-Amin Leghari, "The Concept of Justice and Human Rights in Islam," in ibid., pp. 51–64; Ahmad Zahir, *Huquq al-Insan* (Oman: Dar al-Karmil, 1993). See the articles by Mohamed Abdel Haleem and Ibrahim Al-Marzouqi in *Democracy, the Rule of Law, and Islam*, eds. Eugene Cotran and Adel Omar Sherif (The Hague: Kluwer Law International, 1999), pp. 435–475. 'Abd al-Husayn Sha'ban, *al-Islam wa Huquq al-Insan* (Beirut: Mu'assasat Huquq al-Insan, 2001); Ja'far 'Abd al-Salam Ali, *al-Qanun al-Daw li Huquq al-Insan: Dirasat fi al-Qunun al-Dawli wa al-Shari'a al-Islamiyya* (Cairo: Dar al-Kitab al-Misri, 1999); al-Qutb Muhammad al-Qutb Tabliyya, *al-Islam wa Huquq al-Insan: Dirasa Muqarina* (Cairo: Dar al-Fikr al-'Arabi, 1976); 'Abd al-Lafif al-Ghamidi, *Huquq al-Insan fi al-Islam* (Riyadh: Naif Arab Academy, 2000).

22.   Since the 1940s and to date, there has not been a single systematic and exhaustive treatise by a prominent Muslim jurist on the issue of the relationship of Islam to human rights. Although there was a virtual flood of defensive and apologetic works on the subject, there has been no systematic or serious treatment by an influential theologian.

23.   The foundations of Wahhabi theology were set into place by the eighteenth-century evangelist Muhammad b. 'Abd al-Wahhab (d. 1206/1792). With a puritanical zeal, 'Abd al-Wahhab sought to rid Islam of all the corruptions that he believed had crept into the religion – corruptions such as mysticism, including the doctrine of intercession and rationalism. The simplicity, decisiveness, and incorruptibility of the religious thought of 'Abd al-Wahhab made it attractive to the desert tribes, especially in the area of Najd. 'Abd al-Wahhab's ideas would not have spread even in Arabia had it not been for the fact that in the late eighteenth century the Al Saud family united itself with the Wahhabi movement and rebelled against Ottoman rule in Arabia. The Wahhabi rebellion was considerable, at one point reaching as far as Damascus in the north and Oman in the south. Egyptian forces under the leadership of Muhammad Ali in 1818, however, quashed the rebellion after several failed expeditions and Wahhabism seemed to be on its way to extinction. Nevertheless, Wahhabi ideology was resuscitated once again in the early twentieth century under the leadership of Abd al-Aziz b. Al Sa'ud (r. 1319–1373/1902–1953), who adopted the puritanical theology of the Wahhabis and allied himself with the tribes of Najd, thereby establishing the nascent beginnings of what became Saudi Arabia.

24.   Salafism is a creed founded in the late nineteenth century by Muslim reformers such as Muhammad 'Abduh (d. 1323/1905), Jamal al-Din al-Afghani (d. 1314/1897), Muhammad Rashid Rida (d. 1354/1935), Muhammad al-Shawkani (d. 1250/1834), and al-Jalal al-San'ani (d. 1225/1810). Salafism appealed to a very basic and fundamental concept in Islam, that Muslims ought to follow the precedent of the Prophet and his rightly guided companions (*al-salaf al-salih*). The founders of

Salafism maintained that on all issues Muslims ought to return to the original textual sources of the Qur'an and the Sunna (precedent) of the Prophet. In doing so, Muslims ought to reinterpret the original sources in light of modern needs and demands without being slavishly bound to the interpretive precedents of earlier Muslim generations. Methodologically, Salafism is nearly identical to Wahhabism except that Wahhabism is far less tolerant of diversity and differences of opinion. By the 1980s, however, Wahhabism co-opted the language, symbolisms, and even the very name of Salafism and, therefore, was able to spread in the Muslim world under the Salafi label.

25. For instance see ʿAbd al-Wahhab, "al-Risalah al-Ula," in *Majmuʿat al-Tawhid,* coll. Hamad al-Najdi (Damascus: al-Maktab al-Islami, 1962), pp. 30–31, 68; ʿAbd al-Wahhab, "Bayan al-Najab wa al-Fakak: al-Risala al-Thaniya ʿAshra," in ibid., pp. 394, 400, 421–423, 433.

26. This was, for instance, reproduced in Sayyid Qutb's notion that the world (including the Muslim world) is living in *jahiliyya* (darkness and ignorance associated with the pre-Islamic era). See Sayyid Qutb, *Milestones on the Road* (Indianapolis: American Trust Publications, 1991); and Ahmad S. Mousalli, *Radical Islamic Fundamentalism: The Ideological and Political Discourse of Sayyid Qutb* (Syracuse: Syracuse University Press, 1993). This intellectual and moral isolationism was resisted, perhaps not very successfully, by a variety of jurists in the first half of the twentieth century. For instance, many of the articles published in the Azhar journal, *Nur al-Islam,* in the 1930s and 1940s attempted to engage, interact, and discourse with world thought. It is clear that many Muslim scholars, at that time, tried to stay informed about the latest in European thought and attempted to discuss how the latest ideas in philosophy and sociology would impact upon Muslim culture.

27. See Daryush Shayegan, *Cultural Schizophrenia: Islamic Societies Confronting the West,* trans. John Howe (London: Saqi Books, 1989). See also Louay M. Safi, *The Challenge of Modernity: The Quest for Authenticity in the Arab World* (Lanham, MD: University Press of America, 1994), esp. pp. 153–193; Malise Ruthven, *A Fury for God: The Islamist Attack on America* (London: Granta Books, 2002), pp. 134–168.

28. Timothy McDaniel, "The Strange Career of Radical Islam," in *Human Rights and Revolutions,* eds. Wasserstrom, Hunt, and Young, pp. 211–229.

29. "Westoxification" is a derogatory expression used to describe self-hating Muslims who are in awe of everything Western to the point that they seem to be intoxicated by the West.

30. For an overview of the Islamic response to international human rights, see Eva Brems, *Human Rights: Universality and Diversity* (The Hague: Martinus Nijhoff, 2001), pp. 183–293; Ann E. Mayer, "The Dilemmas of Islamic Identity," in *Human Rights and the World's Religions,* ed. Leroy S. Rouner (Notre Dame: University of Notre Dame Press, 1988), pp. 94–110.

31.   See the discussion on this point by Michael Ignatieff, *Human Rights: As Politics and Idolatry* (Princeton: Princeton University Press, 2001), pp. 53–94.

32.   See, for instance, William F. Felice, *Taking Suffering Seriously: The Importance of Collective Human Rights* (Albany: State University of New York Press, 1996).

33.   Charles Taylor, "Conditions of an Unenforced Consensus on Human Rights," in *The Politics of Human Rights*, ed., the Belgrade Circle (London: Verso, 1999), pp. 101–119; Antonio Cassese, "Are Human Rights Truly Universal?" in ibid., pp. 149–165; Brian Tierney, "Religious Rights: An Historical Perspective," in *Religious Human Rights in Global Perspective: Religious Perspectives*, eds. John Witte and Johan van der Vyver (The Hague: Martinus Nijhoff, 1996), pp. 17–45. See also Michael J. Perry, *The Idea of Human Rights: Four Inquiries* (Oxford: Oxford University Press, 1998), pp. 57–106.

34.   For instance, one can speak of a right to education because of the fact that such a right has been demanded and often denied. On the other hand, one normally does not speak of a right to go to the toilet because that function is normally not demanded and then denied. However, one might start articulating such a right if, for instance, state or non-state actors are torturing a prisoner by denying him or her access to such facilities. I am not necessarily articulating a sociological understanding of human rights. A right could exist as a perennial right or eternity, but it is not recognized or claimed until human experience demonstrates the need to recognize or claim it. On the social recognition and promotion of rights, see Rex Martin, *A System of Rights* (Oxford: Clarendon, 1993), pp. 24–97.

35.   Reference here is typically made to *jus cogens* or customary international law as the reason that non-signatory states are still bound by international human rights standards.

36.   See A.J.M. Milne, *Human Rights and Human Diversity: An Essay in the philosophy of Human Rights* (Albany: State University of New York Press, 1986), pp. 62–78. See also Richard Falk, "A Half Century of Human Rights: Geopolitics and Values," in *The Future of International Human Rights*, ed. Burns H. Weston and Stephen P. Marks (Ardsley, NY: Transnational, 1999), pp. 1–24. Criticizing what he calls "personalisms," Yves Simon argues that the natural law tradition is at its weakest when it functions as ideology instead of as philosophy. He asserts that there is a tendency to use the natural law tradition in highly politicized ways, and that this trend has greatly damaged the credibility of this moral tradition. See Yves Simon, *The Tradition of Natural Law: A Philosopher's Reflections* (New York: Fordham University Press, 1992).

37.   This is well exemplified by the unfortunate practice of retaliatory "political" rapes that exist in some countries. Once a woman's right to be

free of sexual molestation is recognized, political rapes become indefensible regardless of the applicability of the legal argument. Whether rape is mentioned in an international declaration or treaty, and whether a particular country is a signatory to a particular covenant or not, is treated as irrelevant to assessing the moral wrong of retaliatory rapes. On retaliatory rapes, see Shahla Haeri, "The Politics of Dishonor: Rape and Power in Pakistan," in *Faith and Freedom*, ed. Afkhami, pp. 161–174.

38. By an exercise of personal volition, an individual may resolve most, if not all, conflicts between religious conviction and human rights claims. For instance, although the divine law may decree that the hands of a thief be severed, I may refuse to sever anyone's hands, or even refuse to prosecute anyone if the punishment is so harsh. Likewise, I may abstain from stoning an adulterer or adulteress to death, or refuse to take part in a proceeding that would result in a stoning. Of course, the more a system is compulsory and the more it denies individual volition, the more exasperated the tension becomes between the subjective experience and human rights standards.

39. On the dynamics between religion and human rights, see Martin Marty, "Religious Dimensions of Human Rights," in *Religious Human Rights in Global Perspective*, ed. Witte and van der Vyver pp. 1–16.

40. See Basil Mitchell, *Law, Morality and Religion in a Secular Society* (Oxford: Oxford University Press, 1967), pp. 103–118; Richard Tuck, *Natural Rights Theories: Their Origin and Development* (Cambridge: Cambridge University Press, 1979), pp. 5–31. On the religion and the natural rights tradition, see Paul E. Sigmund, *Natural Law in Political Thought* (Lanham, MD: University Press of America, 1971), pp. 36–89; Leo Strauss, *Natural Right and History* (Chicago: University of Chicago Press, 1965), pp. 81–164; Robert Gordis, "Natural Law and Religion," in Center for the Study of Democratic Institutions, *Natural Law and Modern Society* (Cleveland: World Publishing Company, 1963), pp. 240–276.

41. See Mahmood Monshipouri, *Islamism, Secularism, and Human Rights in the Middle East* (Boulder: Lynne Rienner, 1998), pp. 207–235.

42. On the issue of hypocrisy in international human rights practices and its impact upon the credibility of the field, see Richard Falk, *Human Rights Horizons: The Pursuit of Justice in a Globalizing World* (London: Routledge, 2000).

43. For the Iranian context, see Abdolkarim Soroush, *Reason, Freedom and Democracy in Islam*, trans. M. Sadri and A. Sadri (Oxford: Oxford University Press, 2000), pp. 61–64, 122–130, 132–133; Ziba Mir-Hosseini, *Islam and Gender: The Religious Debate in Contemporary Iran* (Princeton: Princeton University Press, 1999).

44. For instance, see Abdulaziz Sachedina, *The Islamic Roots of Democratic Pluralism* (Oxford: Oxford University Press, 2001); Farid Esack, *Qur'an,*

Liberation, and Pluralism (Oxford: Oneworld, 1997); Abdullahi A. An-Na'im, *Toward an Islamic Reformation: Civil Liberties, Human Rights, and International Law* (Syracuse: Syracuse University Press, 1996); Abdullahi A. An-Na'im, *Human Rights, Religion, and the Contingency of Universalist Projects* (Syracuse: Syracuse University Press, 2001); Abdullahi An-Na'im, "Islamic Foundations of Religious Human Rights," in *Religious Human Rights in Global Perspective*, eds. Witte and van der Vyver, pp. 337–359; Mohammad Hashim Kamali, *The Dignity of Man: An Islamic Perspective* (Cambridge: Islamic Texts Society, 2002); Ahmad Moussalli, *The Islamic Quest for Democracy, Pluralism, and Human Rights* (Gainesville: University Press of Florida, 2001).

45.   For elaboration on this, see Khaled Abou El Fadl, *Speaking in God's Name: Islamic Law, Authority, and Women* (Oxford: Oneworld, 2001), pp. 32–33.

46.   Nizam Barakat, *Muqaddima fi al-Fikr al-Siyasi al-Islami* (Riyadh: Jami'at al-Malik Su'd, 1985), p. 119.

47.   See Abu al-Hasan 'Ali b. Muhammad b. Habib al-Mawardi, *al-Ahkam al-Sultaniyya* (Beirut: Dar al-Kutub al-'Ilmiyya, 1985), pp. 19–21; al-Qadi Abu Ya'la Muhammad b. al-Husayn al-Farra', *al-Ahkam al-Sultaniyya* (Beirut: Dar al-Kutub al-'Ilmiyya, 1983), p. 28; Ann Lambton, *State and Government in Medieval Islam: An Introduction to the Study of Islamic Political Theory: The Jurists* (Oxford: Oxford University Press, 1981), p. 19; W. Montgomery Watt, *Islamic Political Thought: The Basic Concepts* (Edinburgh: Edinburgh University Press, 1968), pp. 102–103; Hanna Mikhail, *Politics and Revelation: Mawardi and After* (Edinburgh: Edinburgh University Press, 1995), pp. 20–21; H.A.R. Gibb, "Constitutional Organization," in *Law in the Middle East*, vol. 1: *Origin and Development of Islamic Law*, eds. Majid Khadduri and Herbert J. Liebesny (Washington, DC: Middle East Institute, 1955), pp. 3–27, esp. 9, 12; Khaled Abou El Fadl, *Rebellion and Violence in Islamic Law* (Cambridge: Cambridge University Press, 2001); Muhammad Jalal Sharaf and 'Ali 'Abd al-Mu'ti Muhammad, *al-Fikr al-Siyasi fi al-Islam: Shakhsiyyat wa Madhahib* (Alexandria: Dar al-Jami'at al-Misriyya, 1978), p. 399; Yusuf Ibish, *Nusus al-Fikr al-Siyasi al-Islami: al-Imama 'ind al-Sunna* (Beirut: Dar al-Tali'ah, 1966), p. 55.

48.   Abu al-Faraj al-Baghdadi Ibn al-Jawzi, *al-Shifa' fi Mawa'iz al-Muluk wa al-Khulafa*, ed. Fu'ad Ahmad (Alexandria: Dar al-Da'wa, 1985), p. 55; idem., *al-Misbah al-Muda fi al-Khilaf al-Mustada'*, ed. Ibrahim Najiyya (Baghdad: Matba'at al-Awqaf, 1979), 1:298.

49.   Ibn al-Jawzi, *al-Shifa'*, pp. 55, 57; idem., *al-Misbah*, 1:298. As discussed later, torture, according to Muslim jurists, was never justified. Interestingly, in their view, the divine law cannot sanction torture. But it is anachronistic to assume that what we would consider torture today was also considered as such in the premodern juristic culture.

50. So for instance, Ibn al-Jawzi states: "Religion is the origin, and government is its protector." Ibn al-Jawzi, *al-Shifa'*, pp. 46–47. See also, Barakat, *Muqaddima*, pp. 102–103.

51. Shams al-Din Abi 'Abd allah Muhammad b. Abi Bakr Ibn Qayyim al-Jawziyya (d. 751/1350), *I'lam al-Muwaqqi'in 'an Rabb al-'Alamin*, ed. Taha 'Abd al-Ra'uf Sa'd (Beirut: Dar al-Jil, n.d.), 1:10.

52. Abu Hamid al-Ghazali (d. 505/1111), *Fada'ih al-Batiniyya*, ed. 'Abd al-Rahman Badawi (Cairo: Dar al-Qawmiyya, 1964), pp. 191, 193; Sharaf and Muhammad, *al-Fikr al-Siyasi*, 351, pp. 399–403; Ibn al-Jawzi, *al-Shifa'*, p. 55; Abu Ya'la Muhammad b. al-Husayn al-Farra' (d. 458/1066), "al-Mu'tamad fi Usul al-Din," in Ibish, *Nusus al-Fikr al-Siyasi al-Islami*, p. 221; Abu Ya'la, *al-Ahkam*, p. 20; Ibn Qayyim al-Jawziyya, *I'lam al-Muwaqqi'in*, 1:10. In this context, al-Ghazali concluded: "Despotic, non-consultative, decision-making, even if from a wise and learned person is objectionable and unacceptable." Al-Ghazali, *Fada'ih*, pp. 186, 191.

53. Afaf Lutfi al-Sayyid Marsot, "The Ulama of Cairo in the Eighteenth and Nineteenth Century," in *Scholars, Saints, and Sufis*, ed. Nikki Keddie (Berkeley: University of California Press, 1972), p. 149.

54. Ibid., p. 150. For a study on the role of the *'ulama'* in legitimizing rulers and rebellions through the use of their moral weight, see Abou El Fadl, *Rebellion and Violence in Islamic law*, pp. 32–99. On the social and political roles played by the *'ulama'*, see Edward Mortimer, *Faith and Power: The Politics of Islam* (New York: Vintage, 1982), pp. 299–307; Malcolm H. Kerr, *Islamic Reform: The Political and Legal Theories of Muhammad 'Abduh and Rashid Rida* (Berkeley and Los Angeles: University of California Press, 1966), p. 196; Louis J. Cantori, "Religion and Politics in Egypt," in *Religion and Politics in the Middle East*, ed. Michael Curtis (Boulder: Westview, 1981), pp. 77–90.

55. Marsot, "The Ulama of Cairo," p. 159.

56. After the evacuation of the French in Egypt in 1801, 'Umar Makram with the assistance of the jurists overthrew the French agent left behind. Instead of assuming power directly, the jurists offered the government to the Egyptianized Albanian Muhammad 'Ali. See Marsot, "The Ulama of Cairo," pp. 149–165, esp. 162–163.

57. Modernity, however, through a complex dynamic, turned the *'ulama'* from "vociferous spokesmen of the masses" into salaried state functionaries that play a primarily conservative, legitimist role for the ruling regimes in the Islamic world. See Daniel Crecelius, "Egyptian Ulama and Modernization," in, *Scholars, Saints, and Sufis*, ed. Keddie, pp. 167–209, esp. p. 168. Crecelius makes this point about the *'ulama'* of Egypt in the modern age. However, see, Fouad Ajami, "In the Pharaoh's Shadow: Religion and Authority in Egypt," in *Islam in the Political Process*, ed. James Piscatori (London: Cambridge University Press, 1983), p. 18; Mortimer, *Faith and Power*, pp. 91, 95; Malise Ruthven, *Islam in the World*

(Oxford: Oxford University Press, 1984), p. 179. Of course, there are notable exceptions in contemporary Islamic practice. Many clerics became prominent opponents of the present Muslim regimes, and suffered enormously for their troubles. To my mind, the disintegration of the role of the 'ulama' and their co-optation by the modern praetorian state, with its hybrid practices of secularism, has made Islamic normative determinations all the less rich. On the idea of the praetorian state, see Amos Perlmutter, Egypt: The Praetorian State (New Brunswick: Transaction Books, 1974).

58.   Structurally, Shari'a is comprised of the Qur'an, Sunna, and fiqh (juristic interpretive efforts). Substantively, the Shari'a refers to three different matters: (1) general principles of law and morality; (2) methodologies for extracting and formulating the law; and (3) the ahkam, which are the specific positive rules of law. In the contemporary Muslim world, there is a tendency to focus on the ahkam at the expense of the general principles and methodology. It is entirely possible to be Shari'a-compliant, in the sense of respecting the ahkam, but to ignore or violate the principles and methodologies of Shari'a.

59.   Of course, I realize that this claim is quite controversial for Muslims and non-Muslims alike. Nevertheless, I believe that this argument is supported by the fact that the rebellion of the Khawarij took place in the context of an overall search for legitimacy and legality after the death of the Prophet. Furthermore, the research of some scholars on the dogma and symbolism of the early rebellions lends support to this argument. See Hisham Ja'i, al-Fitnah: Jadaliyyat al-Din wa al-Siyasah fi al-Islam al-Mubakkir (Beirut: Dar al-Tali'ah, 1989).

60.   Muhammad b. 'Ali b. Muhammad al-Shawkani, Nayl al-Awtar Sharh Muntaqa al-Akhbar (Cairo: Dar al-Hadith, n.d.), 7:166; Shihab al-Din Ibn Hajar al-'Asqalani, Fath al-Bari bi Sharh Sahih al-Bukhari (Beirut: Dar al-Fikr, 1993), 14:303.

61.   According to the Qur'an, as a symbol of the honor due to human beings, God commanded the angels, who are incapable of sin, to prostrate before Adam. The angels protested that God was commanding them to honor a being that is capable of commiting evil, and causing mischief. God conceded as much, but explained that the miracle of the intellect, in and of itself, deserves to be honored, and that God has made human beings the vicegerents of divinity. On this, see Fazlur Rahman, Major Themes of the Qur'an (Minneapolis: Bibliotheca Islamica, 1994), pp. 17–36.

62.   The four surviving Sunni schools of law and legal thought are the Hanafi, Maliki, Shafi'i, and Hanbali schools. On the history of these schools, as well as those which are now extinct, such as the Tabari and Zahiri schools, see Christopher Melchert, The Formation of the Sunni Schools of Law, 9th-10th Centuries C.E. (Leiden: Brill, 1997). On the organization, structure, and curriculum of legal learning, see George Makdisi, The Rise

of Colleges: Institutions of Learning in Islam and the West (Edinburgh: Edinburgh University Press, 1981).

63. The literature on the history, theory, and practices of secularism is vast. Most theoretical treatments understandably have remained wedded to the Western historical experience. See, Blandine Kriegel, *The State and the Rule of Law*, trans. Marc A. LePain and Jeffrey C. Cohen (Princeton: Princeton University Press, 1995), pp. 123–134; Horace M. Kallen, *Secularism is the Will of God: An Essay in the Social Philosophy of Democracy and Religion* (New York: Twayne, 1954); Harvey Cox, *The Secular City: Secularization and Urbanization in Theological Perspective* (New York: Macmillan, 1965); *The Secular City Debate*, ed. Daniel Callahan (New York: Macmillan, 1966).

64. Christian Duquoc, ed., *Secularization and Spirituality* (New York: Paulist Press, 1969); Seyyed Hossein Nasr, *Islam and the Plight of Modern Man* (London: Longman, 1975); Stephen L. Carter, *The Culture of Disbelief: How American Law and Politics Trivialize Religious Devotion* (New York: Basic Books, 1993); Harold J. Berman, *Faith and Order: The Reconciliation of Law and Religion* (Atlanta: Scholars Press, 1993); Timothy L. Fort, *Law and Religion* (Jefferson, NC: McFarland & Co., 1987); Kent Greenawalt, *Private Consciences and Public Reasons* (Oxford: Oxford University Press, 1995); John Finnis, *Natural Law and Natural Rights* (Oxford: Clarendon, 1980); Milner S. Ball, *The Word and the Law* (Chicago: University of Chicago Press, 1993).

65. I am simplifying this sophisticated doctrine in order to make a point. Muslim jurists engaged in lengthy attempts to differentiate between the two concepts of Shari'a and *fiqh*. See Subhi Mahmasani, *Falsafat al-Tashri' fi al-Islam*, 3rd ed. (Beirut: Dar al-'Ilm li al-Malayin, 1961), pp. 21–24, 199–200; Bernard G. Weiss, *The Spirit of Islamic Law* (Athens, G: University of Georgia Press, 1998), pp. 119–121; Muhammad Abu Zahrah, *Usul al-Fiqh* (Cairo: Dar al-Fikr al-'Arabi, n.d.), p. 291; Mustafa Zayd, *al-Maslahah fi al-Tashri' al-Islami wa Najm al-Din al-Tufi*, 2nd ed. (Cairo: Dar al-Fikr al-'Arabi, 1964), p. 22; Yusuf Hamid al-'Alim, *al-Maqasid al-'Amma li al-Shari'a al-Islamiyya* (Herndon, V.A.: International Institute of Islamic Thought, 1991), p. 80; Muhammad b. 'Ali b. Muhammad al-Shawkani, *Talab al-'Ilm wa Tabaqt al-Muta'allimin: Adab al-Talab wa Muntaha al-'Arab* (n.p.: Dar al-Arqam, 1981), pp. 145–151.

66. The Arabic is "kull mujtahid musib" and "li kulli mujtahid nasib." See Abu al-Husayn Muhammad b. 'Ali b. al-Tayyib al-Basri, *al-Mu'tamad fi Usul al-Fiqh* (Beirut: Dar al-Kutub al-'Ilmiyya, 1983), 2:370–372; 'Ala' al-Din 'Abd al-'Aziz b. Ahmadi al-Bukhari, *Kashf al-Asrar 'an Usul Fakhr al-Islam al-Bazdawi*, ed. Muhammad al-Mu'tasim bi Allah al-Baghdadi, 3rd ed. (Beirut: Dar al-Kitab al-'Arabi, 1997), 4:30–55; Abu Hamid Muhammad b. Muhammad al-Ghazali, *al-Mustasfa min 'Ilm al-Usul*, ed. Ibrahim Muhammad Ramadan (Beirut: Dar al-Arqam, n.d), 2:363–367;

Abu al-Ma'ali 'Abd al-Malik b. 'Abd Allah b. Yusuf al-Juwayni, *Kitab al-Ijtihad min Kitab al-Talkhis* (Damascus: Dar al-Qalam, 1987), pp. 26–32; Abu Muhammad 'Ali b. Ahmad b. Sa'id b. Hazm al-Zahiri, *al-Ihkam fi Usul al-Ahkam* (Cairo: Dar al-Hadith, 1984), 5:68–81, 8:589–592; Muhammad b. Ahmad b. 'Abd al-'Aziz b. 'Ali al-Fatuhi Ibn al-Najjar, *Sharh al-Kawkab al-Munir al-Musamma Mukhtasar al-Tahrir aw al-Mukhtabar al-Mubtakar Sharh al-Mukhtasar fi Usul al-Fiqh*, eds. Muhammad al-Zuhayli and Nazir Hamma (Riyadh: Maktabat al-'Ubaykan, 1993), 4:488–492; Abu Bakr Ahmad b. 'Ali b. Thabit al-Khatib al-Baghdadi, *Kitab al-Faqih wa al-Mutafaqqih wa Usul al-Fiqh* (Cairo: Zakariyya 'Ali Yusuf, 1977), pp. 245–250; Abu al-Thana' Mahmud b. Zayd al-Lamishi, *Kitab fi Usul al-Fiqh*, ed. 'Abd al-Majid Turki (Beirut: Dar al-Gharb al-Islami, 1995), pp. 201–202; Shihab al-Din Abu al-'Abbas Ahmad b. Idris al-Qarafi, *Sharh Tanqih al-Fusul fi Ikhtisar al-Mahsul fi al-Usul*, ed. Taha 'Abd al-Ra'uf Sa'd (Beirut: Dar al-Fikr, 1973), pp. 438–441; Fakhr al-Din al-Razi Muhammad b. 'Umar b. al-Husayn, *al-Mahsul fi 'Ilm Usul al-Fiqh*, ed. Taha Jabir Fayyad al-'Alwani, 3rd ed. (Beirut: Mu'assasat al-Risalah, 1997), 6:29–36; Muhammad b. 'Ali b. Muhammad al-Shawkani, *Irshad al-Fuhul ila Tahqiq al-Haqq min 'Ilm al-Usul* (Beirut: Dar al-Kutub al-'Ilmiyyah, n.d.), pp. 383–389; Abu Ishaq Ibrahim b. 'Ali b. Yusuf al-Fayruzabadi al-Shirazi, *Sharh al-Lum'a*, ed. 'Abd al-Majid Turki (Beirut: Dar al-Gharb al-Islami, 1988), 2:1043–1071; idem, *al-Tabsirah fi Usul al-Fiqh*, ed. Muhammad Hasan Haytu (Damascus: Dar al-Fikr, 1980), pp. 496–508. In this context, Muslim jurists also debated a report attributed to the Prophet in which he says, "whoever performs *ijtihad* and is correct will be rewarded twice and whoever is wrong will be rewarded once." See Jalal al-Din 'Abd al-Rahman b. Abi Bakr al-Suyuti, *Ikhtilaf al-Madhahib*, ed. 'Abd al-Qayyum Muhammad Shafi' al-Bastawi (Cairo: Dar al-I'tisam, 1404 AH), p. 38. Ibn Hazm, *al-Ihkam*, 5:73–74, 8:591; idem, *al-Nubadh fi Usul al-Fiqh al-Zahiri*, ed. Muhammad Subhi Hasan Hallaq (Beirut: Dar Ibn Hazm, 1993), pp. 119–120; Abu al-Hasan 'Ali b. 'Umar Ibn al-Qassar, *al-Muqaddima fi al-Usul*, ed. Muhammad b. al-Husayn al-Sulaymani (Beirut: Dar al-Gharb al-Islami, 1996), pp. 114–115; Mahfuz b. Ahmad b. al-Hasan Abu al-Khattab al-Kaluzani, *al-Tamhid fi Usul al-Fiqh*, ed. Muhammad b. 'Ali b. Ibrahim (Mecca: Markaz al-Bahth al-'Ilmi wa Ihya' al-Turath al-Islami, 1985), 4:317–318; al-Qarafi, *Sharh*, p. 440; Abu 'Abd Allah Muhammad b. Idris al-Shafi'i, *al-Risalah*, ed. Ahmad Muhammad Shakir (n.p.: Dar al-Fikr, n.d.), p. 494; al-Shirazi, *al-Tabsira*, p. 499; Muhammad b. 'Abd al-Hamid al-Asmandi, *Badhl al-Nazar fi al-Usul*, ed. Muhammad Zaki 'Abd al-Barr (Cairo: Maktabat Dar al-Turath, 1992), pp. 702–703.

67.   For discussions of the two schools, see al-Bukhari, *Kashf*, 4:18; Abu Hamid Muhammad b. Muhammad al-Ghazali, *al-Mankhul min Ta'liqat al-Usul* (Damascus: Dar al-Fikr, 1980), p. 455; idem, *al-Mustasfa*, 2:

550–551; Fakhr al-Din Muhammad b. 'Umar b. al-Husayn al-Razi, *al-Mahsul fi 'Ilm Usul al-Fiqh* (Beirut: Dar al-Kutub al-'Ilmiyya, 1988), 2: 500–508; al-Qarafi, *Sharh,* 438; Wahbah al-Zuhayli, *al-Wasit fi Usul al-Fiqh al-Islami,* 2nd ed. (Beirut: Dar al-Fikr, 1969), pp. 638–655; 'Ali Hasab Allah, *Usul al-Tashri' al-Islami,* 3rd ed. (Cairo: Dar al-Ma'arif, 1964), pp. 82–83; Badran Abu al-'Aynayn Badran, *Usul al-Fiqh* (Cairo: Dar al-Ma'arif, 1965), p. 474.

68. Al-Juwayni, *Kitab al-Ijtihad,* pp. 50–51.

69. Ibid., p. 61.

70. Sayf al-Din Abu al-Hasan 'Ali b. Abi 'Ali b. Muhammad al-Amidi, *al-Ihkam fi Usul al-Ahkam,* ed. 'Abd al-Razzaq 'Afifi, 2nd ed. (Beirut: al-Maktab al-Islami, 1402 AH), 4:183; Jamal al-Din Abi Muhammad 'Abd al-Rahim b. al-Hasan al-Asnawi, *al-Tamhid fi Takhrij al-Furu' 'ala al-Usul,* 3rd ed. (Beirut: Mu'assasat al-Risalah, 1984), pp. 531–534; Muhammad b. al-Hasan al-Badakhsi, *Sharh al-Badakhshi Manahij al-'Uqul ma'a Sharh al-Asnawi Nihayat al-Sul* (Beirut: Dar al-Kutub al-'Ilmiyyah, 1984), 3:275–281; Abu Hamid al-Ghazali, *al-Mustasfa,* 2:375–378; al-Juwayni, *Kitab al-Ijtihad,* p. 41; Abu al-Thana' Mahmud b. Zayd al-Lamishi, *Kitab fi Usul al-Fiqh,* ed. 'Abd al-Majid Turki (Beirut: Dar al-Gharb al-Islam, 1995), pp. 202–203; al-Qarafi, *Sharh,* p. 440; Fakhr al-Din al-Razi, *al-Mahsul* (1997), 6: 34–35, 6: 43–50; Zaki al-Din Sha'ban, *Usul al-Fiqh al-Islami* (Cairo: Matba'at Dar al-Ta'lif, 1965), pp. 418–419; Badran, *Usul al-Fiqh,* 474; al-Zuhayli, *al-Wasit,* p. 643.

71. I deal with these two schools of thought more extensively elsewhere. See Abou El Fadl, *Speaking in God's Name,* pp. 145–165.

72. I am ignoring in this context the role of *ijma'* (consensus) because of the complexity of the subject. Some modern Muslims have argued that the doctrine of consensus is the normative equivalent of majority rule. I think this is a gross oversimplification, and, in any case, whether a presumed consensus can foreclose moral inquiry is highly contested in Islamic jurisprudence. In my view, consensus can help establish derivative moral standards, but cannot be the basis for foundational moralities.

73. Contemporary Islamic discourses suffer from a certain amount of hypocrisy in this regard. Often, Muslims confront an existential crisis if the enforced, so-called, Islamic laws result in social suffering and misery. In order to solve this crisis, Muslims will often claim that there has been a failure in the circumstances of implementation. This indulgence in embarrassing apologetics could be avoided if Muslims would abandon the incoherent idea of Shari'a state law.

74. This proposal is nonsense unless the *'ulama'* regain their institutional and moral independence.

75. See Robert Kane, *Through the Moral Maze: Searching for Absolute Values in a Pluralistic World* (New York: Paragon House, 1994).

76. As to basic values, I am advocating a foundational approach. As to derivative values and specific applications, my approach is more socio-logical, but it does not exclude the possibility of achieving consensus, and that some forms of human consensus might sanctify and elevate a value from a derivative status to a foundational status. An example of this would be the practice of a human legally owning another human (i.e. slavery). But unlike slavery, there are many forms of human bondage that have not risen to the status of foundational values, and are therefore morally contested acts (for instance, twelve-year-old girls working as household servants in the homes of rich families in Egypt). Believing that this form of bonded relationship is highly immoral, I will try to objec-tificate my subjective belief by convincing fellow Muslims of my view, and I will even argue that my understanding of morality is more Islamic than any other competing vision. If I am fortunate, the day will come when it will become core to Islamic beliefs that twelve-year-old girls should not be made by their parents to work as maids in foreign house-holds. This is significant because the vast majority of Muslims now consider slavery to be immoral and unlawful, and they also consider this to be fundamental to their faith and moral commitments. Only a hundred years ago, one could not say that the immorality of slavery was core to the Muslim faith. I should note that this foundational approach is open to the criticism, which all foundational approaches must confront, and that is: foundational approaches affirm principles, but cannot provide moral applications. In the words of some, they plant the seed, but never produce a flower. For this type of criticism against natural law orientations, see Pauline Westerman, *The Disintegration of Natural Law Theory: Aquinas to Finnis* (Leiden: Brill, 1998). This criticism, however, ignores the fact that the planting of the seed is a great moral act. Producing a flower needs a lot of sociology (and skill). On the embar-rassment of slavery and natural law, see Margaret Macdonald, "Natural Rights," in *Theories of Rights*, ed. Jeremy Waldron (Oxford: Oxford University Press, 1984), pp. 21–40. For somber reflections on the often-artificial dynamic between the subjective and objective in moral discourses, see Jeremy Waldron, "The Irrelevance of Moral Objectivity," in *Natural Law Theory: Contemporary Essays*, ed. Robert George (Oxford: Clarendon Press, 1992), pp. 158–184.

77. Abu al-Maʿali al-Juwayni, *Ghiyath al-Umam fi Iltiyath al-Zulam*, eds. Mustafa Hilmi and Fuʾad Ahmad (Alexandria: Dar al-Daʿwa, 1978), p. 15.

78. Shams al-Din Abu Bakr Ibn Qayyim al-Jawziyya, *Iʿlam al-Muwaqqiʿin ʿan Rabb al-ʿAlamin*, ed. ʿAbd al-Rahman al-Wakil (Cairo: Maktabat Ibn Taymiyya, n.d.), 4:452.

79. On the obligation of justice in the Qurʾan, see Rahman, *Major Themes of the Qurʾan*, pp. 42–43; Toshihiko Izutsu, *The Structure of Ethical Terms in the Quran* (Chicago: ABC International Group, 2000), pp. 205–261. On

the various Muslim theories of justice, see Majid Khadduri, *The Islamic Conception of Justice* (Baltimore: John Hopkins University Press, 1984).

80. The Qur'an also demands adherence to a large number of moral virtues such as mercy, compassion, truthfulness, equity, generosity, modesty, and humility.

81. Sharaf and Muhammad, *al-Fikr al-Siyasi,* pp. 209, 212, 377, 380–381, 514–515; Barakat, *Muqaddima,* pp. 107, 116; Ridwan al-Sayyid, *al-Umma wa al-Jamaʿa wa al-Sulta* (Beirut: n.p., 1984), pp. 207–208; ʿAli b. Muhammad al-Mawardi, *Adab al-Dunya wa al-Din,* ed. Mustafa al-Saqqa (Cairo: n.p., 1950), pp. 116–127; Abu Hamid al-Ghazali, *al-Iqtisad fi al-Iʿtiqad* (Cairo: n.p., 1320 AH), p. 106. In Islamic jurisprudence, government is contractual. In theory, a ruler should come to power through a contract between the governor and governed, or the people who represent the governed.

82. Qur'an 49:13.

83. Qur'an 11:119.

84. In the approach I am advocating, deontology is prior to law, and moral commitments preempt legal rules. I distinguish my approach from the reformative efforts of a large number of modern Muslim scholars. Several Islamic reformers have argued that Islamic laws must be changed in the contemporary age in accord with the *maslaha* (public welfare) – whatever is good for Muslims is good for Islamic law. I must confess that I find this functionalist view of law, and perhaps teleological view of ethics, opportunistic and troubling. It seems to me that there are moral values, such as the wrongfulness of torture, that are absolute and right, in and of themselves, regardless of the good that comes out of following such moral rules. In this regard, among other things, I would argue that moral rules are based on *potentialities* of harm and good, and that, when thinking about moral rules, such potentialities are more important than the *actual* harm suffered or good achieved. For instance, torture is wrong because of the potential for injustice that it creates, and that it is morally irrelevant, whether in a given situation torture does, in fact, generate more good than harm. In contrast to a deontological view of morality, a teleological view tends to look to the consequences of acts in order to ascertain what is good, and also right. Some theorists have argued that in a deontological view, right is prior to good, and in a teleological view, good is prior to right. A deontological view does not interpret "the right" as that which maximizes "the good"; rather, a moral constraint is considered right regardless of the utilitarian consequences to which it might lead. Although I am not prepared to develop this point in this chapter, for the sake of clarity I should note that I tend to think that deontological views of morality are more consistent with Islamic theology than teleological views. However, in my opinion, even under a deontologial view, it is possible to realize moral virtues imperfectly, and

it is also possible to have higher-order and lower-order moralities, as well as inherent and derivative moralities.

Importantly, in this chapter, I have avoided reengaging the old debate between two premodern Muslim sects, the Mu'tazila and Ash'ariyya, about whether, in cases of conflict between morality and the text, which of the two gets priority. The Mu'tazila argued that morality is prior to the text, and therefore it should always take priority over the text. On the other hand, arguing that the text is prior to morality, the Ash'ariyya maintained that the text defined morality. According to the Ash'ariyya, there is no such thing as morality that exists outside the text. Furthermore, the Mu'tazila tended to adopt a deontological view of morality, while the Ash'ariyya leaned toward a teleological view of right and wrong. The debate between the two schools of thought focused on whether God is obligated to give effect to morality, and whether God is bound by moral standards. The Ash'ariyya maintained that since God is not bound by any moral standards, there is no need to investigate moral issues other than through the text. The text will clearly explicate, and strictly define, morality. The Mu'tazila, however, contended that morality is recognizable by reason or intuition, and not by text alone. According to the Mu'tazila, God, as well as human beings, is bound by moral rules, and therefore any religious text that is inconsistent with universal moral standards must have been either inaccurately transmitted or imperfectly understood. In other words, in the view of the Mu'tazila, God does not violate morality, and it is human error of transmission or comprehension that is responsible for the erroneous impression that God has violated a moral rule. For my purposes, I think it is not necessary to resolve this debate. The Qur'an clearly identifies certain moral virtues as binding, and invites humans to explore and study these virtues. In my view, God is not bound by moral virtue; God is the embodiment of moral virtue. Beauty and moral virtues are what God is, and moral virtues are inherent to the very concept of divinity. If God describes Godself as just or merciful then this is what God is. Can God alter God's character and become something other than what God said He is? This possibility is too speculative to be worthy of discussion, and we, as human beings, have no basis for thinking that it is even possible. In many ways, I see the issue in more straightforward terms than the classical approaches adopted by the Mu'tazila or Ash'ariyya. In my view, God's moralities and virtues are inseparable from God, and they are unalterable because God is unalterable. As such God's morality is binding on all, in the same way that God is present for all. Divinity is approached, in my view, through studying the divine moral imperatives, and not the rules of law because morality is prior to law, in the same way that God is prior to anything, including the text, law, or creation. In my view, the primary commitment of a Muslim should be to God, and God's moral essence, and not to the specific rules of law. Therefore, if there is a conflict between the morality of a legal rule, and our moral conception of God, it is the latter that must take priority.

85.   Qur'an 6:12, 54.

86.   Qur'an 21:107, which, addressing the Prophet, states: "We have not sent you except as a mercy to human beings." See also 16:89. In fact, the Qur'an describes the whole of the Islamic message as based on mercy and compassion. Islam was sent to teach and establish these virtues among human beings. I believe that to Muslims, as opposed to Islam, this creates a normative imperative of teaching mercy: Qur'an 27:77; 29:51; 45:20. But to teach mercy is impossible unless one learns it, and such knowledge cannot be limited to text. It is *ta'aruf* (the knowledge of the other), which is premised on an ethic of care, that opens the door to learning mercy, and in turn, teaching it.

87.   In Qur'anic terms, *rahma* (mercy) is not limited to *maghfira* (forgiveness).

88.   The Qur'an explicitly commands human beings to deal with one another with patience and mercy (90:17), and not to transgress their bounds by presuming to know who deserves God's mercy and who does not (43:32). An Islamic moral theory focused on mercy as a virtue will overlap with the ethic of care developed in Western moral theory. See Joan C. Tronto, *Moral Boundaries: A Political Argument for an Ethic of Care* (London: Routledge, 1994), pp. 101–155.

89.   Qur'an 11:119. This idea is also exemplified in a tradition attributed to the Prophet asserting that the disagreement and diversity of opinion of the *umma* (Muslim nation) is a source of divine mercy for Muslims. See Isma'il al-Jirahi, *Kashf al-Khafa' wa Muzil al-Ilbas* (Beirut: Mu'assasat al-Risala, 1983), 1:66–68. Whether the Prophet actually made this statement, or whether it is part of the received wisdom that guided the diverse, and often competing, interpretive traditions within Islam is beside the point. The point is that this tradition, Prophetic or not, was used to justify an enormous amount of diversity within the Islamic juristic tradition, and it played an important role in preventing the emergence of a single voice of authority within the Islamic tradition. On this issue, see Khaled Abou El Fadl, *And God Knows the Soldiers: The Authoritative and Authoritarian in Islamic Discourses* (Lanham, MD: University Press of America, 2001), pp. 23–36.

90.   On tolerance as a moral virtue, and its limits, see Glen Newey, *Virtue, Reason and Toleration* (Edinburgh: Edinburgh University Press, 1999), pp. 85–114. See Jay Newman, *Foundations of Religious Tolerance* (Toronto: University of Toronto Press, 1982); Hans Oberdiek, *Tolerance: Between Forbearance and Acceptance* (Lanham, MD: Rowman & Littlefield, 2001). See also Robert McKim, *Religious Ambiguity and Religious Diversity* (Oxford: Oxford University Press, 2001). See also the collection of articles in *Toleration: An Elusive Virtue*, ed. David Heyd (Princeton:

Princeton University Press, 1996), especially the articles by Bernard Williams, pp. 18–27, John Horton, pp. 28–43, Gordon Graham, pp. 44–59, George Fletcher, pp. 158–172, and T.M. Scanlon, pp. 226–239.

91. On this topic, see Daniel Vokey, *Moral Discourse in a Pluralistic World* (Notre Dame: University of Notre Dame Press, 2001). For a similar approach, see Michelle Moody-Adams, *Fieldwork in Familiar Places: Morality, Culture, and Philosophy* (Cambridge MA: Harvard University Press, 1997). For the argument that cultural pluralism is not necessarily inconsistent with rational moral knowledge, see Alan Gewirth, "Is Cultural Pluralism Relevant to Moral Knowledge," in *Cultural Pluralism and Moral Knowledge*, ed. Ellen Paul, Fred Miller, and Jeffrey Paul (Cambridge: Cambridge University Press, 1994), pp. 22–43.

92. Of course, approximating the divine does not mean aspiring to become divine. Approximating the divine means visualizing the beauty and virtue of the divine, and striving to internalize as much as possible of this beauty and virtue. I start with the theological assumption that God cannot be comprehended or understood by the human mind. God, however, teaches moral virtues that emanate from the divine nature, and that are also reflected in creation. By imagining the possible magnitudes of beauty and its nature, human beings can better relate to the divine. The more humans are able to relate to the ultimate senses of goodness, justice, mercy, and balance that embody divinity, the more they are able to visualize or imagine the nature of divinity, and the more they are able to model their own sense of beauty and virtue as approximations of divinity.

93. On the relationship between justice and human rights, see Hillel Steiner, *An Essay on Rights* (Oxford: Blackwell, 1994), pp. 224–248; David S. Oderberg, *Moral Theory* (Oxford: Blackwell, 2000), pp. 53–63.

94. Debates on individual rights raise questions about the nature, foundations, and universality of such rights. The historical discontinuities of individual rights suggest that, despite the absolutist-moral overtones of some rights talk, individual rights are the product of complex historical processes. See *Legal Rights: Historical and Philosophical Perspectives*, eds. Austin Sarat and Thomas R. Kearns (Ann Arbor: University of Michigan Press, 1997); Louis Henkin, *The Age of Rights* (New York: Columbia University Press, 1990); S.I. Benn and R.S. Peters, *The Principles of Political Thought: Social Foundations of the Democratic State* (1959; repr. New York: Free Press, 1966), pp. 101–120; Carl Wellman, *A Theory of Rights: Persons Under Laws, Institutions, and Morals* (Totowa, NJ: Rowman & Allanheld, 1985).

95. See Virginia Black, "What Dignity Means," in *Common Truths: New Perspectives on Natural Law*, ed. Edward McLean (Wilmington, DE: Intercollegiate Studies Institute, 2000), pp. 119–50.

96   Abu Hamid al-Ghazali, *al-Mustasfa*, 1:286–287; Fakhr al-Din al-Razi, *al-Mahsul* (1997), 5:159–160; Abu Ishaq Ibrahim b. Musa al-Shatibi,

al-Muwafaqat fi Usul al-Fiqh, ed. ʿAbd Allah Daraz and Muhammad ʿAbd Allah Daraz (Beirut: Dar al-Kutub al-ʿIlmiyya, n.d.), 2:7–8; al-Qarafi, *Sharh*, p. 391; Abu Zahrah, *Usul al-Fiqh*, pp. 291–293; Shaʿban, *Usul al-Fiqh*, 382; al-Zuhayli, *al-Wasit*, pp. 500–501; Mohammad Hashim Kamali, *Principles of Islamic Jurisprudence*, rev. ed. (Cambridge: Islamic Texts Society, 1991), pp. 271–273.

97. Muhammad ʿUbayd Allah al-Asʿadi, *al-Mujaz fi Usul al-Fiqh* (n.p.: Dar al-Salam, 1990), p. 247; Badran, *Usul al-Fiqh*, pp. 430–431; Zakariyya al-Birri, *Usul al-Fiqh al-Islami*, 3rd ed. (Cairo: Dar al-Nahdah al-ʿArabiyyah, 1974), pp. 144–145; al-Zuhayli, *al-Wasit*, pp. 498–499; Abu Zahrah, *Usul al-Fiqh*, pp. 291–293; Hasab Allah, *Usul al-Tashriʿ*, p. 260; Shaʿban, *Usul al-Fiqh*, pp. 382–384; Kamali, *Principles*, pp. 271–272.

98. I would argue that the protection of religion should be developed to mean protecting the freedom of religious belief; the protection of life should mean that the taking of life must be for a just cause and the result of a just process; the protection of the intellect should mean the right to free thinking, expression, and belief; the protection of honor should mean the protecting of the dignity of a human being; and the protection of property should mean the right to compensation for the taking of property.

99. See Khaled Abou El Fadl, "Tax Farming in Islamic Law (*Qibalah* and *Daman* of *Kharaj*): A Search for a Concept," *Islamic Studies*, 31, 1 (1992), pp. 5–32.

100. See Abou El Fadl, *Rebellion and Violence in Islamic Law*, pp. 234–294.

101. Jalal al-Din ʿAbd al-Rahman al-Suyuti, *al-Ashbah wa al-Nazaʿir fi Qawaʿid wa Furuʿ Fiqh al-Shafiʿiyya* (Beirut: Dar al-Kutub al-ʿIlmiyya, 1983), p. 53; ʿAli Ahmad al-Nadhwi, *al-Qawaʿid al-Fiqhiyya*, 3rd ed. (Damascus: Dar al-Qalam, 1994), pp. 400–401; Ahmad b. Muhammad al-Zarqa, *Sharh al-Qawaʿid al-Fiqhiyya*, 4th ed. (Damascus: Dar al-Qalam, 1996), pp. 369–389; Mahmasani, *Falsafat al-Tashriʿ*, p. 294.

102. Ibn Hajr al-ʿAsqalani, *Fath al-Bari*, 14:308; al-Shawkani, *Nayl*, 7: 168.

103. See Abu Ishaq Burhan al-Din b. Muhammad b. Muflih, *al-Mubdiʿ fi Sharh al-Muqniʿ* (Beirut: al-Maktab al-Islami, 1980), 9:168; Khaled Abou El Fadl, "Law of Duress in Islamic Law and Common Law: A Comparative Study," *Islamic Studies*, 30, 3 (1991), pp. 305–350.

104. Muslim jurists, however, did not consider the severing of hands or feet as punishment for theft and banditry to be mutilation. Jalal al-Din al-Suyuti, *al-Durr al-Manthur fi al-Tafsir bi al-Maʾthur* (Cairo: Matbaʿat al-Anwar al-Muhammadiyya, n.d.), 2:305–306; Abu al-Fidaʾ al-Hafiz Ibn Kathir al-Dimashqi, *Tafsir al-Qurʾan al-ʿAzim* (Beirut: Dar al-Khayr, 1990), 2:56–57; Abu Bakr Ahmad b. ʿAli al-Razi al-Jassas, *Ahkam al-Qurʾan* (Beirut: Dar al-Kitab al-ʿArabi, 1986), 2:407–408; Ahmad b. Muhammad al-Sawi, *Hashiyat al-ʿAllama al-Sawi ʿala Tafsir al-Jalalayn* (Beirut: Dar Ihyaʾ al-Turath al-ʿArabi, n.d.), 1:280; Abu al-Fadl Shihab al-

Din al-Sayyid Mahmud al-Alusi, *Ruh al-Ma'ani fi Tafsir al-Qur'an al-'Azim wa al-Sab' al-Mathani* (Beirut: Dar Ihya' al-Turath al-'Arabi, 1985), 6:121–122; Abu Ja'far Muhammad b. Jarir al-Tabari, *Jami' al-Bayan fi Tafsir al-Qur'an* (Beirut: Dar al-Ma'rifah, 1989), 5:134–135; 'Imad al-Din b. Muhammad al-Taba'i al-Kiya al-Harasi, *Ahkam al-Qur'an* (Beirut: Dar al-Kutub al-'Ilmiyya, 1985), 3:65; Abu Bakr Muhammad b. 'Abd Allah b. al-'Arabi, *Ahkam al-Qur'an*, ed. 'Ali Muhammad al-Bajawi (Beirut: Dar al-Jil, 1987), 2:594; Abu 'Abd Allah Muhammad b. Ahmad al-Ansari al-Qurtubi, *al-Jami' li Ahkam al-Qur'an* (Cairo: n.p., 1952), 6:149–150; 'Abd al-Rahman b. Muhammad b. Makhluf al-Tha'alabi, *al-Jawahir al-Hisan fi Tafsir al-Qur'an* (Beirut: Mu'assasat al-A'lami li al-Matbu'at, n.d.), 1:459; Qutb al-Din Sa'id b. Hibat Allah al-Rawandi, *Fiqh al-Qur'an*, ed. al-Sayyid Ahmad al-Husayni (Qum: Matba'at al-Wilayah, 1405 AH), 1:366; Abu Muhammad 'Ali b. Ahmad b. Sa'id Ibn Hazm, *al-Muhalla bi al-Athar*, ed. 'Abd al-Ghaffar Sulayman al-Bandari (Beirut: Dar al-Kutub al-'Ilmiyya, n.d.), 12:285–288; Abou El Fadl, *Rebellion and Violence in Islamic Law*, pp. 32, 50–57, 73–77, 340–341.

105. A considerable number of jurists in Islamic history were persecuted and murdered for holding that a political endorsement (*bay'u*) obtained under duress is invalid. Muslim jurists described the death of these scholars under such circumstances as a death of *musabara*. This had become an important discourse because caliphs were in the habit of either bribing or threatening notables and jurists in order to obtain their *bay'a*. See Ibn Khaldun, *al-Muqaddima*, p. 165; Abou El Fadl, *Rebellion and Violence in Islamic Law*, pp. 86–87. On the Islamic law of duress and on coerced confessions and political commitments, see Abou El Fadl, "Law of Duress in Islamic Law," pp. 305–350.

106. Abu Bakr Ahmad b. 'Amr b. Munir al-Shaybani al-Khassaf, *Kitab Adab al-Qadi*, ed. Farhat Ziyadah (Cairo: American University of Cairo Press, 1978), pp. 364–365; Abu al-Hasan 'Ali b. Muhammad b. Habib al-Mawardi, *Adab al-Qadi*, ed. Muhyi Hilal al-Sarhan (Baghdad: Matba'at al-Irshad, 1971) 1:233; idem, *al-Ahkam*, p. 58; Abu al-Qasim 'Ali b. Muhammad al-Rahbi al-Simnani, *Rawdat al-Qudah wa Tariq al-Najah* (Beirut: Mu'assasat al-Risalah, 1984) 1:157–8; *al-Fatawa al-Hindiyya* (Beirut: Dar Ihya' al-Turath al-'Arabi, 1986), 6:430; Fakhr al-Din 'Uthman b. 'Ali al-Zayla'i, *Tabyin al-Haqa'iq Sharh Kanz al-Daqa'iq* (Medina: Dar al-Kitab al-Islamiyya, n.d.), 3:240.

107. Some modern Muslim commentators tried to equate the rights of God with the idea of public rights. Muhammad Abu-Hassan, "Islamic Criminal Law," in *Justice and Human Rights in Islamic Law*, ed. Gerald E. Lampe (Washington, DC: International Law Institute, 1997), pp. 79–89, 81–82; Shaikh Shaukat Hussain, *Human Rights in Islam* (New Delhi: Kitab Bhavan, 1990), pp. 38–39; Mohammad Hashim Kamali, *Freedom of Expression in Islam*, rev. ed. (Cambridge: Islamic Texts Society, 1997),

p. 10. This argument is untenable and it is based on a misunderstanding of the theory behind the concept of God's rights. For a Muslim critique of God's rights as the equivalent of public rights, see Fazlur Rahman, "The Concept of *Hadd* in Islamic Law," *Islamic Studies* 4, 3 (1965): pp. 237–251, esp. pp. 247–249.

108. Abu Zahra, *Usul al-Fiqh*, pp. 256–258; Weiss, *The Spirit of Islamic Law*, pp. 181–184; Kamali, *Principles*, pp. 348–350.

109. Abu Bakr Muhammad b. 'Abd Allah b. al-'Arabi, *Ahkam al-Qur'an*, ed. 'Ali Muhammad al-Bajawi (Beirut: Dar al-Ma'rifah, n.d.), 2:603; Khaled Abou El Fadl, *Conference of the Books* (Lanham, MD: University Press of America, 2001), pp. 105–108. See also Abu 'Abd Allah Muhammad b. Ahmad al-Ansari al-Qurtubi, *al-Jami' li Ahkam al-Qur'an* (Beirut: Dar al-Kutub al-'Ilmiyya, 1993), 6:103; Taqi al-Din Ahmad b. 'Abd al-Halim Ibn Taymiyya, *al-Siyasa al-Shar'iyya fi Islah al-Ra'i wa al-Ra'iyya* (Beirut: Dar al-Kutub al-'Ilmiyya, 1988), pp. 65–144; Hasab Allah, *Usul al-Tashri'*, pp. 293–297; Ahmad Farraj Husayn, *Usul al-Fiqh al-Islami* (Lebanon: al-Dar al-Jami'iyya, 1986), pp. 405–415; Lambton, *State and Government*, pp. 19–20.

110. Abu Muhammad Mahmud b. Ahmad al-'Ayini, *al-Binaya fi Sharh al-Hidaya* (Beirut: Dar al-Fikr, 1990), 6:482.

111. This idea is reflected in the well-known tradition attributed to the Prophet that whenever God commands humans to do something, then they should do of it as much as they can. This tradition represents further recognition of the contingent and aspirational nature of human ability, and that while humans may strive for perfection, God is perfection itself.

112. For this often-repeated claim, see Lawrence Rosen, *The Justice of Islam* (Oxford: Oxford University Press, 2000), pp. 7, 79–80, 156–157; Weiss, *The Spirit of Islamic Law*, pp. 145–185; Rhoda Howard, *Human Rights and the Search for Community* (Boulder: Westview, 1995), pp. 92–104.

113. For the claim that the human rights tradition is Judeo-Christian in origin, see Claudio F. Benedi, *Human Rights: The Theme of our Times* (St. Paul, MN: Paragon House, 1997), pp. 27–32.

114. Salim Rustum Bazz, *Sharh al-Majalla* (Beirut: Dar Ihya' al-Turath al-'Arabi, 1986), p. 31. Muslim jurists also asserted that specific rights and duties should be given priority over general rights and duties. But, again, this was legal principle that applied to laws of agency and trust: ibid., pp. 43–44. Although the principle could be expanded and developed to support individual rights in the modern age, historically it was given a far more technical and legalistic connotation.

115. On this, see Simon, *The Tradition of Natural Law*, pp. 86–109; Alan Gewirth, *Human Rights: Essays on Justification and Applications* (Chicago: University of Chicago Press, 1982), pp. 218–233; John Finnis, *Natural Law and Natural Rights* (Oxford: Clarendon Press, 1980), pp. 205–218.

116. It might be that someone would want to argue that collectivist rights schemes are superior to individual rights schemes. But a collectivist

rights scheme would need to be justified on Islamic grounds as much as an individualist rights scheme. Both types of rights schemes are equally alien, or familiar, to the Islamic tradition. In addition, I do not dispute the morality of some collectivist rights, such as the rights of indigenous people, the right to culture, or development, and that these rights could be justified on Islamic grounds. But from an Islamic perspective, it is much harder to justify the sacrificing of the safety or well-being of individuals in pursuit of a collective right. It seems to me that the collectivist rights mentioned above are justifiable largely when a collectivity is trying to protect its individual and collective interests from aggression coming from outside the collectivity. In other words, it is justifiable when a community of people, sharing common interests, is trying to protect itself from external dangers. But it seems far less justifiable when the community is turning inwards, and trying to target individuals within its own membership, under the auspices of protecting the character of the collectivity against the dangers of dissent. On this issue, see *The Rights of Peoples*, ed. James Crawford (Oxford: Clarendon Press, 1995); Alexandra Xanthaki, "Collective Rights: The Case of Indigenous Peoples," in *Human Rights in Philosophy and Practice*, cds. Burton Leiser and Tom Campbell (Burlington, VT: Ashgate, 2001), pp. 303–313; Emily R. Gill, "Autonomy, Diversity, and the Right to Culture," pp. 285–300 in ibid.

117. On the relationship between duty and right in Roman law, and the subsequent Western legal tradition, see Finnis, *Natural Law*, pp. 205–210. The dynamic that Finnis describes is very similar to that which took place in classical Islamic law. Also see on rights and responsibilities: Lloyd L. Weinreb, "Natural Law and Rights," in *Natural Law Theory*, ed. George pp. 278–305.

118. On this subject, see Abou El Fadl, *Rebellion and Violence in Islamic Law*, pp. 280–287.

119. Qur'an 5:32.

120. Some premodern jurists did differentiate between Muslim, and non-Muslim, especially in matters pertaining to criminal liability and compensation for torts.

121. Qur'an 2:105; 3:74; 35:2; 38:9; 39:38; 40:7; 43:32.

SELECT BIBLIOGRAPHY

Abou El Fadl, K. *And God Knows the Soldiers: The Authoritative and Authoritarian in Islamic Discourse.* Lanham, MD, University Press of America, 2001

Abou El Fadl, K. *Speaking in God's Name: Islamic Law, Authority and Women.* Oxford, Oneworld, 2001

Adams, R.M. *Finite and Infinite Goods: A Framework for Ethics.* New York and Oxford, Oxford University Press, 1999

Adler, M. *The World of the Talmud.* New York, Schocken, 1958

Afkhami, M. (ed.) *Faith and Freedom: Women's Human Rights in the Muslim World.* Syracuse, Syracuse University Press, 1995

Ahmed, L. *Women and Gender in Islam.* New Haven, Yale University Press, 1992

Aiken, W. and LaFollette, H. (eds.) *World Hunger and Morality.* Upper Saddle River, NJ, Prentice Hall, 1996

Ali, S.S. *Gender and Human Rights in Islam and International Law: Equal Before Allah, Unequal Before Man?* The Hague, Kluwer Law International, 2000

Allen, T. and Seaton, J. (eds.) *The Media of Conflict: War Reporting and Representations of Ethnic Violence.* London and New York, Zed Books, 1999

An-Na'im, A.A. (ed.) *Human Rights in Cross-Cultural Perspective.* Philadelphia, University of Pennsylvania Press, 1992

An-Na'im, A.A. *The Politics of Memory: Truth, Healing, and Social Justice.* London and New York, Zed Books, 2000

An-Na'im, A.A. *Toward an Islamic Reformation: Civil Liberties, Human Rights, and International Law.* Syracuse, Syracuse University Press, 1990

An-Na'im, A.A., Gort, J., Jansen, H., and Vroom, H. (eds.) *Human Rights and Religious Values: An Uneasy Relationship?* Grand Rapids, Eerdmans, 1995

Astor, C. *"...Who Makes People Different: " Jewish Perspectives on the Disabled.* New York, United Synagogue of America, 1985

Audi, R. and Wolterstorff, N. *Religion in the Public Square: The Place of Religious Convictions in Political Debate.* Lanham, MD, Rowman & Littlefield, 1997

Barber, B.R. *Jihad vs. McWorld*. New York, Ballantine, 1996

Baron, S.W. *The Jewish Community*. Philadelphia, Jewish Publication Society, 1942

Bauer, J. and Bell, D. (eds.) *The East Asian Challenge for Human Rights*. Cambridge, Cambridge University Press, 1999

Bauman, Z. *Modernity and the Holocaust*. Cambridge, Polity Press, 1989

Beck, U. *What is Globalization?* Cambridge, Polity Press, 2000

Bell, D. *East Meets West: Human Rights and Democracy in East Asia*. Princeton, Princeton University Press, 2000

Berthrong, J. *All Under Heaven: Transforming Paradigms in Confucian–Christian Dialogue*. New York, State University of New York Press, 1994

Black, G. (ed.) *Islam and Justice: Debating the Future of Human Rights in the Middle East and North Africa*. New York, Lawyers' Committee for Human Rights, 1997

Bloom, I., Martin, J.P., and Proudfoot, W.L. (eds.) *Religious Diversity and Human Rights*. New York, Columbia University Press, 1996

Brems, E. *Human Rights: Universality and Diversity*. The Hague, Martinus Nijhoff Publishers, 2001

Bulmer, M. *Censuses, Surveys and Privacy*. London, Macmillan, 1979

Carman, J.B. "Duties and Rights in Hindu Society." In *Human Rights and the World's Religions*, ed. L.S. Rouner. Notre Dame, University of Notre Dame Press, 1988

Chappell, C. *Nonviolence to Animals, Earth, and Self in Asian Traditions*. New York, State University of New York Press, 1993

Chappell, D. *Buddhist Peacework: Creating Cultures of Peace*. Boston, Wisdom Publications, 2000

Cohen, A. *Everyman's Talmud*. New York, Schocken, 1949

Cohn, H. *Human Rights in Jewish Law*. New York, Ktav, 1984

Cotran, E. and Yamani, M. *The Rule of Law in the Middle East and the Islamic World: Human Rights and the Judicial Process*. London, I.B. Tauris, 2000

Dalacoura, K. *Islam, Liberalism and Human Rights*. London, I.B. Tauris, 1998

Dalai Lama. *Ethics for the New Millennium*. New York, Riverhead Books, 1999

Dalai Lama. *A Policy of Kindness: An Anthology of Writings by and about the Dalai Lama*. Ithaca, Snow Lion Publications, 1990

Danieli, Y., Stamatopoulos, E., and Dias, C.J. (eds.) *The Universal Declaration of Human Rights: Fifty Years and Beyond*. Amityville, NY, Baywood Publishing Company, 1999

Das, V. (ed.) *Mirrors of Violence: Communities, Riots and Survivors in South Asia*. Delhi, Oxford University Press, 1992

Davis, M. *Human Rights and Chinese Values: Legal, Philosophical, and Political Perspectives*. Oxford, Oxford University Press, 1995

de Bary, W.T. *Asian Values and Human Rights: A Confucian Communitarian Perspective*. Cambridge, MA, Harvard University Press, 1998

de Bary, W.T. *The Liberal Tradition in China*. Hong Kong, Chinese University Press, 1983 de Bary, W.T. and Tu, Weiming (eds.) *Confucianism and Human Rights*. New York, Columbia University Press, 1998

Des Forges, A. *Leave None to Tell the Story: Genocide in Rwanda*. New York, Human Rights Watch, 1999

Doctorow, E.L. *City of God*. New York, Random House, 2000

Donnelly, J. *International Human Rights: Dilemmas in World Politics*, 2nd ed. Boulder, Westview Press, 1998

Donnelly, J. *Universal Human Rights in Theory and Practice*. Ithaca, Cornell University Press, 1989

Dorff, E.N. *Matters of Life and Death: A Jewish Approach to Modern Medical Ethics*. Philadelphia, Jewish Publication Society, 1998

Dorff, E.N. *To Do the Right and the Good: A Jewish Approach to Modern Social Ethics*, 1st ed. Philadelphia, Jewish Publication Society, 2002

Dunne, T. and Wheeler, N. (eds.) *Human Rights in Global Politics*. Cambridge, Cambridge University Press, 1999

Duyzings, G. *Religion and the Politics of Identity in Kosovo*. London, Hurst & Co., 1999

Dwyer, K. *Arab Voices: The Human Rights Debate in the Middle East*. Berkeley and Los Angeles, University of California Press, 1991

Edwards, R., Henkin, L., and Nathan, A. (eds.) *Human Rights in Contemporary China*. New York, Columbia University Press, 1986

Ellis, S. *The Mask of Anarchy: The Destruction of Liberia and the Religious Dimension of an African Civil War*. London, Hurst & Co., 1999

Esack, F. *Qur'an, Liberation and Pluralism: An Islamic Perspective of Interreligious Solidarity Against Oppression*. Oxford, Oneworld, 1997

Esposito, J.L. (ed.) *Political Islam: Revolution, Radicalism, or Reform?* Boulder and London, Lynne Riener, 1997

Esposito, J.L. and Voll, J.O. (eds.) *Makers of Contemporary Islam*. Oxford, Oxford University Press, 2001

Finkelstein, L. *Jewish Self-Government in the Middle Ages*. New York, Jewish Theological Seminary of America, 1924

Fowl, S.E. and Jones, L.G. *Reading in Communion: Scripture and Ethics in Christian Life*. Grand Rapids, Eerdmans, 1999

Frye, M. *The Politics of Reality: Essays in Feminist Theory*. Trumansburg, NY, The Crossing Press, 1983

Ghandhi, P.R. (ed.) *Blackstone's International Human Rights Documents*. London, Blackstone Press Ltd., 1995

Glover, J. *Humanity: A Moral History of the Twentieth Century*. London, Jonathan Cape, 1999

Goodman, L.E. *God of Abraham*. New York and Oxford, Oxford University Press, 1996

Goodman, L.E. *Judaism, Human Rights, and Human Values*. New York and Oxford, Oxford University Press, 1998

Harlow, J. *Siddur Sim Shalom*. New York: Rabbinical Assembly and United Synagogue of America, 1985

Harvey, P. *An Introduction to Buddhist Ethics*. Cambridge, Cambridge University Press, 2000

Haynes, J. *Religion in Global Politics*. London and New York, Longman, 1998

Henkin, L. "Religion, Religions, and Human Rights." *Journal of Religious Ethics*, 26.2, Fall 1998

Hertz, J.H. *Pentateuch and Haftorahs*, 2nd ed. London, Soncino Press, 1960

Hick, J. *Truth and Dialogue in World Religions: Conflicting Truth-Claims*. Philadelphia, Westminster Press, 1975

Hicks, D. *Inequality and Christian Ethics*. Cambridge, Cambridge University Press, 2000

Howland, C. *Religious Fundamentalisms and the Human Rights of Women*. New York, St. Martin's Press, 1999

Jacobson, M. and Bruun, O. (eds.) *Human Rights and Asian Values: Contesting National Identities and Cultural Representations in Asia*. Richmond, Curzon, 2000

Jordan, J. and Howard-Snyder, D. (eds.) *Faith, Freedom, and Rationality*. Lanham, MD, Rowman & Littlefield, 1996

Kant, I. *The Conflict of the Faculties*, trans. by M.J. Gregor. Lincoln and London, University of Nebraska Press, 1992

Kelsay, J. and Twiss, S.B. (eds.) *Religion and Human Rights*. New York, The Project on Religion and Human Rights, 1995

Kellenberger, J. *Moral Relativism, Moral Diversity, and Human Relationships*. Philadelphia, Pennsylvania State University Press, 2001

Kellenberger, J. *Relationship Morality*. Philadelphia, Pennsylvania State University Press, 1995

Kent, A. *Between Freedom and Subsistence: China and Human Rights*. Hong Kong and New York, Oxford University Press, 1993

Keown, D., Prebish, C., and Husted, W. (eds.) *Buddhism and Human Rights*. Richmond, Curzon, 1998

Kierkegaard, S. *Fear and Trembling*, trans. W. Lowrie. Princeton, Princeton University Press, 1968

Kierkegaard, S. *Works of Love*, trans. H. Hong and E. Hong. New York, Harper Torchbooks, 1962

King, S. "Human Rights in Contemporary Engaged Buddhism." In *Buddhist Theology: Critical Reflections by Contemporary Buddhist Scholars*, eds. R. Jackson, and J.J. Makransky. Richmond, Curzon, 1999

King, S. and Ingram, P. (eds.) *The Sound of Liberating Truth: Buddhist–Christian Dialogues in Honor of Frederick J. Streng*. Richmond, Curzon, 1999

Korten, D.C. *When Corporations Rule the World*. San Francisco, Berrett-Koehler, 1995

Lamm, N. *Faith and Doubt: Studies in Traditional Jewish Thought*. New York, Ktav, 1971

Laursen, J.C. (ed.) *Religious Toleration: The Variety of Rites from Cyrus to Defoe*. New York, St. Martin's, 1999

Laytner, A. *Arguing with God: A Jewish Tradition*. Northvale, NJ, Jason Aronson, 1990

Leahy, M. and Cohn-Sherbok, D. (eds.) *The Liberation Debate: Rights at Issue*. London and New York, Routledge, 1996

Lepard, Brian D. *Rethinking Humanitarian Intervention: A Fresh Legal Approach Based on Fundamental Ethical Principles in International Law and World Religions*. University Park, PA, Pennsylvania State University Press, 2002

Lerner, N. *Religion, Beliefs, and International Human Rights*. Maryknoll, Orbis Books, 2000

Lindholm, T. and Vogt, K. (eds.) *Islamic Law Reform and Human Rights: Challenges and Rejoinders*. Olso, Nordic Human Rights Publications, 1993

Little, D., Kelsay, J., and Sachedina, A. *Human Rights and the Conflict of Cultures*. Columbia, University of South Carolina Press, 1988

Lopez, D. *Prisoners of Shangri-La: Tibetan Buddhism and the West*. Chicago, University of Chicago Press, 1998

MacIntyre, A. *After Virtue*, 2nd ed. Notre Dame, University of Notre Dame Press, 1984

Majumdar, R.C. (ed.) *The Age of Imperial Unity*. Bombay, Bharatiya Vidya Bhavan, 1951

Majumdar, R.C. *The Classical Accounts of India*. Calcutta, Firma KLM Private Ltd., 1981

Maritain, J. *The Rights of Man and Natural Law*, trans. D. Anson. New York, Charles Schribner & Sons, 1943

Mayer, A. *Islam and Human Rights: Tradition and Politics*, 3rd ed. Boulder, Westview Press, 1999

Mitra, K. "Human Rights in Hinduism." In *Human Rights in Religious Traditions*, ed. A. Swidler, New York, Pilgrim Press, 1982

Monshipouri, M. *Democratization, Liberalization, and Human Rights in the Third World*. Boulder, Lynn Rienner, 1995

Morsink, J. *The Universal Declaration of Human Rights: Origins, Drafting, and Intent*. Philadelphia, University of Pennsylvania Press, 1999

Ngor, H. and Warner, R. *Haing Ngor: A Cambodian Odyssey*. New York, Macmillan, 1987

Norchi, C. "The National Human Rights Commission of India as a Value-Creating Institution." In *Human Rights in Religious Traditions*, ed. J.D. Montgomery. Hollis, NH, Hollis Publishing Co., 1998

Novak, D. *The Image of the Non-Jew in Judaism*. New York and Toronto, Edwin Mellen Press, 1983

Olupona, J.K. (ed.) *African Traditional Religions in Contemporary Society*. New York, Paragon House, 1991

Perera, L.P.N. *Buddhism and Human Rights: A Buddhist Commentary on the Universal Declaration of Human Rights*. Columbo, Karunaratne & Sons, 1991

Peters, J. and Wolper, A. (eds.) *Women's Rights, Human Rights: International Feminist Perspectives*. London, Routledge, 1995

Platvoet, J.G. and Molendijk, A.L. (eds.) *The Pragmatics of Defining Religion: Contexts, Concepts and Contests*. Leiden, Brill, 1999

Pliskin, Z. *Guard Your Tongue*. Jerusalem, Aish Ha-Torah, 1975

Pollis, A. and Schwab, P. (eds.) *Human Rights: New Perspectives, New Realities*. Boulder, Lynne Rienner, 2000

Rai, L.D. *Human Rights in the Hindu–Buddhist Tradition*. Jaipur, Nirala Publications, 1995

Rawls, J. *Political Liberalism*. New York, Columbia University Press, 1993

Regan, T. *The Case for Animal Rights*. Berkeley and Los Angeles, University of California Press, 1983

Regan, T. (ed.) *Matters of Life and Death: New Introductory Essays in Moral Philosophy*. New York, Random House, 1980

Reid, T.R. *Confucius Lives Next Door: What Living in the East Teaches us Living in the West*. New York, Random House, 1999

Robertson, G. *Crimes Against Humanity: The Struggle for Global Justice*. London, Penguin Books, 2000

Rosas, A. (ed.) *Economic, Social, and Cultural Rights*. Dordrecht, Martinus Nijhoff, 1995

Rouner, L. (ed.) *Human Rights and the World's Religions*. Notre Dame, University of Notre Dame Press, 1988

Sangay, L. "Education Rights for Tibetans in Tibet and India." In *Human Rights in Religious Traditions*, ed. J.D. Montgomery. Hollis, NH, Hollis Publishing, 1998

Sangharakshita. *Ambedkar and Buddhism*. Glasgow, Windhorse Publications, 1986

Schmale, W. (ed.) *Human Rights and Cultural Diversity: Europe, Arabic-Islamic World, Africa, China*. Goldbach, Keip, 1993

Schochet, E.J. *A Responsum of Surrender*. Los Angeles, University of Judaism, 1973

Sharma, A. "India's Reservation Policies as Affirmative Action." In *Human Rights: Positive Policies in Asia and the Pacific Rim*, ed. J.D. Montgomery. Hollis, NH, Hollis Publishing, 1998

Sidorsky, D. (ed.) *Essays on Human Rights: Contemporary Issues and Jewish Perspectives*. Philadelphia, Jewish Publication Society, 1979

Silverman, M. *Sabbath and Festival Prayerbook*. New York, Rabbinical Assembly of America and United Synagogue of America, 1945

Singer, P. *Animal Liberation*, 2nd ed. New York, New York Review, 1990

Sivaraksa, S. *A Socially Engaged Buddhism*. Bangkok, Khana Radom Tham, 1982

Smart, N. and Thakur, S. (eds.) *Ethical and Political Dilemmas of Modern India*. New York, St. Martin's Press, 1993

Spitz, E. *Jewish and American Law on the Cutting Edge of Privacy: Computers in the Business Sector*. Los Angeles, University of Judaism, 1986

Steiner, H. and Alston, P. *International Human Rights in Context: Law, Politics, Morals*. Oxford, Clarendon Press, 1996

Stock, J. *Debating Human Rights in the Middle East.* Cambridge, Cambridge University Press, forthcoming

Subramuniyaswami, S.S. "Hinduism's Human Rights Dilemma." *Hinduism Today,* Feb. 1995

Ter Haar, G. *Halfway to Paradise: African Christians in Europe.* Cardiff, Cardiff Academic Press, 1998

Tabandeh, S. *A Muslim Commentary on the Universal Declaration of Human Rights,* trans. Francis J. Goulding. London, F.T. Goulding, 1970

Tesón, Fernando R. *Humanitarian Intervention: An Inquiry into Law and Morality,* 2nd ed. Irvington-on-Hudson, Transnational Publishers, 1997

Traer, R. *Faith in Human Rights: Support in Religious Traditions for a Global Struggle.* Washington, DC, Georgetown University Press, 1991

Tu, Weiming. *Centrality and Commonality: An Essay on Confucian Religiousness.* Albany, State University of New York Press, 1989

Tu, Weiming. *Confucian Thought: Selfhood as Creative Transformation.* Albany, State University of New York Press, 1985

Turkson, P. and Wijsen, F. (eds.) *Inculturation: Abide by the Otherness of Africa and Africans.* Kampen, Kok, 1994

Twiss, S.B. "Moral Grounds and Plural Cultures: Interpreting Human Rights in the International Community." *Journal of Religious Ethics,* 26.2, Fall 1998

Twiss, S.B. and Grelle, B. (eds.) *Explorations in Global Ethics: Comparative Religious Ethics and Interreligious Dialogue.* Boulder and Oxford, Westview Press, 1998

Twiss, S.B. and Kelsay, J. *Religion and Human Rights.* Boulder and Oxford: Westview Press, 2003

UNESCO. *Human Rights: Comments and Interpretations.* London, Allan Wingate, 1949

Van Ness, P. *Debating Human Rights: Critical Essays from the United States and Asia.* London, Routledge, 1999

Veatch, R.M. (ed.) *Medical Ethics.* Boston and Portola Valley, Jones & Bartlett, 1989

Walsh, T.G. and Olupona, J. (eds.) *Religion and Social Transformation in Southern Africa.* Minnesota, Paragon House, 1999

Westin, P. and Allan, F. *Privacy and Freedom.* New York, Atheneum, 1967

Wilson, R.A. (ed.) *Human Rights, Culture and Context: Anthropological Perspectives.* London and Chicago, Pluto Press, 1997

Witte, J. and van de Vyver, J. (eds.) *Religious Human Rights in Global Perspective,* vol. 1: *Religious Perspectives.* The Hague, Kluwer, 1996

Wolgast, E. *The Grammar of Justice.* Ithaca and London, Cornell University Press, 1987

Young, I.M. *Justice and the Politics of Difference.* Princeton, Princeton University Press, 1990

INDEX

Numbers in *italics* refer to photographs